Quantitative methods for business studies

Quantitative methods for business studies

RICHARD THOMAS

FINANCIAL TIMES
Prentice Hall
An imprint of Pearson Education

Harlow, England · London · New York · Reading, Massachusetts · San Francisco
Toronto · Don Mills, Ontario · Sydney · Tokyo · Singapore · Hong Kong · Seoul
Taipei · Cape Town · Madrid · Mexico City · Amsterdam · Munich · Paris · Milan

Pearson Education Limited
Edinburgh Gate
Harlow
Essex, CM20 2JE
England

and Associated Companies throughout the world

Visit us on the World Wide Web at:
http://www.pearsoned.co.uk

First published 1997 by Prentice Hall Europe

©Prentice Hall Europe 1997

Typeset in $9\frac{1}{2}$ on 12pt Sabon
by Mathematical Composition Setters Ltd, Salisbury, Wiltshire

Printed and bound in Great Britain
by Ashford Colour Press Ltd, Hampshire

Library of Congress Cataloging-in-Publication Data

Thomas, Richard.
    Quantitative methods for business studies / Richard Thomas.
        p.   cm.
    Includes index.
    ISBN 0-13-231119-4
    1. Commercial statistics.   I. Title.
    HF1017.T44 1997   96-34934
    519.5—dc20   CIP

British Library Cataloguing in Publication Data

A catalogue record for this book is available from the British Library

ISBN-10: 0-13-231119-4
ISBN-13: 978-0-13-231119-9

---

10 9 8 7 6
05

Contents

Pecentages, ratios, powers and roots, arithmetic operations, substitution, simple equations, summation notation

Answers to all odd numbered questions

Preface

This book is intended to introduce the reader to a wide range of quantitative techniques used in business and management. Such methods are becoming increasingly important in management decision making where rational and logical arguments are expected to justify any decisions made. In practice, this often leads to consideration of the costs and budgetary implications though many analytical techniques are not solely concerned with financial data. It is hoped that this book will give the reader an insight into many of the analytical tools currently available. The increasing importance and application of computer systems in this field is highlighted and a number of computer software packages are described and illustrated in appropriate sections in the text. A computer disk is also available containing a range of files referred to in the text, where they are represented by this icon:

The book is particularly appropriate for students in business and management. Those currently taking undergraduate or MBA courses will find that the text provides an excellent grounding for the variety of analytical techniques likely to be covered. In particular, the book contains an extensive range of case studies, worked examples and exercises in order to assist the acquisition of the required skills. However, it should be stated that the book does not solely concentrate on the techniques involved but seeks to underline their application in a work-based context. Thus the book should enable the student to not only perform the appropriate calculations and processes, but also interpret the results obtained and make relevant decisions incorporating all the information at his/her disposal.

The main thrust of this book is in the Quantitative Methods/Management Science areas and additional statistical chapters are included in order to provide a good foundation for later sections. The chapters are designed to be reasonably self-contained and can, with only a few exceptions, be read in any order. This enables considerable flexibility of treatment for the topics in any course design. Furthermore, each chapter is structured to facilitate learning and includes the following features:-

- Statement of learning objectives and Introduction
- Two business related case studies
- Numerous graded worked examples
- Exercises following each major topic area
- Description of appropriate computer application packages with examples
- Chapter summary and further exercises

Questions given in the *Exercises* at the end of each chapter are characterised as easy (E), intermediate (I) and difficult (D). These classifications are clearly subjective and relate to the specific topic being considered.

The book also includes appropriate statistical tables, additional reference material for each chapter and answers to all the odd numbered questions given in the text.

I would like to thank the numerous reviewers of this book who have given invaluable help and suggestions on modifications and additions to the text. In particular, the following have provided excellent advice:

Kirsty Davidson, Napier University
Gwyn Jones, London Guildhall University
Mr W E Platt, Halton College, Widnes
Ray Kent, University of Stirling
Edwin Romeijn, Erasmus University

I would like to thank Melanie Brooks for all her hard work in checking the mathematical examples throughout the book.

I would also like to thank John Yates and Carrie Hoy for their help and encouragement in the development of this book. Finally, I would like to thank my wife Lisa for her support during this project.

This book is dedicated to Lisa Jayne who has given me love and support over many years.

Further reading

The table below indicates where further material on the topics covered in each chapter can be found in background reading.

Background reading	Thomas Ch 1	Ch 2	Ch 3	Ch 4	Ch 5	Ch 6	Ch 7	Ch 8	Ch 9	Ch 10
Anderson et al., *An Introduction to Management Science*, West Publishing Company, St Paul, USA, 1994		Ch 14					Ch 11	Ch 2–7	Ch 13	Ch 9 & 10
Ball, *Quantitative Approaches to Management*, Butterworth-Heinemann, Oxford, 1991		Ch 4 & 5				Ch 6				
Black, *Business Statistics – An Introductory Course*, West Publishing Company, St Paul, USA, 1992		Ch 4–9								
BPP, *Quantitative Methods – Business Basics*, BPP Publishing, London, 1955			Ch 9							
Carter/Williamson, *Quantitative Modelling for Management and Business*, Pitman, London, 1996			Ch 9			Ch 9 & 10	Ch 12			
Curwin/Slater, *Quantitative Methods for Business Decisions*, Chapman & Hall, London, 1991	Ch 1–4			Ch 9	Ch 5					
Eppen et al., *Introductory Management Science*, Prentice Hall, New Jersey, USA, 1993		Ch 14				Ch 18	Ch 10 & 16		Ch 13	Ch 9 & 15
Keller et al., *Statistics for Management and Economics*, Duxbury Press, 1994					Ch 20					

Reference									
Kvanli et al., *Introduction to Business Statistics*, West Publishing Company, St Paul, USA, 1992						Ch 16			
Mathur/Solow, *Management Science – The Art of Decision Making*, Prentice Hall, New Jersey, USA, 1994			Ch 4–6	Ch 12	Ch 16				
Morris, *Quantitative Approaches in Business Studies*, Pitman, London, 1993			Ch 17			Ch 7	Ch 15		Ch 3–6
Oakshott, *Quantitative Approaches to Decision Making*, DP Publications, 1993					Ch 14				
Piascik, *Applied Mathematics for Business and the Social and Natural Sciences*, West Publishing Company, St Paul, USA, 1991							Ch 4		
Targett, *Analytical Decision Making*, Pitman, London, 1996			Ch 7 & 8					Ch 14 & 15	
Toh/Hu, *Basic Business Studies – An Intuitive Approach*, West Publishing Company, St Paul, USA, 1991						Ch 18			Ch 2 & 3
Waters, *A Practical Introduction to Management Science*, Addison Wesley, 1994	Ch 5	Ch 11		Ch 3					
Winston, *Operations Research – Applications and Algorithms*, Duxbury Press, 1991	Ch 8	Ch 23							
Wisniewski, *Quantitative Approaches for Decision Makers*, Pitman, London, 1994				Ch 12	Ch 11	Ch 4	Ch 15	Ch 10	Ch 3 & 4

Summary Statistics

CHAPTER OBJECTIVES

At the end of this chapter you will be able to:

▶ understand techniques used in data collection
▶ use appropriate methods to tabulate and graph data
▶ calculate a range of descriptive statistics
▶ understand the reasons for using these statistics
▶ use statistics in interpreting business information

Introduction

The use of basic data presentation techniques and summary statistics is becoming increasingly important for today's decision makers. The presentation and interpretation of business data form a vital part of many companies' marketing and public relations strategies. It is only necessary to refer to any company's annual report to realise the extent to which statistics and data presentation have become part of everyday business processes. Such company literature without the incorporation of data analysis and graphical presentations is increasingly rare. Internally, as well as externally, data presentation techniques are used to assist in communication. Good information is the

▷ **Figure 1.1** The role of data analysis in decision making.

lifeblood of good decisions, and good information is greatly enhanced by the appropriate use and representation of data. Consequently, the ability to derive, present and interpret data is an important skill for the modern manager.

Figure 1.1 illustrates the role of data analysis in management decision making. Appropriate data are collected in order to address a specific business problem. By the use of data analysis techniques, relevant information is provided to the manager to assist in the decision making process.

In this chapter the basic methods of presenting data, both graphically and numerically, will be introduced and, where appropriate, these techniques will be related to practical business situations and areas in management decision making.

CASE STUDY   The Hartwoods pharmaceutical company

The Hartwoods company is a large multi-national pharmaceutical company with regional headquarters in New York, London, Bonn and Sydney. The company is divided into a number of sectors including Research & Development, Production, and Marketing & Sales. Each of these sectors is independently managed at the regional headquarters. Hartwoods achieved high profit levels during the mid and late 1980s, based largely on a new range of drugs developed by the company. Some of the drugs developed and produced by Hartwoods include an antidepressant drug, arthritis medication, female contraceptive pills, and a series of drugs to combat HIV.

Hartwoods is a publicly owned company, with shares traded on the London Stock Exchange. Share prices reached an all-time high during 1993 at £11.40 per share. Since that time the share price gradually dropped down to a five-year low of £8.25 in mid 1995 owing to doubts concerning some of the Hartwoods products, including the anti-HIV drugs.

The company produces a range of quantitative and financial analyses for publication in the annual reviews, financial statements, and internal communications. The range of analyses would include details of profitability, revenue, expenditure, and production output. The techniques described in this chapter can be used in these analyses and they will be described in the appropriate sections.

CASE STUDY   Spitz & Kohl (Market Research) Ltd

The Spitz & Kohl company is a market research organisation established in 1978. With headquarters in Munich, and subsidiary offices located in San Francisco and Hong Kong, the company has an extensive list of corporate and government clients. The company is primarily involved in conducting market research surveys for public and private organisations, and developing and managing promotional campaigns for new and existing products and services.

Currently, Spitz & Kohl employ around 2000 staff worldwide. The company prides itself on providing excellent customer service and client care. Each client is assigned a specific member of staff or team to handle the account. The same staff would generally be used throughout the lifetime of any project so that the client receives consistent and effective support. All client accounts are managed centrally from one of the three main locations in order that project costs are monitored and a consistent approach to the clients is maintained.

The staff at Spitz & Kohl have a wide range of skills and expertise. In addition to the graphic artists, designers and advertising specialists, there are large teams in each of the main locations involved in survey design and analysis. These teams include those involved in designing questionnaire and interview surveys, and statisticians who provide expertise on data analysis methods. Such methods will be discussed in this chapter and illustrative examples will be provided when required.

1.1   Data collection methods

The first stage of any quantitative analysis is the collection of appropriate data. Such data can be collected in many ways, including the following methods:

1.1.1   Reference to existing material

Such material would include internal and external information. For instance, internal company records on production, sales and personnel may contain the required data. Such information could be text-based but is increasingly likely to be stored as part of a computerised company database enabling ease of access to specific details. Furthermore, external publications such as the *Monthly Digest of Statistics*, the *Annual Abstract of Statistics* or the *Economic Trends*, all published by the Central Statistical Office, are readily available. These publications cover a wide range of national data such as population and demographic trends, earnings and prices, sales, production output and consumer trends. Other external publications such as local government statistics, marketing survey reports, and company reports may be of use in obtaining the required information. Data obtained from such sources are referred to as **secondary data** since they have not been collected with a specific purpose in mind. Data are also considered to be secondary if they have been collected for a specific purpose other than the current analysis.

1.1.2   Questionnaires

In the absence of existing data, methods must be utilised to collect information with a specific purpose in view. One obvious method of collecting the so-called **primary data** involves the use of questionnaires. This method of data collection provides a relatively cost-effective means of obtaining information from a large sample. For example, questionnaires may be used to gain information on attitudes of a company's workforce to changes in conditions and remuneration. Questionnaires can be of various types such as the common self-administered type (e.g. as used in postal surveys), or administered type (e.g. where the person conducting the survey is able to help with interpretation of questions). Extreme care must be taken in the design of the questionnaire to avoid misleading, ambiguous, or leading questions.

Good design of questionnaires is a vital element in the collection of reliable and valid information. The design of a successful questionnaire is notoriously difficult; however, there are a number of points that may assist in the process. The design involves a number of basic steps including:

1. **Initial interviews** or brain-storming sessions to discuss the type and range of information required.
2. **First draft** of the questionnaire.
3. **Internal testing** of the draft questionnaire, including initial examination of the framing of questions to ensure that they are understandable and answerable.
4. **Conduct pilot study**. This would involve sending questionnaires to a small sample of respondents in order to further test the questionnaire format and design.
5. **Produce final questionnaire** using the results from previous testing and pilot.
6. **Conduct final survey** on the full sample.

The formulation of effective questionnaires and framing of appropriate questions can be aided by the following guidelines:

▶ The purpose of the questionnaire should be explained at the start of the question-naire or in a covering letter.
▶ Language used in the questions should be as simple as possible, avoiding any jargon or technical terms.
▶ The number of questions should be kept to a minimum.
▶ Multi-choice or Yes/No questions should be used whenever possible.
▶ Open-ended questions should be used sparingly and preferably only towards the end of the questionnaire.
▶ Leading questions should not be used.
▶ Ambiguous or double questions should be avoided.
▶ Personal or potentially embarrassing questions should not be used unless necessary.

1.1.3   Interviews

Another method of obtaining primary data, the interview, is a more expensive, time-consuming approach to data collection. Interviews are often used in preference to questionnaires when sensitive information is to be collected. Any embarrassing, controversial information is usually considered unsuited for the questionnaire approach. Thus, it may be more suitable to use interviews as the main method of data collection in the example given in the previous section concerning employees' remuneration and conditions. The disadvantages of using this approach include the increased costs, timescales and use of appropriately trained interviewing staff. Furthermore, the amount of data collected is likely to be less since a smaller sample size will be necessary in order to complete interviews within a given time.

1.1.4 Observations

Some situations lend themselves to the use of observation in order to collect relevant data. For instance, when collecting data on the use of a variety of facilities available to employees such as restaurant, staff lounge and recreation areas it may be more appropriate to observe such use rather than to ask employees for details. Furthermore, the observation or tracking of items through a production environment may yield more reliable data than requesting information from the staff involved.

It is beyond the scope of this book to describe in detail the processes involved in data collection. However, this is undoubtedly the single most important element in the process of data analysis. Inappropriate data collection methods can easily produce poor data, resulting in inaccurate and misleading analysis. The techniques and methodologies described throughout this book are based on the assumption that reliable data have been collected. The process of data collection involves careful identification of a number of elements including the following:

Specific business problem. This will be affected by management and organisational objectives. The problem to be considered may also be determined by the financial limitations, time constraints and the expertise available to conduct the appropriate research.

Identification of the population. The so-called 'parent population' includes all of the individuals who could possibly be included in the research. The identification of the specific population is not always as easy as it seems. Consider an analysis of the employees' remuneration and working conditions. What is the population under consideration? It could be that the population includes all employees, or just employees on certain grades or working in specific locations. Alternatively, a wider population may be considered such as prospective employees, e.g. all adults in the region with particular skills. This needs to be clearly defined before relevant data collection can take place.

Sampling frame. This is used to select a representative sample from the population already defined. The sampling frame for all employees would simply be the employee records' system. Other sampling frames can be used such as membership lists of professional institutions, social club membership lists or, more widely, telephone directories, or even the electoral registers. The sampling frame is an important element in the process and, if poorly chosen, may drastically affect the validity of the data collected. For instance, the telephone directory is a biased frame if we are attempting to consider all households. Indeed it may be misleading even when we only wish to consider those households with telephones, since a small proportion of those will be 'ex-Directory'.

Sample size. The number of items of data collected depends on a variety of factors, including the methods of data collection used, the available budget, the specific population to be considered, and the required accuracy of the results. In general, provided that the sampling is unbiased, an increase in the sample size is likely to improve the reliability of the results obtained.

Response rate. The response rate is an important factor in determining the reliability of the data collected. For example, if a sample size of 1000 is chosen and the survey only achieves a response rate of 10%, then the actual data collected only covers 100 members of the population. Furthermore, the returns may form a biased sample which would not be truly representative of the population. Response rates for self-administered questionnaire surveys are notoriously low, with rates below 10% not uncommon.

Sampling method. Usually some type of 'random sampling' method will be used unless the population is small enough for all members to be included in the research. Simple random sampling involves a pure random selection from the population. This could be achieved by numbering each member, and picking the numbers out randomly. Stratified sampling is a modification of this approach. In stratified sampling the population is split into a number of groups in which members have a common characteristic, and a random selection is obtained from each group. This ensures that the final sample contains a reasonable representation from each of the groups defined. For example, the workforce in a company can be split into bands to include managers, administrators and technical staff. Random samples from each group are taken to comprise the final sample. Other sampling methods such as multi-stage, cluster and quota sampling can be used in certain circumstances.

1.2   Tabulation of data

Data collected as the result of the methods outlined in the previous section are initially in 'raw' form. These raw data can be simplified considerably if they are tabulated by grouping items together. The following examples illustrate the basic techniques involved in this process.

EXAMPLE 1

The raw data shown below give the weekly earnings of a sample of forty technicians in a large manufacturing organisation. (The figures are given in £.)

750	410	520	604	810	610	770	690
670	505	370	660	515	860	654	550
446	725	632	720	590	694	424	649
760	535	756	682	330	785	575	835
802	625	437	520	440	584	610	710

Data in this format are difficult to analyse. In order to make any sense of the earnings displayed, the data will need to be put into a tabular form. The standard method to represent these data would be to construct a frequency table, as shown below. Data values will need to be grouped together in order to simplify the process. The following steps will be taken:

(i) Find the largest and smallest values in the data collected. In the data shown above the highest figure is £860 and the lowest is £330. Thus, the frequency table will need to contain at least the range indicated.

(ii) A decision must be made on how this range of values can be split into groups or class intervals. As a general rule it is usual to split the full range into approximately 5 to 10 groups. Of course, this is only a guide and in many circumstances it is appropriate to use more or fewer groups than this. Furthermore, the specific groups will normally be of the same width, though sometimes this is not convenient. The class intervals for the data could be grouped in £100 intervals. Thus, we could count the number of employees earning between £300 and £400, and between £400 and £500, and so on.

Weekly earnings	Tally	Number of employees
£300 and above, and under £400	//	2
£400 and above, and under £500	////	5
£500 and above, and under £600	//// ////	9
£600 and above, and under £700	//// //// //	12
£700 and above, and under £800	//// ///	8
£800 and above, and under £900	////	4

▷ **Figure 1.2** Tally chart.

(iii) A tally chart can then be used to count the values in the selected range as shown in Figure 1.2.

Thus the original raw data can be tabulated using the frequency table as shown below:

Weekly earnings (£):	300–	400–	500–	600–	700–	800–
No. of employees:	2	5	9	12	8	4

Note the notation used to represent the class intervals. The range 300– indicates a wage of £300 and over but below the beginning of the next class, e.g. below £400. Unless otherwise stated it will be assumed that the classes are all of the same width. Thus, each class in this table indicates a wage band of £100. Consequently, the last group, 800–, indicates a wage of £800 and over, up to anything below £900.

EXAMPLE 2

The daily output of the Horgonol antidepressant drug produced by the Hartwoods company over the past fifty working days are given in the following table. The drug is produced in 20 milligram tablets and packaged in boxes each containing 36 tablets. The figures below give the number of boxes produced per week in 1000s.

```
24.1  26.3  22.9  28.4  22.2  24.5  22.7  21.3  22.8  25.6
22.6  29.1  25.4  24.5  25.3  23.2  24.2  23.7  26.7  23.6
23.0  24.6  20.2  23.0  26.3  23.7  21.1  23.0  24.0  25.8
27.5  24.0  25.2  24.4  22.2  20.9  25.1  23.0  24.0  23.8
23.4  24.5  21.4  22.5  27.6  23.1  28.9  21.8  23.9  25.7
```

The table shows that in the first day studied the output was 24.1 thousands of packets. In other words, 24 100 packets were produced. Similarly, in the second day 26 300 packets were produced, and so on for the period of 50 days as shown.

The data production output ranges between 20.2 and 29.1. Figure 1.3 shows the tally chart produced from these data using suitable class intervals.

Thus, the resulting frequency table is as shown:

Daily production (1000s of packets):	20–	22–	24–	26–	28–
Number of days:	6	19	17	5	3

This table can then be used for further analysis of the daily production output, as described in the following sections in this chapter.

EXAMPLE 3

The Personnel Manager at the Harwoods Pharmaceutical Company has been requested to provide an analysis of the absence rates of its workforce. The number of

Daily production (1000s of packets)	Tally	Number of days
20–	//// /	6
22–	//// //// //// ////	19
24–	//// //// //// //	17
26–	////	5
28–	///	3

▷ **Figure 1.3** Tally chart of production output.

employees who were absent from work over the past thirty days is shown in the following table:

$$
\begin{array}{cccccccccc}
5 & 0 & 15 & 1 & 23 & 6 & 5 & 18 & 8 & 10 \\
2 & 10 & 6 & 0 & 0 & 11 & 2 & 13 & 6 & 3 \\
19 & 7 & 12 & 1 & 5 & 16 & 0 & 14 & 4 & 8
\end{array}
$$

This type of data is called **discrete** since the variable (number of absentees) can only take on specific values, i.e. whole numbers. The class intervals in the frequency table of such a variable would normally be specified by both the upper and lower limits, unlike the previous examples, where only the lower limit has been stated. The tally chart given

Number of absentees	Tally	Number of days
0–4	//// ////	10
5–9	//// ////	9
10–14	//// /	6
15–19	////	4
20–24	/	1

▷ **Figure 1.4** Tally chart for number of absentees.

in Figure 1.4 enables the frequencies for each class to be evaluated. The tally chart yields the following frequency table:

Number of absentees:	0–4	5–9	10–14	15–19	20–24
Number of days:	10	9	6	4	1

Having obtained the frequency table shown here, the absentee rates can then be further analysed as described in the following sections.

1.3   Graphical representation

An illustration of the data obtained is one of the primary methods of analysis most frequently used. In this section a variety of graphical methods will be introduced to illustrate specific data types. The following graph types are most common for business analysis:

▶ Histograms
▶ Bar charts
▶ Line graphs
▶ Pie graphs

Other graphical approaches used are often variations on the four types listed here. The following examples indicate where each of these graph types is used in the representation of data.

1.3.1   The histogram

The histogram is the most important diagram for use in illustrating frequency tables.

> **Definition:** *A histogram is a graph used to represent data from a frequency table where each frequency is represented by a block.*

Figure 1.5 shows a histogram of the wages data tabulated in the previous section:

Weekly earnings (£):	300–	400–	500–	600–	700–	800–
No. of employees:	2	5	9	12	8	4

Each block on the histogram represents a frequency for a specific class interval. For example, the two employees earning between £300 and £400 are illustrated by the first block in the diagram. In general, the area of each block in a histogram is proportional to the frequency it represents.

A slight complication arises when drawing a histogram of discrete data. Usually there are no gaps between blocks in the diagram. However, when considering a frequency table of discrete data such as the absentee information shown below there seem to be gaps between successive class intervals.

Number of absentees:	0–4	5–9	10–14	15–19	20–24
Number of days:	10	9	6	4	1

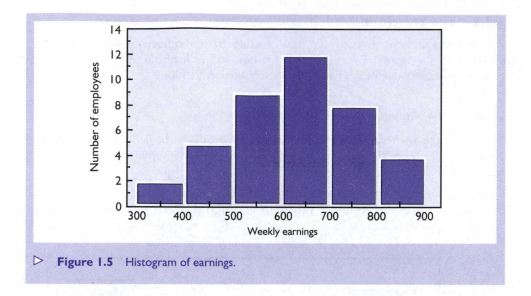

▷ **Figure 1.5** Histogram of earnings.

For instance, the first class ends at 4 and the second class commences at 5. However, there are actually no gaps between these classes, and this must be illustrated on the histogram. This is achieved by closing the gaps and joining the respective blocks midway. Thus the blocks 0–4 and 5–9 are joined together on the diagram at $4\frac{1}{2}$ on the horizontal scale. Figure 1.6 illustrates the resulting histogram of the absentee data. This sounds complicated, and in practice the values on the horizontal scale where the blocks meet (i.e. $4\frac{1}{2}$, $9\frac{1}{2}$, $14\frac{1}{2}$, etc.) are not displayed. It is more likely that the class intervals themselves will simply be specified along the axis as indicated.

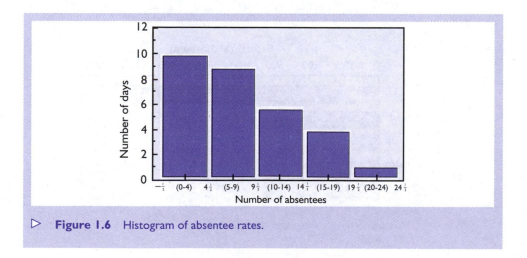

▷ **Figure 1.6** Histogram of absentee rates.

1.3.2 The bar graph

The bar graph is often used for data relating to non-numerical (or 'qualitative') variables. For example, Figure 1.7 shows a bar graph illustrating the daily output of four production companies. (The figures are quoted in $1000s.)

Company:	A	B	C	D
Production output:	12	6	9	14

The bar graph is one of few graphs that can be produced horizontally or vertically. Figure 1.8 illustrates the value of exports from a number of countries during a given month. (The figures quoted are given in $10 millions.)

Country:	USA	Canada	UK	France	Germany
Exports:	700	350	170	210	480

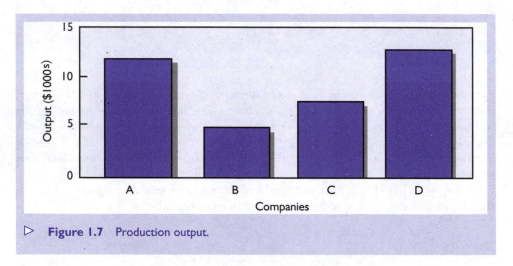

▷ **Figure 1.7**   Production output.

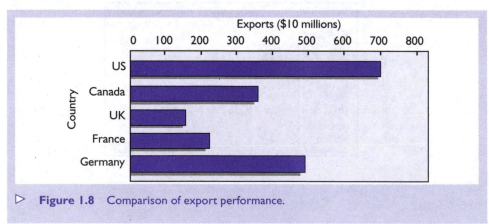

▷ **Figure 1.8**   Comparison of export performance.

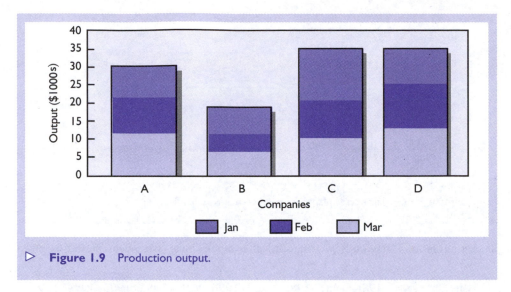

▷ **Figure 1.9** Production output.

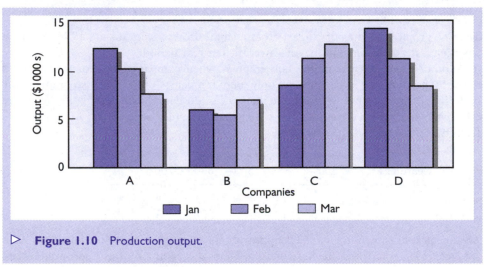

▷ **Figure 1.10** Production output.

This type of graph has a number of variations such as the stacked bar graph and the multiple bar graph illustrated in Figures 1.9 and 1.10, based on the production output of four companies over three successive months.

1.3.3 The line graph

The line graph (otherwise referred to as the frequency polygon) can be used to illustrate data in two main situations. Firstly, the line graph is often used to illustrate data given over a time period. For instance, Figure 1.11 illustrates a line graph of the

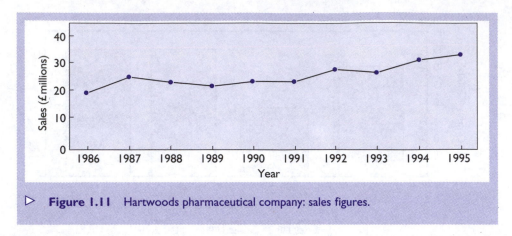

▷ **Figure 1.11**   Hartwoods pharmaceutical company: sales figures.

sales figures for Hartwoods pharmaceutical company over a ten-year period as given below:

Year:	1986	1987	1988	1989	1990	1991	1992	1993	1994	1995
Sales (£millions):	19	25	22	21	23	23	28	26	32	34

The line graph illustrates that apart from a slight drop in sales during 1988–89 there has been a steady increase in the sales over the ten-year period.

Another important use of the line graph is when comparing two or more sets of data. In general, when illustrating only one frequency table the histogram is the preferred diagram. However, for more than one set of data the line graph is much more effective. For example, consider the weekly earnings of a sample of forty employees from two companies as shown below:

	No. of employees:					
Weekly earnings (£)	300–	400–	500–	600–	700–	800–
Co. A:	2	5	9	12	8	4
Co. B:	7	14	8	7	3	1

The line graphs shown in Figure 1.12 illustrate the earnings in the two companies. Each frequency is represented by a point drawn in the centre of the appropriate class interval. The line graph provides an ideal method of comparing sets of data. For instance, it can be seen from the graph that the earnings of employees in company A are generally higher than those in company B. If required, the same graph could be used to illustrate the earnings for additional companies by the incorporation of extra lines.

1.3.4   The pie graph

The pie graph gives an alternative method of illustrating data. The primary application of this type of graph is to illustrate individual values related to the total amount. For

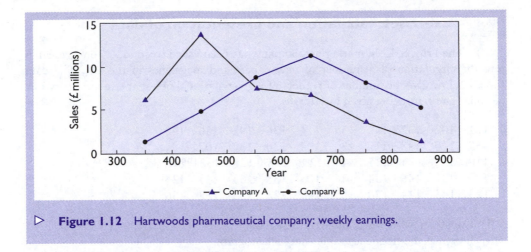

▷ **Figure 1.12** Hartwoods pharmaceutical company: weekly earnings.

example, the data in the following table give the annual costs incurred by a number of departments in a specific product range.

Departments:	Production	Sales	Marketing	Research	Logistics
Expenditure (£millions):	17	9	3	5	2

The pie graph shown in Figure 1.13 illustrates the proportion of expenditure in each department compared to the total expenditure. For instance, it can be seen from the graph that almost half the total expenditure on the product relates to Production costs.

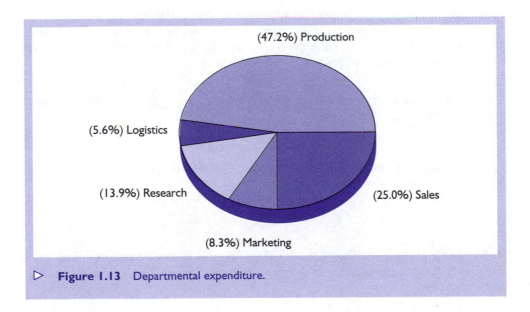

▷ **Figure 1.13** Departmental expenditure.

| **1.4** | **Exercises: tabulation and presentation of data** |

1.(E)   The Fritz & Kohl marketing company has been asked to conduct some research into the circulation of a number of newspapers and magazines in the UK. The data shown below give the number of readers of a given national newspaper over a fifty-day period. (The figures are given in 10 000s.)

```
121  102  132  142  139  114  136  142  156  145
135  140  148  117  125  134  120  137  107  134
110  150   94  135  144  111  145  128  133  146
137  127  146  154  136  105  138  153  143  124
123  145  114  130  125  149  128  133  118  136
```

(i)   Construct a frequency table of these data.
(ii)   Illustrate the frequency table using a histogram.
(iii)   Comment on the use of other diagrams, such as the line graph, in illustrating this type of data.

2.(I)   The table given below shows the sales figures (in £1000s) for a small clothing company over a forty-day period.

```
16.8  15.6   8.0  14.0  10.2   9.2  10.4   7.5  10.9  17.4
13.6   6.3  12.5  15.3   8.1  12.0  16.2  12.7  14.6  19.0
17.0   9.7  15.1  10.2  17.9  11.0  14.2  10.7   8.6  11.2
15.7  11.5   8.3  13.2  12.2  11.5   6.9  11.7  18.3  14.9
```

(i)   Tabulate the data given and illustrate using an appropriate graph.
(ii)   Comment on the shape of the graph. Do you find this surprising? What could cause such a shape, and how could you check whether this is the correct distribution of sales values?

3.(I)   Use a suitable diagram to compare the weekly sales of the two companies over the past 100 weeks as shown below.

| | | | | No. of weeks | | | |
Weekly sales (£1000s)	20–	25–	30–	35–	40–	45–	50–
Co. A:	15	26	19	15	11	9	5
Co. B:	10	22	25	22	10	7	4

4.(E)   Use a pie graph to illustrate the volume of sales in world markets during 1996 for the Hartwoods pharmaceutical company as shown below. The figures are given in $tens of millions.

Global sector	Sales volumes
Europe	70
Australasia	25
Asia	40
N. America	130
S. America	20
Africa	15

1.5   Averages

The average value (sometimes referred to as the measure of location or measure of centre) is the most important single statistic used to summarise data. The average value provides an idea of the most 'typical' or 'central' value in the variable range. It is common to read published material such as company reports and financial statements that quote averages for a variety of variables. For instance, the average earnings, average production, average working hours and average sales are frequently quoted in various forms. When considering such statistics, care must be taken to discover exactly how these averages have been calculated. There are a variety of methods used to evaluate averages, and each method can often produce differing values. The methods described in this section are the three most commonly used measures of 'averages' in most practical situations.

> **Definition:** *An average is a statistic giving the estimate of the 'middle' or 'centre' of the data under consideration.*

1.5.1   The arithmetic mean

The arithmetic mean, usually referred to as simply the mean, is the most commonly used estimate of the average. Indeed, for many people it is the only average that is ever considered. The main advantage of using this measure is that there is a standard mathematical formula that can be applied. This at least ensures the objectivity of the value obtained. The following give a range of examples to illustrate the calculation of the arithmetic mean.

> **Definition:** *An arithmetic mean is obtained by finding the sum of all values divided by the number of values.*

EXAMPLE 1

The weekly earnings of a group of five employees are as follows:

£400, £350, £520, £440, £490

The mean of these values is obtained by adding the values up and dividing by the number of values.

Thus, the mean $= \dfrac{400 + 350 + 520 + 440 + 490}{5}$

$= \dfrac{2200}{5}$

$= 440$

Therefore the mean wage for this group of employees is £440 per week.

In general, given a list of n values of x, the mean is obtained by the formulae

$\bar{x} = \Sigma x / n$

The Σ (based on the Greek letter *sigma*) means 'the sum of'. Therefore this formula is read as the sum of x divided by n.

EXAMPLE 2

Consider the frequency table below, giving the number of absentees from work over the past 20 days.

Number of absentees:	1	2	3	4	5
Number of days:	4	7	5	2	2

The mean number of absentees per day is calculated by adding up the values and dividing by the number of days. In this table, on 4 days there was only one absence, on 7 days there were 2 absences, and so on. To obtain the mean we must add up all these values and divide by the number (20) as shown below:

$\text{Mean} = \dfrac{1+1+1+1+2+2+2+2+2+2+2+3+3+3+3+3+4+4+5+5}{20}$

A simplified way of writing this would be:

$\text{Mean} = \dfrac{4 \times 1 + 7 \times 2 + 5 \times 3 + 2 \times 4 + 2 \times 5}{20}$

$= \dfrac{4 + 14 + 15 + 8 + 10}{20}$

$= \dfrac{51}{20} = 2.55$

Thus, on average, as estimated by the mean, there are just over $2\frac{1}{2}$ absences per day in this company.

Consider the notation for the formula calculated. We are given a frequency table as shown:

Number of absentees (x):   1   2   3   4   5
Number of days (f):   4   7   5   2   2

The variable (the number of absentees) is denoted by x, and the frequency (the number of days) is denoted by f.

The mean is obtained by multiplying the values of f by the corresponding values of x and summing. This value is then divided by the total number of values, which is obtained by finding the sum of the frequencies.

Thus, given a frequency table, the mean is obtained by the following formula:

$$\bar{x} = \frac{\sum fx}{\sum f}$$

EXAMPLE 3

The formula specified in the previous example can be used for any data given in the form of a frequency table. However, when class intervals are specified in the table then it is necessary to use the mid-points of each class to represent the values of x. Consider the following frequency table of earnings of a group of employees.

Weekly earnings (£):   300–   400–   500–   600–   700–   800–
No. of employees: 2   5   9   12   8   4

The calculations for the mean of these data are generally tabulated in columns, as shown below:

x (Mid values)	f	fx
350	2	700
450	5	2250
550	9	4950
650	12	7800
750	8	6000
850	4	3400
Totals	$\sum f = 40$	$\sum fx = 25\,100$

The mean is then obtained as follows:

$$\bar{x} = \frac{\sum fx}{\sum f} = \frac{25\,100}{40} = 627.5$$

Thus, the mean wage for this group of employees is £627.50.

This value can be used in a variety of ways. First, it is used purely as a way of describing the data. Thus, quoting the mean wage will give an indication of the earnings of employees in this company. Secondly, the value can be used in comparing two or more sets of data. For instance, if the mean wage in a second company was found to be £700, then this would tell us something concerning the relative earnings of the two groups of employees. Consequently, such information could, for example, provide a guide and a useful starting position in negotiations between employees and management over increased pay. However, the mean can be distorted by extreme values and must therefore be used with care. For instance, if one employee in the group given above earns £2000 per week then the resulting mean would be considerably changed.

1.5.2   The mode

The average of a set of values can be obtained by estimating the mode. The mode can briefly be defined as the most frequent value in a set of data. This estimate gives the most 'typical' value in the data, and is often regarded as more representative than the arithmetic mean. The following examples illustrate the procedure of estimating the mode given data in different formats.

Definition: *The mode is a measure of the 'average' obtained by finding the most frequent value in the data.*

EXAMPLE 1

The list of values below show the number of employees absent from work over a ten-day period:

   3, 5, 2, 1, 4, 3, 2, 0, 3, 6

From this list of values it can be seen that 3 occurs more often than any other single value. Therefore the mode = 3 employees. Thus the 'average' number of employees absent from work can be stated as 3.

EXAMPLE 2

The table below shows the number of absentees from work over the last three weeks (21 days).

Number of absentees:	0	1	2	3	4
Number of days:	2	8	6	3	2

From this frequency table it can be seen that the most frequent value is 1. That is, there are more days in which only one employee was absent than any other number of absences.

   Thus, the mode = 1 employee

It can be seen that with a simple frequency table such as given in this example the estimation of the mode is trivial. We simply find the highest frequency and then quote the value of the corresponding variable. When the frequency table contains class intervals the process is more difficult, as shown in the following example.

EXAMPLE 3

Consider the weekly earnings for a group of 40 employees as previously discussed.

Weekly earnings (£):	300–	400–	500–	600–	700–	800–
No. of employees:	2	5	9	12	8	4

In the process of grouping values together in class intervals as in this example, we have lost much of the detail from the original raw data. For instance, it is impossible to find precisely the most frequent single value. There may be no two employees earning the same wage and thus no unique mode. Alternatively, the mode could be in any of the class intervals in this table. For instance, if two employees earned exactly £300 and no other employees earned the same wage then strictly speaking the mode would be £300. This would not be a very appropriate estimate of the average! However, since much of the detail has been lost we need to estimate the most likely value for the mode from the data given. We see that the most frequent class interval in this table is £600 and above. Thus it is reasonable to assume that the mode will lie within this group. One estimate of the mode would be the centre of this class, i.e. £650. Although this is reasonable, a better estimate can be obtained with reference to the frequencies on either side of the highest value. We can see that there are more values below 600– than there are above. Therefore it is more likely that the mode is in the lower half of this class interval. For instance, instead of £650 it may be £640, or £630. One accepted method of obtaining

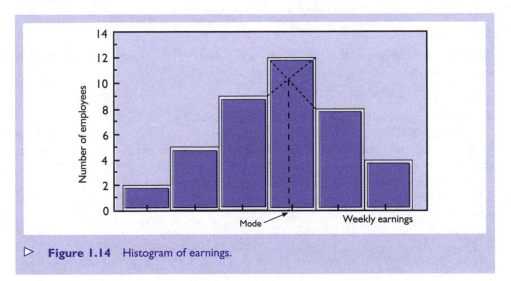

▷   **Figure 1.14**   Histogram of earnings.

a reasonable estimate of this value is to use a histogram as shown in Figure 1.14. The histogram shown in Figure 1.14 has a construction on the highest block in order to obtain an estimate of the mode. Essentially, a straight line is drawn from the top right hand corner of the tallest block down to where the left hand block joins. Similarly, a line is drawn from the top left hand corner down to where the right hand block joins. The intersection of these two lines is then extended down to the horizontal axis in order to obtain an estimate of the mode.

As can be seen from the graph, the estimate of the mode = £643.

It should be stated that the original definition of the mode as the most frequent value has now been superseded. Any estimate of the mode obtained in the way described is unlikely to be the most frequent value for the reasons already expressed. However, this method of estimating the mode is still valid, and in many practical examples provides a better way of expressing the 'average' than other methods such as the mean.

1.5.3   The median

The median is an additional method of obtaining the average of a set of data. In some ways this is the most sensible and obvious way of finding an estimate of the centre of values. The median is literally the middle value, assuming that the data are listed in numerical order. The following examples will indicate the method of obtaining the median.

> **Definition:**   *The median is a measure of the average obtained by locating the 'central' value in the list of data when sorted into numerical order.*

EXAMPLE 1

Find the median wage from the list of earnings given:

  £500, £450, £290, £760, £375, £430, £410

To obtain the median of this set of values, the data should be sorted into numerical order as shown:

  £290, £375, £410, £430, £450, £500, £760

The middle value of this list is the fourth value, i.e. £430. Thus, the median = £430.

The median is the value that splits the data into halves. Therefore, in general, there should be the same number of values above and below the median. In this example, there are three values above and three values below the median.

It is useful to consider a general formula that will give the position of the median in a list. For instance, in this example the median was the fourth value out of a total of seven numbers.

In general, given n values the median $= \left(\dfrac{n+1}{2}\right)$th number

Thus, given a list of 5 values the median $= \left(\dfrac{5+1}{2}\right)$ th number

$$= 3\text{rd number}$$

Similarly, given a list of 10 values the median $= \left(\dfrac{10+1}{2}\right)$ th number

$$= 5\tfrac{1}{2}\text{th number}$$

That is halfway between the 5th and the 6th values.

EXAMPLE 2

Consider the frequency table illustrating the number of absentees from work over a period of three weeks (21 days).

Number of absentees:	0	1	2	3	4
Number of days:	2	8	6	3	2

In this table the total number of days $= n = \Sigma\, f = 21$

Therefore the median $= \left(\dfrac{n+1}{2}\right)$ th value $= \left(\dfrac{21+1}{2}\right)$ th $= 11$ th value

Now we should search for the 11th value in these data. There are 2 days in which no absences occurred; another 8 days in which 1 absence occurred. Therefore the first ten values are either 0 or 1. Thus, the 11th value will be a 2.

Therefore, the median $= 2$ employees.

EXAMPLE 3

This process of first finding the position of the median in order to obtain the estimate can be extended to a frequency table containing class intervals as shown in the following example. Consider the earnings of the group of employees previously tabulated.

Weekly earnings (£):	300–	400–	500–	600–	700–	800–
No. of employees:	2	5	9	12	8	4

In this table the number of values $= n = \Sigma f = 40$

Therefore the median $= \left(\dfrac{n+1}{2}\right)$ th value $= \left(\dfrac{40+1}{2}\right)$ th $= 20\tfrac{1}{2}$ th value

It can be seen that the first three classes contain a total of 16 employees; the next class (£600 and above) contains the next 12 employees. Thus, the $20\frac{1}{2}$th value must be included in this class. Therefore, the median is in the class £600 and above. In addition to locating the class interval, it is necessary to estimate the actual value of the $20\frac{1}{2}$th number. This can be achieved with the aid of a cumulative frequency curve (or **ogive**).

Definition: *An ogive is a graphical representation of the cumulative frequencies.*

The cumulative frequencies shown in the following table are evaluated by finding the frequency **below** a given value. For example, the frequency below 300 (i.e. the number of employees earning below £300) is zero. Similarly, the frequency below 400 is 2, and the frequency below 500 is 7 (i.e. there are seven employees earning below £500 in the table). The complete table of cumulative frequencies is shown below:

Weekly earnings (£)	Cumulative frequency (frequency under given value)
300	0
400	2
500	7
600	16
700	28
800	36
900	40

The values in the cumulative frequency table can be plotted onto a graph as shown in Figure 1.15.

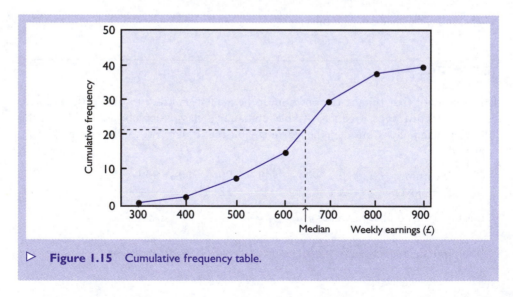

▷ **Figure 1.15** Cumulative frequency table.

The process of drawing a curve connecting the points plotted is the way in which we can estimate non-tabular values. The $20\frac{1}{2}$th value is estimated as shown on the graph by extending a line from 20.5 on the vertical scale across to the ogive, and then drawing down to the horizontal axis. The value obtained is the estimate of the median. It should be noted that in practice, if the cumulative frequency points are connected with straight lines, then a reasonable median estimate is still obtained. Theoretically, the best-fitting curve through the points drawn will provide the best estimate. However, it is usually difficult to obtain this accurately.

The graph illustrated in Figure 1.15 yields an estimate of the median = £638.

Thus, we can say that £638 is the central weekly wage. Therefore, half the employees earn less than £638 and half the employees earn more. Again, this can be a very useful method of expressing the 'average'. Indeed, with a number of variables, including earnings, the median is thought to be the most realistic method.

1.6   Comparison of averages

The three methods of obtaining an 'average' described in this section are all perfectly valid alternatives. Each method has its own advantages and limitations, as summarised in the table shown in Figure 1.16.

Method	Advantages	Disadvantages
Arithmetic mean	▶ Calculated using a formula ▶ The obvious choice for most people	▶ Can be distorted by extreme values ▶ Not always representative of data
Mode	▶ Simple to obtain ▶ The best way of specifying a 'typical' value in the data	▶ Estimation based on graph (though there is a mathematical alternative) ▶ Unsuitable for 'non-standard' distributions, i.e. those incorporating two or more peaks
Median	▶ The actual 'central' value ▶ Usually considered as the most representative value	▶ Estimation based on graph or corresponding mathematical method

▷ **Figure 1.16** Comparison of average methods.

The arithmetic mean (or simply the mean) is usually regarded as the primary method of calculation of the average. The obvious method of estimating the average of a list of numbers is to add up the values and then divide by the number of items. This is the basic method of calculating the arithmetic mean, which can be extended for frequency tables. However, although this estimate is the most obvious method, it is often the least appropriate in many circumstances. Consider the distribution of wages shown in Figure 1.17. This graph illustrates a typical distribution of earnings of the total workforce in a large organisation. This is a positively skewed distribution since there is a longer tail on the right hand end of the scale. The earnings of the bulk of employees are situated towards the lower end of the range. Only a few employees have earnings at the top end of the range. These few employees at the top end tend to distort the value of the mean. Thus the 'average' quoted using the mean value tends to be higher than is reasonably representative. The mode value corresponds to the peak of the frequencies displayed in the distribution. With this type of shape of the distribution this value tends to be at the lower end of the earnings range and is therefore not totally representative either. The median value, being the central value, is a compromise between the other measures, and is often regarded as being the best measure. Figure 1.17 illustrates the values of the mean, median and mode. The three estimates will only correspond when the distribution of data is symmetrical. If the distribution is negatively skewed then these values are reversed. Thus the mean will be the lowest value, and the mode the highest. Figure 1.18 illustrates three types of distribution with appropriate estimates of the three 'averages'. The illustrations simply show the shape of each distribution. Thus the curves drawn indicate the outline of the corresponding histogram. For instance, Figure 1.18(i) shows a shape representing the same distribution as that displayed in Figure 1.17.

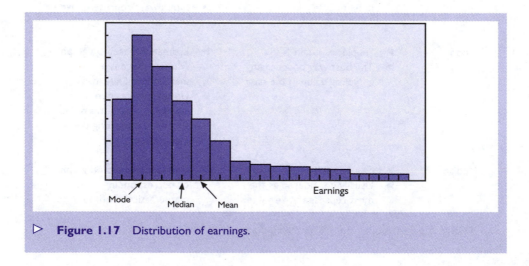

▷   **Figure 1.17**   Distribution of earnings.

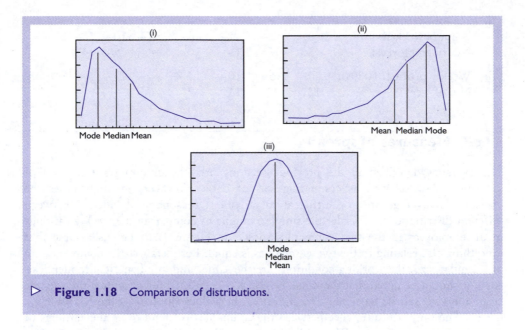

▷ **Figure 1.18**   Comparison of distributions.

| 1.7 | **Exercises: averages** |

1.(E) The table below shows the number of absentees in a company each day over a period of 60 working days.

Number of absentees: 0   1   2   3   4   5   6
Number of days: 12 16 11   6   8   3   4

Calculate the mean, median and mode for this set of data. What would you say is the most appropriate measure of average in this type of data?

2.(I) Given the following data on the bank balances of 50 customers who are in credit.

Balance (£):   0– 200– 400– 600– 800– 1000–
No. of accounts: 12   18   10   6   3   1

Find the average bank balance by using the:

(a) mean   (b) mode   (c) median

Comment on the differences between these values.

3.(I) Find the mean, median and mode for each of the following frequency tables

(i) Wages(£):   200– 300– 400– 500– 600–
     No. of earners: 4   7   6   5   3

(ii) No. of overtime

hours worked:	0–	2–	4–	6–	8–	10–	12–
No. of employees:	3	7	13	10	8	5	4

(ii)

Weekly profit (£1000s):	0–	5–	10–	15–	20–	25–
No. of weeks:	13	17	11	9	6	4

1.8	**Measures of spread**

The averages described in the previous sections provide an important method of describing data as well as comparing sets of data. However, in many cases the measures of average are not sufficient to provide a reasonable distinction between different distributions. Consider the simple example of comparing the weekly earnings of all employees in the two companies shown in Figure 1.19. Let us assume that everything else relating to the two companies is equal. For instance, the companies are of a similar size, the working conditions are the same, and any benefits are identical. Also, it should be noted that the same method has been used for obtaining the average from the two sets of earnings. For instance, the values quoted are both arithmetic means. The only real difference between the companies is found to be the earnings of their respective employees. The table shows that the average wage in company B is slightly higher than that in company A. Thus, given a choice, most of us would wish to work for company B given this information. However, the averages do not show us the complete picture. For instance, it would be useful to know the highest and lowest earnings in the two companies in order to gain a better comparison. Thus, the table in Figure 1.20 gives a comparison of the two companies incorporating this additional information. With reference to the additional information given in this table, company A may now be considered in a more favourable light. It can be seen that the minimum earnings are similar in the two companies, and the maximum earnings are considerably higher in company A. Thus, although the average in B is slightly higher than in A for many employees, the earnings potential in A is much better. The employees in company B all earn a similar wage. This means that there is little room for an employee's development, and there are minimal incentives for progressing up through the organisation. Alternatively, in company A there seems to be considerable scope for development. The range of earnings is significantly higher, indicating that the pay

Weekly earnings (£)	Company	
	A	B
Averages	400	420

▷ **Figure 1.19**   Comparison of averages.

Weekly earnings (£)	Company	
	A	B
Averages	400	420
Highest	1000	500
Lowest	350	350

▷ **Figure 1.20** Comparison of companies.

scales of different employee grades in the company could be wide, and therefore there is considerable incentive for high achievers in this organisation. Given this information, the choice between the two companies is more complex. The more ambitious employees would choose to work in company A whereas the lower paid employees are better off in B.

This example shows a situation in which the averages do not present the total picture. It can be seen that in addition to the average measures, some indication of the spread in the two sets of data can be useful. In this section we will consider a number of measures of spread that can be used for this purpose.

1.8.1   The range

The range is the simplest measure of spread of a set of data. The range is the distance between the highest and lowest values in the distribution. The following examples illustrate the calculation of the range.

> **Definition:**   *The range is a simple measure of spread found by calculating the difference between the highest and lowest values in the data.*

EXAMPLE 1

Find the range of the following values giving the weekly revenue obtained by a small retail organisation over the past ten weeks. (The figures are given in £1000s.)

12, 20, 15, 8, 5, 14, 22, 13, 10, 17

To obtain the range we find the largest and smallest values in the data. In this example the maximum value is 22, and the minimum value is 5. Therefore, the range is calculated as:

Range = 22 − 5 = 17

Thus, the range for these data is £17 000.

EXAMPLE 2

The table below shows the number of absentees in an organisation taken over the past 50 days.

Number of absentees:	3	4	5	6	7	8	9	10
Number of days:	2	5	7	12	11	6	4	3

In this table, the largest number of absentees in a given day is 10, and the smallest number is 3. Thus, the range = 10 − 3 = 7 absentees.

EXAMPLE 3

The table below shows the weekly production figures for a small electronics company taken over a 40-week period.

Production output ($1000s):	20–	24–	28–	32–	36–	40–
Number of weeks:		3	9	12	15	7	4

In this table the highest possible value is below $44 000 (assuming that the class intervals are all of the same width). Similarly, the lowest possible value is $20 000. Therefore, for these data the range = 44 000 − 20 000 = $24 000.

1.8.2   The inter-quartile range

The range described in the previous section has a number of limitations. In general, the range cannot be satisfactorily used to compare sets of data since it can be easily distorted by extreme isolated values. For example, the table below shows the weekly earnings of a group of 100 employees in two companies, A and B.

Weekly earnings (£s):		200–	300–	400–	500–	600–	700–	800–	900–
No. of	Co. A:	25	38	23	13	0	0	0	1
employees	Co. B:	25	38	23	14	0	0	0	0

The ranges for the two sets of data are as follows:

Range for Co. A = 1000 − 200 = £800
Range for Co. B = 600 − 200 = £400

It can be seen that the spread as indicated by the range for company A is double that of company B. However, when the original frequency tables are investigated, this difference can be attributed to a single employee who earns in the 900– class, compared to an extra employee in the 500– class for company B. Thus, one extreme value has totally distorted the value of the range. Therefore, the range cannot be relied upon to provide a reasonable comparison of sets of data. Consequently, an alternative method of measuring spread is required. The inter-quartile range (IQR) is found to be a suitable value. The IQR is obtained by only considering the 'range' for the central 50% of values in the data. Figure 1.21 illustrates the distribution of a set of data. If we ignore the lowest 25%, and the highest 25% of values, then the range containing the central 50% of values is called the inter-quartile range, as shown in the diagram. The two values at the extremes of the central 50% are called the quartiles. The inter-quartile range is the distance between the lower quartile (Q_1) and the upper quartile (Q_3) shown on the graph. These quartiles can be obtained in much the same way as the median was found in an earlier section. Effectively, the median is half way through the distribution and is the $((n+1)/2)$th value.

Similarly, the lower quartile is located a quarter of the way through the distribution, and the upper quartile is three-quarters of the way through the data. Thus, these quartiles can be obtained as follows:

Lower quartile, $\quad Q_1 = \left(\dfrac{n+1}{4}\right)$th value

Upper quartile, $\quad Q_3 = \frac{3}{4}(n+1)$th value

Having obtained these two values the inter-quartile range can be obtained as follows:

$$IQR = Q_3 - Q_1$$

Definition: *The inter-quartile range is the difference between the upper and lower quartiles. This value gives the range containing the central 50% of data.*

The following examples illustrate the estimation of the IQR.

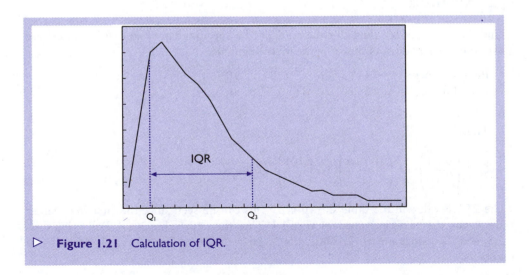

▷ **Figure 1.21** Calculation of IQR.

EXAMPLE 1

The data below show the values of a random sample of 15 shares listed on the London Stock Exchange.

2.20 1.50 3.00 5.55 4.42
3.17 0.96 7.83 1.65 2.58
2.10 0.58 1.75 1.20 3.74

Sorting these values into numerical order we have:

0.58, 0.96, 1.20, 1.50, 1.65, 1.75, 2.10, 2.20, 2.58,
3.00, 3.17, 3.74, 4.42, 5.55, 7.83

In this example, the value of $n = 15$.
Thus,

$$Q_1 = \left(\frac{n+1}{4}\right)\text{th} = \left(\frac{15+1}{4}\right)\text{th} = \left(\frac{16}{4}\right)\text{th} = \text{4th value}$$

The 4th value in the sorted list shown is 1.50. Therefore, $Q_1 = £1.50$.
Similarly,

$$Q_3 = \tfrac{3}{4}(n+1)\text{th} = \tfrac{3}{4}(15+1)\text{th} = \tfrac{3}{4}(16)\text{th} = \text{12th value}$$

The 12th value in the sorted list is 3.74. Thus, $Q_3 = £3.74$. Finally, having obtained the values of the quartiles, we can estimate the inter-quartile range (IQR) $= Q_3 - Q_1 = 3.74 - 1.50 = £2.24$

EXAMPLE 2

Find the inter-quartile range for the number of a specific item of stock in a warehouse over the last 100 days as shown in the following table:

Items of stock:	3	4	5	6	7	8	9	10
No. of days:	4	12	22	20	16	12	8	6

In this example, $n = 100$.
Thus,

$$Q_1 = \left(\frac{n+1}{4}\right)\text{th} = \left(\frac{100+1}{4}\right)\text{th} = \left(\frac{101}{4}\right)\text{th} = 25\tfrac{1}{4}\text{th value}$$

The $25\tfrac{1}{4}$th value in the table shown is 5. This can be seen since the first four values are 3, and the next twelve values are all 4. Thus the 16th value is a 4. Following this, the next 22 values are all 5. Thus, the $25\tfrac{1}{4}$th value is 5. Therefore, $Q_1 = 5$ items of stock.

Similarly,

$$Q_3 = \tfrac{3}{4}(n+1)\text{th} = \tfrac{3}{4}(100+1)\text{th} = \tfrac{3}{4}(101)\text{th} = 75\tfrac{3}{4}\text{th value}$$

Consideration of the frequency table shows that the 74th value is a 7, and the 75th value is an 8. The $75\tfrac{3}{4}$th value is therefore 8.

Consequently, $Q_3 = 8$ items of stock.

Finally, the inter-quartile range can be estimated. $\text{IQR} = Q_3 - Q_1$
$$= 8 - 5 = 3 \text{ items}$$

EXAMPLE 3

Find the IQR for the table of weekly earnings for a group of employees given below.

Weekly earnings (£):	300–	400–	500–	600–	700–	800–
Number of employees:	28	47	49	17	9	5

In this example, $n = $ total number of employees $= 155$.
Thus

$$Q_1 = \left(\frac{n+1}{4}\right)\text{th} = \left(\frac{155+1}{4}\right)\text{th} = \left(\frac{156}{4}\right)\text{th} = 39\text{th value}$$

Similarly,

$$Q_3 = \tfrac{3}{4}(n+1)\text{th} = \tfrac{3}{4}(155+1)\text{th} = \tfrac{3}{4}(156)\text{th} = 117\text{th value}$$

These values can be estimated using an ogive in the same way as the median was estimated in an earlier section. Figure 1.22 illustrates the ogive for the set of data based

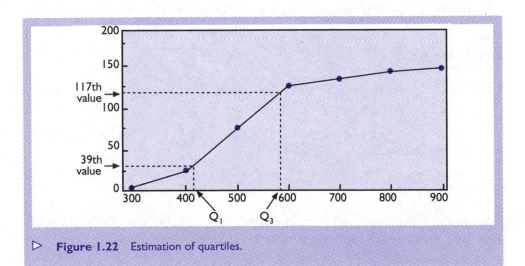

▷ **Figure 1.22** Estimation of quartiles.

on the cumulative frequencies shown below:

Weekly earnings (£):	300	400	500	600	700	800	900
Cumulative frequency:	0	28	75	124	141	150	155

The values of the quartiles obtained from the ogive as illustrated in Figure 1.22 are:

Lower quartile, Q_1 = £425
Upper quartile, Q_3 = £585

Therefore, the inter-quartile range is = $Q_3 - Q_1 = 585 - 425 = £160$

1.8.3   The standard deviation

One of the most important measures of spread is the standard deviation (usually denoted by s or σ). A major advantage of the standard deviation is that it can be calculated by an objective mathematical formula rather than using estimation methods as required for the inter-quartile range. The standard deviation of a sample of values can be calculated by the following formula:

$$\text{Standard deviation} = s = \sqrt{\frac{\sum (x - \bar{x})^2}{n}}$$

Alternatively, the standard deviation can be obtained from a frequency table using either of the following formulae:

$$\text{Standard deviation} = s = \sqrt{\frac{\sum f(x - \bar{x})^2}{\sum f}} = \sqrt{\frac{\sum fx^2}{\sum f} - (\bar{x})^2}$$

The following examples illustrate the calculation of the standard deviation.

Definition: *The standard deviation is a measure of spread found by the square root of the average sum of squares of deviations between each value and the mean.*

EXAMPLE 1

The number of hours of overtime worked by a group of ten employees is shown below:

2   3   5   1   0   1   7   4   2   5

The number of overtime hours is the variable (denoted by x) that we wish to find the standard deviation of. Firstly, we find the mean

$$\bar{x} = \frac{\sum x}{n} = \frac{30}{10} = 3$$

Now we can calculate the values of $(x - \bar{x})$ by subtracting the value of the mean ($\bar{x}$) away from each value of x as given below:

$x - \bar{x}$:   −1   0   2   −2   −3   −2   4   1   −1   2

Now we can square all these values to obtain:

$(x - \bar{x})^2$: 1 0 4 4 9 4 16 1 1 4

Finally the total of these values is found:

$$\sum (x - \bar{x})^2 = 44$$

Thus, the standard deviation can be calculated as follows:

$$s = \sqrt{\frac{\sum (x - \bar{x})^2}{n}} = \sqrt{\frac{44}{10}} = \sqrt{4.4} = 2.1 \text{ correct to one decimal place.}$$

EXAMPLE 2

Consider the table giving the number of stock items available on each day over a period of one hundred days.

Items of stock: 3   4   5   6   7   8   9 10
No. of days: 4 12 22 20 16 12   8   6

The mean and standard deviation of these data can be obtained by the tabulation as shown below. The number of items in stock is the variable under consideration (denoted by x) and the number of days is the corresponding frequency (denoted by f). Firstly, the mean ($\bar{x}$) is calculated using the formulae $\sum fx / \sum f$. Then the remaining three columns in the table can be obtained.

x	f	fx	$x - \bar{x}$	$(x - \bar{x})^2$	$f(x - \bar{x})^2$
3	4	12	−3.3	10.89	43.56
4	12	48	−2.3	5.29	63.48
5	22	110	−1.3	1.69	37.18
6	20	120	−0.3	0.09	1.8
7	16	112	0.7	0.49	7.84
8	12	96	1.7	2.89	34.68
9	8	72	2.7	7.29	58.32
10	6	60	3.7	13.69	82.14
	100	**630**			**329**

Now using the second and third columns from the above table we have:

$$\sum fx = 630 \text{ and } \sum f = 100$$

Therefore, the mean $= \bar{x} = \sum fx / \sum f = 630/100 = 6.3$ items.

Using this value for $\bar{x}$ the remaining columns are calculated as shown.
Finally, the value of $\sum f(x - \bar{x})^2$ is found to be equal to 329.
Thus the standard deviation is calculated as:

$$\text{Standard deviation} = s = \sqrt{\frac{\sum f(x - \bar{x})^2}{\sum f}} = \sqrt{\frac{329}{100}} = \sqrt{3.29} = 1.81 \text{ items}$$

It is generally considered to be simpler to use the alternative formula for the standard deviation:

$$\text{Standard deviation} = \sqrt{\frac{\sum fx^2}{\sum f} - (\bar{x})^2}$$

Using this formula it is only necessary to calculate the mean, and then evaluate an additional column for the calculation of $\sum fx^2$ as shown below:

x	f	fx	fx^2
3	4	12	36
4	12	48	192
5	22	110	550
6	20	120	720
7	16	112	784
8	12	96	768
9	8	72	648
10	6	60	600
Totals	**100**	**630**	**4298**

Using this table we can obtain the mean $= \dfrac{\sum fx}{\sum f} = \dfrac{630}{100} = 6.3$ items

Similarly, the standard deviation $= \sqrt{\dfrac{\sum fx^2}{\sum f} - (\bar{x})^2}$

$$= \sqrt{\frac{4298}{100} - (6.3)^2}$$

$$= \sqrt{42.98 - 39.69}$$

$$= \sqrt{3.29}$$

$$= \mathbf{1.81} \textbf{ items} \text{ as shown using the previous formula.}$$

EXAMPLE 3

Finally, consider the grouped frequency table of weekly earnings given below.

Weekly earnings (£): 300– 400– 500– 600– 700– 800–
No. of employees: 2   5   9   12   8   4

The calculations for the mean and standard deviation of these data are tabulated in the following table:

x (Mid values)	f	fx	fx^2
350	2	700	245 000
450	5	2250	1 012 500
550	9	4950	2 722 500
650	12	7800	5 070 000
750	8	6000	4 500 000
850	4	3400	2 890 000
Totals	$\Sigma f = 40$	$\Sigma fx = 25\ 100$	$\Sigma fx^2 = 16\ 440\ 000$

The mean is then obtained as follows:

$$\bar{x} = \frac{\Sigma fx}{\Sigma f} = \frac{25\ 100}{40} = 627.5$$

Similarly, the standard deviation is found as follows:

$$\text{standard deviation} = \sqrt{\frac{\Sigma fx^2}{\Sigma f} - (\bar{x})^2}$$

$$= \sqrt{\frac{16\ 440\ 000}{40} - (627.5)^2}$$

$$= \sqrt{411\ 000 - 393\ 756.25}$$

$$= \sqrt{17\ 243.75}$$

$$= £131.32$$

1.9 Interpretation of measures of spread

The previous section looked at a variety of measures of spread which could be used in summarising data. In particular, these values can provide a useful comparison of sets of data as shown in the following examples.

EXAMPLE 1

The market research company Spitz & Kohl have conducted a survey on the earnings in two industrial sectors, electronics and construction. The results shown below are based on a random sample of 1000 employees in each industry sector.

Statistics (Weekly earnings)	Industrial sectors	
	Electronics	Construction
Mean	£500	£400
Standard deviation	£80	£120

The means shown in the table show that the average earnings in the electronics industry are higher than in the construction industry. Thus, generally, electronics employees earn more than construction employees. However, the standard deviation of earnings in the construction industry is greater. This indicates that the spread of earnings in construction is more than in electronics. Thus, there is a wider dispersion of earnings in construction, and electronics employees earnings are bunched closer together. The standard deviation indicates the amount of spread for a given set of data. Therefore, a larger standard deviation shows a wider spread of values. According to the results shown in the table, earnings in the electronics industry are more consistent, and are generally closer to the mean than those in construction.

A similar comparison could be made by looking at different statistical measures such as those shown in the following table obtained from the same set of data.

Statistics (Weekly earnings)	Industrial sectors	
	Electronics	Construction
Median	£470	£350
Inter-quartile range	£140	£220

The medians indicate that the 'average' earnings in electronics are higher than in construction. The figures show that in the electronics industry half the employees sampled earn less than £470 and the other half earn more. Similarly, in construction the £350 figure is the central point splitting the employees sampled into halves. The inter-quartile range gives the range containing the 'central' 50% of employees. The employees in construction have a higher IQR, thus indicating that the spread of earnings in this sector is wider.

EXAMPLE 2

The production sector of the Hartwoods pharmaceutical company based in London produces a range of drugs including Butrothomine, a drug designed to relieve the symptoms of arthritis. The use of 'team working' at Hartwoods requires that the performances of individual production teams are monitored and carefully analysed. There are currently three teams (A, B and C) involved in the production of the Butrothomine drug, and the results shown below give an analysis of the daily output of these teams over the past three months.

Production output	Production teams		
(1000s of tablets)	Team A	Team B	Team C
Mean	45	48	39
Standard deviation	2.5	8.2	4.0

Firstly, consider a comparison of the mean output for the three teams. From the values shown it seems that team B is performing best, with team A close behind, and team C with the lowest output. Of course, a comparison of this type assumes that all other attributes are equal. For instance, it is assumed that the teams are all using the same machinery, with the same output capacities, and that other facilities, such as availability of raw materials, are equitable.

The comparison between the teams is more complicated when considering the standard deviation. The values shown indicate that the spread of daily output is much higher for team B, and is lowest in team A. This shows that the production output is relatively consistent in team A and very erratic for team B. The spread of output values for team C is between these two. This indicates that there may be a serious problem in team B. Production output for this team would be difficult to predict on a daily basis since the possible spread is very high. Conversely, team A is very consistent, and therefore it would be much easier to predict the output from this team. In management terms, there may be a problem with team B. For example, the high spread of output may be caused by disruptive staff, of high rates of sickness, or poor supervision. It seems that team B potentially can produce a higher output, and thus if the consistency can be improved an even higher average output could be achieved.

1.10   Comparison of measures of spread

The three measures of spread outlined in the previous sections are compared in the Figure 1.23.

In general, the inter-quartile range or the standard deviation is a reasonable estimate of the spread, and either value can be used as a means of comparison of two or more

Method	Advantages	Disadvantages
Range	▶ Simple to estimate ▶ Obvious interpretation of value	▶ Poor method of comparison of data ▶ Easily distorted by extreme isolated values
IQR	▶ Relatively easy to estimate ▶ Reasonable as a method for comparison of sets of data ▶ The determination of quartiles gives an indication of 'shape' for the distribution	▶ Evaluation requires graphical or alternative estimation method
Standard deviation	▶ Calculated by a mathematical formula ▶ Can be used to uniquely define some data distributions	▶ Formula can be offputting! ▶ Difficult to interpret single values

▷ **Figure 1.23**   Comparison of measures of spread.

sets of data. Alternatively, instead of quoting the IQR, more information can be simply expressed by stating the values of the upper and lower quartiles. The range is rarely used to compare sets of data since as demonstrated in the previous sections it can be easily distorted by extreme, isolated values. The standard deviation is not only an excellent way of comparing the spread in sets of data, but can also be used to actually uniquely define some distributions (see Chapter 2 on Probability).

1.11   Exercises: measures of spread

1.(E)   Find the range and inter-quartile range for each set of values given below:

  (i)   10, 4, 7, 12, 3, 2, 15, 8, 9, 6, 7, 4, 10, 30, 9, 8, 13, 10, 16
 (ii)   4, 20, 5, 28, 12, 7, 8, 3, 1, 10, 16, 19, 8, 5, 3, 22, 19, 12, 30

Comment on the difference between these two sets of data as indicated by the measures of spread that you have obtained.

2.(I)   The table below shows the weekly earnings of a sample of 50 employees from the Randolph company.

Weekly earnings (£):	300–	400–	500–	600–	700–
Number of employees:	5	20	15	7	3

(i) Find the median and inter-quartile range for earnings in this company.

(ii) By finding the median and inter-quartile range for the earnings in a second organisation (the Swartzkof company) compare the differences between the two companies.

Weekly earnings (£):	200–	300–	400–	500–	600–	700–	800–
Number of employees:	3	7	12	13	9	4	2

3.(D) Find the mean and standard deviation for the following sets of data:

(i) The weekly production output from a medium-sized steel plant over a period of 50 weeks:

Production output: (1000 tonnes)	20–	30–	40–	50–	60–	70–
Number of weeks:	7	14	11	9	6	3

(ii) The monthly profitability of a company over the past 100 months:

Monthly profit: (£100 000s)	2–	4–	6–	8–	10–
Number of months:	19	35	26	14	6

(iii) The weekly sales figures for an electronics retailer taken over a period of 80 weeks:

Weekly sales (£10 000s):	10–	14–	18–	22–	26–	30–	34–
Number of weeks:		10	7	15	23	17	5	3

4.(D) The share price at close of trading on the London Stock Exchange at the end of each week is recorded for future analysis. The table below shows the distribution of share prices over two years, 1993 and 1995, for the Hartwoods pharmaceutical company.

Share price (£)	1993	1995
8.00–	0	5
8.50–	2	12
9.00–	9	18
9.50–	11	14
10.00–	14	3
10.50–	9	0
11.00–	7	0

By finding suitable measures of average and spread for the two sets of data given in this table, comment on the differences in the share prices between the two years given.

5.(I)   The table below compares the output of two production lines in terms of the weight of items produced. The target weight for each item is 50 grams, and a sample of 100 items from each production line gave the following data.

Production line	Mean	Standard deviation
A	50.1	0.2
B	50.0	1.1

Comment on the differences between the output produced on the two production lines. Would you say that production line B is 'better' than A?

1.12   Further data analysis methods

The previous sections have summarised a wide range of data analysis techniques. However, there are a number of additional measures that are occasionally used in business applications and these will be briefly considered in this section.

1.12.1   The variance

The variance is sometimes quoted as the measure of spread in place of the standard deviation. This value is simply the square of the standard deviation. Thus it can be obtained by following the formula:

$$\text{Variance} = \frac{\sum fx^2}{\sum f} - (\bar{x})^2$$

The variance can be used in complex analyses when combining different sets of data together. Variances can be combined together directly whereas standard deviations cannot. However, an advantage of the standard deviation is that it is stated in the units of measurement for the variable being analysed (e.g. £s for revenue or salaries). Generally, the standard deviation is the preferred value in most applications.

Definition: *The variance is a measure of spread found by squaring the standard deviation.*

1.12.2   The coefficient of variation

When considering different distributions with significantly different means, the coefficient of variation can be used as a more realistic comparison. For example, a distribution with a higher mean is likely to have a wider spread. Thus, a basic comparison of the spread by using the standard deviation or quartiles may not yield any additional information. The coefficient of variation provides a method of comparison of spread related to the magnitude of data under consideration. The value can be found as follows:

$$\text{Coefficient variation} = \frac{\text{Standard deviation}}{\text{Mean}} * 100$$

Definition: *The coefficient of variation is a particular measure of spread obtained by the ratio of the standard deviation to the mean expressed as a percentage.*

The resulting value gives the standard deviation as a percentage of the mean. For example, consider the following sets of data:

Data values	Mean	Standard deviation
A	200	50
B	300	60

The table shows that the average in data B is higher than in data A. Also, as would normally be expected, the spread in data B is higher than in data A. However, if the coefficient of variation is calculated for each set of data, a different perspective is shown:

$$\text{Data A:} \quad \text{coefficient of variation} = \frac{50}{200} * 100 = 25\%$$

$$\text{Data B:} \quad \text{coefficient of variation} = \frac{60}{300} * 100 = 20\%$$

The analysis shows that the variation in B is less than in A when related to the average values.

It should be noted that the coefficient of variation is a 'dimensionless' measure of spread unlike other values introduced in this section. For example, when considering salaries most measures of spread would be in the form of the currency (e.g. £s) being used. Conversely, the coefficient of variation is independent of the unit being used.

1.12.3   Percentiles

We have previously considered the calculation of quartiles for a set of data. In practice, the values of percentiles may be quoted. In this case, the raw data are split into 1/100ths. Thus, the 10th percentile is a value that is 10% of the way through the set of data. For example, if the 10th percentile for a distribution of weekly wages is found to be £300 then this implies that 10% of the employees earn less than £300 and 90% earn

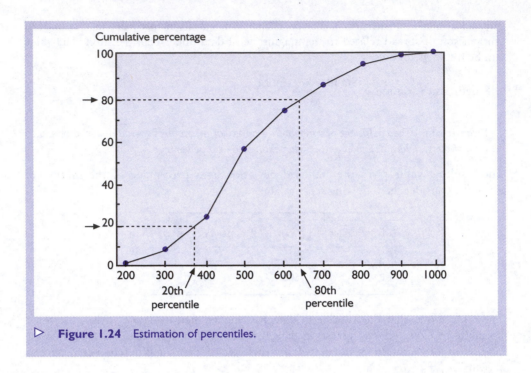

▷ **Figure 1.24**   Estimation of percentiles.

more. The percentiles can be obtained by the use of an ogive as shown in the following example. Consider the distribution of weekly earnings in a large organisation as shown below:

Earnings (£):	200–	300–	400–	500–	600–	700–	800–	900–
% of employees:	5	20	30	19	14	7	4	1

The ogive is illustrated in Figure 1.24 and the 20th and 80th percentiles have been estimated from the graph. The values obtained are as follows:

20th percentile = £375,   80th percentile = £645

Thus only 20% of employees earn less than £375, and 20% of employees earn over £645. Such values can be used to summarise data as well as compare sets of data.

1.12.4   Measure of skewness

As discussed in an earlier section, the values of the different types of 'averages' can change in relation to the shape of the distribution. Figure 1.18 illustrates three typical distributions. When the data are symmetrical then the three values (mean, median and mode) are the same. Alternatively, when the distribution is positively skewed (i.e. there is a longer tail on the right hand side of the distribution) then the mean is the largest estimate, and the mode the smallest. The reverse is true for a negatively skewed distribution where there is a longer tail on the left of the scale. This indicates a way of measuring the shape (or skewness) of the data. The following values show two similar measures of skewness:

$$\text{Skewness} = \frac{\text{mean} - \text{mode}}{\text{standard devn}} \quad \text{or} \quad \frac{3 * (\text{mean} - \text{median})}{\text{standard devn}}$$

This value is zero for a symmetrical distribution. Furthermore, these values are positive for a positively skewed distribution and negative for negatively skewed data.

Definition: *Skewness is a measure of the shape (degree of symmetry) of the distribution.*

1.13   Computer applications

There are a range of computer packages that can be utilised for basic statistical analysis. Spreadsheet packages such as Excel and Lotus 123 provide excellent facilities for simple analyses and graphical output. Other packages specifically designed for analysis of data such as SPSS provide much more sophisticated wide-ranging analytical tools. The following examples illustrate the use of such packages in basic data analysis as described in this chapter.

EXAMPLE 1

An example outlined earlier in this chapter considered a comparison of the output of a selection of production teams in the Hartwoods pharmaceutical company. The output of the teams in this company is closely monitored, and feedback is given to the teams on a monthly basis. The daily output of these teams is entered using the SPSS for Windows package. This package is then used to provide basic statistical analysis in order to compare the team's performances. The SPSS package can provide a range of analyses such as a graphical output of the data entered. The screen shown in Figure 1.25 gives a bar graph obtained from the daily figures of a specific production team taken over the past 40 working days.

In addition to the bar graph illustrated in Figure 1.25 the SPSS software provides a range of graph types including line graphs, pie charts, multiple and stacked bar charts. Further data analysis can be performed on these figures, including the construction of frequency tables, calculation of averages and measures of spread. The resulting values are then placed in a report format for easy printing as shown in the screen displayed in Figure 1.26. The screen displayed in Figure 1.26 shows a range of values such as the mean, median and mode, and the minimum, maximum and standard deviation values. The quartiles are also displayed and are referred to as the 25th percentile (1st quartile) and 75th percentile (3rd quartile).

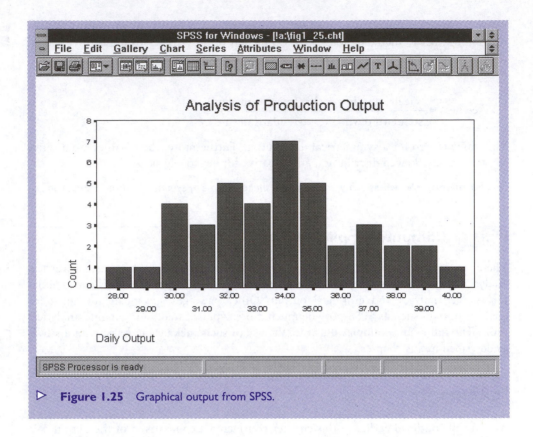

▷ **Figure 1.25** Graphical output from SPSS.

EXAMPLE 2

The table below shows the weekly earnings of a sample of forty employees as described in an earlier example.

Weekly earnings (£):	300–	400–	500–	600–	700–	800–
No. of employees:	2	5	9	12	8	4

These data can be set up in a spreadsheet package, and basic data analysis and graphical representation can be achieved.

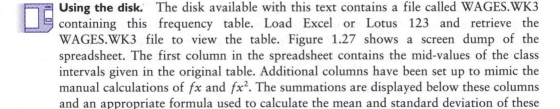

Using the disk. The disk available with this text contains a file called WAGES.WK3 containing this frequency table. Load Excel or Lotus 123 and retrieve the WAGES.WK3 file to view the table. Figure 1.27 shows a screen dump of the spreadsheet. The first column in the spreadsheet contains the mid-values of the class intervals given in the original table. Additional columns have been set up to mimic the manual calculations of fx and fx^2. The summations are displayed below these columns and an appropriate formula used to calculate the mean and standard deviation of these

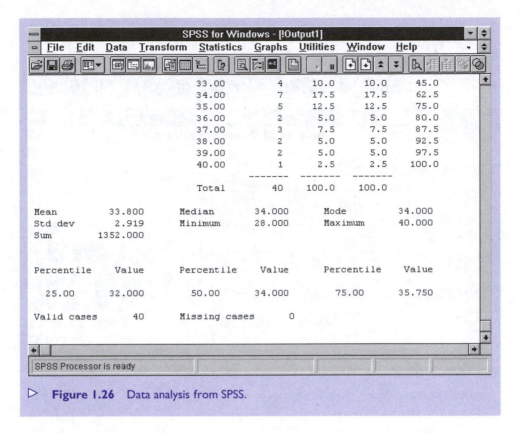

33.00	4	10.0	10.0	45.0
34.00	7	17.5	17.5	62.5
35.00	5	12.5	12.5	75.0
36.00	2	5.0	5.0	80.0
37.00	3	7.5	7.5	87.5
38.00	2	5.0	5.0	92.5
39.00	2	5.0	5.0	97.5
40.00	1	2.5	2.5	100.0
	-------	-------	-------	
Total	40	100.0	100.0	

```
Mean        33.800    Median    34.000    Mode       34.000
Std dev      2.919    Minimum   28.000    Maximum    40.000
Sum       1352.000


Percentile   Value     Percentile   Value     Percentile   Value

  25.00      32.000      50.00      34.000      75.00      35.750

Valid cases     40     Missing cases     0
```

SPSS Processor is ready

▷ **Figure 1.26** Data analysis from SPSS.

data. The screen also displays a graph that has been created and added into the spreadsheet.

You may wish to change the data given in the table. For example, the spreadsheet can be used to analyse different frequency tables. For instance, consider the following table on earnings:

Weekly earnings (£):	300–	400–	500–	600–	700–	800–
No. of employees:	4	11	17	5	2	1

By changing the frequency values in column B of the spreadsheet you will be able to obtain an analysis of the new data. Changes in the frequency values will automatically change the results of the mean and standard deviation, and the graphical output displayed. The type of graph displayed can also be changed by the use of the spreadsheet options. For instance, in Lotus, if you press '/' and then choose **Graph** and the **Type** you will be given a list of graph types such as **Line, Bar** and **Pie**. Similarly, in Excel, you can choose **Format** and **Chart Type** and select from a range of chart types. Try experimenting with these different graph types. Finally, you can save the amended spreadsheet using a different file name (eg WAGES2) or simply exit the spreadsheet without saving.

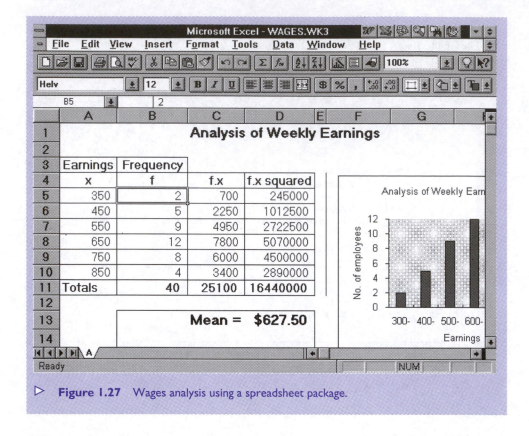

EXAMPLE 3

There are a range of statistical functions available in the Lotus and Excel packages that can be used to analyse raw data. In particular, the following functions can be used to obtain a simple data analysis:

Lotus function	Excel function	Result
@COUNT	= COUNT	Count the number of values
@SUM	= SUM	Calculate the sum of a range of values
@AVG	= AVERAGE	Calculate the mean of a list of values
@MIN	= MIN	Display the lowest value in a list
@MAX	= MAX	Display the highest value in a list
@STDS	= STDEV	Calculate the standard deviation of a list of values

Using the disk.   The file called HOURS.WK3 on the sample disk contains details on the overtime hours worked for a sample of 20 employees. The raw data are displayed in column A. Load the HOURS.WK3 file into your spreadsheet to display these data. The screen displayed is illustrated in Figure 1.28. The spreadsheet

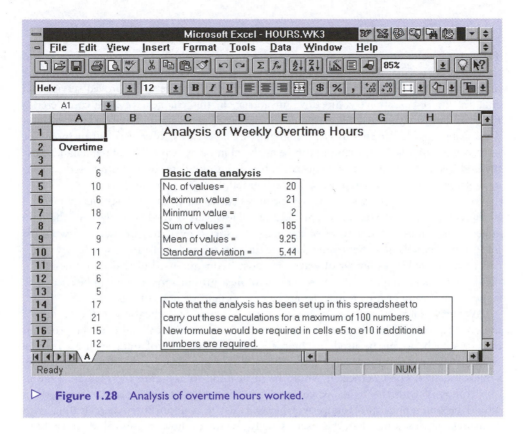

▷ **Figure 1.28** Analysis of overtime hours worked.

functions have been used to calculate the basic statistics as shown in column E of the spreadsheet. As in the previous example, you can change the raw data by altering any of the cells in column A. The number of values in the raw data can also vary. One approach to editing the data in column A would be to erase the data range before entering new values. To do this in Lotus, highlight the range containing the numbers in column A, then press '/' and choose **Range** and then **Erase**. Alternatively, in Excel select the range of cells and then choose **Edit** and **Delete**. Column A is now blank, and you can enter new values. For example, enter the following values relating to the overtime hours worked by a group of ten employees in a different department in the company:

3   10   5   8   0   2   4   7   4   1

Look at the new values for the mean and standard deviation. Comment on the differences between these data and the original values displayed on the screen in Figure 1.28.

Experiment by entering other sets of data as required.

| 1.14 | **Chapter summary** |

The accurate and effective use of data is important for today's managers and businesses. Raw data obtained and analysed in a correct way will give vital information to assist in the management decision making process and thus help to provide an improved service and enhance the organisation's competitive advantage. In this chapter we have considered a range of data analysis methods including tabulation of raw data and graphical representation. Data collected from surveys, questionnaires, interviews, observational methods, or reference to published information, can be analysed in many ways. The initial data analysis methods include production of frequency tables from raw data, and illustrating data with an appropriate graph such as a histogram, bar graph, line graph or pie chart.

Often basic data analysis of this type provides sufficient detail for in-company memos, business reports and external communications. However, if further analysis of the data collected is required then a range of summary statistics is available for use. The two most important methods of summarising data are the average and measure of spread. Averages can be calculated in a number of ways, the most frequently used of which are the mean, median or mode. Similarly, there are a range of measures of spread that can be used. The standard deviation or use of quartiles are two important methods of this measure.

Averages (sometimes called measures of centre) give an indication of the middle of the data collected. The average gives an idea of the most 'typical' value in the group of data. As such, it can be used to compare and contrast sets of data such as average wages, production output, sales, and profitability. Care must be taken to compare the same measures. For instance, it would be misleading to compare the median wage in one company with the mean wage from a second organisation. Such a comparison would be ambiguous and totally worthless. Thus, it is important when dealing with measures of this kind that the user is fully aware of how these values have been obtained. A report stating simply that 'the average wage is £450' without reference to the method used can be misleading and subjective.

Measures of spread such as the standard deviation or inter-quartile range can be used to compare sets of data in terms of their 'spread' or 'dispersion'. Such measures give an added dimension to the comparison of data and can be vital in distinguishing distributions with similar averages.

Finally, the chapter has concluded with a brief view of the use of computer packages in data analysis. Spreadsheet packages such as Excel or Lotus 123 provide a variety of statistical and graphical facilities. Bespoke software such as SPSS enables additional analysis to be performed and provides a vast array of extra tools to analyse and summarise the data collected.

| 1.15 | **Further exercises** |

1.(E) Use appropriate graphs to illustrate the following sets of data:

(i) The results of a survey on the mode of transport for employees travelling to work yielded the following results:

Method of travel:	Car	Train	Bus	Motor-cycle	Walk	Others
Number of employees:	78	12	22	8	30	10

(ii) Show how the total expenditure of a large district hospital is split into the following categories:

Category:	Staff	Equipment	Buildings	Services
Percentage of total expenditure:	40	25	20	15

(iii) The monthly revenue of a medium-sized organisation in electronics retailing taken over the past 36 months:

Revenue (£10 000s):	40–	50–	60–	70–	80–
No. of months:		3	7	14	8	4

(iv) Compare the three companies' sales figures over the past four years:

Year:	1995	1996	1997	1998
Co. A:	30	25	26	32
Co. B:	18	22	28	33
Co. C:	24	26	19	14

2. (I) The number of employees arriving late for work over the past fifty days is recorded and displayed below. (The numbers shown were more than 5 minutes late according to their contracted time of starting.)

```
15  22   8  26  10   6   1  16  10  17
12  18   7   2  12  15   7  23  13   3
20   9   0  12  16  10  20  11   7   9
11   4  10  19   6   3   8  14  28  14
 5  24   9  15  11  13  16  11   8  14
```

(i) Construct a frequency table from these data and illustrate using a histogram.
(ii) Find the mean and standard deviation from the table obtained.
(iii) Compare this with a second company where the lateness data over the same period gave the mean = 18 employees late, with a standard deviation = 3.5 employees.

3. (I) Find the mean, median, and mode for each of the data tabulated below:

(i) The age distribution of a sample of 40 employees:

Age range (years):	20–	30–	40–	50–	60–
No. of employees:	6	15	10	7	2

(ii) The proportion of defects found in 30 samples from a production line.

Percentage defects:	0–	2–	4–	6–	8–	10–
No. of samples:	2	5	9	8	5	1

(iii) The hourly pay rates of all employees (other than management grades) in a large manufacturing company:

Hourly pay (£):	3.00–	4.00–	5.00–	6.00–	7.00–	8.00–	9.00–
Percentage of staff:	20	34	30	10	4	1	1

4.(I) Find the median and inter-quartile range in order to compare the following data:

Weekly earnings (£):	200–	300–	400–	500–	600–	700–	800–	900–
No. of employees: Co. A:	25	38	23	14	0	0	0	0
Co. B:	18	22	24	17	10	5	3	1

Comment on the differences between the earnings of the two companies.

5.(D) Calculate the mean and standard deviation for the following sets of data:

(i) The price of the Yellow Tram Co. quoted at the end of trading on the New York Stock Exchange over a period of 20 consecutive days:

Peak share price (£):	5.00–	5.20–	5.40–	5.60–	5.80–	6.00–
Number of days:	2	3	7	4	3	1

(ii) The diameter of a sample of 80 alloy washers used in a bridge construction:

Dimension (mm):	20–	22–	24–	26–	28–
No. of items:	16	26	18	12	8

(iii) The distance recorded by a group of sales representatives during a specific week in June 1996:

Distance travelled (miles):	200–	300–	400–	500–	600–	700–
No. of salesmen:		3	4	10	3	4	2

6.(I) Comment on the differences between the share prices of the two companies given in the following table. (The figures are given in £s, and the prices are based on those found at the close of trading each day over the past 60 days).

Company	Hopes Ltd	Swartz Co.
Mean	£4.00	£4.40
Standard deviation	£1.50	£0.60

Would you say that the shares in the Hopes Ltd company are more volatile than those from Swartz Co.?

7.(I) The table below shows an analysis of the performance of three production teams in terms of their daily output over the past year. The figures are given in terms of 1000s of units produced per day.

Production team	A	B	C
Median	18	16	19
IQR	2	5	10

8.(D) Would you agree with the statement that team C is best? If not, why not? The file STATS on the disk contains a simple frequency distribution on the number of staff absent for work each day over a sample of 100 days.

(i) Load the STATS file and set up appropriate formulae to calculate the mean and standard deviation of these data.
(ii) Use the spreadsheet facilities to draw a line graph of these data, and experiment with other graph types.
(iii) Try to set up cells containing the cumulative frequencies and illustrate them on a line graph. Can you estimate the quartiles from this graph?

9.(I) Draw histograms of the following sets of data:

(i) The weekly earnings of a random sample of employees:

Weekly wages (£):	200–	250–	300–	350–	400–	450–	500–
No. of employees:	4	14	20	17	11	7	3

(ii) The number of overtime hours worked in a given week by a sample of employees:

Number of hours overtime:	0–	2–	4–	6–	8–	10–
No. of workers:	2	6	13	15	8	5

(iii) The number of employees arriving late for work over a period of 65 days:

Number of employees arriving late:	0	1	2	3	4	5	6	7
No. of days:	25	13	7	9	5	2	3	1

10.(I) (i) Use a multiple bar graph to illustrate the production figures for five companies over a three-year period as shown below.

Company	Production output (£1000 000s)		
	1996	1997	1998
A	20	26	32
B	15	19	14
C	7	12	22
D	30	26	19
E	16	13	17

(ii) Would a stacked bar graph be more useful to illustrate these data? Draw this alternative graph and comment on the differences between the two methods of representation.

11.(D)   From a recent market survey of customer preferences for a range of television programmes, the table below shows information on the ages of viewers for two major series shown during 1996 on the US network. The figures given are percentages of viewers in each age category.

Age (Years):	10–	20–	30–	40–	50–	60–	70–	80–	90–
Programme A:	0	2	7	34	23	19	9	5	1
Programme B:	13	40	34	12	1	0	0	0	0

Find the mean and standard deviation of age ranges for the viewers of these two programmes. Comment on the differences in ages between the two groups, and give possible reasons for these differences.

Probability and Decisions

CHAPTER OBJECTIVES

At the end of this chapter you will be able to:

► understand and use the basic rules of probability
► use techniques such as decision trees in making business decisions
► calculate probabilities using discrete and continuous distributions
► apply the ideas of confidence limits in significance
► understand the applications of hypothesis testing on means

Introduction

The study of probability can assist the manager in making appropriate decisions in a wide range of applications. In many business situations there is often an element of uncertainty when dealing with a problem. For example, will the customers buy the latest product range? Will our competitors match our prices? Will our advertising campaign improve our sales? Will the employees accept the proposed pay awards? Will our training programme help to improve effectiveness? So many of the problems requiring management decision making involve uncertainties of these types. The study of probability looks at uncertainty, and attempts to assign objective measurements to a range of potential events. Specific areas such as risk management and quality assurance incorporate a wide range of probability tools.

A knowledge of the rules of probability can assist the manager in assessing the likelihood of particular events occurring and enhance the decision making process. An appreciation of probability will also help the manager to understand the applications of sampling. It is necessary to understand the relationship between results obtained from a sample compared with the actual attributes of the population. For example, in a market research survey it has been found that 20% of a sample of 50 potential customers preferred brand X. In order to make an informed decision on the potential of this brand it would be necessary to realise the implications of this sample for the total population of customers. For instance, does this result mean that 20% of all customers will prefer brand X? How likely is it that the actual percentage is less than 10%? These issues involve a knowledge of basic probability distributions which will be discussed later in this chapter.

CASE STUDY   The Downbrooks Corporation

Downbrooks is a confectionery producer based in Manchester, England. The company produces a range of chocolate products including the popular 'Big-Bite' bar, and the 'Troofle' – a large bar of truffle chocolate. The company was established in 1876, and has been trading continuously since that time. The company employs over 300 staff at the Manchester production site, and an additional 60 management and administrative staff at their headquarters located three miles away.

The company sells to a range of wholesalers as well as direct to a number of large retail chains. In 1985 Downbrooks opened its first retail shop in Manchester, specialising in selling its own products, including a range of 'hand made' sweets. Since that time, the company has opened an additional fifteen shops spread throughout the UK including sites in Liverpool, Bristol, Edinburgh and Canterbury.

The company uses a range of decision making tools incorporating probability to assist in areas such as product development, marketing and quality control. For example, the company must assess the chance of a new product being successful, and on the basis of this make decisions relating to the existing and future production plans. Furthermore, the quality of products is closely examined and controlled. In particular, with the mass produced items such as the 'Big-Bite' bar, samples are taken at regular intervals and examined. The proportion of rejects in these samples then indicates the chance of a number of rejects in the complete batch. Pricing of these products and quality promises included in contracts with Downbrooks customers are partly based on these probabilistic elements. Details of a range of applications relating to this company will be included in examples throughout this chapter.

| CASE STUDY | **St. Joseph's general hospital** |

The St. Joseph's hospital located in New York has over 1400 staff catering for as many as 2000 patients at any one time. The private hospital includes a Research Department attached to the city's Medical Training Centre. Patient facilities include 1000 single rooms, and over 600 rooms containing multiple beds (usually two or four beds per room). The hospital also has an Accident & Emergency unit catering for patients admitted 24 hours per day every day throughout the year.

The management at St. Joseph's have recently hired the services of external consultants to consider a range of problems, including staffing, patient care and the dramatic increases in medical expenses in recent years, and corresponding fees charged to patients. One specific problem that St. Joseph's has along with many other hospitals in the New York region is that currently, the utilisation of beds is approximately 80%. Thus, on average 20% of the beds in the hospital are unoccupied on any given day. However, despite this there are occasions when owing to increased demand, particularly in the emergency areas, beds cannot be found for patients. This has resulted in seriously ill patients being rushed to different hospitals to obtain treatment. The management regard this problem area as a priority, and a consideration of patient arrivals and the chances of the number of patients exceeding the beds available must be considered. The application of probability in the study of bed utilisation and general areas of supply and demand will be considered in examples throughout this chapter.

2.1 Basic probability

The probability of an event occurring can be described as the chance or likelihood expressed as a numerical value. This can be given as either a percentage (between 0% and 100%) or an actual value (between 0 and 1). For example, in a recent survey of employees' attitudes at the Downbrooks company it was found that 30 employees out of the 50 sampled were satisfied with the new organisation structure introduced in 1996.

> **Definition:** *The probability of an event is expressed as a value between the limits 0 and 1. A probability of 0 indicates that the event cannot happen, and a probability of 1 shows that the event is certain to occur.*

This information can be expressed in probabilistic terms as follows:

Out of the sample taken, the percentage of satisfied employees is $\frac{30}{50} * 100 = 60$.

Thus we can say that there is a 60% chance of an employee in the sample being satisfied. Alternatively, the probability of an employee in the sample being satisfied is $30/50 = 0.6$. In general, the basic method of calculating the probability of an event occurring is outlined by the following formula

$$\text{Probability of an event} = \frac{\text{Number of ways the event can occur}}{\text{Total number of possible outcomes}}$$

This can be written in a more general way. The probability of an event X occurring is given by

$$P(\text{event } X) = \frac{\text{Number of ways } X \text{ can occur}}{\text{Total no. of possible outcomes}}$$

Thus, related to the previous problem,

$$\text{Probability of an employee being satisfied} = \frac{\text{Number of satisfied employees}}{\text{Total number of employees}}$$

$$= \frac{30}{50}$$

$$= 0.6$$

Similarly, consider another problem related to the Downbrooks company. For instance, from a sample of 140 customers at the Canterbury store, 35 customers said that they preferred the 'Big-Bite' chocolate bar rather than the 'Troofle' bar. This information can be expressed in probability terms as follows:

Probability of customer preferring 'Big-Bite'

$$= \frac{\text{No. of customers stating their preference for 'Big-Bite'}}{\text{Total number of customers questioned}}$$

$$= \frac{35}{140} = 0.25$$

(Alternatively, this can be stated as a percentage $= 0.25 * 100 = 25\%$.)

As has been stated, the actual value of a probability lies between 0 and 1. A probability of 0 indicates that the event is impossible. At the other extreme, a probability of 1 (100%) implies that the event is certain to happen.

Understanding the basic ideas of probability may help the manager to make decisions based on simple data. For instance, it would be interesting for the Personnel Manager at Downbrooks to have the information relating to satisfaction with the new organisational structure. From the sample of 50 employees previously outlined, only 60% were satisfied. This may lead the manager to review the structure and build in additional improvements, or improve the communications systems so that the employees are more aware of the benefits of these changes.

Similarly, the Sales Manager would be interested in the popularity of the alternative products. A probability equal to 0.25 (i.e. 25%) of customers preferring the 'Big-Bite' bar could lead to a method of estimating the potential sales of these products. These basic probability estimates will be used in the later sections to analyse a range of business problems.

2.2   Combination of events

Often, the calculation of probabilities involves the consideration of a number of different events. The relationship between these events will then affect the evaluation of appropriate probabilities. In particular, the following definitions should be understood:

Complementary events. Two events are said to be complementary if together they cover the entire range of possibilities. For instance, complementary events in the survey of employees' attitudes are 'satisfaction with the changes' and 'dissatisfaction with the changes'. One of these two outcomes is certain to happen (providing the employees are not given any other alternatives!). Consider a simple question in a survey requiring a Yes/No answer. These two responses are complementary providing that there are no other possible outcomes (such as 'Don't Know') available.

Mutually exclusive events. Two events are mutually exclusive if they cannot possibly occur at the same time. For instance, related to the customer survey customers respond with their preferences. Two mutually exclusive events are first, a preference for 'Big-Bite' bars, and secondly, a preference for 'Troofle' bars. They are mutually exclusive because the customers could not express a preference for both. They are forced to state one or other of the two options. Similarly, a 'satisfied' statement and a 'dissatisfied' statement from employees relating to the organisation structure changes are mutually exclusive. Employees cannot be both satisfied and dissatisfied at the same time.

Independent events. Two events are independent if each event is not affected in any way by the occurrence of the other event. Thus, if one event occurs, then this does not change the chance of the second event happening. For instance, consider the first event being an employee expressing satisfaction, and the second event being a customer stating preference for 'Big-Bite' bars. These two events are unrelated, and the chance of one happening does not affect the other. Thus, the events are said to be independent.

Knowledge of the relationship between events will enable us to determine the probability of a combination of events. The probability of a number of events occurring can be obtained by one of the formulae shown in the following sections.

2.2.1   The addition rule

If two events (X and Y) are mutually exclusive then the probability of one or other event occurring is obtained by adding the individual probabilities. Thus, Prob(event X or event Y) = Prob(event X) + Prob(event Y) or, more simply,

$P(X \text{ or } Y) = P(X) + P(Y)$

Definition: *The probability of an event X or event Y occurring is found by: Prob(X or Y) = Prob(X) + Prob(Y) provided that the events X and Y are mutually exclusive.*

EXAMPLE 1

If 25% of customers expressed a preference for the 'Big-Bite' bar, and 50% expressed a preference for 'Troofles', then the probability of a customer expressing a preference for either Big-Bite or Troofles is found as follows:

We are given, Prob(Big-Bite) = 25% = 0.25
Similarly, Prob(Troofles) = 50% = 0.5.

Therefore, since these two events are mutually exclusive,

Prob(Big-Bite **or** Troofles) = Prob(Big-Bite) + Prob(Troofles)
$$= \quad 0.25 \quad + \quad 0.5$$
$$= 0.75 \ (\text{or } 75\%)$$

EXAMPLE 2

In a quality inspection of the handmade products at Downbrooks, the following results have been obtained for a sample of 200 sweets:

Quality:	Superior	Acceptable	Rejects
Number of sweets:	140	40	20

Thus, based on this sample, $P(\text{Superior}) = 140/200 = 0.7$.
Similarly, $P(\text{Acceptable}) = 40/200 = 0.2$ and $P(\text{Rejects}) = 20/200 = 0.1$.

The three categories of quality for these products are all mutually exclusive. Thus, for example, the probability of obtaining a superior or acceptable product is obtained by:

$$P(\text{Superior } \textbf{or } \text{Acceptable}) = P(\text{Superior}) + P(\text{Acceptable})$$
$$= \quad 0.7 \quad + \quad 0.2$$
$$= 0.9 \ (\text{or } 90\%)$$

EXAMPLE 3

The example above can be related to complementary events. For instance, consider the probability of 'obtaining a reject' or 'not obtaining a reject'. These two events are complementary, since one or other event must happen. They are also mutually exclusive since both cannot happen simultaneously: it is not possible to obtain a sweet that is at the same time a reject and not a reject! Thus, the combined probability of obtaining a reject or not obtaining a reject must be 1 (or 100%). We can write this as follows:

$$P(\text{Reject } \textbf{or } \text{not Reject}) = P(\text{Reject}) + P(\text{not Reject}) = 1$$

Therefore, rearranging this expression we have:

$$P(\text{not Reject}) = 1 - P(\text{Reject})$$

Now, from the previous example, $P(\text{Reject}) = 0.1$. Therefore, $P(\text{not Reject}) = 1 - 0.1 = 0.9$

(or 90%). This example illustrates another rule, which can be generally stated as follows:

$P(\text{not } X) = 1 - P(X)$

So, for example, if the probability of obtaining a superior quality product is 0.7, then the probability that the product is not superior will be $1 - 0.7 = 0.3$ (or 30%).

2.2.2 The multiplication rule

If two events are independent then the probability of both events occurring is obtained by multiplying the individual probabilities. Thus,

Prob(event X **and** event Y) = Prob(event X) * Prob(event Y).

Or, simply, this can be abbreviated to

$P(X \text{ and } Y) = P(X) * P(Y)$

Definition: *Given two events X and Y, the probability of both X and Y occurring is found by: Prob(X and Y) = Prob(X) * Prob(Y), provided that the events X and Y are independent.*

EXAMPLE 1

We already know that 25% of customers expressed a preference for 'Big-Bite', and that 60% of employees are satisfied with the new organisational structure. We can summarise this information as:

$P(\text{Big-Bite preferred}) = 0.25, \qquad P(\text{Satisfied employee}) = 0.6$

Since these two events are independent then the probability that both events will occur is as follows:

$P(\text{Big-Bite preferred } \textbf{and} \text{ Satisfied employee})$
$= P(\text{Big-Bite preferred}) * P(\text{Satisfied employee})$
$= 0.25 * 0.6$
$= 0.15 \text{ (or 15\%)}$

EXAMPLE 2

In the Downbrooks company there are 70% male employees and 30% female. As previously stated, 60% of employees expressed satisfaction with the organisational changes. Assuming that there is no relationship between gender and attitudes to the changes then the probability of an employee taken at random being male and unhappy with the changes can be found as follows.

P(Dissatisfied employee) = $1 - P$(Satisfied employee)

$$= 1 - 0.6$$
$$= 0.4$$

Also, P(Male employee) = 0.7 (= 70%).

Thus P(Dissatisfied **and** Male) = P(Dissatisfied) $* P$(Male)

$$= 0.4 * 0.7$$
$$= 0.28 \text{ (or 28%)}$$

EXAMPLE 3

Orders arrive regularly at the Downbrooks headquarters for a range of confectionery goods. Over the past year it has been found that 24% of orders include the 'Big-Bite' bar, and that 30% of orders are for goods valued at over £5000. There seems to be no relationship between the value of orders and whether or not they include the 'Big-Bite' bar. To estimate the chance of the next order including the 'Big-Bite' bar and being valued at over £5000 we use the multiplication rule as shown below.

We know that P(Order including 'Big-Bite') = 0.24 (or 24%)
Also P(Order value over £5000) = 0.3 (or 30%)

Thus, P(Order including 'Big-Bite' **and** Value over £5000)
   $= P$('Big-Bite') $* P$(Over £5000)
   $= 0.24 * 0.3$
   $= 0.072$ (or 7.2%)

2.2.3   Complex events

In many examples it is necessary to use a combination of the multiplication and addition rules introduced in the previous section. Consider the elementary examples shown below.

EXAMPLE 1

Consider orders arriving at Downbrooks. 24% of orders include the 'Big-Bite' bar, and 20% of orders include the 'Troofle'. Assuming that there is no relationship between these two products, let us estimate the chance of a single order containing only one, and not both, of the items. In other words we wish to consider the possibility of an order containing Big-Bite and not Troofle or, alternatively, Troofle and not Big-Bite.

Now P(Big-Bite) = 0.24 and P(Troofle) = 0.2
Similarly, P(not Big-Bite) = $1 - 0.24 = 0.76$ and P(not Troofle) = $1 - 0.2 = 0.8$

The probability of an order containing only one of these items (and not both) is obtained as follows:

  P(only one item included)
    = P(Big-Bite **and** not Troofle **or** not Big-Bite **and** Troofle)

Essentially wherever '**and**' appears in combining events we multiply the probabilities (assuming that they are independent) and whenever there is an '**or**' the probabilities are added (provided that they are mutually exclusive).

  Thus, *P*(only one item)
    = *P*(Big-Bite) * *P*(not Troofle) + *P*(not Big-Bite) * *P*(Troofle)
    = 0.24 * 0.8 + 0.76 * 0.2
    = 0.192 + 0.152
    = 0.344 (or 34.4%)

Thus, over a third of all orders are likely to contain just one of these products.

EXAMPLE 2

The Downbrooks company uses a range of assessment methods when selecting new management staff, including tests on numeracy and verbal reasoning. From past experience it has been found that 60% of candidates pass the numeracy test and 80% pass the verbal test. Assuming that passing one test has no bearing on success or failure in the other we can find the chance of various results of a candidate taken at random. For instance, let us look at the probability of this candidate: (i) passing both tests, (ii) passing just one test, or (iii) failing both tests.
We are given the probabilities for success in individual tests:

  P(pass Numeracy) = 0.6, *P*(pass Verbal) = 0.8
  Thus, *P*(fail Numeracy) = 0.4, and *P*(fail Verbal) = 0.2

(i) *P*(Passing both tests)

    = *P*(pass Numeracy **and** pass Verbal)
    = *P*(pass Numeracy) * *P*(pass Verbal)
    (since these two tests are independent)
    = 0.6 * 0.8
    = 0.48 (or 48%)

Therefore, 48% of candidates are likely to pass both tests.
(ii) *P*(passing only one test)

    = *P*(pass Numeracy **and** fail Verbal **or** fail Numeracy **and** pass Verbal)
    = *P*(pass Numeracy) * *P*(fail Verbal) + *P*(fail Numeracy) * *P*(pass Verbal)
    = 0.6 * 0.2 + 0.4 * 0.8
    = 0.12 + 0.32
    = 0.44 (or 44%)

Therefore, 44% of candidates are likely to pass just one of the tests.

(iii) P(failing both tests)

$= P$(fail Numeracy **and** fail Verbal)
$= P$(fail Numeracy) $*$ P(fail Verbal)
$= 0.4 * 0.2$
$= 0.08$ (or 8%)

Therefore, only 8% of candidates fail both tests.

Note: The three possibilities considered here are the only ones available. The candidate must pass both, pass one, or fail both tests. There are no other alternatives. This is demonstrated when looking at the probabilities. The sum of the three probabilities obtained is $0.48 + 0.44 + 0.08 = 1$ (or 100%).

2.3	**Exercises: basic probability**

1.(E) From past results it is known that approximately 20% of items from a production line are defective. If two items are taken at random from this production, find the probability that:

(a) neither is defective,
(b) both are defective,
(c) only one item is defective.

2.(E) 30% of trainee managers in the St. Joseph's hospital fail to complete their two-year training period. If two trainees commence the training on the same day, what is the chance that:

(a) both trainees will complete their course,
(b) only one trainee will complete the course.

3.(I) It has been found that 55% of patients arriving at the Accident & Emergency unit of St. Joseph's hospital are male. Furthermore, 10% of all arrivals are required to return for extra treatment.

  (i) Find the probability that the next patient arriving at the unit will:
    (a) be female,
    (b) require no further treatment,
    (c) be male and require further treatment,
    (d) be female and not require further treatment.
 (ii) Given two patients taken at random from the arrivals on a particular day, estimate the probability that:
    (a) both are male,
    (b) both require additional treatment,
    (c) only one patient requires additional treatment,
    (d) the first patient requires treatment and the second patient is female,
    (e) only one patient is female.

| 2.4 | **Probability trees** |

The use of probability trees can simplify the evaluation of complex probabilities involving a number of interrelated events. The probability tree provides a pictorial method of illustrating the probabilities involved. The following examples will demonstrate the use of this approach.

| **EXAMPLE 1** |

Consider patients arriving at the Accident & Emergency unit of St. Joseph's hospital. It has been found that 80% of patients are sent home within the first few hours after a medical examination and minor assistance. Of the remaining 20% of patients, these are transferred to one of two wards (A and B). 60% of patients got to Ward A and 40% are sent to Ward B. These wards are visited on a daily basis by two consultants, Mr Hals and Mrs Elder. Mr Hals covers 70% of the patients on ward A and only 10% of patients on ward B. Mrs Elder consults all the remaining patients. What is the chance of a patient arriving in the Accident & Emergency unit being seen by Mr Hals?

This complicated situation can be illustrated by a probability tree, as shown in Figure 2.1. The diagram displayed shows the arrival of the patient at the top of the tree. The patient is then either sent home or admitted, illustrated by the two branches. Following admittance, the patient goes to one of the two wards as shown, and is consequently seen by the appropriate consultant. The probabilities of each event are shown on the probability tree. The individual probabilities can be multiplied to obtain the likelihood of arriving at the end of any branch. For instance, the probability of a patient being admitted into ward B and being seen by Mrs Elder is

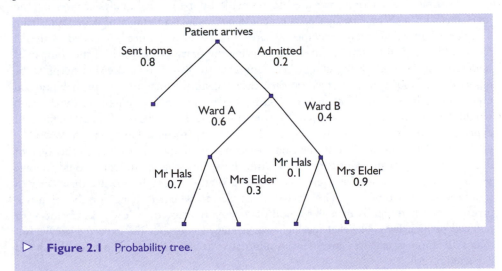

▷ **Figure 2.1** Probability tree.

obtained by multiplying all the probabilities on this route through the tree. Thus the probability is $= 0.2*0.4*0.9 = 0.072$ (or 7.2%). Similarly, the probability of a patient arriving at the Accident & Emergency unit being seen by Mr Hals is found by adding all the probabilities on the appropriate branches of the tree. In this example, there are two branches which end with patients being seen by Mr Hals. Thus, this probability is:

$$(0.2*0.6*0.7) + (0.2*0.4*0.1)$$
$$= 0.084 + 0.008$$
$$= 0.092$$

Thus, 9.2% of patients arriving at the unit will eventually see Mr Hals.

It is left to the reader to find the probability of a patient seeing the other consultant, Mrs Elder.

2.5   Decision analysis

Decision analysis involves using a range of techniques to assist the manager in choosing the most appropriate decisions in given circumstances. As outlined in the introduction to this chapter the techniques of probability can be utilised to assist the manager in making decisions. There are a number of practical decision making techniques using probabilistic ideas. Such methods are necessary since there are many circumstances in decision making where relevant information is not known with any degree of certainty. These probabilistic problems generally involve the consideration of a range of decision alternatives. The manager must make a decision from the list of alternatives, which may then lead to a new set of alternatives to be analysed.

For instance, a decision may need to be made by a financial analyst concerning an investment for a client. The first decision could be to select a number of companies from a range of investment opportunities. There may be probabilities associated with the likelihood of a profit from the investment during the first year for each of the companies under consideration. Having chosen the companies to invest in, a decision needs to be made on the amount of investment in each case. Again, this may involve probabilities on outcomes such as profitability and long-term investment yields. One basis of the decision would be to maximise the **expected profit** from the investments. The calculation of expected values will be demonstrated in the following section. However, there can be other considerations involved in the final decision. An additional attribute in this type of decision making is the consideration of **risk**. Some investment strategies could involve significant risk of a loss. However, such high-risk ventures may also involve the chance of significantly higher profits. The analyst must decide whether to go for the high-risk investments on the basis of a likelihood of greater returns, or a low-risk scheme with reduced profits. It may be that the high-risk strategy maximises the expected profit, but that a decision is made to invest in an alternative lower-risk portfolio with a reduced expected return.

2.6	**Expected values**

In many simple examples the expected value of a variable is obtained by multiplying a probability by the total number of values. For instance, in an earlier example, the probability of an employee being satisfied by changes in the organisational structure was found to be 0.6. Thus, out of a total workforce of 360 employees, the expected number of satisfied employees would be equal to $360 * 0.6 = 216$. Similarly, if the probability of the 'Big-Bite' bar being included in any order is 0.24, then out of a batch of 50 orders, the expected number including orders for the 'Big-Bite' is equal to $50 * 0.24 = 12$.

The above process can be extended to relate to more complex problems. In general, the expected value of a variable is obtained by multiplying each probability by the corresponding value and obtaining the sum of these products. This can be written using the summation notation as follows:

Expected value of X denoted by

$$E(X) = \sum X.P(X)$$

where $P(X)$ is the probability of X occurring.

The expected value can be regarded as being an estimate of the average value for the variable.

EXAMPLE I

The number of patients arriving at the Accident & Emergency unit of St. Joseph's hospital has been monitored over the past month. The number arriving every five minutes was found to range between 0 and 4 patients. The following table shows the probability of a given number of patients arriving within a five-minute period.

Number of patients arriving:	0	1	2	3	4
Probability:	0.1	0.3	0.3	0.2	0.1

The table shows that there is a 10% chance of no patient arriving in this period, a 30% chance of one patient arriving, and so on for the remaining values. The number of patients arriving can be denoted by X, and the related probabilities by $P(X)$. The expected number of patients arriving within this period is:

$$
\begin{aligned}
E(X) = \sum X.P(X) &= 0 * 0.1 + 1 * 0.3 + 2 * 0.3 + 3 * 0.2 + 4 * 0.1 \\
&= 0 + 0.3 + 0.6 + 0.6 + 0.4 \\
&= 1.9
\end{aligned}
$$

Thus, according to this information, we would expect just under 2 patients on average to arrive during any five-minute period.

EXAMPLE 2

The quantity of 'Troofle' bars sold daily over the past three months by the

Downbrooks company varied between 2 and 8 boxes, as shown in the following table. Each box contains 144 bars.

Number of boxes sold:	2	3	4	5	6	7	8
Probability:	0.04	0.07	0.32	0.26	0.16	0.09	0.06

The expected number of boxes sold in any one day can be calculated by:

$$E(X) = \sum X.P(X)$$
$$= 2*0.04 + 3*0.07 + 4*0.32 + 5*0.26 + 6*0.16 + 7*0.09 + 8*0.06$$
$$= 0.08 + 0.21 + 1.28 + 1.30 + 0.96 + 0.63 + 0.48$$
$$= 4.94 \text{ boxes.}$$

Thus, the expected number of boxes sold is found to be slightly under 5 per day.

2.7   Decision trees

The use of decision trees can help to represent a given problem and to ascertain the likelihood and expected values of given situations occurring. These diagrams are an extension of the simpler probability trees which were used to illustrate specific probabilities relating to a sequence of outcomes. The decision tree illustrates the results of specific decisions being made and the likely result in terms of critical factors, such as projected profit or costs.

A Decision Tree consists of two main elements: Decisions and 'Chance' events. These are represented by squares and circles as shown in Figure 2.2. These decisions and chance events are connected, as shown in the following examples.

Definition: *A decision tree is a pictorial representation of a situation involving a number of decision alternatives. By the calculation of expected values, the decision tree can be used to ascertain the most appropriate decision at each stage.*

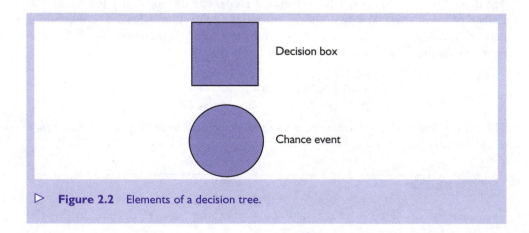

Decision box

Chance event

▷   **Figure 2.2**   Elements of a decision tree.

EXAMPLE I

Consider that you own £1000 worth of shares. You must make a decision about whether to keep the shares, sell them all, or buy an additional £500 worth. The chance of a 20% rise in the share price is 0.6, and the chance of a 20% fall is 0.4. What decision should you make in order to maximise your expected assets?

The initial decision is whether to buy, sell, or stay with the existing shares. This is indicated by the decision tree shown in Figure 2.3. The diagram incorporates the income and expenditure incurred as a result of each decision. For instance, the 'sell' option will give an income of £1000 (indicated by +1000 on the tree). Alternatively, the 'buy' option will involve an expenditure of £500 (indicated by −500). If you sell your shares then you will end up with zero shares remaining. Alternatively, if you just keep the shares then a 20% rise in the market will give you £1200 worth of shares, or a 20% fall will leave you with £800 worth. Alternatively, buying an additional £500 worth of shares will leave you with £1800 if the market rises and £1200 if it falls. These values are shown at the end of each branch on the right hand side of the decision tree shown in Figure 2.4. The tree also shows the probabilities of the chance events (i.e. a rise or fall in the share price), as well as the money spent or received during this process. For instance, buying shares will cost £500 (i.e. the diagram includes a −£500 at this point). Similarly, selling the shares will result in a gain of £1000 and this is included on the relevant branch of the decision tree.

Starting from the right hand side and progressing left, the expected values are calculated as shown in Figure 2.5. Thus, the expected value at the chance event box A is calculated by multiplying each probability by the value at the end of the branch, i.e. expected value at event A is $0.6*1800+0.4*1200=£1560$. Similarly, the expected value at the event B is $0.6*1200+0.4*800=£1040$.

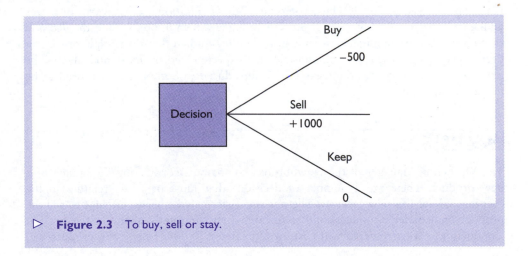

▷ **Figure 2.3**   To buy, sell or stay.

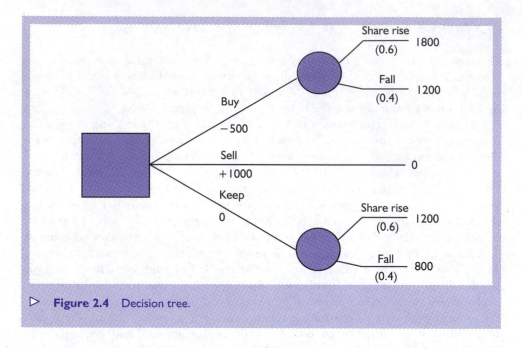

▷ **Figure 2.4**   Decision tree.

Finally, a decision can be made by considering the expected values following each branch back to the decision box C. The three possible routes back into this box give the following values:

Option 1: $1560 - 500 = £1060$
Option 2: $0 + 1000 = £1000$
Option 3: $1040 + 0 = £1040$

Therefore using this criterion in order to maximise the expected value of your shares you would choose option 1. Thus, you would buy an additional £500 worth of shares giving an expected net value of £1060. This value is shown in box C, and the decision route is marked or highlighted as shown. It should be noted that this simple process of decision making based on maximising the expected return may not always be appropriate. For instance, the ideas of risk introduced in Section 2.5 also need to be taken into account.

EXAMPLE 2

The Marketing Manager of the Downbrooks company is considering the launch of a new product. There are a number of decisions that must be made relating to the eventual sale of this new product. The initial decision is whether to attempt to sell the product immediately, conduct market research first, or totally abandon the project. Conducting market research will cost an estimated £50 000. Selling the product will

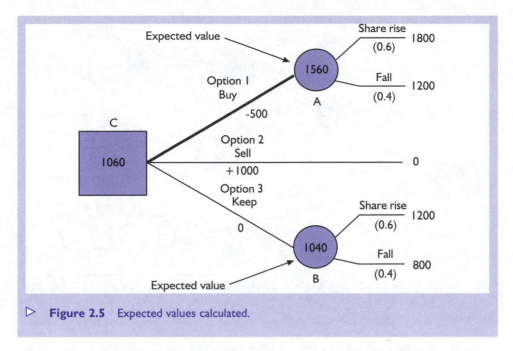

▷ **Figure 2.5** Expected values calculated.

cost £100 000 in terms of extra equipment and setup costs. Abandoning the product will eventually save the company £250 000 in staff costs.

   If the company decides to conduct market research then there is still a decision to be made regarding whether to sell or abandon the new product. The likelihood of estimated sales will depend on whether or not market research has been conducted, and also on the results of such research which could turn out to be either positive or negative. The table below shows the chances of a range of sales for this new product, depending on the market research conducted. The company estimates that a high level of sales will give a gross income of £1 million, a medium level will gross £500 000, and a low level will obtain only £200 000.

   The decision tree shown in Figure 2.6 illustrates the range of decisions to be made and includes estimates of the probabilities of chance events.

Estimated probability of sales levels			
		Market research conducted	
Level of sales	No market Research	Positive response	Negative response
High	0.2	0.4	0.1
Medium	0.4	0.4	0.1
Low	0.4	0.2	0.8

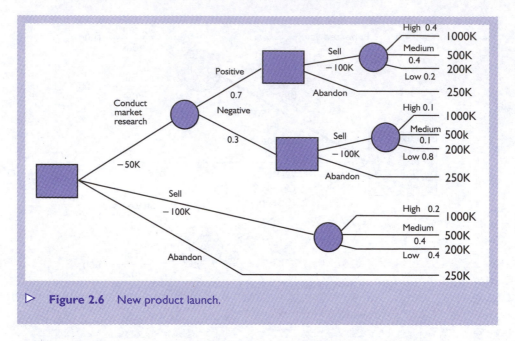

▷ **Figure 2.6** New product launch.

The probabilities given in the table have been included in this decision tree, and the various costs have been incorporated. For example, conducting market research costs £50 000 (abbreviated as 50K) and is included in the diagram as a negative figure.

Finally, starting at the right hand side of the tree and working backwards, the expected values are calculated. For example, the expected value in box A indicated in Figure 2.7 is obtained by $0.4 * 1\,000\,000 + 0.4 * 500\,000 + 0.2 * 200\,000 = £640\,000$. Progressing backwards from this chance event, the decision box (labelled B) contains the maximum expected value from the two branches (sell or abandon). The 'sell' option produces an expected value of £540 000 (i.e. the £640 000 already calculated minus the £100 000 selling costs). Alternatively, the 'abandon' option yields an expected value of £250 000. Thus, the decision at this stage would be to sell, giving an expected value of £540 000 (shown on box B as 540K).

In the same way the chance event (box C) contains an expected value estimated by $0.7 * 540\,000 + 0.3 * 250\,000 = £453\,000$.

The final result shows that in order to maximise the expected profit, the company should do the following:

(i) conduct market research, and
(ii) if the result of the market research is positive then sell the product, and if a negative result is obtained, then abandon the product.

The decision tree shows that the expected profit based on these decisions (in box D) is equal to £403 000.

These examples illustrate the processes involved in determining the 'best' decision based on maximising the expected values. This approach is most likely to be appropriate

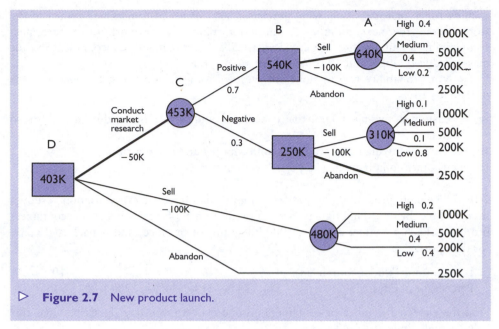

in circumstances where similar decisions are being repeatedly made. The expected value will then provide an estimate of the average (e.g. average profit) over a long run of decisions. However, in situations requiring one-off decisions the approach involving expected values may not be effective. For instance, in Example 1, the 'buy' option produces the highest expected value of £1060. However, we see that if this option is chosen, at a cost of £500, the final value of shares will be either £1800 or £1200, depending on the rise or fall in the market. Thus, subtracting the £500 expenditure, the net value will be £1300 or £700. These compare with values of £1200 or £800 if option 3 (keeping existing shares) is chosen, and a certain £1000 for option 2.

It can be seen that different decision criteria could result in a variety of alternatives. For instance, a decision could be based on maximising the minimum possible return. In this case option 3 (where the minimum return is £800) would be better than option 1, where it is possible to end up with only £700. In fact, option 2 (selling the shares) is the safest route since the return is certain to be £1000. This simple example shows that the use of expected values is not always the best or most appropriate method. Thus, decision trees must be used with care, and a good deal of judgement, and reference should always be made to the exact decision criteria adopted.

2.8	**Exercises: decision trees**

1.(E) Consider a customer arriving in a Downbrooks store. The proportion of customers buying specific items from the store is as follows: 60% buy handmade chocolates, 20% buy mass-produced confectionery, and the remainder buy other items such as fudge or toffee. Following purchase, 30% of all customers will return to the store within the next month. Of those returning, the proportion of customers complaining about the goods purchased is: 5% for handmade chocolates, 15% for mass-produced range, and 10% for the remaining goods.

Draw a probability tree to represent these customers, and use it to determine the probability of:

(a) a customer buying handmade chocolates and returning within a month to complain,
(b) a customer buying mass-produced confectionery and not returning,
(c) a customer complaining.

2.(E)   The daily production output from a large manufacturing organisation is shown in the table below. The figures are given in terms of the number of containers produced. Each container contains 1000 kilograms of produce, and is packaged ready for transport.

Daily output (No. of containers):	4	5	6	7	8	9	10
Percentage of days:		7%	14%	21%	34%	12%	8%	4%

Find the expected number of containers produced in a given day. Describe what this value actually indicates.

3.(I)   A company must decide which of two products to produce. Resources are only available for one of the products. The setup costs for product A are £10 000, and for product B are £15 000. Other expenses, including staff and material costs, are the same. The results of a market research study have been used to predict the likely sales of the two products. The probabilities of the predicted gross profit, excluding setup costs for the two products, are shown in the following table:

Gross profit	Product A	Product B
High (£50 000)	0.7	0.8
Low (£20 000)	0.3	0.2

(i) Using a decision tree, which product would you produce in order to maximise your expected profit?
(ii) Repeat the exercise using a value of £70 000 for a 'high' profit estimate. Does this make any difference to your recommendations?

2.9   The binomial distribution

Consider a quality inspection at the 'Big-Bite' chocolate bar production line in the Downbrooks company.

The proportion of unusable (defective) chocolate bars is known to be 1 in 10. Thus, 10% of the production must be discarded and cannot be sold. This information can be written as:

Prob(defective bar) $= \frac{1}{10} = 0.1$

Similarly, Prob(not defective) $= \frac{9}{10} = 0.9$

The 'Big-Bite' bars are sometimes sold in packs of four 'Family Packs'. The probability of one defective bar being found in a pack of four is obtained as follows. Consider the four bars as being labelled A, B, C and D. The probability of one bar being defective in the pack is described as follows:

$$
\begin{aligned}
\text{Prob(one defective)} = {} & \text{Prob(A defective } \textbf{and } \text{B\&C\&D not defective)} \\
& + \text{Prob(B defective } \textbf{and } \text{A\&C\&D not defective)} \\
& + \text{Prob(C defective } \textbf{and } \text{A\&B\&D not defective)} \\
& + \text{Prob(D defective } \textbf{and } \text{A\&B\&C not defective)} \\
= {} & 0.1 * 0.9 * 0.9 * 0.9 \\
& + 0.9 * 0.1 * 0.9 * 0.9 \\
& + 0.9 * 0.9 * 0.1 * 0.9 \\
& + 0.9 * 0.9 * 0.9 * 0.1 \\
= {} & 4 * 0.1 * (0.9)^3 \\
= {} & 0.2916
\end{aligned}
$$

Similarly, we can obtain the probability of no defectives in the pack as follows:

$$
\begin{aligned}
\text{Prob(no defectives)} = {} & \text{Prob(A\&B\&C\&D all not defective)} \\
= {} & 0.9 * 0.9 * 0.9 * 0.9 \\
= {} & (0.9)^4 \\
= {} & 0.6561
\end{aligned}
$$

The probability of two bars being defective, or three bars, or four bars being defective can be calculated in the same way. The results of these calculations are shown in the following table.

Number of defectives:	0	1	2	3	4
Probability:	0.6561	0.2916	0.0486	0.0036	0.0001

This illustrates a specific example of the **binomial distribution**. The binomial distribution can be identified by the following criteria:

      1. Only two outcomes are possible (e.g. defective or not, Yes or No).
And 2. There are a fixed number of repeated trials (denoted by n).
And 3. The trials are independent of each other.
And 4. The probability of an outcome remains unchanged through all the trials (denoted by p).

The above example illustrates a binomial situation because:

(1) There are only two possible outcomes, i.e. obtaining a defective bar or obtaining a good bar.

(2) The number of repeated independent trials is four (the number of bars in each pack)

(3) The probability of a defective bar is always 0.1.

Thus, in this example, we have a binomial distribution with $n = 4$ and $p = 0.1$.

The probability of obtaining r successes in n trials in a binomial distribution is obtained by:

Prob$(r$ successes$) = {}^nC_r p^r (1 - p)^{n-r}$.
where $r = 0, 1, 2, 3, \ldots, n$.

One expression in this formula for the binomial probability needs further explanation. The number of combinations of n items taken r at a time is denoted by ${}^nC_r$. The value of ${}^nC_r$ is obtained by the expression:

$${}^nC_r = \frac{n!}{r!(n-r)!}$$

where $n!$ ('n factorial') $= n(n-1)(n-2) \ldots 3.2.1$. Note that this rule for the evaluation of factorials applies to positive whole numbers. The value of $0! = 1$ is an exception to this rule.

> **Definition:** *The binomial distribution can be used to calculate probabilities in circumstances where: (i) there are only two possible outcomes in a trial (e.g. success or failure); (ii) independent trials are repeated a number of times (n); (iii) the probability of a success (p) is the same in each trial.*

EXAMPLE 1   (factorials)

Find values of the following factorial expressions:

(i) $5!$, (ii) $2! \, 3!$, (iii) $\dfrac{6!}{4! \, 2!}$

The calculations of these expressions are shown below:

(i) $5! = 5.4.3.2.1 = \mathbf{120}$

(ii) $2!3! = (2.1)(3.2.1) = (2)(6) = \mathbf{12}$

(iii) $\dfrac{6!}{4! \, 2!} = \dfrac{6.5.4.3.2.1}{(4.3.2.1)(2.1)} = \dfrac{720}{24.2} = \dfrac{720}{48} = \mathbf{15}$

EXAMPLE 2   (combinations)

Find the following number of combinations:

(i) ${}^3C_2$, (ii) ${}^6C_4$, (iii) ${}^5C_5$

These combinations are calculated as follows

(i) $^3C_2 = \dfrac{3!}{2!\ 1!} = \dfrac{3.2.1}{(2.1)(1)} = \dfrac{6}{2} = 3$

(ii) $^6C_4 = \dfrac{6!}{4!2!} = \dfrac{6.5.4.3.2.1}{4.3.2.1.2.1} = \dfrac{720}{48} = 15$ (see (iii) above)

(iii) $^5C_5 = \dfrac{5!}{5!\ 0!} = \dfrac{5.4.3.2.1}{(5.4.3.2.1)1} = \dfrac{120}{120} = 1$

(Note that $0! = 1$)

EXAMPLE 3   (binomial probabilities)

From a production line it has been found that one chocolate bar in ten is defective. In a batch of four bars, find the probability of obtaining a given number of defective bars.
   This is a typical binomial distribution problem, with the following parameters:

$p = \text{Prob(obtaining a defective)} = 1$ in $10 = 0.1$
$n = \text{number of trials} = \text{number of bars sampled} = 4$

Using this information we can calculate the probabilities of any number of defective bars being obtained using the binomial formula:

$\text{Prob}(r \text{ successes}) = {}^nC_r p^r (1 - p)^{n-r}$

For instance, the probability of obtaining no defective bars in the batch of four is found by substituting $n=4$, $p=0.1$ and $r=0$ into this expression as shown below:

$\text{Prob}(0) = {}^4C_0 (0.1)^0 (1 - 0.1)^{4-0}$

$\qquad = \dfrac{4!}{0!\ 4!}\ (0.1)^0 (0.9)^4$

$\qquad = \dfrac{4.3.2.1}{1.4.3.2.1}\ 1(0.6561)$

$\qquad = 1.1.(0.6561)$

$\qquad = 0.6561$

Similarly, the probability of obtaining one defective bar from the batch of four is:

$\text{Prob}(1) = {}^4C_1 (0.1)^1 (1 - 0.1)^{4-1}$

$\qquad = \dfrac{4!}{1!\ 3!}\ (0.1)^1 (0.9)^3$

$\qquad = \dfrac{4.3.2.1}{1.3.2.1}\ (0.1)(0.729)$

$\qquad = 4.(0.1)(0.729)$

$\qquad = 0.2916$

Continuing with this method we find:

$$\text{Prob}(2 \text{ defectives}) = {}^4C_2(0.1)^2(1-0.1)^{4-2}$$

$$= \frac{4!}{2! \ 2!}(0.1)^2(0.9)^2$$

$$= 0.0486$$

and

$$\text{Prob}(3 \text{ defectives}) = {}^4C_3(0.1)^3(1-0.1)^{4-3}$$

$$= \frac{4!}{3! \ 1!}(0.1)^3(0.9)^1$$

$$= 0.0036$$

$$\text{Prob}(4 \text{ defectives}) = {}^4C_4(0.1)^4(1-0.1)^{4-4}$$

$$= \frac{4!}{4! \ 0!}(0.1)^4(0.9)^0$$

$$= 0.0001$$

The results of these calculations give the binomial distribution introduced at the beginning of this section and reproduced below:

Number of defectives:	0	1	2	3	4
Probability:	0.6561	0.2916	0.0486	0.0036	0.0001

EXAMPLE 4

At the St. Joseph's Hospital, New York, the probability of any bed being unoccupied is 20%. Given a random sample of five beds find the probability that the number of beds unoccupied is:

(i) at most one,   (ii) more than two.

Again, these probabilities can be obtained using the binomial formula. In this example, we have:

$p = \text{Prob}(\text{unoccupied bed}) = 0.2,$ $n = \text{number of beds} = 5$

(i) The probability of at most one bed being unoccupied is equivalent to the probability of no beds or only one bed being unoccupied, i.e. $\text{Prob}(\text{at most } 1) = \text{Prob}(0 \text{ or } 1) = \text{Prob}(0) + \text{Prob}(1)$

$$\text{Now, Prob}(0) = {}^5C_0(0.2)^0(1-0.2)^{5-0}$$

$$= \frac{5!}{0! \ 5!}(0.2)^0(0.8)^5$$

$$= \frac{5.4.3.2.1}{1.5.4.3.2.1}(1)(0.32768)$$

$$= 0.32768$$

Similary, $\text{Prob}(1) = {}^5C_1 (0.2)^1 (1 - 0.2)^{5-1}$

$$= \frac{5!}{1! \, 4!} (0.2)^1 (0.8)^4$$

$$= 0.4096$$

Therefore, $\text{Prob}(\text{at most } 1) = \text{Prob}(0) + \text{Prob}(1)$

$$= 0.32768 + 0.4096$$

$$= 0.73728$$

Thus, there is approximately a 74% chance that at most one bed out of five will be unoccupied.

(ii) $\text{Prob}(\text{more than } 2) = \text{Prob}(3 \text{ or } 4 \text{ or } 5 \text{ beds being unoccupied})$

This can be written as $1 - \text{Prob}(2 \text{ or fewer beds being unoccupied})$
$= 1 - \text{Prob}(0 \text{ or } 1 \text{ or } 2 \text{ beds})$
$= 1 - \{\text{Prob}(0) + \text{Prob}(1) + \text{Prob}(2)\}$

Now the probabilities of 0 and 1 have already been calculated in part (i). Therefore it is only necessary to use the binomial formula to obtain the probability of two beds being unoccupied.

$\text{Prob}(2) = {}^5C_2 (0.2)^2 (1 - 0.2)^{5-2}$

$$= \frac{5!}{2! \, 3!} (0.2)^2 (0.8)^3$$

$$= 0.2048$$

Therefore, the probability of more than two beds being unoccupied is:

$\text{Prob}(\text{more than } 2) = 1 - \{\text{Prob}(0) + \text{Prob}(1) + \text{Prob}(2)\}$

$$= 1 - (0.32768 + 0.4096 + 0.2048)$$

$$= 1 - 0.94208$$

$$= 0.05792$$

Thus, there is almost a 6% chance of more than two beds being unoccupied.

2.10   The Poisson distribution

The Poisson distribution can be used to evaluate probabilities of a number of events occurring in the following circumstances:

1. the number of events occurring is considered over a specified time interval.
2. The independent events occur at random,
3. The average (mean) number of events occurring is known and is constant.

In general, the probability of r events occurring can be found by the Poisson formula:

$$\text{Prob}(r \text{ events}) = \frac{e^{-\mu}\mu^r}{r!}$$

where μ = average number of events occurring and $r = 0, 1, 2, 3, \ldots$. This Poisson formula includes the exponential function $e^{-\mu}$, which can be found from exponential tables for given values of μ.

> **Definition:**   *The Poisson distribution can be used to evaluate probabilities in which events occur at random, and the average number of events occurring (μ) is known.*

EXAMPLE 1

Consider the example of defective chocolate bars in the Downbrooks production line. It has been noted that there is an average of two defective bars every minute from the production line. The defectives occur at random and so cannot be predicted.

In this example, events (i.e. defectives) occur at random, and we know the average number ($\mu = 2$) of defectives. Therefore the probability of obtaining no defectives in a given minute is obtained by the Poisson formula:

$$\text{Prob}(0) = \frac{e^{-\mu}\mu^r}{r!} = \frac{e^{-2}.2^0}{0!}$$

The value of $e^{-2} = 0.13534$ can be obtained from exponential tables.

Therefore,

$$\text{Prob}(0) = \frac{(0.13534).1}{1} = 0.13534$$

Thus there is a 13.534% chance of obtaining no defectives in any one minute. Similarly, the probability of any number of defectives can be obtained. For instance, the probability of getting three defectives is:

$$\text{Prob}(3) = \frac{e^{-2}.2^3}{3!} = \frac{(0.13534).8}{6} = 0.1805$$

EXAMPLE 2

The Health & Safety Manager in a large manufacturing organisation has been asked to analyse the accident rate of employees in the production teams. On average there is one serious accident every two years in this organisation. Find the chance that in a given year more than two accidents occur.

Assuming that the accidents occur at random, we have a Poisson distribution with the average $\mu = 0.5$ accidents per year.

The probability of more than two accidents occurring is:

Prob(more than 2) = 1 – {Prob(0 or 1 or 2)}
$$= 1 - \{Prob(0) + Prob(1) + Prob(2)\}$$

Now, using the Poisson probability formula we have:

$$Prob(0) = \frac{e^{-0.5}.0.5^0}{0!} = \frac{(0.60653).1}{1} = 0.60653$$

Similarly,

$$Prob(1) = \frac{e^{-0.5}.0.5^1}{1!} = \frac{(0.60653)(0.5)}{1} = 0.30327$$

and

$$Prob(2) = \frac{e^{-0.5}.0.5^2}{2!} = \frac{(0.60653)(0.25)}{2} = 0.07582$$

So the required probability is obtained by:

Prob(more than 2) = 1 – (0.60653 + 0.30327 + 0.07582)
$$= 1 - 0.98562$$
$$= 0.01438$$

This shows that there is a 1.4% chance of more than two accidents occurring in any one year.

2.11 Exercises: binomial and Poisson distributions

1.(E)   One in ten of the patients arriving at the Accident & Emergency department in St. Joseph's hospital need to be kept in overnight for observation and further tests. From a group of six patients arriving, what is the chance that the number of patients being kept in for observation is:

  (i)   only one,
 (ii)   more than two,
(iii)   less than two.

2.(E)   The Sales Manager in a large wholesale organisation estimates that one in three 'cold calls' from his salespersons will result in a sale. If a salesperson makes five such calls to prospective customers what is the probability that he/she obtains:

  (i)   no sales,
 (ii)   only one sale,
(iii)   two sales,
 (iv)   more than two sales.

3.(I)   The Personnel Manager in a large organisation has found that when recruiting for middle management staff, only one in four of the applicants satisfies all the requirements for shortlisting. From a batch of ten applications, find the probability that the number of candidates shortlisted is:

  (i)   less than 2,
 (ii)   two or more,
(iii)   over two.

| 2.12 | **Continuous probability distributions** |

The previous sections have introduced the ideas of discrete probability distributions in which a variable under consideration can only take specific (discrete) values. For instance, variables such as the number of defects, number of arrivals, and the number of accidents can all only be whole number values. In this section we will consider continuous distributions, where a variable can theoretically equal any value within a given range.

In an earlier section in this chapter the idea of expected values has been introduced. The examples shown in Section 2.6 involved the use of simple probability distributions which could have been obtained from observation of previous values. For instance, the daily sales of a company over the last 50 days is shown in the table below:

Daily sales (£):	1000–	2000–	3000–	4000–	5000–	6000–
Number of days:	2	6	18	13	7	4

This information can be converted into a probability distribution. For instance, on 2 days in the last 50 (i.e. 4% of days) the sales were £1000 and over. Therefore, the probability of obtaining sales of £1000 and over could be expressed as 0.04. Similarly, the remaining probabilities are found as shown in the probability distribution given below.

Daily sales (£):	1000–	2000–	3000–	4000–	5000–	6000–
Probability:	0.04	0.12	0.36	0.26	0.14	0.08

The graph of this distribution is shown in Figure 2.8. The area of each block in this diagram is proportional to the probability. For instance, the area of the shaded block is 12% of the total area. Similarly, the area of the blocks representing the last three classes (4000–, 5000– and 6000–) would be 48% of the total area. This approach gives a different method of finding probabilities from a probability distribution. The diagram shown in Figure 2.9 gives an alternative way of illustrating the same data. A line graph is used to indicate the overall shape of the distribution rather than a histogram outlining each individual class interval. This graph can be used in the same way to represent probabilities. The area under the line can be used to determine the probabilities. For instance, the area shaded on the diagram in Figure 2.9 illustrates the

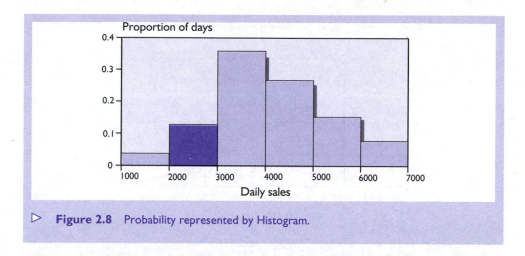

▷ **Figure 2.8** Probability represented by Histogram.

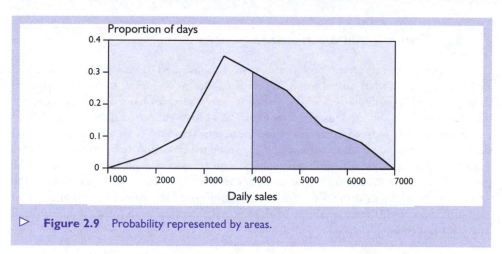

▷ **Figure 2.9** Probability represented by areas.

probability of sales exceeding £4000 (i.e. incorporating all the values along the horizontal scale over £4000). If we consider that the total area under the line drawn is equal to 1, then any area found would directly equate to the probability. Thus the area shaded in Figure 2.9 would be equal to 0.48 (48% of the total area).

Figure 2.10 illustrates a probability distribution of weekly earnings in a company. Assuming that the total area under the curve is equal to 1, then the area under the graph shaded represents the probability of an employee earning between £400 and £500 per week.

Definition: *The area under the graph of a continuous probability distribution can be used to estimate the probability of a variable lying between given limits.*

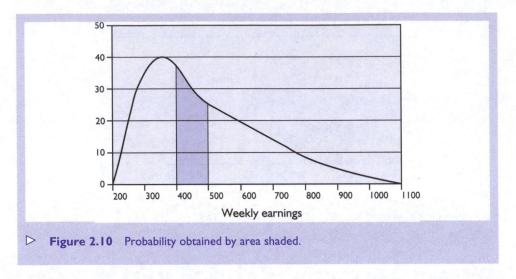

Weekly earnings

▷   **Figure 2.10**   Probability obtained by area shaded.

| 2.13 | ## The normal distribution |

One of the most important probability distributions used in management decision making is the **normal distribution**. This distribution is found in many practical examples, and is particularly useful when considering samples from a large population. The normal distribution, illustrated in Figure 2.11, is symmetrical, bell-shaped, and can be completely defined by values of the mean and standard deviation. The mean (μ) defines the centre of the distribution, and the standard deviation (σ) defines its spread. Figure 2.12 illustrates how differences in the mean will change the position of the graph, and Figure 2.13 shows how increases in the standard deviation will alter the spread of the curve as displayed. However, regardless of the values for the mean and standard deviation, the basic shape of the normal distribution defined by the normal curve is preserved.

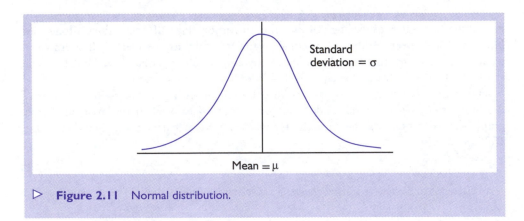

Standard
deviation = σ

Mean = μ

▷   **Figure 2.11**   Normal distribution.

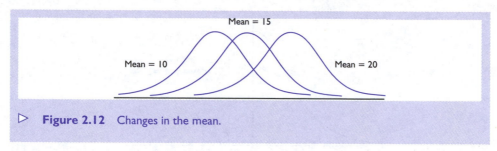

▷ **Figure 2.12**   Changes in the mean.

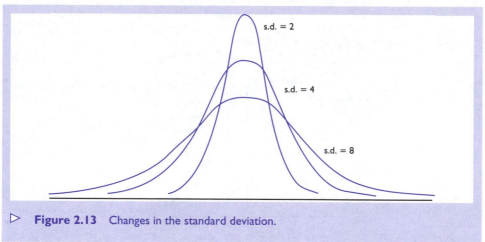

▷ **Figure 2.13**   Changes in the standard deviation.

As described in the previous section, probabilities can be obtained by finding the area under the curve. Consequently, the total area under any normal curve is equal to the total probability (=1). Consider the normal curve with a mean equal to 200 and a standard deviation of 50. This distribution is illustrated in Figure 2.14 and the probability of a value being between 240 and 280 is shown by the area shaded.

The evaluation of areas under the normal curve involves a complex mathematical formula. The use of normal tables simplifies this process. Usually, tables are published of the 'standard normal distribution' where the mean is zero with a standard deviation of 1. Any normal distribution with a given mean (μ) and given standard deviation (σ) can be transformed to this standardised distribution by the following calculation:

$$z = \frac{x - \mu}{\sigma}$$

The value of z found by this formula gives the distance between the value (x) and the mean (μ) expressed in terms of the number of standard deviations.

The normal distribution tables, such as those given at the end of this text, can give the area under the standard normal curve above a specific value of z, as shown in Figure 2.15. Any probability can be found by the use of a combination of these values,

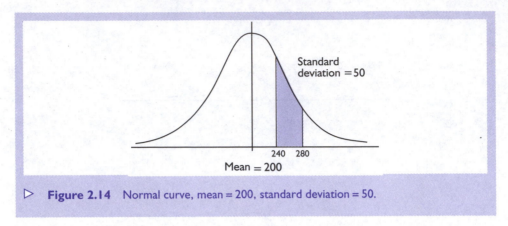

▷ **Figure 2.14**   Normal curve, mean = 200, standard deviation = 50.

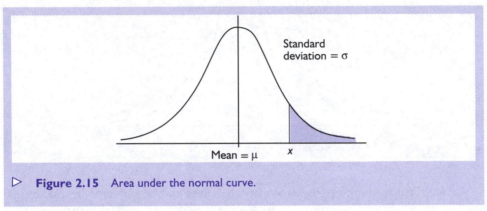

▷ **Figure 2.15**   Area under the normal curve.

as shown in the following examples. The area illustrated in Figure 2.15 equates to the probability of the variable being over a given value (x).

Definition: *The normal distribution is represented by a symmetrical, bell-shaped curve defined in terms of the mean (μ) and standard deviation (σ).*

EXAMPLE 1

The weights of a sample of chocolate boxes produced by Downbrooks are found to be normally distributed with an average of 400 grams and a standard deviation of 20 grams. Find the probability of a box of chocolates, taken at random, weighing:

(i)   over 425 grams,
(ii) under 410 grams,
(iii) under 380 grams,
(iv) over 395 grams,
(v)   between 390 and 412 grams.

The solutions to these separate problems will illustrate the use of the standard normal distribution tables.

(i) Figure 2.16 illustrates the required probability as the shaded area over 425 grams. The values of the mean (μ) and standard deviation (σ) are shown on the diagram. The first step is to evaluate the standard variate:

$$z = \frac{x - \mu}{\sigma}$$

$$= \frac{425 - 400}{20}$$

$$= \frac{25}{20} = 1.25$$

Now using the normal tables, when $z = 1.25$, the shaded area is 0.1057. Thus, the probability of obtaining a box of chocolates over 425 grams is 0.1057 (or a 10.57% chance).

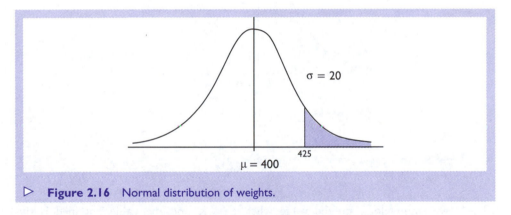

$\sigma = 20$

425

$\mu = 400$

▷ **Figure 2.16** Normal distribution of weights.

(ii) Figure 2.17 illustrates the required probability under 410 grams. Again, we calculate the value of $z = (x - \mu)/\sigma = (410 - 400)/20 = 10/20 = 0.5$. The area obtained directly from tables corresponding to $z = 0.5$ is equal to 0.3085. This is the area **above** the given value. To find the area below this value we simply subtract it from 1 (the total area under the curve). Therefore, the required area $= 1 - 0.3085 = 0.6915$. Thus, the probability of obtaining a box of chocolates weighing less than 410 grams is 0.6915 (or 69.15%).

(iii) Figure 2.18 illustrates the required area and the calculation of the value of z.

Although the value of z is negative, we can still use the normal tables, where only positive values are published. The normal curve is symmetrical and therefore the area in the left hand tail is exactly equal to the area in the right hand tail. Therefore, given that

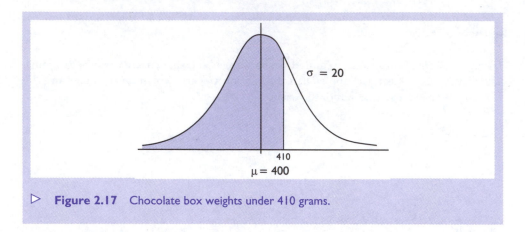

▷ **Figure 2.17**   Chocolate box weights under 410 grams.

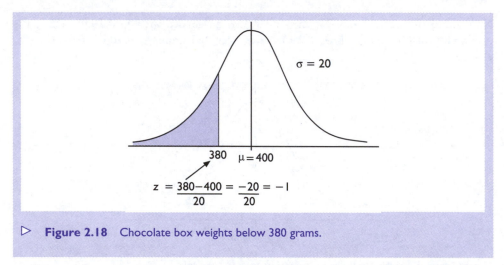

▷ **Figure 2.18**   Chocolate box weights below 380 grams.

$z = -1$, we simply look up the value when $z = +1$, and the value obtained is the required probability.

Thus, the probability of obtaining a box of chocolates weighing less than 380 grams is 0.1587 (or 15.87%).

(iv) Figure 2.19 illustrates the required area and shows the calculation of the value of z. Again, the value of z is negative. However, finding the area corresponding to the positive value of z will find the area in the left hand tail. Thus, from the tables, the area in this tail is 0.4013. Therefore, the required area = $1 - 0.4013 = 0.5987$. The required probability is 0.5987 (or a 59.87% chance).

(v) The area between two limits (390 to 412 grams) requires two values of z to be calculated, and the area between these values estimated by a combination of the

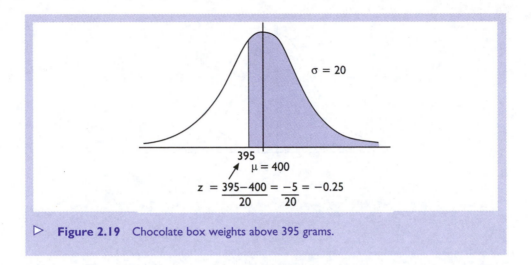

$$z = \frac{395-400}{20} = \frac{-5}{20} = -0.25$$

▷ **Figure 2.19**   Chocolate box weights above 395 grams.

tabulated values obtained. The two values of z are calculated on Figure 2.20 together with the required area shaded.

The areas in the two tails are found directly from tables. For instance, the area above 412 grams is found by using the value of $z = 0.6$. Similarly, the area below 390 grams is found by using $z = 0.5$. Thus, using $z = 0.6$ area above 412 grams is 0.2743. Similarly, using $z = 0.5$, the area below 390 grams is 0.3085.

The required area between 390 and 412 grams is obtained by subtracting these two areas away from the total area of 1. Thus,

$$
\begin{aligned}
\text{required area} &= 1 - (0.2743 + 0.3085) \\
&= 1 - (0.5828) \\
&= 0.4172
\end{aligned}
$$

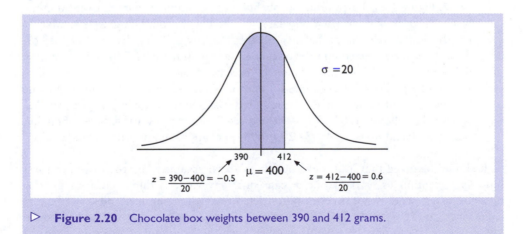

▷ **Figure 2.20**   Chocolate box weights between 390 and 412 grams.

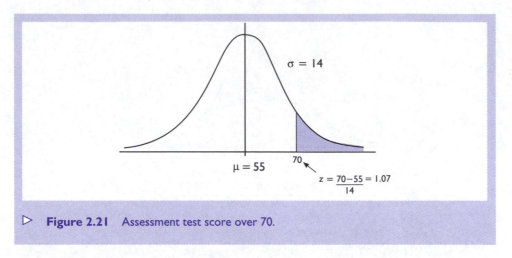

$\sigma = 14$

$\mu = 55$

70

$z = \dfrac{70-55}{14} = 1.07$

▷ **Figure 2.21**   Assessment test score over 70.

Thus, the probability of obtaining a box of chocolates weighing between 390 and 412 grams is 0.4172 (or 41.72% chance).

EXAMPLE 2

St. Joseph's hospital uses a range of assessment methods in the selection of management staff. One assessment test used has been validated using the results of over 3000 tests nationwide over the past five years. The results of this test are normally distributed with an average score of 55 and a standard deviation of 14.

In a shortlist of 20 candidates, estimate how many you would expect to obtain a score for this assessment test of:

  (i)   over 70,   and (ii) between 40 and 60.

 (i) Now, Figure 2.21 illustrates the probability of obtaining a score of over 70 in the test. The value of z has been calculated on the illustration. Using normal tables it can be found that the probability of obtaining over 70 in the test is $= 0.1423$. Therefore, the expected number of candidates obtaining over 70 will be found by $0.1423 * 20 = 2.846$, i.e. approximately three candidates.

 (ii) Figure 2.22 shows the required area between 40 and 60, and gives the calculations of the two values of z required. Using normal tables, the area shaded is found to be $= 0.4983$. Thus the expected number of candidates obtaining between 40 and 60 is $= 0.4983 * 20 = 9.966$, i.e. approximately ten candidates.

It should be noted that in this example it has been assumed that the assessment test score is a 'continuous' variable, i.e. it can equal **any** value within a given range. For instance, a test score is not necessarily restricted to a whole number and could be any value such as 52.6 or 49.861. Alternatively, if the test score is considered to be 'discrete', e.g. it can only be a whole number, then the 'continuity correction' needs to be used in order to use the normal distribution to estimate probabilities. For instance,

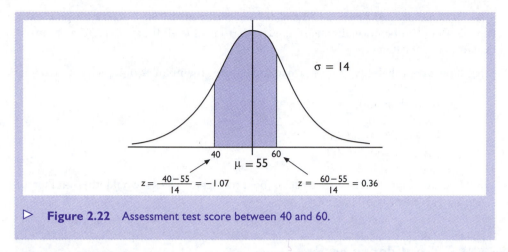

$$z = \frac{40-55}{14} = -1.07 \qquad z = \frac{60-55}{14} = 0.36$$

$\triangleright$ **Figure 2.22**   Assessment test score between 40 and 60.

the probability of obtaining a score of 40 would be obtained by finding the area under the normal curve between 39.5 and 40.5. Similarly, the probability of a score between 40 and 50 would be found by the area between 39.5 and 50.5.

2.14	**Exercises: the normal distribution**

1.(E)   Given a normal distribution with mean equal to 40 and standard deviation equal to 10, find the area under the normal curve:

    (a) above 45,
    (b) below 30,
    (c) between 42 and 52,
    (d) below 48,
    (e) between 28 and 55,

2.(I)   Hourly pay rates for a group of skilled employees in all industries across the US are found to be normally distributed with an average of $12 per hour and a standard deviation of $2 per hour.

  (i) Find the probability of an employee with these skills, taken at random, receiving an hourly pay rate of:
    (a) over $16,
    (b) over $10,
    (c) below $12,
    (d) between $10 and $14,
    (e) between $7 and $11.
 (ii) What is the chance of such an employee earning within one standard deviation of the mean?
(iii) Out of a group of 50 such employees how many would you expect to earn over $15 per hour?

3.(I) The number of patients arriving for treatment at the St. Joseph's hospital each week is found to be normally distributed with a mean of 400 patients and a standard deviation of 90 patients.

  (i) Find the probability that on a particular week the number of patients arriving at the hospital is:
   (a) more than 500,
   (b) less than 250,
   (c) between 350 and 450,
   (d) between 400 and 480,
   (e) between 420 and 520.
  (ii) During a given year (52 weeks), on how many weeks would the number of arrivals exceed 550 patients?

2.15	**Confidence limits**

Consider the problem of determining the number of beds required in a specialist department in the St. Joseph's hospital. The total number of beds required each day is normally distributed with a mean of 60 and a standard deviation of 10. The management wish to be reasonably certain that there are enough beds to satisfy requirements on a daily basis. In fact, the management have stated that the number of available beds should be sufficient for at least 99 days out of every 100.

  The problem is to determine how many beds the department should have available in order to satisfy this condition. The distribution of the number of beds required each day is illustrated in Figure 2.23. The problem, as outlined, is that we need to find the value of x, such that the area above this value is at most 1%, as illustrated in the diagram. Using the same approach as in the previous section, we can attempt to calculate z as follows:

$$z = \frac{x - \mu}{\sigma} = \frac{x - 60}{10}$$

Now, the value of x is unknown. However, the value of z that corresponds to an area in the tail of 1% (=0.01) can be obtained from using normal tables. The nearest value of z is 2.33 corresponding to an area of 0.0099. Thus, we have the equation

$$z = \frac{x - 60}{10} = 2.33$$

Rearranging the equation we have: $x - 60 = 2.33 * 10$
                                    i.e. $x - 60 = 23.3$
                                    and so $x = 23.3 + 60 = 83.3$

Thus, if the department has 84 beds then there is less than a 1% chance of not being able to satisfy demand.

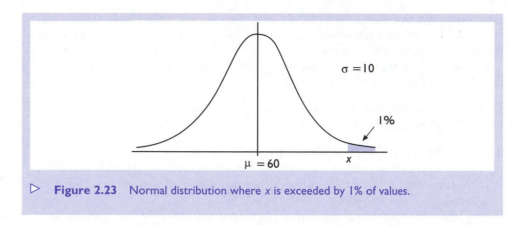

▷   **Figure 2.23**   Normal distribution where x is exceeded by 1% of values.

This method can be adapted for use in the calculation of **confidence limits**. Such limits indicate the range of values containing a specified proportion of all values around the mean. For example, the 95% confidence limits in a normal distribution can be obtained by the formula $\mu \pm 1.96\sigma$. These limits, illustrated in Figure 2.24, define the two values containing the central 95% of the distribution. Thus, the area in each tail either side of the limits is only 2.5% of the total. With this area in the tail the value of z from normal tables is 1.96. Therefore the value of z is $(x - \mu)/\sigma = 1.96$. Rearranging this expression we have $x - \mu = 1.96\sigma$, and so $x = \mu + 1.96\sigma$. Similarly, the lower confidence limit is $\mu - 1.96\sigma$.

For example, the 95% confidence limits for the weight of the chocolate boxes produced by Downbrooks, where the mean weight is 400 grams and the standard deviation is 20 grams, are $\mu \pm 1.96\sigma = 400 \pm 1.96 * 20 = 400 \pm 39.2$ or 360.8 to 439.2. Thus, we can be 95% confident that the weight of a box of chocolates is between 360.8 and 439.2 grams.

This approach forms the basis of a range of quality control techniques used in manufacturing and production. The confidence limits provide a guide to the expected

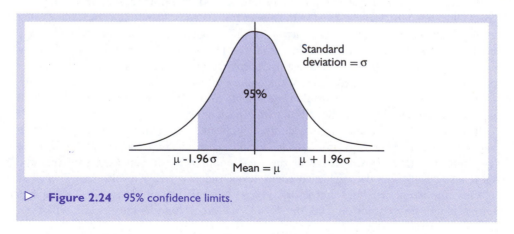

▷   **Figure 2.24**   95% confidence limits.

range for given variables. Any value sampled that is found to be outside this expected range can be viewed with suspicion, and thus the overall 'quality' of the production could be subject to further scrutiny.

In addition to the 95% values, other confidence limits are sometimes used in circumstances, including the following:

> **99% confidence limits:** $\mu \pm 2.58\sigma$
> **99.8% confidence limits:** $\mu \pm 3.09\sigma$

Thus, for example, the 99% confidence limits for the weight of chocolate boxes previously discussed are $\mu \pm 2.58\sigma = 400 \pm 2.58 * 20 = 400 \pm 51.6 = 348.4$ to 451.6.

Therefore, we can be 99% confident that the weight of a chocolate box will be within the range 348.4 to 451.6 grams.

It is left to the reader to obtain the 99.8% confidence limits for this distribution.

The use of alternative confidence limits is important in problems that require greater or lesser degrees of accuracy. For example, an overweight or underweight box of chocolates is less important than variations in the weight of a vital chemical component in a drug. Thus, appropriate confidence limits will be used, dependent on the importance of the variable under consideration.

> **Definition:** *Confidence limits define the upper and lower values containing the central proportion from the population. For example, the 95% confidence limits define the limits containing 95% of values.*

2.16   Significance and sampling

In many circumstances a sample is taken from a population in order to make inferences relating to that population. This is often the case when the population is simply too large for all items to be included. For instance, in the quality control problem at Downbrooks, the company produced millions of 'Big-Bite' bars each year. It would be impossible to check every item being produced and therefore a sample of items is checked at regular intervals. Even with smaller populations, sampling is necessary, such as in situations that involve destruction of the original product. For example, one quality check on the Downbrooks products is to examine the items following packaging. This involves unpacking the chocolates and investigating that the correct number of items are included and that the quality of display is acceptable. Clearly, with such a check it would be impossible for all items to be examined, otherwise the whole production will need to be unboxed following packaging.

The reliability of samples to accurately indicate the attributes of a population depends on a number of factors. These include ensuring that the samples taken are 'random' and thus representative of the total population, and making sure that the sample size is sufficiently large in an attempt to avoid any 'freak' results.

One important attribute that is often considered is the sample mean. A sample is taken from the population and the mean (average) found. This result will then enable us to draw conclusions about the total population. In general, if a population has a mean of μ then a sample mean is likely to be relatively close to this value. Indeed, if many samples are taken, then the mean of the sample means will be μ. It is useful to look at the distribution of these sample means in order to resolve practical problems such as those presented in quality control. The sample means will be spread around the value of μ. Can the spread of these means be predicted? It is known that if the population has a standard deviation of σ then the distribution of sample means will have a standard deviation of $\sigma/\sqrt{n}$ where n is the sample size.

Definition: *If samples of size n are taken from a population with a mean* $= \mu$ *and standard deviation* $= \sigma$, *then the distribution of sample means has a mean* $= \mu$ *and standard deviation* $= \sigma/\sqrt{n}$.

EXAMPLE 1

Consider the population of 400 gram chocolate boxes produced by Downbrooks. The total production has a mean of 400 grams with a standard deviation of 20 grams. Samples of 25 boxes are examined every hour from this production and weighed, and the sample average recorded. This information can be used to determine how we would expect these sample averages to be distributed. We are given that the population mean $\mu = 400$ and the population standard deviation $\sigma = 20$. Samples of size $n = 25$ are taken.

These details enable us to determine the likely attributes of the sample means. The distribution of sample means will conform to the following:

Mean of sample means, $\mu = 400$ grams

Standard deviation of sample means, $\dfrac{\sigma}{\sqrt{n}} = \dfrac{20}{\sqrt{25}} = \dfrac{20}{5} = 4$ grams

Thus, this information could enable us to determine the probability of sample means being within given ranges. For instance, the probability of the sample mean being over 405 grams is shown by the shaded area under the curve in Figure 2.25.

Notice that the standard deviation used in the evaluation of z is the standard deviation of the sample means $\sigma/\sqrt{n}$

$$z = \frac{405 - 400}{4} = 1.25$$

Using normal tables the area shaded is equal to 0.10565. Thus, there is a 10.565% chance that the sample mean is over 405 grams.

Using the same information, we can evaluate an expected range for the sample means. For instance, assuming the normal distribution, the 95% confidence limits for the sample means are obtained as follows:

$400 \pm 1.96 * 4 = 400 \pm 7.84 = 392.16$ to 407.84 grams

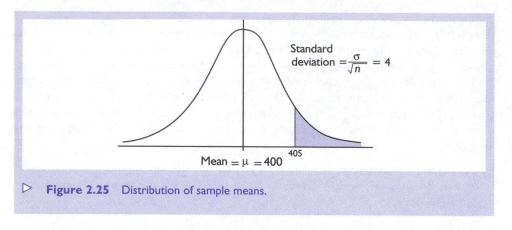

Standard
deviation $= \dfrac{\sigma}{\sqrt{n}} = 4$

405

Mean $= \mu = 400$

▷ **Figure 2.25** Distribution of sample means.

Thus, we can be 95% certain that any sample of 25 boxes taken from this production will have a mean between 392.16 and 407.84 grams. This gives a basis for determining the **significance** of a sample mean. If the calculated mean is outside this expected range then it is said to be 'significant'. A value outside the range is fairly unlikely, and therefore this may tell us that there is a problem with the production. For instance, if a sample of 25 boxes is found to have a mean of 410 grams then it looks as though the weights of boxes are significantly higher than required. Therefore, we must re-examine the production process and make adjustments where necessary.

<hr>

EXAMPLE 2

The daily output of the 'Troofle' bar is known to be normally distributed with a mean of 2500 bars and a standard deviation of 300 bars per day. Following the introduction of a new machine in production, a sample of 50 days gave an average daily production of 2600 bars. The Production Manager says that this is evidence that the new machine has improved the production output. To verify this we could look at the distribution of sample means and investigate whether the new average is significantly different.

The original population mean is $\mu = 2500$, and the population standard deviation is $\sigma = 300$. If samples of 50 values are taken from this population then the distribution of sample means will have a mean $= \mu = 2500$, and a standard deviation of $\sigma/\sqrt{n} = 300/\sqrt{50} = 300/7.07 = 42.43$.

Now, with this population the 95% confidence limits for the sample means are found by the formula: $2500 \pm 1.96 * 42.43 = 2500 \pm 83.16 = 2416.8$ to 2583.2 grams.

Thus, with the original machine, any sample of the production over 50 days is likely to have a mean in this range. It follows that a sample mean outside this range is not likely to occur. Thus, a mean of 2600 is significant, which indicates that it is very unlikely to occur with the original machinery. Therefore, it seems that the population of daily production figures may have changed. Therefore, this evidence backs up the Production Manager's claim that the output using the new machinery is different.

| 2.17 | **Hypothesis testing** |

The processes described in the previous section led on to a consideration of **hypothesis testing**. In many practical situations, we make assumptions concerning the population that may need to be tested objectively. Such assumptions are referred to as 'hypotheses' and may be proved or disproved by the use of an appropriate hypothesis test involving probabilities. In this section we will consider assumptions involving the mean of a population and introduce a test that can be used to examine such assumptions.

| EXAMPLE I | **(known standard deviation)** |

In the Downbrooks company it is assumed that the average weight of a particular chocolate product is 400 grams. The standard deviation of these weights is known to be 20 grams. A sample of 100 items is taken from the production line and found to have a mean of 402 grams. Does this sample disprove the assumption about the population average?

In this example we have the following:

In the sample: mean $\bar{x} = 402$, sample size $n = 100$
In the population: standard deviation $\sigma = 20$

The initial assumption (called the **null hypothesis**) is that the population mean (μ) is equal to 400. If this is false then an alternative assumption could be that the mean is not 400.

The process of stating the null hypothesis and an alternative hypothesis can be denoted as follows:

$H_0: \mu = 400$ (the null hypothesis)
$H_1: \mu \neq 400$ (the alternative hypothesis)

If the null hypothesis is correct then the population has a mean $\mu = 400$ and standard deviation $\sigma = 20$. If samples of 100 items are taken then the distribution of sample means (as shown in the previous section) will have a mean $\mu = 400$ and standard deviation $\sigma/\sqrt{n} = 20/\sqrt{100} = 20/10 = 2$.

The hypothesis is tested by considering whether the sample mean obtained is 'significant', i.e. whether the value is outside the confidence limits. Instead of actually calculating the confidence limits and comparing them with the value obtained we can adopt a new approach. It is only necessary to calculate the following formula:

$$z = \frac{\bar{x} - \mu}{\sigma/\sqrt{n}}$$

This value can then be compared with a critical value such as 1.96 if using the 95% confidence limits.

Thus, in this example

$$z = \frac{\bar{x} - \mu}{\sigma/\sqrt{n}} = \frac{402 - 400}{20/\sqrt{100}} = \frac{2}{20/10} = 1$$

Now the value of z (=1) is less than 1.96 and is therefore 'not significant' at the 95% level of confidence. (Relating to the previous section this means that the sample mean is **inside** the 95% confidence limits.)

Therefore, we can accept the null hypothesis (i.e. we accept H_0).

Consequently, this sample has not caused us to doubt the assumption that the average weight from the production line is 400 grams. Thus, we cannot use the evidence from this sample to show that the production is off-target.

EXAMPLE 2   (standard deviation unknown)

In practice, when using an hypothesis test of this type it is unlikely that the population standard deviation is known. Usually, the standard deviation will be estimated based on a sample value. The population standard deviation is usually denoted by σ and the sample standard deviation is denoted by s.

The formula for z used to test the hypothesis for large samples can be modified to incorporate a sample standard deviation as shown below:

$$z = \frac{\bar{x} - \mu}{\sigma/\sqrt{n}} = \frac{\bar{x} - \mu}{s/\sqrt{n-1}}$$

This modified formula incorporating the sample standard deviation (s) is obtained by finding the 'best' estimate of a population standard deviation (σ) as follows.

The population variance is likely to be slightly larger than the sample variance and the following expression gives the best estimate:

$$\sigma^2 = \frac{n}{n-1} s^2$$

Rearranging this expression we obtain

$$\frac{\sigma^2}{n} = \frac{s^2}{n-1}$$

Finally, square rooting both sides of the equation we have

$$\frac{\sigma}{\sqrt{n}} = \frac{s}{\sqrt{n-1}}$$

Thus, the amended formula for z as shown above can be used.

The value of z can then be compared with 1.96 at the 5% significance level (i.e. using 95% confidence limits), or other values such as 2.58 at the 1% significance level (obtained from 99% confidence limits).

Consider the following example: The average daily sales income in a company is assumed to be $2000. Over a sample of 20 days the sales incomes average $1800 per day, with a standard deviation of $300 per day. Use a suitable hypothesis test to examine the assumption.

We have that the null hypothesis is $H_0: \mu = 2000$

with the alternative hypothesis as $H_1: \mu \neq 2000$.

We can test this based on the sample obtained where the sample size $n = 20$, the sample mean $\bar{x} = 1800$, and the sample standard deviation $s = 300$.

Using these values we can calculate the expression for z as shown:

$$z = \frac{\bar{x} - \mu}{s/\sqrt{n-1}} = \frac{1800 - 2000}{300/\sqrt{20-1}} = \frac{-200}{300/\sqrt{19}} = \frac{-200}{300/4.359}$$

$$= \frac{-200}{68.82} = -2.91$$

The value of $z = 2.91$ is greater than 1.96 and is therefore significant at the 5% significance level. (Note that the negative sign can be ignored when considering the significance of a value of z in this type of test.)

This shows that the null hypothesis is likely to be false. We therefore reject the null hypothesis and accept the alternative hypothesis. We conclude from this sample that the population mean is unlikely to be equal to $2000. In other words the average daily income for this company is probably not $2000.

By the use of hypothesis tests of this type we can examine the characteristics of a population based on sample data.

2.18   Exercises: confidence limits and significance

1.(E) Given a normal population with mean equal to 240 and standard deviation equal to 60.

(i) Find the 95% confidence limits for the values in this population.
(ii) If a sample of 100 items is taken from this population, find the 95% confidence limits for the mean of this sample.

2.(I) Values of orders received by a company tend to be normally distributed with an average value of £20 000 and a standard deviation of £5000. Given a batch of 100 orders, find the probability that the average order (sample mean) is over £21 000. What are the 95% and 99% confidence limits for the mean of this sample?

3.(I) The number of orders received by a company tends to be normally distributed with a mean of 120 orders per week and a standard deviation of 42 orders per week.

(i) Over a period of ten weeks, find the probability that the average number of orders received per week is:
    (a) over 140,
    (b) under 135,
    (c) between 115 and 130.
(ii) Find the 95% confidence limits for the average number of orders received over this ten-week period.
(iii) Would you be surprised if the average number of orders received over the ten-week period is 150? Give reasons for your answer, and state any conclusions that you would draw from such a value.

4.(D)   During 1996 the number of beds required at St. Joseph's hospital was normally distributed with a mean of 1800 per day and a standard deviation of 190 per day. During the first fifty days of 1997, the average daily requirement for beds was 1830. A senior hospital manager has claimed that this gives evidence that the requirements for beds has changed since 1996. Would you agree? Is the sample average taken during 1997 significant?

2.19   Computer applications

This section highlights the use of packages such as spreadsheets to evaluate basic probabilities and determine the significance of values based on confidence limits.

EXAMPLE 1

Consider the evaluation of basic probability. Packages such as Microsoft Excel or Lotus 123 will enable you to enter appropriate formulae such as the addition and multiplication of probabilities. Consider three different events labelled A, B and C. If we know the probabilities of the separate events, then it is a relatively easy task to evaluate the probability of a combination of these events occurring.

Using the disk   The disk available includes a file called PROB.WK3. Using Excel or Lotus, load this file to display the screen illustrated in Figure 2.26. The left hand side of the spreadsheet contains an evaluation of the probability of a combination of the events A, B and C. You are able to change the probability of the individual events displayed in cells C4 to C6. The remaining probabilities shown in the two boxes below these values will automatically be recalculated.
    For example, consider the following probabilities:

$P(\text{event A}) = 0.1$, $P(\text{event B}) = 0.3$ and $P(\text{event C}) = 0.6$

Enter these values in the appropriate cells in the spreadsheet and look at the resulting values displayed calculated on the assumptions that the events are either independent or

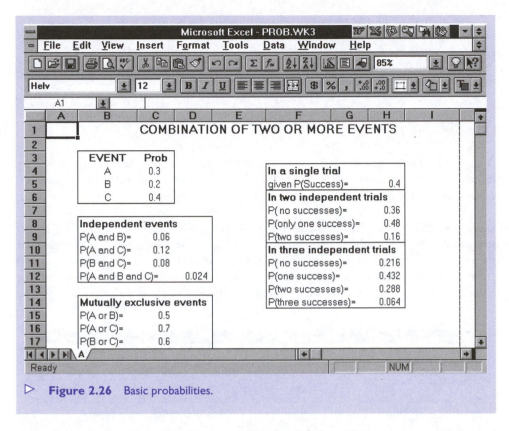

△ **Figure 2.26** Basic probabilities.

mutually exclusive. Note that it is impossible for both conditions to be satisfied, and therefore at most only one of the boxes displayed will be valid.

The boxes displayed on the right hand side of the screen illustrate the calculation of probabilities in a different situation. Here we have the probability of a single event (a success), and from this we can evaluate the probability of a number of successes in several trials. For example, consider a sales representative employed by Downbrooks. She has estimated that the probability of obtaining a sale on a visit to a customer is 0.4. In other words, 40% of visits result in sales for this employee. On this basis we can determine the chance of a number of sales in multiple visits. For instance, if she visits two customers in one day, then the probability of obtaining no sales is 0.36. This is shown in cell H7 of the spreadsheet as the probability of no successes in two independent trials. Similarly, if the sales representative makes three visits in a given day, then the chance of obtaining two sales is 0.288, and for three sales it is 0.064. These values are given in the box headed 'In three independent trials'.

By changing the value of the probability given in cell H5 you can look at the resulting probabilities for multiple sales. For instance, a second salesperson achieves sales in 30% of visits. Input the new value into cell H5 and determine the probability of obtaining only one sale in three visits. Experiment with other values in cell H5.

Note that the majority of cells in this spreadsheet are protected. This ensures that any formulae that have been inserted cannot be easily overwritten. The only cells that you can change are those containing the basic information. The cells C4 to C6 contain the probabilities for events A, B and C, and the cell H5 giving the probability of a 'success' can all be changed if required.

EXAMPLE 2

A spreadsheet package such as Excel or Lotus 123 can be used to determine confidence limits assuming a normal distribution. The significance of a sample mean can then be established on the basis of these limits found.

Using the disk   Load the spreadsheet file SAMPLE.WK3 from the disk. The screen that should be displayed is illustrated in Figure 2.27. The screen contains estimates of the population mean and standard deviation given in cells C3 and C4. Values obtained from a sample are displayed in the first column starting at cell A10. These sample values are then used to evaluate the sample mean and sample size shown in cells F12

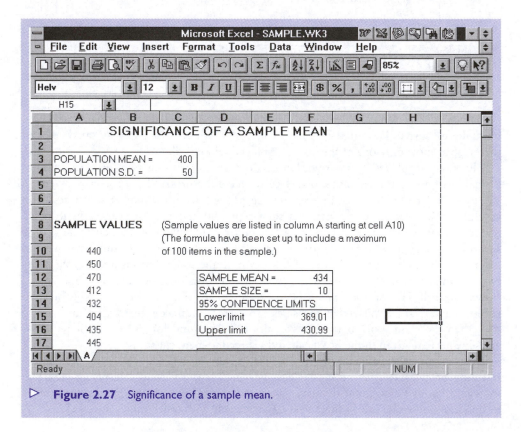

▷   **Figure 2.27**   Significance of a sample mean.

and F13. The population mean and standard deviation (μ and σ) and sample size (n) are used to determine the confidence limits for the sample means using the normal distribution formula: $\mu \pm 1.96\sigma/\sqrt{n}$. These limits are displayed in cells F15 and F16 in the spreadsheet.

Using the confidence limits for the sample mean enables us to determine whether a specific sample mean is 'significant' or not. If the sample mean obtained is inside the confidence limits then the value is not significant. However, if the value is outside the limits then it is said to be 'significant', and therefore we can conclude that a change may have occurred.

Consider a new sample containing the following 20 values:

395	420	415	430	390	400	412	407	399	435
402	450	386	404	402	414	420	396	403	401

Now input these values into the column A starting at cell A10. Now look at whether this new sample is significant or not. Try changing the population mean to 350, or 450, and look at whether the result changes.

This spreadsheet is set up to accept a maximum of 100 values in the sample. In general, before inputting a new set of sample values, it is preferable to erase the existing range of values. Do this by selecting the **Range** and **Erase** options, and specifying the cell range A10 to A109. Following this procedure you can enter new sample values as required.

EXAMPLE 3

The formula for the 95% confidence limits of sample means assumes that we know the values of the mean (μ) and standard deviation (σ) for the population. In most circumstances these values may not be known. In particular, it is likely that the value of σ is not known. This value can be estimated from a sample standard deviation (s). This means that the formula for the confidence limits for sample means can be written in terms of the sample standard deviation instead of the population standard deviation as shown below:

95% confidence limits for sample means are:

$$\mu \pm 1.96\sigma/\sqrt{n} = \mu \pm 1.96s/\sqrt{n-1}$$

 Using the disk   The file entitled SAMPLE2.WK3 contains an example similar to the spreadsheet outlined in the previous example. Load this file into a blank Excel or Lotus spreadsheet. Figure 2.28 shows this new spreadsheet. The table can be used in the same way. Thus, by entering sample values into the cells in the first column we can investigate the significance of a sample mean. Using the sample values displayed in the first column of this table, the sample mean and sample standard deviation are found and displayed in cells F11 and F12. The population mean and sample standard deviation are then used to evaluate the 95% confidence limits displayed in cells F15

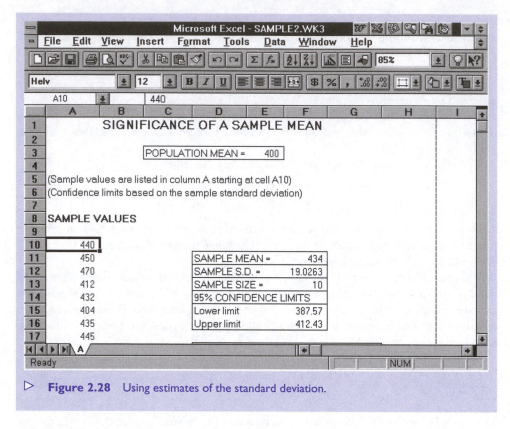

> **Figure 2.28**   Using estimates of the standard deviation.

and F16. The spreadsheet then compares the sample mean against these limits and determines whether the value is significant or not.

Try to experiment with a new set of data, or a different population mean, to investigate the significance of the sample mean. The data used in the previous example can be entered if required.

2.20   Chapter summary

This chapter has introduced the concept of probability and its use in a range of business applications. Probability is used to represent the chance of alternative events occurring in uncertain situations. It can be advantageous for the manager to be aware of probability techniques to assist in areas of decision making. In this context, the decision tree has been introduced as one approach. The decision tree can be used to illustrate a range of possible decisions and their impact in numerical terms such as implications for costs, profit and revenue. It should be noted that, although useful in formulating the range of possible decisions, this tool provides a restricted viewpoint of the total problem area. For example, it is assumed that the user has knowledge of the probabilities of any chance events incorporated into the decision tree. In general, decision trees can only be effectively utilised in conjunction with a number of other tools to formulate realistic decisions using all the information available.

Probability distributions have also been introduced in this chapter. In particular, the normal distribution, defined in terms of the mean and standard deviation, has been described. This important continuous probability distribution occurs in a range of practical situations, and is particularly useful when considering sampling. For example, whatever shape of distribution the parent population describes, if large samples are taken and the means found, it is known that these means tend to approximate to the normal distribution. Knowledge of this important distribution enables the evaluation of probabilities of a range of variables such as results in assessment tests, critical dimensions in production, customer arrivals, and project durations. Furthermore, the normal distribution can be used to predict the likely range of values occurring by the evaluation of areas under the normal curve. This provides a basis for applications such as quality control, where samples are compared with expected values, and action taken depending on the sampling results. Values lying outside the 'expected' range are referred to as being significant. These ideas on significance can be used in the process of hypothesis testing. This chapter has summarised one hypothesis test involving the population mean.

Finally, this chapter has considered a number of computer-based examples in the evaluation of probabilities, confidence limits and the determination of significance of a sample mean.

2.21   Further Exercises

1.(E)   It is known from past experience that 10% of employees arrive late for work, and a further 4% of employees are absent from work each day.

(i) Find the probability that on a given day an employee is:
   (a) not late for work,
   (b) not absent.
(ii) On two unrelated days, find the probability that an employee is:
   (a) late on both days,
   (b) late on the first and absent on the second day,
   (c) in attendance on both days,
   (d) absent on one day,
   (e) absent on one day and not late on the other.

2.(E)   The chance of a patient arriving in the reception area at St. Joseph's hospital in any given minute is 0.4.

(i) Find the probability that in two successive minutes:
   (a) no patient will arrive,
   (b) a patient will arrive only in the second minute,

    (c) patients will arrive in both minutes,

    (d) only one patient will arrive.

(ii) The receptionist leaves the area for a five-minute period to attend to an administrative problem. What is the chance that there will be patients waiting when the receptionist returns?

3.(I) A risk manager is employed by the Walker & Schmidt industrial group to assess the risk of a range of occurrences and to instigate backup systems that will ensure that the company will be able to cope if any serious complications arise. In performing this role, the manager must consider a range of potential disasters that would adversely affect the performance of the company, particularly in relation to the production and transportation systems. In this capacity the manager assesses the likelihood of particular events occurring in order to prioritise the protection and backup measures required.

  (i) The manager has found that the chance of a serious fire in a given month resulting in a halt to production is approximately 2%. This is thought to be unacceptable, as evidenced by consideration of the following probabilities. Find the probability that there are no fires over:

    (a) a three-month period,

    (b) a six-month period,

    (c) two years.

  What are the implications of this for the company?

 (ii) The chance of a break-in and theft of goods in any week is 1%. What is the probability of:

    (a) no break-ins during a four-week period,

    (b) at least one break-in during a four-week period.

4.(I) (i) The machines used in the main production area at Walker & Schmidt each produce an estimated $300 000 worth of finished goods per day. It can be seen, therefore, that a halt in production on any single machine for a significant length of time can prove to be disastrous for the company. The probability of a machine stoppage on any day is estimated to be 0.03. The company has five such machines.

    Use the binomial distribution to find the chance that on a given day:

    (a) no machine breaks down,

    (b) only one machine breaks down,

    (c) at least two machines break down.

    How could the company improve this situation?

 (ii) The average number of minor industrial accidents occurring within the company is 2 per month. Use the Poisson distribution to estimate the probability that in any given month the number of minor accidents is:

    (a) less than two,

    (b) more than three.

5.(I) At the Downbrooks company an automatic machine packages chocolates with an average weight of 500 grams and a standard deviation of 5 grams. If the weights of these boxes are normally distributed:

  (i) Find the probability that a box of chocolates taken at random will weigh:
     (a) under 496 grams,
     (b) under 486 grams,
     (c) over 510 grams.
 (ii) Find the 95% confidence limits for the weight of these boxes.
(iii) The company aims to ensure that any box is within 10 grams of the stated weight displayed on the side of the box. If not, then a customer is able to obtain a full refund of the purchase price. What proportion of customers are likely to be able to claim?
(iv) Downbrooks supplies a large retail chain with these boxes. The retailer has strict quality control measures, including the regular checking of samples being delivered. This involves checking the weight of a crate (including 144 boxes) and determining the average box weight. The complete delivery is returned to Downbrooks if the average weight of this batch is below 499 grams. What proportion of deliveries are likely to be returned on this basis? What are the implications of this for the Downbrooks management? How could they improve the situation?

6.(I) The Zendall company produces and markets a range of household products, including a range of washing powders. The company has recently designed a new detergent product which it wishes to promote. The company estimates that an advertising campaign for the product costing an estimated £2 million will give the product a 80% chance of success. From market research the company estimates that with this advertising support the product would give the company a return of £6 million, whereas if unsuccessful the return would only be £1.5 million. The same research and previous product launches have suggested that without such advertising there would only be a 40% chance of success. Also, without the initial advertising campaign, even if successful, the product will only provide a return of £4.5 million, and if unsuccessful, then the return would be as low as £0.7 million.

   Use a decision tree to advise the company on whether to go ahead with the advertising campaign.

7.(D) A large management consultancy company based in London must make a decision on a new computer system to be installed. The company has a shortlist of three systems (A, B or C) that they consider to be appropriate. However, the systems are significantly different in their performance and price. The costs of purchasing the three systems are: system A: £1.5 million, system B: £2 million, System C: £4 million. However, the expected income over the next five years that could be generated by these systems also varies: system A: £3 million, system B: £5 million, system C: £6.5 million. System C has already been installed at other offices and is known to be totally reliable.

The chances of the other systems being totally successful are: system A: 60%, system B: 80%.

If the company installs either system A or system B and it is found that they are not satisfactory, then a decision will need to be made to either modify the systems, or buy one of the other systems instead. The cost of modifying either of the systems is £1 million. Again, if the new system is successful then there is no problem, but if unsuccessful then a decision will need to be made whether to modify this second system or to install system C.

Use a decision tree to illustrate this situation and give recommendations to the company on the best course of action. Comment on the suitability of this technique. What other issues would you consider to be relevant in this decision?

8.(I) In the Downbrooks company, 6% of staff are managers, 10% are administrators and 30% are involved with sales. The remaining staff are involved in the production process. If two employees are taken at random from the staff list, find the probability that:

(a) both are managers,
(b) neither is sales staff,
(c) only one is involved with production,
(d) only one is not an administrator,
(e) one is a manager, and one is in sales.

9.(D) The St. Joseph's hospital is considering the purchase of a new scanner in the Research Department to replace the existing machine that requires major upgrading. The hospital has one of three options: (i) buy a new scanner at a cost of $1 million, (ii) modify the existing scanner at a cost of $0.6 million, or (iii) keep the existing scanner and do not upgrade. If a new scanner is purchased, then the estimated revenue from this facility will be $2 million.

However, there is a 20% chance that the new scanner will still require further modifications at an extra cost of $0.2 million before becoming fully operational. Similarly, if the existing scanner is modified there is still a 10% chance of further work needing to be carried out at an additional cost of $0.1 million. The estimated revenue from the modified scanner is $1.5 million, since it would still be a slower machine and would not be able to cater for the same quantity of patients. If the existing scanner is used without modifications then the estimated revenue is only $0.6 million.

What would you recommend the hospital do in this situation?

10.(I) The number of employees absent from work averages three per day. Absences at the company tend to be random. Using the Poisson distribution, find the probability that on a given day, the number of absentees is:

 (i) none,
 (ii) only one,

(iii) less than two,

(iv) at least three.

11.(I) Patients arrive at random at the Maternity Department of the St. Joseph's hospital at the rate of six per hour. During a half-hour period, what is the probability that:

(i) no patients arrive,

(ii) fewer than two patients arrive,

(iii) more than three patients arrive.

12.(D) The average weekly production output from an assembly line is known to be 1200 units. Following the introduction of a new pay and benefits package for the production workers, a sample of 50 days gave an average daily output of 1240 with a standard deviation of 150 units. The Personnel Director claims that the new pay and benefits package has caused a change in the production output. Use a suitable hypothesis test to examine the assumption that the average daily production is still 1200 units. Comment on your result.

 13.(I) **(Using the disk)** Load the spreadsheet file called HYPOTH.WK3 contained on the disk.

This spreadsheet contains cells in which you can enter the values required in order to conduct a test of the hypothesis concerning the population mean based on data obtained from a sample. The spreadsheet will conduct the test and confirm whether to accept or reject the hypothesis.

Consider the following hypothesis H_0: $\mu = 200$, with sample values of:

Sample size $n = 100$, sample mean $= 210$, sample standard deviation $= 40$

Insert these values into the appropriate cells in the spreadsheet and check on whether the assumption has been accepted or not. Try other values, such as just changing the sample standard deviation to 80. Has the conclusion changed? Why do you think this happens?

CHAPTER

3

Relationships

SUMMARY OF CHAPTER CONTENTS

▷ Illustrating relationships

▷ Linear and non-linear relationships

▷ Correlation coefficient

▷ Rank correlation

▷ Interpretation of correlation
coefficient

▷ Coefficient of determination

▷ Line of 'best fit'

▷ Regression techniques

▷ Non-linear relationships

▷ Multiple regression

▷ Computer applications

CHAPTER OBJECTIVES

At the end of this chapter you will be able to:

▶ analyse the relationship between two variables using graphical methods

▶ evaluate correlation coefficients in order to determine the strength of relationship

▶ use regression methods to obtain simple forecasts

▶ understand the differences between linear and non-linear relationships

▶ use relationships in a business context for management decision making

Introduction

In the earlier chapters we have considered basic analyses of single variables such as wages, production output, profitability, or sales. In many business applications, in order to obtain a realistic analysis it is necessary to consider the relationship between such values. It is often the case that two or more variables are related in any given circumstance. For instance, earnings may be connected to production, sales determined by advertising expenditure, profit related to costs. A knowledge of the relationship between a number of variables can be beneficial in terms of management decision making. For example, questions such as how does the advertising expenditure affect sales, or does an increase in pay result in an improvement in production, can assist in determining management strategies. Furthermore, such relationships can be useful in obtaining basic forecasts. For instance, if advertising expenditure is increased by a given amount, how will this affect sales? Alternatively, how much should advertising expenditure be increased by in order to increase sales by 5%? Such questions will be considered in this chapter.

CASE STUDY | The Petlocks cereal company

The Petlocks company, founded in 1876 in Boston, Massachusetts, produce a range of breakfast cereal products. Popular products in the company's range include Wheat Flakes, Barley Krisps and Rice Pops. In recent years the company has developed new products including the 'Petlocks Swiss Muesli', which has become the second most popular brand behind Wheat Flakes.

The primary production site for Petlocks is still located on the outskirts of Boston, with other production and warehousing at Jackson, Mississippi; Tucson, Arizona; and Minneapolis, Minnesota. The Boston headquarters includes Marketing, Sales, Logistics, and Research & Development specialists. The company employs over 2000 people, including those in the production and warehousing divisions.

The Marketing Director, Joe Simmons, has monitored the performance of all the company's products over the past four years, and has requested a study of the relationship between the level of sales for each item. Furthermore, information on Petlocks' main competitors in the breakfast cereal market has been collected. In particular, the level of sales for the main brands has been recorded and analysed. Using this information has enabled Joe to obtain useful predictions of sales of some of the products based on previous sales of Petlocks' and Petlocks' competitors. Furthermore, Simmons has requested that the Sales team produce a report on the effectiveness of past advertising, including an analysis of the relationship between advertising expenditure and sales performance.

CASE STUDY | The Quick-Time Coach company

QTC owns a fleet of 240 buses and coaches located in six regional sites across the UK. The sites are at Newcastle, Southampton, Cardiff, Dundee, Lancaster and Birmingham. Each site has between 30 and 50 vehicles located there at any point in time. The vehicles (with the QTC drivers) are available for private hire. Many of the buses are rented by local organisations and are used for regular journeys such as transporting employees to and from work. Other buses are rented on an *ad hoc* basis to private individuals and companies. A number of travel companies rent the coaches at various times of the year for excursions, day trips, and longer one-week or two-week trips to Europe.

QTC's main offices are located at the Lancaster site, and include 350 administrative, sales and managerial staff. Each regional site has a management team, including Site Manager,

Transport Manager, and Sales & Promotions Manager. The company employs a total of 800 staff on permanent and temporary contracts.

The Personnel Director, based at Lancaster, is reviewing the recruitment and selection procedures that are currently being used by QTC. For example, all first-line managers are selected by a series of aptitude tests, interviews and assessment centres. The Personnel Director, Lisa Gregory, feels that the company's current approaches to selection can be streamlined without any deterioration in the quality of selection decisions made. Lisa has employed consultants to consider this problem. She has asked the consultants to prepare a report on a range of issues including the relationship between the results obtained by candidates at various stages in the selection process, and whether some results could have been predicted from earlier performances. Furthermore, Lisa has requested an analysis of the validity of the current selection methods, by consideration of the candidates' results compared with their current job performance.

3.1   Illustrating relationships

As with many analytical methods, at the first stage it is often useful to attempt to illustrate the data obtained. This approach can lead to the solution of a range of problems, without the necessity of complex analytical techniques. As a tool in business reporting and communications, the graphical representation of data is often underutilised. The scatter diagram provides a useful graph to illustrate possible relationships between sets of data. The following examples show the use of such a diagram.

EXAMPLE 1

The data below show the monthly sales figures for two popular brands of breakfast cereal produced by the Petlocks company. The values shown are in $millions.

Month	Jan	Feb	Mar	Apr	May	Jun
Barley Krisps	3.0	3.4	3.8	4.1	3.9	4.4
Rice Pops	2.6	2.4	2.8	3.2	2.7	3.2

The volume of sales for the two products can be illustrated by using a scatter diagram. The scatter diagram illustrated in Figure 3.1 contains a series of points representing pairs of values from the table. Each axis on the graph represents a single variable. In Figure 3.1 the horizontal axis represents the sales of 'Barley Krisps', and the vertical axis shows the sales of 'Rice Pops'. Each point represents the sales of the two products on a given month. For instance, in January, when the sales of 'Barley Krisps' reached $3.0 million, the 'Rice Pops' sales were $2.6 million. This is shown by a single point on the graph.

The scatter diagram shows that there seems to be some relationship between the two

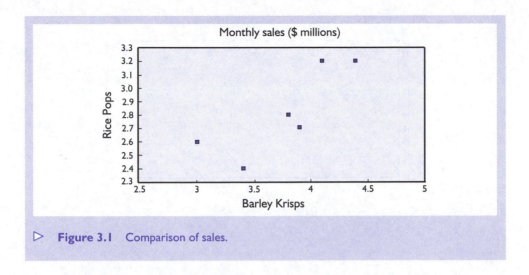

▷ **Figure 3.1** Comparison of sales.

sets of figures. The points lie in a narrow band spreading from the bottom left of the graph, up to the top right hand side. This indicates that low monthly sales in 'Barley Krisps' generally correspond to low values in 'Rice Pops'. Thus an increase in the sales figures for one product will usually correspond to an increase in the performance of the second product. The relationship is certainly not perfect, as illustrated by the January and February sales figures. During these two months, the sales in 'Barley Krisps' rose whilst the other product's performance declined.

The graph does not conclusively show whether or not there is a definite relationship between the sales figures. However, the graph does indicate that a connection between the two products is likely.

EXAMPLE 2

A group of eight candidates shortlisted for a supervisory post in QTC have been given a range of assessment tests. The results of two tests measuring the candidates' aptitude in numeracy and verbal reasoning are shown in the following table.

Candidate	A	B	C	D	E	F	G	H
Numeracy	12	14	15	15	18	19	20	23
Verbal reasoning	16	19	21	15	22	17	13	21

The scatter diagram of this set of data is shown in Figure 3.2. The horizontal axis represents the scores of candidates for the numeracy test, and the vertical axis shows the verbal reasoning scores. The points are scattered over a wide part of the graph indicating that there is no obvious relationship between the two sets of scores. For example, the candidate obtaining the highest score in verbal reasoning gains an

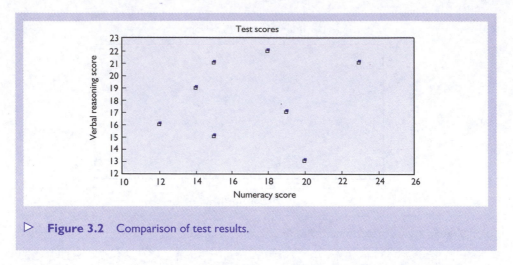

▷   **Figure 3.2**   Comparison of test results.

'average' score in numeracy. Similarly, the candidate with the lowest score in verbal reasoning has performed well in the numeracy test. Thus, the graph shows that the two aptitude tests yield vastly differing results. A candidate who performs well in one test will not necessarily do well in the second test. Generally, then, the results of one test will not help to predict the results in the other.

This evidence brings into question the relevance of the two tests for the use of selection for the post offered. If the results obtained are unrelated then it may be that the tests provide invalid information which would not be helpful in selecting the best candidate for the post offered. The graph shows that the two tests are examining unrelated skills. Thus, the Personnel Director at QTC may conclude that it is not appropriate to use both of these tests in the selection process. Conversely, the tests may be used deliberately to examine different skills. The QTC policy could be that candidates will only be considered if they perform well in both tests. Thus, in this example, only candidate H seems to possess the necessary skills.

3.2   Linear and non-linear relationships

As described in the previous section, the scatter diagram can assist in determining whether or not there is a relationship between two sets of values. If a relationship does exist then it is either linear or non-linear. Linear relationships are illustrated by straight lines, whereas a non-linear relationship could be represented by a curve. The following examples show relationships of both types.

EXAMPLE 1

Consider the table below, showing the volume of sales in the Petlocks company over a

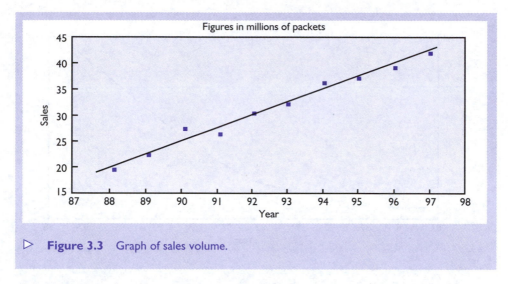

Figures in millions of packets

ten-year period. The figures shown give the number of packets of the 'Barley Krisps' product sold in millions.

Year:	1988	1989	1990	1991	1992	1993	1994	1995	1996	1997
Sales:	19	22	27	26	30	32	36	37	39	42

Figure 3.3 illustrates these data using a scatter diagram. The horizontal axis is used to represent the years, and the vertical axis gives the volume of sales in millions of packets.

The diagram shows that there seems to be some relationship between the years and volume of sales. Essentially, the sales are increasing as the years progress. The relationship is not perfect, though the points lie very close to the straight line as shown on the diagram. Thus, it is likely that the relationship between the years and volume of sales is **linear**.

EXAMPLE 2

Rather than considering the volume of sales as in the previous example, let us look at the sales revenue at Petlocks. The table below shows the annual total sales revenue obtained from the sale of 'Barley Krisps' during the same ten-year period. The figures shown are in $millions.

Year:	1988	1989	1990	1991	1992	1993	1994	1995	1996	1997
Sales:	14	15	17	20	24	30	48	49	59	67

These figures are illustrated in Figure 3.4. The scatter diagram again seems to show that there is a relationship between the years and sales revenue. The points plotted on this graph seem to conform to a curve, rather than a straight line, as illustrated on the diagram. This type of non-linear relationship is often found in economic data, where

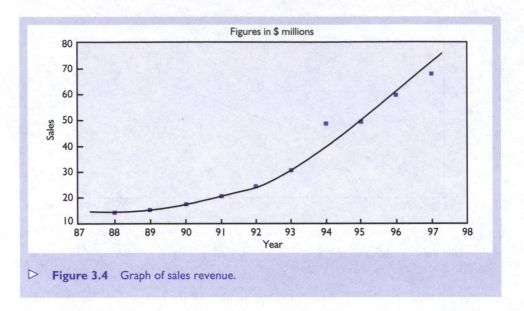

Figures in $ millions

Figure 3.4   Graph of sales revenue.

inflationary effects distort the original set of figures. It may be that if the sales figures shown here are compared in real terms, without the effects of inflation, then the resulting graph may show a linear relationship. Further analysis of the actual data will need to be conducted in order to confirm this.

3.3 | The correlation coefficient

As shown in the previous sections, the scatter diagram can be used to illustrate whether there is a relationship between two variables. However, the graph produced can be fairly subjective. Using the graph, it is still often a matter of judgement as to whether or not there exists a real relationship between the data. For instance, consider the graph shown in Figure 3.1, comparing the sales of two products. The points are scattered over a fairly wide range. It seems that the high values of one variable correspond to high values of the other and, similarly, the low values of the two variables correspond. However, the relationship is not perfect, and it may be that if a few more points are plotted there could be an even greater scattering of points. Conversely, any extra points on the graph may indicate a stronger relationship. Thus, we see that the graph cannot provide a definitive answer on whether there is a relationship between the variables. The scatter diagram is a subjective analytical method, and what is required is a more objective approach. Such an approach can involve the calculation of the correlation coefficient described in this section.

The degree of 'straight line' relationship can be measured by **Pearson's product moment correlation coefficient**. This value, usually referred to as simply the **Correlation coefficient**, measures the degree of linear relationship between two variables x and y, and is obtained by the following formula:

$$r = \frac{\sum xy - n\bar{x}\bar{y}}{\sqrt{\{\sum x^2 - n\bar{x}\}\{\sum y^2 - n\bar{y}^2\}}}$$

The value of the correlation coefficient, denoted by r, lies between -1 and $+1$. Values near $+1$ or -1 indicate a good correlation between the two variables. The scatter diagrams shown in Figure 3.5 illustrate a variety of values of the correlation coefficient for different sets of data. These diagrams should help us to understand and interpret the range of likely values of r.

Figure 3.5(i) shows the situation where there is a perfect correlation between the two variables. All the points on the scatter diagram lie exactly on a straight line. There is a direct (or positive) correlation between the two variables since an increase in one variable always corresponds to an increase in the other. This can be illustrated by a straight line with positive slope. The correlation coefficient obtained in this situation will be equal to $+1$.

The scatter diagram in Figure 3.5(ii) shows a situation in which there is some degree of positive correlation. The points lie on a narrow band spread from the bottom left up to the top right of the graph. The diagram is similar to that shown in Figure 3.1.

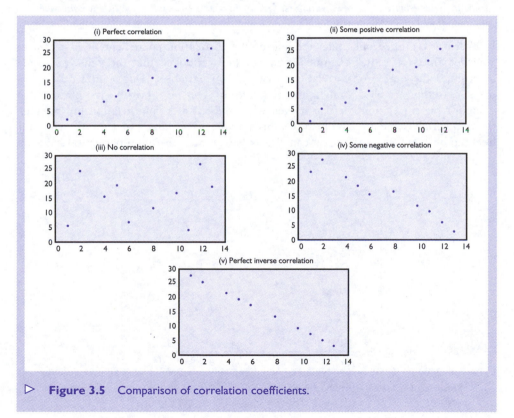

▷ **Figure 3.5** Comparison of correlation coefficients.

The diagram in Figure 3.5(ii) indicates that increases in one variable will generally correspond to increases in the second. In this case, the value of the correlation coefficient will be near to +1, e.g. values such as 0.8 or 0.9 would be likely. The correlation coefficient approaches +1 as the points get closer to the straight line.

Figure 3.5(iii) illustrates a situation where there is no relationship between the two variables. The points are scattered all over the diagram, with no identifiable pattern. In this example, the correlation coefficient will be close to, or equal to, zero.

Figure 3.5(iv) shows some degree of negative (or inverse) correlation. The points lie on a narrow band dispersed from the top left to the bottom right of the graph. This shows that as one variable increases, the other variable tends to decrease. In this case, the value of the correlation coefficient will be negative, and tends towards −1, e.g. values such as −0.7, −0.8 may be obtained.

The final diagram, Figure 3.5(v), shows a perfect inverse correlation between the two variables. All the points lie on a straight line with negative slope. This shows that when one variable increases we can be sure that the value of the other variable will decrease. Such data would give a correlation coefficient equal to −1.

> **Definition:** *The correlation coefficient provides a method of measuring the strength of linear relationship between two variables. The value of the correlation coefficient is between − 1 and + 1.*

In order to reinforce our understanding of the correlation coefficient, it is useful to consider an extra scatter diagram. It cannot be overlooked that the value of r only determines the degree of correlation between two variables. This simply provides a measure of the variables' 'straight line' relationship. Thus, it is possible to obtain a zero value for the correlation coefficient even when there is a definite relationship between the two variables. Figure 3.6 illustrates this situation. The value of r from these data is likely to be near zero, although it can clearly be seen that there is a perfect relationship

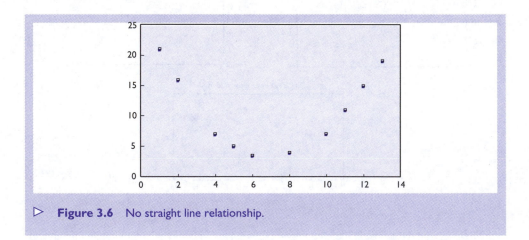

▷   **Figure 3.6**   No straight line relationship.

between the variables. However, the relationship illustrated can be seen to be non-linear; a smooth curve can be drawn linking all of the points on the scatter diagram. Thus, although there exists a definite relationship between the variables, this relationship is not a straight line, and therefore there is zero correlation.

EXAMPLE 1

Consider the values of x and y given in the following table.

x: 1 2 3 4   5
y: 3 5 7 9   11

It is left to the reader to draw a scatter diagram to illustrate the pairs of values of x and y. It can be seen that there is a direct relationship between the two variables. The points all lie on a straight line, showing perfect correlation. Thus, from the previous notes, the value of the correlation coefficient, r, should be equal to $+1$. This example will be used to illustrate the methods of calculation for the correlation coefficient. The correlation coefficient is calculated by finding the relevant summations $\sum x^2$, $\sum y^2$ and $\sum xy$. Also, the summations $\sum x$ and $\sum y$ will be used to evaluate the means, $\bar{x}$ and $\bar{y}$.

The following table is used to evaluate the required summations. The values of x and y are listed in the first two columns, and the remaining columns used to calculate the required values.

x	y	x^2	y^2	xy
1	3	1	9	3
2	5	4	25	10
3	7	9	49	21
4	9	16	81	36
5	11	25	121	55
Totals 15	35	55	285	125

The summations obtained from this table are as follows:

$$\sum x = 15, \ \sum y = 35, \ \sum x^2 = 55, \ \sum y^2 = 285, \ \sum xy = 125$$

Thus, the means for the values of x and y can be calculated:

$$\bar{x} = \frac{\sum x}{n} = \frac{15}{5} = 3$$

$$\bar{y} = \frac{\sum y}{n} = \frac{35}{5} = 7$$

Now, we can calculate the correlation coefficient as follows:

$$r = \frac{\sum xy - n\bar{x}\bar{y}}{\sqrt{\{\sum x^2 - n\bar{x}^2\}\{\sum y^2 - n\bar{y}^2\}}}$$

$$= \frac{125 - 5.3.7}{\sqrt{\{55 - 5.3^2\}\{285 - 5.7^2\}}}$$

$$= \frac{125 - 105}{\sqrt{\{55 - 45\}\{285 - 245\}}}$$

$$= \frac{20}{\sqrt{\{10\}\{40\}}}$$

$$= \frac{20}{\sqrt{400}}$$

$$= \frac{20}{20}$$

Therefore, as expected, the value of r is +1. This indicates a perfect correlation between the two variables.

EXAMPLE 2

Consider the scores of eight candidates in two aptitude tests introduced in an earlier example. The results from the two tests were as follows:

Candidate	A	B	C	D	E	F	G	H
Numeracy (x)	12	14	15	15	18	19	20	23
Verbal reasoning (y)	16	19	21	15	22	17	13	21

The degree of correlation can be calculated using the correlation coefficient described in this section. We are given two sets of values: scores for numeracy and verbal reasoning tests. These can be denoted by the two variables x and y as shown in the table. The correlation coefficient can be calculated using the following table.

To summarise, this table gives values of the following summations:

$$\sum x = 136, \; \sum y = 144, \; \sum x^2 = 2404, \; \sum y^2 = 2666, \; \sum xy = 2460$$

Thus, the means for the values of x and y can be calculated:

$$\bar{x} = \frac{\sum x}{n} = \frac{136}{8} = 17$$

$$\bar{y} = \frac{\sum y}{n} = \frac{144}{8} = 18$$

x	y	x^2	y^2	xy
12	16	144	256	192
14	19	196	361	266
15	21	225	441	315
15	15	225	225	225
18	22	324	484	396
19	17	361	289	323
20	13	400	169	260
23	21	529	441	483
Totals 136	144	2404	2666	2460

The value of the correlation coefficient is

$$r = \frac{\sum xy - n\bar{x}\bar{y}}{\sqrt{\{\sum x^2 - n\bar{x}^2\}\{\sum y^2 - n\bar{y}^2\}}}$$

$$= \frac{2460 - 8.17.18}{\sqrt{\{2404 - 8.17^2\}\{2666 - 8.18^2\}}}$$

$$= \frac{2460 - 2448}{\sqrt{\{2404 - 2312\}\{2666 - 2592\}}}$$

$$= \frac{12}{\sqrt{92.74}}$$

$$= \frac{12}{\sqrt{6808}}$$

$$= \frac{12}{82.511}$$

Therefore, $r = 0.145$

Thus, the value of r is 'near' zero, indicating that there is unlikely to be correlation between the two sets of aptitude test scores. This could lead to a reconsideration of the tests for use in the selection of candidates for the post offered at QTC. A more detailed interpretation for the actual value of the correlation coefficient will be considered in later sections in this chapter. In particular, the precise evaluation of a given correlation coefficient involves a consideration of the sample size used.

3.4 | Exercises: correlation

1.(E) The following sets of data show the results of a group of candidates in two tests. Use a scatter diagram to illustrate the sets of results, and find the correlation coefficient in each case. Comment on the relationship between the results of the two tests in each example.

(i)	Candidate:	A	B	C	D	E
	Test X:	2	3	5	6	9
	Test Y:	3	5	9	11	17
(ii)	Candidate:	A	B	C	D	E
	Test L:	2	2	4	5	7
	Test M:	8	7	6	5	4
(iii)	Candidate:	A	B	C	D	E
	Test S:	2	3	5	7	8
	Test T:	1	1	3	4	6

2.(I)   The Marketing Director of the Petlocks company has requested an analysis of the monthly advertising expenditure and corresponding sales of the complete product range. The table below shows the total monthly sales revenue for the 'Barley Krisps' product, together with the amount spent on advertising this item.

Month:	Jan	Feb	Mar	Apr	May	Jun	Jul	Aug
Sales ($millions):	3.0	3.4	3.8	4.1	3.9	4.4	4.5	4.9
Advertising ($100 000s):	2.2	2.5	2.1	2.7	2.6	2.9	2.6	2.4

Calculate the degree of correlation between these two sets of values, and comment on the relationship between advertising and sales of the 'Barley Krisps' product.

3.5   Rank correlation

The correlation coefficient formula previously described assumes that the two variables can be measured precisely. These measurements are then used as the values of x and y in the correlation formulae. In many circumstances, it is likely that accurate measurements cannot be obtained for specific variables. Furthermore, even when such measurements are obtained it is possible that the values found are not always reliable. For instance, consider the results obtained in the two aptitude tests by the group of job applicants. One candidate obtained 19 in the numeracy test and 17 for verbal reasoning. Does this really show that this candidate performs better in the numeracy skills than in verbal reasoning? Are the two results directly comparable? Also, consider the results obtained in the numeracy test. Candidate A obtained 12 marks in this test, and candidate E scored 18. In other words, E scored 50% more marks than A. Does this show that E is 50% better than A? It is doubtful whether this is the case. It is likely that all we can deduce from these marks is that E has performed better than A. The actual difference between the scores is less relevant, and can be misleading. At best, the test results can provide an indication of the relative differences between the candidates. Thus, the test scores may enable the company to place the candidates in order of their performances. For instance, in the numeracy test, candidate H came top, G was second, and at the other end of the scale, candidate A was last. The results, then, enable us to rank the candidates in order of performance. Thus, we could rank the candidates based on their performance in the numeracy test, and perform a similar ranking process for verbal reasoning. The relationship between these two sets of rankings can be obtained by calculating **Spearman's rank correlation coefficient** by using the following formula:

$$r = 1 - \frac{6 \sum d^2}{n(n^2 - 1)}$$

In this formula, n = number of values and d = difference between pairs of rankings.

   This formula produces the same value as the product moment correlation coefficient formula calculated on the rankings. It can be seen that the formula is much simpler, and yet still provides us with an objective measure of the correlation between two sets of values. The following examples will illustrate the calculation of the rank correlation coefficient.

> **Definition:** *The rank correlation coefficient provides a method of measuring the strength of linear relationship between two sets of rankings. The value of the rank correlation coefficient is between -1 and $+1$.*

EXAMPLE 1

Consider the sales figures for two sales representatives over a six-month period as shown below. The figures given are in £1000s sales revenue.

Month:	Mar	Apr	May	Jun	Jul	Aug
Salesperson A:	20	30	17	34	27	25
Salesperson B:	15	20	23	29	19	16

In some cases the figures are only estimates, but it can be assumed that they are correct to within a £1000 error.

   Instead of considering the actual values, let us look at the rankings over the six months for each sales representative. For instance, salesperson A achieved their highest sales during June. Thus, in June the ranking for A is 1. Similarly, the second highest sales were achieved in April, and therefore this is assigned a ranking of 2. In this way, the ranks for the six months can be obtained for salesperson A. Similarly, the rankings for B can be found. These ranks are shown in the following table:

Month:	Mar	Apr	May	Jun	Jul	Aug
Salesperson A:	5	2	6	1	3	4
Salesperson B:	6	3	2	1	4	5

It can be seen that both sales representatives obtained their best sales in June. The relationship between the performance of the two sales persons can be measured using the rank correlation coefficient.

   To evaluate this coefficient, the values of n and d should be obtained. Clearly, the number of pairs of values in these data, n, is 6. The values of d (the differences between the corresponding rankings) are shown below:

Month: Mar   Apr   May   Jun   Jul   Aug
Difference (d):   −1   −1   4   0   −1   −1

The values of d^2 are as follows:

d^2: 1 1 16 0 1 1

Thus, the sum of d^2 is $\sum d^2 = 20$.

Finally, the rank correlation coefficient formula can be calculated:

$$r = 1 - \frac{6 \sum d^2}{n(n^2 - 1)}$$

$$= 1 - \frac{6.20}{6(6^2 - 1)}$$

$$= 1 - \frac{120}{6.35}$$

$$= 1 - \frac{120}{210}$$

$$= 1 - 0.571$$

Therefore, $r = 0.429$.

The value of r is fairly low, showing that there does not seem to be any correlation between the two sets of ranks. Thus, the correlation between the two sets of sales figures is not strong. Further data, such as the sales figures over a longer period of time, are required in order to carry out any further analysis on the relationship between the rankings for the two sales representatives.

EXAMPLE 2

Consider the results obtained by the eight candidates in the aptitude tests, as shown below:

Candidate	A	B	C	D	E	F	G	H
Numeracy	12	14	15	15	18	19	20	23
Verbal reasoning	16	19	21	15	22	17	13	21

These test scores can be used to rank the candidates in order of performance for each of the tests. Thus, in numeracy, candidate H came first and is ranked as 1, G has a rank of 2 and F has a rank of 3. However, there is a slight complication where two candidates obtained the same score in a specific test. This is the case in numeracy, where candidates C and D both obtained scores of 15. In such a case, both candidates should be assigned the same ranking. The ranking given is obtained by finding the average rank assuming that the values are distinguishable. For instance, candidates C and D would have had rankings of 5th and 6th. Thus, the average ranking for these two candidates is $5\frac{1}{2}$. In the same way, in the verbal reasoning test, candidates C and H both scored 21 and will each be assigned ranks of $2\frac{1}{2}$. The table below shows the rankings of the candidates in the two tests.

Candidate:	A	B	C	D	E	F	G	H
Numeracy ranking:	8	7	$5\frac{1}{2}$	$5\frac{1}{2}$	4	3	2	1
Verbal ranking:	6	4	$2\frac{1}{2}$	7	1	5	8	$2\frac{1}{2}$

The differences between these ranks are calculated below:

d: 2　3　3　$-1\frac{1}{2}$　3　-2　-6　$-1\frac{1}{2}$

The values of d^2 are:

d^2: 4　9　9　2.25　9　4　36　2.25

Thus, we have $\sum d^2 = 75.5$.

Finally, the rank correlation coefficient formula is calculated:

$$r = 1 - \frac{6 \sum d^2}{n(n^2 - 1)}$$

$$= 1 - \frac{6(75.5)}{8(8^2 - 1)}$$

$$= 1 - \frac{453}{8.63}$$

$$= 1 - \frac{453}{504}$$

$$= 1 - 0.899$$

Therefore, $r = 0.101$.

This value of r shows that there is little correlation between the two sets of values. Thus, a candidate with a high ranking in one test is likely to obtain any ranking in the other test.

It should be noted that the product moment correlation coefficient has previously been calculated for this set of data and has been found to be 0.145. Thus, we see that the two correlation coefficients can yield similar results. However, this is not always the case. It is possible that there is correlation between the rankings of two sets of data, at the same time there being little correlation between the actual values. In such circumstances the results become difficult to analyse, and the collection of further data will often be required to obtain more conclusive results.

3.6   Interpretation of the correlation coefficient

In previous sections it has been stated that if the correlation coefficient is 'near' +1 or −1, then this indicates that the two variables under consideration are correlated. The question is how near is 'near'? For example, most of us would agree that a value of $r = 0.99$ indicates a significant correlation between the variables. Similarly, a value of $r = 0.003$ is close to zero and therefore we would expect that it indicates little correlation. Intermediate values of r such as +0.5, or −0.4, or +0.3 are not as easy to interpret and require further investigation.

In practice, the significance of a value of r largely depends on the sample size. This can be illustrated with a simple example. Remember that the correlation coefficient is a measure of how close the points on the scatter diagram are to a straight line. If all the points are on a straight line, then the correlation coefficient equals ±1. Now consider a situation where only two points have been drawn. In such a case, the points must lie on straight line. It is left to the reader to try to draw two points on a scatter diagram that cannot be connected by a straight line! Consequently, with only two points it is certain that the correlation coefficient $r = 1$ (or −1). However, clearly this value of r does not necessarily imply that the two variables are correlated. It would require at least three points on the scatter diagram to obtain a reasonable analysis of the degree of correlation. Thus, for small samples, even values of r close to ±1 may not indicate significant correlation. At the other extreme, given a very large sample, a small value of r may indicate correlation. For example, given a thousand points on the scatter diagram, a value of $r = 0.1$ is enough to show some correlation between the variables.

There are a number of statistical tests that can be performed to demonstrate the significance of a given value of r. These are outside the scope of this text. However, it should be stated that such tests are based on the consideration of confidence limits for the values of r. For example, it can be shown that assuming there is no correlation between two variables, the 95% confidence limits for the value of r where $n = 10$ are −0.632 to +0.632. Therefore, without any relationship between the two variables, it is likely that r will lie within this range of values. Thus, in order to indicate a 'significant' correlation between the two variables, the value of r will need to be outside this range, i.e. above +0.632, or under −0.632.

The table given in Figure 3.7 shows significant values of r using the 95% confidence limits for a range of values of n. Note that these values of r can be applied to positive or negative results. It can be seen from the table in Figure 3.7 that as the sample size (n)

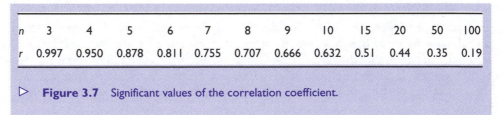

n	3	4	5	6	7	8	9	10	15	20	50	100
r	0.997	0.950	0.878	0.811	0.755	0.707	0.666	0.632	0.51	0.44	0.35	0.19

▷ **Figure 3.7** Significant values of the correlation coefficient.

increases the critical value of r decreases. Thus, for example, for $n = 3$ the value of r would need to be at least 0.997 for us to conclude that there is correlation between the two variables. Alternatively, with a sample size of 100, a value of r over 0.19 indicates a significant correlation.

It should be noted that the significant values shown in Figure 3.7 can be used to analyse both the product moment correlation coefficient and the rank correlation coefficient introduced in earlier sections.

Definition: *If the value of the correlation coefficient (r) is found to be significant then this shows that there is likely to be some degree of linear relationship between the two sets of values under consideration.*

EXAMPLE 1

From a sample of twenty candidates, the correlation coefficient between two sets of test results is found to be +0.5. The Personnel Manager claims that these data show that the two tests are not correlated since the correlation coefficient is not near 1. What would you say concerning this claim?

At first sight, a value of $r = 0.5$ does not seem to show correlation. However, looking at the significant values given in Figure 3.7 we see that when $n = 20$ any value of r of 0.44 or over is significant. Thus, a correlation coefficient of 0.5 does indicate correlation. Therefore, it is likely that there is a relationship between the two sets of test results, i.e. a candidate who scores well in one test is more likely to perform better in the second test.

EXAMPLE 2

An analysis of the effectiveness of advertising on sales revenue has been conducted. Over the past ten months, the sales revenue and corresponding advertising expenditure have been recorded. The product moment correlation coefficient of these data is found to be 0.6. Does this indicate that the two variables are correlated?

In this situation, we need to investigate whether a value of $r = 0.6$ obtained from a sample size of $n = 10$, is significant. From the table shown in Figure 3.7, a significant value of r for this sample size is 0.632. Therefore, the value of r obtained ($= 0.6$) is said to be not significant using the 95% limits. Thus, this value does not conclusively show that there is any correlation between the expenditure on advertising and the monthly sales figures. However, the value of r obtained is so close to the 'significant' value that there may well be some relationship between the data. Further information needs to be collected, such as the advertising and sales values over a longer period of time.

It should be stated that in this example, the correlation value calculated may not be the most appropriate one to use. Intuitively, it seems likely that there is some relationship between advertising and sales. If there is no relationship, then presumably it can be concluded that the company is wasting money on advertising. However, the relationship is likely to be more complex than could be demonstrated with this simple analysis. For example, expenditure on advertising during a given month may not generate any improvement in sales for several months. Thus, there can be a lag between the advertising employed and the resulting change in sales. The duration of the delay between advertising expenditure and resulting sales depends on the product promoted. For example, products such as newspapers and cigarettes may be immediately influenced by advertising. Conversely, the sales of items such as cars, washing machines, televisions and microcomputers may take longer to be affected. Thus, when investigating the correlation between these two variables, some reference to the 'lag' factor may be necessary. In other words, we could investigate the correlation between monthly advertising expenditure and the sales figures one month or two months later. In this way, we may be able to show how effective the advertising really is, and determine the likely delay between advertising and resulting sales.

3.7   Coefficient of determination

The coefficient of determination is an alternative way of expressing the degree of relationship between two variables. This value is calculated by squaring the correlation coefficient (r).

Thus,

Coefficient of determination = r^2

The coefficient of determination is often quoted in preference to the correlation coefficient, as it can be used to quantify a tangible attribute relating the two variables. This value gives the proportion of the total variation in one variable (y) which can be explained by the variation in the second variable (x). The value is often expressed as a percentage. For instance, consider a situation where the correlation coefficient between the sales and advertising expenditure of a company is found to be 0.8. Thus, $r = 0.8$, and the coefficient of determination $r^2 = 0.8^2 = 0.64$ ($= 64\%$). Therefore, this shows that 64% of the variation in sales can be explained by changes in the advertising expenditure.

This way of describing the relationship between the two variables leads us to consider cause and effect. Of the two variables being analysed, one is the cause (x) and the other is the effect (y). For instance, it is hoped that advertising causes a change in the sales. In particular, a change in the advertising expenditure will cause a change in the sales income. Thus, we say that advertising expenditure is the 'cause' and sales income is the 'effect'. Consider the likely situation in which the correlation coefficient between these two variables is +1. Thus, $r = +1$, and the coefficient of determination $r^2 = 1$. This implies that 100% of the variation in sales is caused by a variation in the advertising expenditure. In such a case, changes in the advertising expenditure automatically cause changes in the sales revenue, providing an ideal situation for any marketing manager. Of course, in practice it is extremely unlikely that the degree of correlation will be quite so perfect. Even when the relationship between these variables is significant, many other factors will be involved. Thus, in this type of example, it would be fairly commonplace for the coefficient of determination to be in the range 0.1 to 0.3. For instance, a coefficient of determination equal to 0.2 (20%) shows that 20% of the changes in sales revenue is caused by the changes in the advertising expenditure. In many commercial situations, a 20% effect would be more than adequate justification for continuing with the advertising.

Care must be taken in the interpretation of values such as the correlation coefficient and coefficient of determination. It is possible to obtain very high values of the correlation coefficient without any direct relationship between the two variables being present. For instance, consider the following example where data have been collected over ten years on the value of exports from the UK and the average price of washing machines in France.

Year:	1990	1991	1992	1993	1994	1995	1996	1997	1998	1999
Exports (£millions):	20	24	30	28	32	36	39	50	48	53
Prices (1000 FFr):	1.5	1.6	1.9	2.0	2.5	2.5	2.6	2.9	3.0	3.5

These variables have been chosen since there is virtually no direct relationship between them. Now the correlation coefficient can be calculated between these two variables where x = the value of exports from the UK and y = washing machine prices in France. The correlation coefficient is found to be $r = 0.9635$. Thus, the coefficient of determination is $r^2 = 0.9635^2 = 0.928 = 92.8\%$.

Thus, the coefficient of determination seems to indicate that 92.8% of the changes in washing machine prices in France are caused by the fluctuations in UK exports. Such a relationship is said to be spurious since there is clearly little direct relationship between the variables. The correlation coefficient is significant in this case because both variables are linked to a third variable related to the time period. This effect is common in the consideration of economic data taken over a long period of time, as inflation can be an important factor. To consider the true relationship between the two variables, the inflation element will need to be removed from the values considered and the correlation re-calculated. The example shown above is slightly more complex since the amount of inflation may vary between the two countries. However, in general there is likely to be correlation between the two inflation rates, which will then cause spurious correlation between a range of financial and economic data taken over a long period of time.

Definition: *The coefficient of determination, found by squaring the correlation coefficient, shows the amount of variation of the y variable attributable to changes in the other variable (x).*

3.8 **Exercises: rank correlation and significance**

1.(I) The table below shows the rankings awarded to 10 employees during the interview stage of the recruitment process during which they were selected. The table also shows the rankings given to these employees by their line managers, who were asked to rate their employers' relative job performances over the last financial year.

Employee:	A	B	C	D	E	F	G	H	I	J
Interview ranking:	1	2	3	4	5	6	7	8	9	10
Job performance:	3	5	2	8	1	4	9	6	10	7

(i) Investigate the degree of correlation between these two sets of rankings using Spearman's rank correlation coefficient.

(ii) Is this correlation coefficient significant using the 95% limits? What do you conclude from this analysis in terms of the suitability of the interview in the selection process?

2.(I) The predictions of four financial analysts on weekly changes in the stock market have been compared to the actual fluctuations, and the product moment correlation coefficient calculated in each case. The analysts were asked to estimate changes in each of the following share price indicators: the Dow-Jones index, Nikkei-Dow index, *Financial Times* 100 index. The table below shows the correlation coefficient between the analysts' predictions and the actual values over a twenty-week period.

Correlation between analysts' predictions and actual values				
	Analyst A	Analyst B	Analyst C	Analyst D
Dow–Jones	0.8	0.85	0.55	0.77
Nikkei–Dow	0.4	0.72	0.84	0.82
FT 100	0.5	0.36 .	0.15	−0.15

(i) Comment on the degree of correlation in each case and interpret these values in terms of the performance of the four analysts in predicting the market fluctuations.

(ii) Would you say that one analyst is clearly better at these predictions? Give reasons for your answer.

(iii) Comment on the predictability of the three share price indicators in this table. Which one seems to be the easiest value to predict?

(iv) Confirm the significance of these correlation coefficients by using a suitable test.

3.9   Line of 'best fit'

When investigating the relationship between two variables we have already seen that a graphical representation of the data can be useful. From the scatter diagram produced, in addition to gauging the strength of connection, we can also analyse the 'shape' of the relationship. We can do this by attempting to draw a line of 'best fit' between all the points on the graph. For example, the graph shown in Figure 3.8

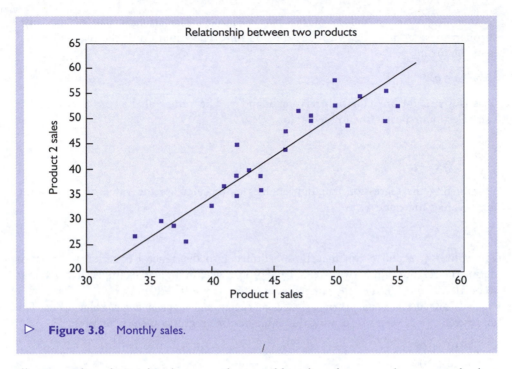

▷ **Figure 3.8** Monthly sales.

illustrates the relationship between the monthly sales of two products over the last two years. The graph illustrates that there is a strong direct correlation between the two sets of sales figures. The 'best' straight line has been drawn through the centre of the points on the scatter diagram. A graph illustrated in Figure 3.4 shows the 'best' curve through a series of values. In these examples, the line of 'best fit' will enable us to estimate other values from the data given. This process is described in the following sections.

3.10 Regression techniques

Regression techniques are used to determine the relationship between two or more variables. In many circumstances, it is useful to be able to express such a relationship in mathematical terms. For instance, there may be a relationship between the advertising expenditure (denoted by x) and the sales revenue (denoted by y). In such a case we would wish to express the value of y in terms of x. For example, a simple expression such as $y = 10x$, would tell us that the value of sales is ten times the amount spent on advertising. Clearly, in practice, the relationships are never as simple as this example. However, the process of finding an equation relating the two variables x and y is important and often achievable.

In general terms we have already considered the use of a scatter diagram to illustrate the relationship between two variables x and y. Points are drawn representing pairs of values of the two variables. The straight line of 'best fit' through these points is called the **regression line**. The equation of the regression line is of the form:

$$y = a + bx$$

This is a straight line equation relating x and y. The values of the constants a and b can be estimated using the following formula:

$$b = \frac{\sum xy - n\bar{x}\bar{y}}{\sum x^2 - n\bar{x}^2}$$

Rearranging the regression equation enables us to calculate the value of a using the mean values for x and y,

$$a = \bar{y} - b\bar{x}$$

The values of a and b can then be substituted into the general equation in order to define the relationship between x and y. For instance, in a given example, if a is found to be 10 and b is 20, then the regression equation is $y = 10 + 20x$.

Such an equation can then be used to determine y for a given value of x. For instance, if $x = 5$, then substituting this value into the regression equation gives

$$\begin{aligned}
y &= 10 + 20.5 \\
&= 10 + 100 \\
&= 110
\end{aligned}$$

Thus, when $x = 5$, $y = 110$. Such estimates form the basis for a range of forecasting examples.

Note that the equation $y = a + bx$ is used to find the expected value of y for given values of x. This should be considered in practical problems, where it is not clear which variable is x and which is y. The variable represented by x is the known value, whereas the y variable is to be evaluated. For example, given a relationship between advertising expenditure and sales revenue, a likely problem would be to estimate the sales from a given advertising expenditure. In this case the known value is advertising and is represented by x, and the unknown variable (sales) is y.

Definition: *The regression line is the 'line of best fit' through the points on a scatter diagram. The equation of this straight line is of the form $y = a + bx$, where a and b can be obtained by the formula as shown.*

EXAMPLE I

Consider the values of x and y given in the following table:

x: 1 2 3 4   5
y: 3 5 7 9   11

The more mathematical reader will recognise that there is a perfect relationship between the two variables. In every case the value of y can be obtained by doubling the value of x and then adding 1. In fact, the equation relating x and y is of the form:

$$y = 1 + 2x$$

Let us use the regression techniques to illustrate how this relationship could be formally obtained.

Firstly, the values of x and y are plotted onto a graph as shown in Figure 3.9. As can be seen, the points all lie on a straight line.

Generally the relationship between the two variables would not be as obvious, and it would usually be necessary to determine the degree of correlation before continuing. Thus, the table below shows the required calculations involved in evaluating the correlation coefficient.

	x	y	x^2	y^2	xy
	1	3	1	9	3
	2	5	4	25	10
	3	7	9	49	21
	4	9	16	81	36
	5	11	25	121	55
Totals	15	35	55	285	125

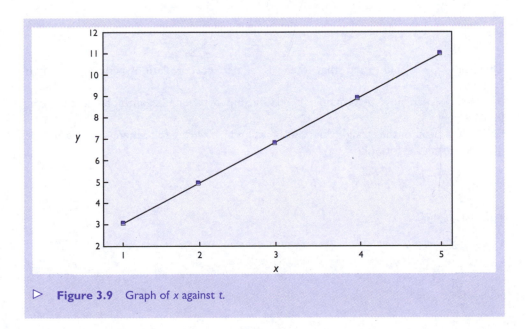

▷ **Figure 3.9**   Graph of x against t.

This table gives the following summations:

$$\Sigma\, x = 15,\ \Sigma\, y = 35,\ \Sigma\, x^2 = 55,\ \Sigma\, y^2 = 285,\ \Sigma\, xy = 125$$

Thus, the means for the values of x and y can be calculated:

$$\bar{x} = \frac{\Sigma\, x}{n} = \frac{15}{5} = 3$$

$$\bar{y} = \frac{\Sigma\, y}{n} = \frac{35}{5} = 7$$

The value of the correlation coefficient is found as follows:

$$r = \frac{\Sigma\, xy - n\bar{x}\bar{y}}{\sqrt{\{\Sigma\, x^2 - n\bar{x}^2\}\{\Sigma\, y^2 - n\bar{y}^2\}}}$$

$$= \frac{125 - 5.3.7}{\sqrt{\{55 - 5.3^2\}\{285 - 5.7^2\}}}$$

$$= \frac{125 - 105}{\sqrt{\{55 - 45\}\{285 - 245\}}}$$

$$= \frac{20}{\sqrt{10.40}}$$

$$= \frac{20}{\sqrt{400}}$$

$$= \frac{20}{20}$$

Therefore, $r = 1$, indicating that there is a perfect correlation between the two variables.

Thus, we can now determine the relationship between the variables x and y as follows.

The equation of the straight line can be written as $y = a + bx$, where a and b can be obtained using the formula:

$$b = \frac{\Sigma\, xy - n\bar{x}\bar{y}}{\Sigma\, x^2 - n\bar{x}^2} \quad \text{and} \quad a = \bar{y} - b\bar{x}$$

Thus, the value of

$$b = \frac{125 - 5.3.7}{55 - 5.3^2}$$

$$= \frac{20}{10}$$

Note that both the numerator and the denominator of the calculation of a have already been calculated in the correlation coefficient formula. Therefore, $b = 2$.

Similarly, the value of

$$a = \bar{y} - b\bar{x}$$
$$= 7 - 2.3$$
$$= 7 - 6$$

Therefore, $a = 1$.

Substituting the values of a and b into the general equation $y = a + bx$ we have the equation of the regression line is $y = 1 + 2x$. This equation could be used to obtain values of y for given values of x. For example, if we wish to find the value of y when x is 6, then we could substitute the value into the regression equation as follows:

$$y = 1 + 2.6$$
$$= 1 + 12$$
$$= 13$$

Therefore, from the regression equation, $y = 13$ when $x = 6$. Similarly, other values of y could be found by substituting given values of x.

EXAMPLE 2

Consider the data giving the volume of sales in the Petlocks company over a ten-year period. The figures shown give the number of packets of 'Barley Krisps' sold in millions.

Year:	1988	1989	1990	1991	1992	1993	1994	1995	1996	1997
Sales:	19	22	27	26	30	32	36	37	39	42

These data were introduced in an earlier example, and are illustrated in a scatter diagram in Figure 3.3. There seems to be a linear relationship displayed on this graph. We can consider the degree of correlation between the years and sales figures using the correlation coefficient. In an example of this type it is useful to simplify the calculations by coding the years. For instance, 1988 can be regarded as year 1, 1989 as year 2, and so on. Thus, we can consider the data as shown below:

Year (x):	1	2	3	4	5	6	7	8	9	10
Sales (y):	19	22	27	26	30	32	36	37	39	42

The correlation coefficient between these variables can be calculated as shown in the following table.

To summarise, this table gives the following summations:

$$\Sigma x = 55, \ \Sigma y = 310, \ \Sigma x^2 = 385, \ \Sigma y^2 = 10\ 124, \ \Sigma xy = 1909$$

x	y	x^2	y^2	xy
1	19	1	361	19
2	22	4	484	44
3	27	9	729	81
4	26	16	676	104
5	30	25	900	150
6	32	36	1024	192
7	36	49	1296	252
8	37	64	1369	296
9	39	81	1521	351
10	42	100	1764	420
Totals 55	310	385	10 124	1909

Thus, the means for the values of x and y can be calculated:

$$\bar{x} = \frac{\sum x}{n} = \frac{55}{10} = 5.5$$

$$\bar{y} = \frac{\sum y}{n} = \frac{310}{10} = 31$$

The degree of correlation is obtained by using the correlation coefficient as shown:

$$\text{The value of } r = \frac{\sum xy - n\bar{x}\bar{y}}{\sqrt{\{\sum x^2 - n\bar{x}^2\}\{\sum y^2 - n\bar{y}^2\}}}$$

$$= \frac{1909 - 10.(5.5)(31)}{\sqrt{\{385 - 10(5.5)^2\}\{10\ 124 - 10(31)^2\}}}$$

$$= \frac{1909 - 1705}{\sqrt{\{385 - 302.5\}\{10\ 124 - 9610\}}}$$

$$= \frac{204}{\sqrt{(82.5)(514)}}$$

$$= \frac{204}{\sqrt{42\ 405}}$$

$$= \frac{204}{205.92}$$

$$= 0.99$$

The value of $r = 0.99$ shows a highly significant correlation between the two variables x and y. Therefore, the two variables are likely to be related by a straight line equation.

The equation of the straight line can be written as $y = a + bx$, where a and b can be obtained using the formula:

$$b = \frac{\sum xy - n\bar{x}\bar{y}}{\sum x^2 - n\bar{x}^2} \quad \text{and} \quad a = \bar{y} - b\bar{x}$$

Thus, the value of

$$b = \frac{1909 - 10(5.5)(31)}{385 - 10(5.5)^2}$$

$$= \frac{204}{82.5}$$

Therefore, $b = 2.473$.

Similarly, the value of

$$a = \bar{y} - b\bar{x}$$
$$= 31 - 2.473(5.5)$$
$$= 31 - 13.6015$$

Therefore, $a = 17.3985$. Thus, the regression equation $y = a + bx$ is $y = 17.4 + 2.47x$.

This equation could now be used to forecast future sales values. For example, to estimate the sales figure in 1998 (year 11) we substitute the value of $x = 11$ into the regression equation. Therefore, we obtain $y = 17.4 + 2.47(11) = 17.4 + 27.17 = 44.57$. Thus, this gives an estimate of the volume of sales in 1998 equal to 45. The accuracy of the estimate cannot be greater than that of the original data given, and therefore this value has been rounded off to the nearest whole number. Thus, the estimated volume of 'Barley Krisps' in 1998 is 45 million packets.

Other forecasts could be obtained using the same regression equation. For instance, the sales figure in 1999 (year 12) is estimated as $y = 17.4 + 2.47(12) = 47$. Thus, an estimated 47 million packets of 'Barley Krisps' will be sold in 1999.

The reliability of such estimates is dependent on a range of factors in addition to this simple regression approach. For example, although past performance is a factor in forecasting future sales, other elements such as pricing, competitors and advertising expenditure may be more important. Furthermore, the accuracy of the estimates is likely to deteriorate as the time period from the original data increases. Thus, the 1998 estimate is likely to be more accurate than the 1999 value. Clearly, forecasting the sales revenue in the year 2050 using this method is likely to be totally inaccurate.

| 3.11 | **Exercises: regression methods** |

1.(E) Find the degree of correlation between the following pairs of values of x and y. Determine the regression equation $y = a + bx$ in each case.

(i) x: 2 3 4 5 6
    y: 8 11 14 17 20

(ii) x: 2   3   4   5   6
    y: 10   8   8   5   4

(iii) x: 2   3   4   5   6
    y: 3   7   4   9   6

In each of these examples, use the regression equation to estimate the value of y when x is 7, and comment on the likely accuracy of these forecasts.

2.(I) A previous exercise in Section 3.4 required the calculation of the correlation coefficient for the following data:

Month:	Jan	Feb	Mar	Apr	May	Jun	Jul	Aug
Sales ($millions):	3.0	3.4	3.8	4.1	3.9	4.4	4.5	4.9
Advertising ($100 000s):	2.2	2.5	2.1	2.7	2.6	2.9	2.6	2.4

Determine the regression equation from these data in order to estimate the monthly sales of the product based on a given advertising expenditure. Use this equation to estimate the sales in September, when the company spent $300 000 on advertising.

Is the estimate obtained valid? Comment on the degree of correlation between these two variables.

3.(I) The Personnel Director at QTC, Lisa Gregory, has requested an analysis of the current company selection procedures. It has been suggested that one of the assessment tests used in the selection process is not valid. The table below shows the results in this test for ten employees selected over the past five years, together with the job performance assessments provided by their line managers.

Employee:	A	B	C	D	E	F	G	H	I	J
Test result:	11	13	15	15	16	17	17	18	19	19
Job performance:	4	5	7	7	8	6	9	7	8	9

 (i) Investigate the degree of correlation between the test results and employees' job performance assessments.
 (ii) Use a regression technique to estimate the job performance assessment of an employee who obtained 14 in the test. Comment on the reliability of this estimate.

3.12   Non-linear relationships

In many practical examples the relationship between the two variables may not be linear. There are a number of ways that such relationships can be analysed further. The following examples show two approaches to this situation.

EXAMPLE I

The example illustrated earlier in Figure 3.4 shows the sales revenue conforming to a curve. This situation is typical for economic data, where inflationary factors are involved. These data can be transformed to a linear relationship by using a log transformation. Consider the example illustrated in Figure 3.4, where the following data are illustrated:

Year: 1988 1989 1990 1991 1992 1993 1994 1995 1996 1997
Sales: 14 15 17 20 24 30 48 49 59 67

The 'known' variable (x) is the year and the 'unknown' variable is the sales revenue. Now, taking logs of the sales values will give the values of y. Using the coded year values 1, 2, 3, . . . and taking logs of the sales figures we have the following:

Year (x): 1 2 3 4 5 6 7 8 9 10
Sales: 14 15 17 20 24 30 48 49 59 67
log (sales): 1.15 1.18 1.23 1.30 1.38 1.48 1.68 1.69 1.77 1.83

The graph in Figure 3.10 shows the relationship between the year (x) and the log of sales (y). The degree of correlation can be calculated in the usual way, where x = year and y = log (sales) as shown in the following table:

x	y	x^2	y^2	xy
1	1.15	1	1.3225	1.15
2	1.18	4	1.3924	2.36
3	1.23	9	1.5129	3.69
4	1.30	16	1.69	5.2
5	1.38	25	1.9044	6.9
6	1.48	36	2.1904	8.88
7	1.68	49	2.8224	11.76
8	1.69	64	2.8561	13.52
9	1.77	81	3.1329	15.93
10	1.83	100	3.3489	18.3
Totals 55	14.69	385	22.1729	87.69

To summarise, this table gives the following summations:

$$\Sigma x = 55, \Sigma y = 14.69, \Sigma x^2 = 385, \Sigma y^2 = 22.1729, \Sigma xy = 87.69$$

The means for the values of x and y can be calculated:

$$\bar{x} = \frac{\Sigma x}{n} = \frac{55}{10} = 5.5$$

$$\bar{y} = \frac{\Sigma y}{n} = \frac{14.69}{10} = 1.469$$

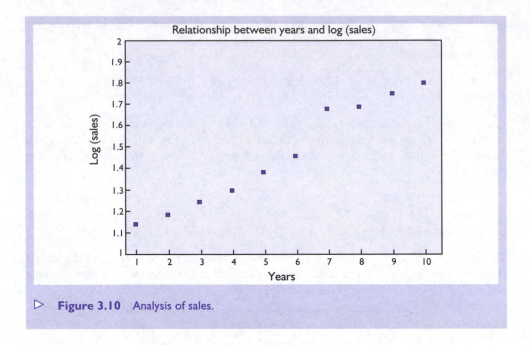

▷ **Figure 3.10**   Analysis of sales.

The degree of correlation is obtained using the correlation coefficient as shown:

$$\text{The value of } r = \frac{\sum xy - n\bar{x}\bar{y}}{\sqrt{\{\sum x^2 - n\bar{x}^2\}\{\sum y^2 - n\bar{y}^2\}}}$$

$$= \frac{89.69 - 10(5.5)(1.469)}{\sqrt{\{385 - 10(5.5)^2\}\{22.1729 - 10(1.469)^2\}}}$$

$$= \frac{87.69 - 80.795}{\sqrt{\{385 - 302.5\}\{22.1729 - 21.5796\}}}$$

$$= \frac{6.895}{\sqrt{(82.5)(0.5933)}}$$

$$= \frac{6.695}{\sqrt{48.947}}$$

$$= \frac{6.895}{6.996}$$

$$= 0.986$$

The value of $r = 0.986$ shows a highly significant correlation between the two variables x and y. Therefore, the two variables are likely to be related by a straight line equation.

The equation of the straight line can be written as $y = a + bx$, where a and b can be obtained using the formula:

$$b = \frac{\sum xy - n\bar{x}\bar{y}}{\sum x^2 - n\bar{x}^2} \quad \text{and} \quad a = \bar{y} - b\bar{x}$$

Thus, the value of $b = 6.895/82.5$. Therefore, $b = 0.0836$.

Similarly, the value of $a = \bar{y} - b\bar{x}$
$$= 1.469 - 0.0836(5.5)$$
$$= 1.0092$$

Therefore, $a = 1.0092$.

Thus, the regression equation $y = a + bx$ is $y = 1.0092 + 0.0836x$. This equation can then be used to estimate the value of y for a given value of x. Thus, to estimate the sales for 1998 (when $x = 11$) we have:

$$y = 1.0092 + 0.0836(11)$$
$$= 0.9196 + 1.0092$$
$$= 1.9288$$

Therefore in year 11 the log of sales is predicted to be 1.9288. Transforming back using anti-logs we obtain an estimate of sales of 84.9. Thus, the sales in 1998 are estimated to be $85 millions, assuming that the straight line relationship still applies.

EXAMPLE 2

An alternative approach to the consideration of non-linear relationships is to attempt to fit a polynomial expression to the data. In other words, the variables x and y may be related by an equation involving powers of x. The general equation can be written as:

$$y = a_0 + a_1 x + a_2 x^2 + a_3 x^3 + \cdots$$

The values of the constants $a_0, a_1, a_2, \ldots$ can be obtained by the solution of simultaneous equations.

To simplify this, we could consider a quadratic relationship between the two variables of the form:

$$y = a_0 + a_1 x + a_2 x^2$$

The values of a_0, a_1 and a_2 can be found by solving the following equations:

$$\sum y = a_0 n + a_1 \sum x + a_2 \sum x^2$$
$$\sum xy = a_0 \sum x + a_1 \sum x^2 + a_2 \sum x^3$$
$$\sum x^2 y = a_0 \sum x^2 + a_1 \sum x^3 + a_2 \sum x^4$$

Consider the original data on sales figures given in the previous example.

x: 1   2   3   4   5   6   7   8   9   10
y: 14 15 17 20 24 30 48 49 59 67

From these data the following values can be obtained:

$n = 10$, $\sum y = 343$, $\sum xy = 2404$, $\sum x^2 y = 19\ 194$,

$\sum x = 55$, $\sum x^2 = 385$, $\sum x^3 = 3025$, $\sum x^4 = 25\ 333$

Substituting these values into the equations we obtain:

$$343 = 10a_0 + 55a_1 + 385a_2$$

$$2404 = 55a_0 + 385a_1 + 3025a_2$$

$$19\ 194 = 385a_0 + 3025a_1 + 25\ 333a_2$$

Solving these equations we obtain the values:

$a_0 = 12.133$, $a_1 = 0.106$, $a_2 = 0.561$

Therefore, the equation relating x and y is as follows:

$$y = 12.133 + 0.106x + 0.561x^2$$

Substituting a value of $x = 11$ into this equation will obtain an estimate of the sales revenue in 1998 of $81 millions. However, as discussed earlier, care must be taken when extrapolating, and estimates outside the range of existing data can be inaccurate.

3.13   Multiple regression

In many practical situations, the linear regression model relating two variables x and y is too simplistic. In general, the value of y may be determined by a number of variables $x_1, x_2, x_3, \ldots$. In such circumstances, a multiple regression equation can be used of the form:

$$y = b_0 + b_1 x_1 + b_2 x_2 + b_3 x_3 + \cdots$$

The values of the regression coefficients $b_0, b_1, b_2, \ldots$ can be obtained by complex mathematical calculations outside the scope of this text. Generally, such analysis can be performed using many of the standard statistical computer packages.

EXAMPLE 1

Consider the monthly sales revenue in the Petlocks company for a particular brand of cereal. The actual sales value in a given month may depend on a number of factors such as unit price, advertising expenditure in preceding month, and number of sales staff employed. In such an example, the value to be predicted, y, is the monthly sales revenue in $ millions. The independent variables used to predict y are:

x_1 = unit retail price ($),
x_2 = advertising expenditure in previous month ($10 000s),
x_3 = total number of sales staff.

A sample of eight months over the past two years gives the following values for the variables:

y	x_1	x_2	x_3
4.0	1.00	8	24
5.2	0.90	9	26
3.8	1.10	6	20
2.9	1.20	5	18
4.6	0.95	7	20
4.5	0.90	6	30
3.7	1.00	6	27
5.0	0.95	10	28

Using the multiple regression model outlined earlier for this set of data gives the following regression equation:

$$y = 9.8 - 5.95x_1 + 0.18x_2 - 0.03x_3$$

This regression equation could then be used to estimate a sales figure given values of the independent variables. For instance, if the unit price is $1.10, the advertising expenditure in the preceding month is $60 000, and there are 30 sales staff employed, then the sales revenue can be forecasted as follows:

Sales $= 9.8 - 5.95(1.10) + 0.18(6) - 0.03(30)$
$= 9.8 - 6.545 + 1.08 - 0.9$
$= 3.435$

Thus, given these circumstances the estimated sales revenue is $3.4 million. A more detailed analysis could be performed to investigate the likely accuracy of such a forecast. However, the regression equation obtained does suggest some useful information. For instance, a consideration of the coefficients of the three variables gives some indication of the relative importance of each variable in the equation. It seems from the data analysed that the unit price (x_1) is most important in forecasting the likely sales in any given month. This is indicated by the relatively large coefficient for this variable. Conversely, the coefficient of x_3 is very small, showing that the number of sales staff employed has little influence on current sales. Clearly, these estimates must be considered with caution. In particular, the model obtained may be reasonably accurate provided that the independent variables x_1, x_2 and x_3 are within a given range, but could be totally unreliable outside the range. For example, in the data given, the ranges of values for the three variables are as follows: x_1 (0.90 to 1.20), x_2 (5 to 10), x_3 (18 to 30). Therefore, for example, the model would not be useful for forecasting sales given a unit price of $2.00 or 50 sales staff.

| 3.14 | **Computer applications** |

The concepts involved in correlation and regression techniques provide important tools in the analysis of data. As such, facilities enabling the evaluation and application of these tools are commonplace in a range of computer packages. In particular, most spreadsheet packages, and any serious data analysis software, would incorporate facilities to conduct simple correlation and regression analyses. The following examples illustrate the use of spreadsheets and the SPSS statistical package in analysing the relationship between variables.

EXAMPLE 1

The data below show details on sales income and advertising expenditure over an eight-month period, as introduced in an earlier exercise in this chapter.

Month:	Jan	Feb	Mar	Apr	May	Jun	Jul	Aug
Sales ($million):	3.0	3.4	3.8	4.1	3.9	4.4	4.5	4.9
Advertising ($100 000s):	2.2	2.5	2.1	2.7	2.6	2.9	2.6	2.4

The SPSS package can be used to provide an analysis of data of this type. The screen displayed in Figure 3.11 shows a number of windows produced in the SPSS software. The screen displayed shows three separate areas created by the user within SPSS. The top left hand window shows where the sales and advertising data have been entered into a table in a similar format to a spreadsheet. Some of the values of both variables shown in two columns are visible in this window. The window on the right of the screen gives a scatter diagram of the data obtained. The advertising values are illustrated along the horizontal axis, and the sales figures are shown on the vertical scale. Finally, the window in the bottom left of the screen has been created to display the correlation coefficient between sales and advertising. The correlation coefficient has been calculated as 0.4531 as shown. As would be expected, it can be seen that the correlation between advertising and advertising is found to be 1!

The SPSS package provides a range of correlation and regression tools, and also gives details on the significance of these calculated values. For example, the window in the bottom left of the screen entitled '!Output1' also gives the probability of obtaining a value of the correlation coefficient obtained. The window shows that assuming there is no relationship between the two variables, the probability of obtaining a correlation coefficient as high as 0.4531 is $p = 0.260$ (26%). Thus, such a value is quite likely, and we could not conclude that there is a significant correlation between these two variables. The value of p in this window would therefore help to ascertain whether the correlation coefficient is significant or not. A lower value of p would indicate a stronger likelihood of correlation between the variables.

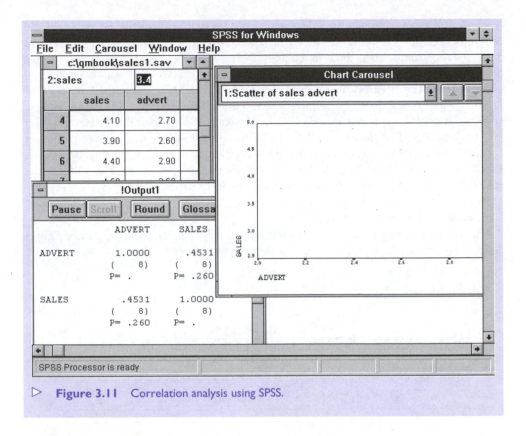

▷ **Figure 3.11** Correlation analysis using SPSS.

EXAMPLE 2

Consider the volume of sales of the 'Barley Krisps' product introduced earlier. The sales figures over a ten-year period are shown below:

Year:	1988	1989	1990	1991	1992	1993	1994	1995	1996	1997
Sales:	19	22	27	26	30	32	36	37	39	42

These data can be analysed using Lotus, Excel or any other convenient spreadsheet, as shown in the following examples.

Using the disk. These sales figures have been placed into the spreadsheet called CORRN1.WK3. Load this file from the disk. The screen displayed is illustrated in Figure 3.12. In this spreadsheet, the two variables have been entered in columns A and B. The years are denoted 1, 2, 3 . . ., instead of the actual figures 1988, 1989, ... In Lotus the / **Data Regression** options will enable the display of the 'Regression Output' as shown on the right of the screen. Similarly, in Excel, the options **Tools, Data**

Analysis and **Regression** will provide a similar output. In both spreadsheet packages the X-Range contains the years as shown in column A (A2 . . . A11), and the Y-Range contains the actual sales data in column B (B2 . . . B11). With these two ranges defined, the output range is specified, where the actual results will be displayed (D1 . . . G9). The 'Regression Output' shown in Figure 3.12 contains a number of familiar values that have been introduced during this chapter. The value of the correlation coefficient is not quoted directly. Instead, the coefficient of determination (r^2) is quoted, and is shown in cell G4 to be equal to 0.981 in this example. Thus, if required the user can obtain the correlation coefficient by square rooting this value. Thus, $r = \sqrt{0.981} = 0.99$. The analysis shown in this output is used to obtain the equation of the regression line in the form $y = ax + b$. In the output displayed, the value of b is the 'Constant' and is found in cell G2. Similarly, the value of a is the 'X coefficient' and is given in cell F8.

The reader can experiment with the regression facility by changing the sales figures given in column B. For example, consider the following sales figures:

Year:	1	2	3	4	5	6	7	8	9	10
Sales:	30	24	32	24	20	25	18	20	16	21

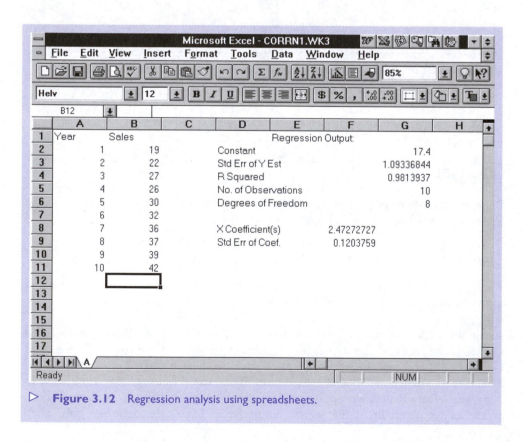

▷ **Figure 3.12** Regression analysis using spreadsheets.

Now using the regression options in your spreadsheet, try to generate a new output, overwriting the previous values obtained.

The 'Constant' and 'X Coefficient(s)' values enable us to obtain the regression equation, which can then be used to estimate other values of the sales figures for given years. This approach is displayed in Figure 3.13, where the cells B15 to B19 contain estimates of the sales in years 11 to 15 based on the regression equation obtained using the original data displayed. For example, the formula entered into the cell B15 is based on the year given in cell A15 and the regression values in cells G2 and F8. The formula entered into cell B15 is obtained as follows:

Estimated sales = 2.47*Year + 17.4
    Thus, B15 = F8*A15 + G2

In fact in order to be able to copy this down to the other cells, the regression values need to be referenced absolutely, and therefore the formula entered into the cell is:

B15 = +F8*A15 + G2

This formula is then copied down to cells B16 to B19 in order to display estimates over

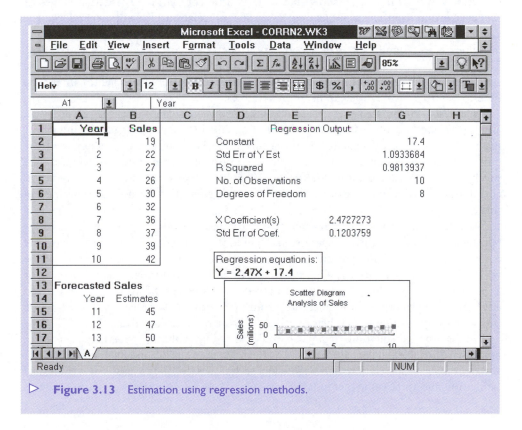

▷   **Figure 3.13**   Estimation using regression methods.

the five-year period. Figure 3.13 also shows the production of a basic graphical output. In this case, the scatter diagram indicating the relationship between the years and sales figures has been produced. The reader can access this file (CORRN2.WK3) from the disk provided if required.

| 3.15 | **Chapter summary** |

This chapter has considered an analysis of the relationships between two or more sets of values. Scatter diagrams can be used to illustrate any connection between two variables. However, the results from such diagrams are largely subjective. In order to further analyse the relationship in detail, an objective measure should be used. The product moment correlation coefficient provides one such measure, which gives an assessment of how close the two variables are related. The coefficient, denoted by r, measures the degree of correlation (or linear relationship) between the two variables. The value of the correlation coefficient ranges between -1 and $+1$. Values of r close to $+1$ or -1 indicate that there is a good correlation between the two variables. Conversely, values near zero show that there is little correlation. The actual values of the correlation coefficient indicating a significant relationship will depend on the sample size. For instance, a correlation coefficient of $r = 0.8$ from a sample of ten pairs of values is less significant than a correlation coefficient of $r = 0.7$ from 100 values. The significance of a coefficient can be ascertained by using confidence limits. The coefficient of determination, found by squaring the correlation coefficient, can also be used to describe the relationship between variables.

In certain circumstances, the rank correlation coefficient can be used as an alternative method of investigating the relationship between two sets of values. For instance, it is often difficult to obtain accurate measures of specific values, and the only reliable method is to place the variables into order, i.e. rank the values. The product moment correlation coefficient of these rankings is known as the rank correlation coefficient and can be obtained using a simplified formula as described in this chapter.

A significant correlation between two variables implies that there is a linear relationship between them. Regression techniques can be used to determine the equation of the 'best' straight line, the regression line. The regression equation can be written in the form $y = a + bx$. This equation can be used to estimate the value of y for a given value of x. Thus, for example, the sales revenue can be estimated for a given advertising expenditure. Non-linear relationships between variables will need to be transformed into straight lines before using the basic regression analysis.

More complex equations can be considered using multiple regression, where an unknown variable y can be estimated from a number of independent variables $x_1, x_2, x_3, \ldots$. Correlation and regression techniques form the basis of a range of estimation and forecasting methods used in business and economics.

3.16 Further exercises

1.(E) The table given below shows the number of vehicles belonging to QTC located at each of six regional sites together with the average monthly income during 1997.

Site:	Newcastle	Southampton	Cardiff	Dundee	Lancaster	Birmingham
No. of vehicles:	30	40	35	38	50	47
Ave. income (£100 000s):	7.1	8.3	6.8	7.3	9.1	9.4

(i) Calculate the correlation coefficient between the number of vehicles and monthly income at the regional sites of QTC. Comment on the significance of this value.

(ii) Find the regression equation relating these two variables and use this to estimate the average monthly income for a proposed seventh site containing 20 vehicles. Comment on the validity of this estimate. What additional factors may determine the accuracy and reliability of such an estimate?

2.(I) In recent negotiations between employees and management, the union representatives have complained about the poor management resulting in loss of time due to materials shortages and machine breakdowns. The company currently operates a productivity pay scheme in which up to 25% of an employee's pay is obtained by additional productivity awards. The union negotiators have stressed that employees are losing productivity payments through no fault of their own. To justify their statements they have provided the following details on the average productivity payments received by a group of fifty employees compared to the amount of lost time over a period of 10 consecutive weeks.

Week	Average productivity bonus (£)	Lost production time (%)
1	40	8
2	35	6
3	20	10
4	25	11
5	45	5
6	60	4
7	75	4
8	40	6
9	20	12
10	50	8

(i) Calculate the correlation coefficient for this set of data in order to investigate whether there is a relationship between the productivity bonuses received by employees and the percentage production time lost.

(ii) Is the correlation coefficient value obtained significant? Comment on the results, and discuss the response from the management negotiators concerning these data.

(iii) Could the data be used to estimate the average productivity bonus received by employees in a given week in which there was a 6% loss of time? Obtain such an estimate using a regression method and comment on the reliability of this value.

3. (I)   In a technical training course provided by a large industrial company for all new production operators, it has been found that there is a relationship between the age of employees and the time required to gain competence in a particular skill. The table below shows the age of a random sample of eight employees and the training time required to achieve competence in one area.

Employee:	A	B	C	D	E	F	G	H
Age (years):	18	19	20	21	22	23	29	38
Training time (hours):	4	3	4	6	5	8	6	7

(i) Use a regression method to estimate the training time required for a new employee aged 30 years.

(ii) By finding the correlation coefficient, discuss the accuracy of your estimate obtained in part (i). What other factors would affect the amount of training time required for each employee?

4. (I)   The table below shows the sales revenue obtained by a company over a ten-year period.

Year:	1988	1989	1990	1991	1992	1993	1994	1995	1996	1997
Revenue ($millions):	20	18	15	19	26	24	30	28	33	37

(i) Draw a scatter diagram of the data given, and draw the 'best' straight line through the points illustrated.

(ii) Use a suitable method to obtain the equation of the regression line of revenue against years. Use this equation to forecast the sales revenue for this company during 1998. Comment on the likely accuracy of this estimate. Compare this value with an estimate obtained from the line of 'best fit' drawn in part (i), and comment on any difference obtained.

5. (I)   The Sales Manager of an electronics company in Melbourne has analysed the performance of the individuals in his sales team. It has been found that there is some relationship between the total sales achieved and the number of personal calls to clients that each sales representative makes. The table below shows these values taken during a one-month period for six sales representatives.

Salesperson:	A	B	C	D	E	F
Average calls per day:	0.9	1.1	1.4	1.7	2.5	3.2
Total sales ($1000s):	22	18	24	21	45	38

(i) Investigate the degree of correlation between these two variables.

(ii) The Sales Manager has used this information to encourage his staff to make more personal calls, saying that this is likely to increase sales. Is this true? Comment on this approach, outlining other factors that would be relevant.

6.(D) It is assumed that the relationship between monthly advertising expenditure and resulting sales revenue is of the form $y = a + b*\sqrt{x}$, where x is the advertising expenditure and y is the sales revenue. Consider the following table, giving information on the sales and advertising expenditure over the previous twelve months.

Month	Advertising expenditure	Sales
(£100s)	(£1000s)	
Jan	4.1	15.6
Feb	6.2	16.8
Mar	5.8	15.9
Apr	7.9	16.6
May	8.6	16.4
Jun	3.0	15.9
Jul	5.0	15.8
Aug	7.2	17.0
Sep	8.4	16.9
Oct	10.6	18.2
Nov	11.0	17.5
Dec	7.0	15.9

(i) Plot these values onto a scatter diagram, and discuss from this graph whether the relationship between x and y is linear or not.

(ii) Calculate the degree of correlation between $\sqrt{x}$ and y, and comment on this relationship.

(iii) Determine the equation of the regression line of y on $\sqrt{x}$, and use this to estimate the sales in a given month in which the advertising expenditure is £2000.

(iv) Comment on your estimate obtained in part (iii), and discuss the reasons why such a forecast may not be accurate.

7.(D) A recent annual appraisal system introduced for all managers in the Petlocks cereal company has been heavily criticised by a wide range of staff. One of the complaints is that an individual's performance appraisal, based on the opinions of two managers, can be highly subjective. Furthermore, an employee's appraisal is very important since it is used as a basis for the individual's annual pay award. It has been suggested that there is little agreement between the appraisals given by the two managers involved. The Personnel Director at Petlocks has requested an investigation into these problems. In order to consider the relationship between different manager's appraisals, two managers have been asked to independently assess the performance of twelve employees in their department. The managers, Mrs Tanton and Mr Wright, have rated the employees on a scale from 1 to 20, where 1 indicates a very poor performance and 20 shows an excellent rating. The results are shown in the table below:

Employee	Manager assessments	
	Mrs Tanton	Mr Wright
A	12	10
B	16	13
C	10	11
D	6	9
E	8	7
F	11	14
G	18	19
H	14	17
I	15	16
J	9	10
K	14	12
L	13	10

(i) Investigate the relationship between the two sets of assessments by using the rank correlation coefficient. (Note that the values given are *not* rankings, but are actual performance measures.)

(ii) Comment on the significance of the rank correlation coefficient, and discuss the relationship between the ratings of the two managers. Would you conclude from this information that the manager's assessments are reliable indicators of the employee's performance?

(iii) A further analysis of the data given could involve the use of the product moment correlation coefficient. Use this to investigate the relationship between the two sets of assessments. Does this provide any additional information? Discuss why this measure may be better or worse than the rank correlation coefficient in this type of example.

8.(I) **Using the Disk.** The file named RELATE.WK3 on the disk contains data relating to the problem outlined in exercise 6 in this section. Load this file into your spreadsheet package. The spreadsheet displays the monthly figures for sales revenue and advertising expenditure.

(i) Use the regression facility in Lotus or Excel to investigate the degree of correlation between the two variables. The X Range will be the cells containing the Advertising expenditure, and the Y Range will be those containing the sales revenue.

(ii) Compare these results with the correlation between y and $\sqrt{x}$. In order to do this you will need to set up a new column of figures in which the values of $\sqrt{x}$ are calculated. The new X Range will be the cells containing these values. Change the

Output range so that the results from this analysis will not overwrite the original values. A new set of correlation and regression statistics will be calculated.

(iii) Comment on the degree of relationship between x and y compared with between $\sqrt{x}$ and y. Compare the regression estimates obtained from the two sets of figures and discuss the reliability of these forecasts.

Financial Mathematics

CHAPTER OBJECTIVES

At the end of this chapter you will be able to:

▶ use a variety of methods to calculate the amount of interest to be paid

▶ understand the application of interest rate calculations in depreciation and discounting

▶ use a range of techniques to evaluate and compare investment choices including net present value and internal rate of return

▶ calculate the value of investments such as annuities and sinking funds

Introduction

The use of financial information is often paramount in business decision making. This chapter considers a variety of techniques in the analysis of financial data and in particular the value of money over a time period. This inevitably leads to the consideration of interest and how changes in interest rates will determine appropriate business decisions. Such decisions will span a broad range of areas such as capital investments, loans and lending, incorporating factors including depreciation, inflation and tax allowances.

The following case studies illustrate a number of applications of this area of financial mathematics.

CASE STUDY   The Thornberry bakery company

Thornberry Bakeries was established in the late 1950s in downtown Los Angeles as a local producer of bread and pastry products. During the 1960s, sales of Thornberry's products grew rapidly, and by 1975 the company had a gross turnover in excess of $300 million. Since that time the company has enjoyed steady growth, with the turnover during 1995 reaching $1.3 billion. In addition to the original location, the company has major production sites throughout the US and Canada, including those in Oakland, New Orleans, Vancouver and Montreal.

The machinery used in these major production sites has evolved since the company's small beginnings into the most sophisticated high-tech systems available. The company regards investment in such plant as essential in order to offer top quality products at a competitive price. Leonard Kilby, the Production Director for Thornberry, needs to make decisions on the best deals for the company in the acquisition of machinery and other systems. These decisions revolve around considerations on the quality of the products being offered, the retail price and any repayment terms offered. Indeed, recent decisions have generally involved leasing the machinery instead of purchasing. The use of basic techniques on the value of money over time (including depreciation and net present value) are vital in determining the optimum strategy for the company.

Similarly, the company has recently started a company car scheme for its middle and senior managers. Initially, Thornberry purchased a range of cars for use by their employees. However, with the aid of financial mathematics techniques the company decided that a rental scheme for the cars including a 'buy-back' clause for employees was the most cost-effective method, enabling the company to upgrade the range of cars being offered to the management group.

CASE STUDY   Parker & Jameson consultancy group

The Parker & Jameson group, based in the UK, includes a Division of Business and Financial Analysts. These analysts offer a wide range of services to individual and corporate clients. This London-based company provides advice and assistance in a range of areas including the following:

Investment advice. The company offers an investment appraisal service and can manage investment portfolios for clients if required.

Loans. The company includes a section specifically involved in providing advice on capital loans and mortgages.

Tax benefits. Advice related to lending, borrowing and investments would be tailored for individual clients, dependent on their tax position and on any taxable benefits available.

Advice on areas such as the likely return on investment, or the likely costs of borrowing, involve knowledge of a range of financial mathematics techniques including net present value, internal rate of return, discounting and amortisation. These areas will be explored in the following sections in this chapter.

4.1   Simple interest

Consider a situation where an initial sum of money is invested in a savings account offering a fixed interest rate, and the interest is paid direct to the investor, rather than being added to the initial capital amount. This gives an example of a scheme offering **simple interest**. For instance, if we invest £200 in an account offering 5% annual interest, then at the end of each year we would obtain interest equal to 5% of the initial investment. Therefore, we would receive 5% of £200 each year, providing that no money is subsequently withdrawn. Thus, we would obtain £10 at the end of each year.

There are a number of calculations related to this simple example, and the following notation will be used for the various elements involved. This line added for sample purposes only.

Let P = the principal (i.e. the amount invested) and r = interest rate as a percentage. Then the amount of interest (denoted by I) earned at the end of each period is found by the formula:

$$I = P * \frac{r}{100}$$

More generally, the amount of interest earned over n periods is found by the formula:

$$I = P * \frac{nr}{100}$$

Finally, the amount of money available to the investor at the end of n periods is the interest earned added to the original investment. This is shown in the following formula where A denotes the amount of money available to the investor.

$$A = P + \frac{Pnr}{100}$$

These formulae are equally valid for evaluating the interest paid through borrowing a fixed sum at simple interest.

The following examples illustrate these formulae involving simple interest calculations.

EXAMPLE 1

An individual invests £800 in a bank account offering simple interest of 4% per year. Investigate how much the investor would have in the account after two years. In this example, using the standard notation, we have:

P = initial investment (the so-called 'principal') = £800
r = rate of interest = 4% per year
n = time period for the investment = 2 years

Therefore the amount of interest earned by this investor is found by

$$I = P * \frac{nr}{100} = 800 * \frac{2*4}{100} = £64$$

Thus, the investor earns £64 interest over the two-year period. Consequently, after two years the investor now has £864 capital.

EXAMPLE 2

Consider a situation where Thornberry, introduced earlier in this chapter in the case study, borrows money at simple interest over a three-year period. The amount borrowed is $200 000 at a fixed interest rate of 6% simple interest over three years.

In this example, we have

P = the amount borrowed = $200 000
r = annual interest rate = 6%
n = the number of years = 3

Therefore the amount of interest paid over the three years is found as follows:

$$I = P * \frac{nr}{100} = 200\,000 * \frac{3*6}{100}$$
$$= 36\,000$$

Thus, the company would pay $36 000 interest on the original loan of $200 000.

4.2 Compound interest

The primary difference between simple interest and compound interest can be described as follows. Interest on an investment is said to be 'simple' if it is not added to the original amount at the end of each period. Conversely, if the interest is added to the initial investment then the actual amount invested will increase and interest earned on this new total amount will therefore increase in the same proportion. This situation is known as compounding, and **compound interest** is earned on such an investment.

For example, if $100 is invested in an account earning 10% compound interest, then at the end of the first year there will be $110 in the account made up from the original $100 investment and $10 interest. During the second year, 10% interest is earned on the compounded amount of $110. This investment will earn $11 during the second year. Thus, after two years the total amount invested has increased to $121. Similarly, during the third year, the investment earns $12.10 (being 10% of $121). It can be seen that each year the investment earns an increasing amount of interest.

Using the same notation as introduced in the previous section we have:

P = principal (i.e. the amount invested)
r = interest rate as a percentage

Then the amount of interest (denoted by I) earned at the end of each period is found by the formula:

$$I = P * \frac{r}{100}$$

Therefore, the amount at the end of the period has been increased to:

$$A = P + P * \frac{r}{100}$$

This expression can be written as

$$A = P\left(1 + \frac{r}{100}\right)$$

Finally, the amount of money available to the investor at the end of n periods is found by the formula:

$$A = P(1 + r/100)^n$$

An alternative formula is sometimes used for this value in which the rate of interest is expressed as a decimal (denoted by R). For example, if the interest rate is 12% then $R = 0.12$. The amount after n periods is then expressed as:

$$A = P(1 + R)^n$$

These formulae assume that payments are made at the end of each period. In many practical examples, additional payments could be made. For instance, if the period under consideration is annual, and payments are made monthly (i.e. twelve times per year), then the formula needs to be modified. Assuming m payments per period then the sum of money available after n periods is:

$$A = P\left(1 + \frac{r}{100m}\right)^{nm}$$

or

$$A = P\left(1 + \frac{R}{m}\right)^{nm}$$

The following examples illustrate these formulae involving compound interest.

EXAMPLE 1

An investment of £500 is made in an account yielding 7% interest per annum. Find the total investment after four years and calculate the amount of interest earned during this period.

Now in this example, we have $P = 500$ and $r = 7\%$. Over a four-year period ($n = 4$) the total amount invested is found as follows:

$$A = P(1 + r/100)^n$$

$$= 500(1 + 7/100)^4$$

$$= 500(1 + 0.07)^4$$

$$= 500(1.3108)$$

$$= 655.4$$

So the value of the investment at the end of four years is £655.40. Consequently, we see that the initial investment has earned £155.40 interest over the four-year period.

EXAMPLE 2

Consider an investment of $1000 at an interest rate of 6% per annum. The interest is paid into the account on a quarterly basis. The amount accrued in the investment after five years is found by the formula:

$$A = P\left(1 + \frac{r}{100m}\right)^{nm}$$

where $P = 1000$, $r = 6\%$, $n = 5$, $m = 4$ (4 periods per year). Therefore,

$$A = 1000\left(1 + \frac{6}{100 * 4}\right)^{4 * 5}$$

$$= 1000(1 + 0.015)^{20}$$

$$= 1000 * 1.3469$$

$$= \$1346.90$$

Notice how this compares with the same investment where the interest is paid annually. In this case the amount after five years would be:

$$A = 1000\left(1 + \frac{6}{100}\right)^5$$

$$= \$1338.20$$

Thus, even when the annual interest rate stays the same, an increase in the number of payment periods will improve the overall return on investment. The reader may wish to calculate the amount accruing for this investment if the interest is paid on a monthly basis.

EXAMPLE 3

Consider an initial investment of £500 in an account that yields 10% annual interest. At the end of each year a further £100 is invested. Consider the amount that has accrued after the first four years.

At end of first year, amount accrued $= 500(1 + 10/100)^1 = 550$

An additional £100 is then invested giving a total of £650.

At the end of year 2 the amount $= 650(1 + 10/100)^1 = 715$

A further £100 is invested, bringing the total up to £815.

At the end of year 3 the amount $= 815(1 + 10/100)^1 = 896.50$

With an additional £100 the amount has increased to £996.50.

At the end of year 4, the amount $= 996.5(1 + 10/100)^1 = 1096.15$

This figure combined with an additional investment of £100 at the end of the fourth year gives a total amount of £1196.15 obtained from investing a total of £900 over the four-year period.

4.3   Exercises: simple and compound interest

1.(E)   Calculate the amount of simple interest earned for each of the following investments over the time periods specified:

  (i) £10 000 at 5% per year over 4 years,
 (ii) £6000 at 12% per year over 18 months,
(iii) £2500 at 8% per year over $6\frac{1}{2}$ years.

2.(I)   The table below shows the projected amounts accumulated in an investment after a given number of years subject to an initial lump sum of £1000 invested.

Value at end of year	Annual compound interest rate			
	2%	4%	6%	8%
1	£1020		£1060	
2	£1040.40	£1081.60		£1166.40
3		£1124.86	£1191.02	£1259.71
4	£1082.43	£1169.86		

(i) Use the compound interest formula to fill the gaps in this table.

(ii) Use the table to find the final accrued value of the following investments:
- (a) £2000 at 4% per annum over three years,
- (b) £10 000 invested over four years at 8% per year,
- (c) £500 over two years at 6% per annum.

3.(I) Find the amount accrued for each of the following investments, assuming that the interest earned is paid monthly and added to the initial investment.

(i) £4000 invested at 6% per annum over 18 months,

(ii) £1000 invested at 2% per month over three years.

4.4   Annual percentage rate (APR)

The annual percentage rate (usually denoted by APR) is the true interest paid for a loan, or earned by an investment, taking into account the compounding of interest over a variety of time periods. For instance, in the previous section we considered a problem of calculating the amount of annual compound interest assuming that quarterly adjustments are made. In many circumstances, an investment will accrue interest on a monthly basis although an annual rate of interest is specified. By law, in the UK, the APR must be specified for such investments, in order that a true comparison of a range of investment opportunities or loan options can be made.

EXAMPLE 1

Consider an investment of £100 at an interest rate of 6% per year in which the interest is calculated and paid monthly. The 6% rate specified is the so-called **nominal rate of interest** and does not realistically indicate the amount of interest earned for such an investment.

In this example, we have the principal $P = £100$, $r = 6\%$ and the number of payments per year is $m = 12$.

Over a one-year period ($n = 1$) the amount accrued is found by the formulae:

$$A = P\left(1 + \frac{r}{100m}\right)^{nm}$$

$$= 100\left(1 + \frac{6}{100 * 12}\right)^{1 * 12}$$

$$= 100(1.005)^{12}$$

$$= £106.17$$

Therefore the £100 investment has earned £6.17 over the year. Therefore, the APR is 6.17%.

EXAMPLE 2

A credit card company charges 2.4% per month on outstanding loans. The nominal interest rate is $2.4 * 12 = 28.8\%$ per year. However, this is not the true rate of interest paid by users of this credit card. The true rate, as specified by the APR, can be found as follows:

Consider a debt of $1 over a year. We have $P = 1$, $n = 1$, $m = 12$ and $r = 28.8\%$, giving an accrued amount of

$$A = P\left(1 + \frac{r}{100m}\right)^{nm}$$

$$= 1 * \left(1 + \frac{28.8}{100 * 12}\right)^{1 * 12}$$

$$= (1.024)^{12}$$

$$= \$1.3292$$

This indicates that the 'true' rate of interest (the APR) charged on this loan is 32.93%.

It should be noted that the basic compound interest formula can be used in this type of example. Here we are given that the monthly interest rate is 2.4%, and with an initial sum of $1 invested over twelve months we have:

$$A = P(1 + r/100)^n$$

$$= 1(1 + 2.4/100)^{12}$$

$$= (1.024)^{12}$$

$$= \$1.3292, \text{ as found using the alternative approach.}$$

4.5   Net present value (NPV)

In this section we will consider the amount of investment required in order to accumulate a specified total investment at a given future point in time. For instance, if we require £500 in two years' time, then what figure needs to be invested now in order to achieve this? This figure is called the present value of the future requirement. The compound interest formula can be used to obtain the present value. The standard formula evaluates the value of a future investment from a given present value. Therefore, if this formula is reversed we can obtain a formula for the present value based on a future requirement.

For instance, we know that $A = P(1 + r/100)^n$, where P is the present value and A is the accumulated (or future) value. Rearranging this formula we obtain:

$$P = A * \frac{1}{(1 + r/100)^n}$$

An alternative expression is the net present value (NPV), which is found by subtracting the initial investment from the future value. Thus, the

$$NPV = A * \frac{1}{(1 + r/100)^n} - P$$

where P denotes the present value and A the future value.

The ideas of present values relate to calculations involved in **discounting**. The process of discounting considers the value of money going backwards in time. This compares with the ideas of compounding where we consider the value of money going forward in time.

EXAMPLE I

An investment offers a fixed rate of return of 8% per annum over five years. Let us consider the figure that would need to be invested now in order to accrue £2000 at the end of the period.

We have $A = 2000$, $r = 8\%$ and $n = 5$

Therefore the present value can be calculated as follows:

$$P = A * \frac{1}{(1 + r/100)^n}$$

$$= 2000 * \frac{1}{(1 + 0.08)^5}$$

$$= 2000 * \frac{1}{1.469328}$$

$$= £1361.17$$

Therefore, if £1361.17 is invested now, then in five years time this will be worth £2000.

EXAMPLE 2

Assuming a compound interest rate of 6% per year consider two alternative schemes for investing a specific lump sum. The first scheme yields £1000 after three years, whereas the second provides £1200 after five years. These two schemes can be compared by considering the NPV in each case.

For the first scheme, the present value,

$$P = A * \frac{1}{(1 + r/100)^n}$$

$$= 1000 * \frac{1}{(1.06)^3} = £839.62$$

Alternatively, in the second scheme, the present value is found by

$$P = A * \frac{1}{(1 + r/100)^n} = 1200 * \frac{1}{(1.06)^5} = £896.71$$

Therefore, it can be seen that the present value for the second scheme is higher than the first. Thus, using these calculations the second investment seems to provide an improved yield. It should be noted that in practice a number of factors need to be considered before determining the most appropriate investment. These ideas will be explored in later sections in this chapter.

EXAMPLE 3

Consider an investment of $1000 that provides a lump sum of $2000 after four years. Assuming an annual discount rate of 8% the net present value can be evaluated as follows:

$$NPV = A * \frac{1}{(1 + r/100)^n} - P$$

where P = present value = initial investment = $1000
A = final value of investment = $2000
r = discount rate = 8%
n = number of periods = 4

Therefore the NPV is found as follows:

$$NPV = A * \frac{1}{(1 + r/100)^n} - P$$

$$= 2000 * \frac{1}{(1 + 8/100)^4} - 1000$$

$$= \frac{2000}{(1.3605)} - 1000$$

$$= 1470.05 - 1000$$

$$= \$470.05$$

Thus, assuming the 8% discount rate is a reasonable estimate, the investment is still a profitable project, though of course this may need to be compared with alternative investments to determine whether the NPV is optimised.

EXAMPLE 4

Consider a situation where £100 is required at the end of a period of investment. To calculate the amount required to invest now, we use the present value formula as shown in the previous examples.

Thus, assuming an annual interest rate of 10% over three years, the present value is found as follows:

$$P = A * \frac{1}{(1 + r/100)^n} = 100 * \frac{1}{(1.1)^3} = 100 * \frac{1}{1.331} = 100 * 0.751 = £75.10$$

Thus, an investment of £75.10 now would yield £100 in three years' time. There is a **discount factor** of 0.751 associated with this investment. The discount factor is simply the value of $1/(1 + r/100)^n = 0.751$ in this example.

In general, the calculations involved with discounting can be complex and discount tables can be used to assist in the process. The discount table would simply provide discount values corresponding to a variety of interest rates over a range of time periods. For instance, the following table shows the discount factors for interest rates between 4% and 10%, over periods from 1 to 5 years.

Number of years	Annual interest rate			
	4%	6%	8%	10%
1	0.962	0.943	0.926	0.909
2	0.925	0.890	0.857	0.826
3	0.889	0.840	0.794	0.751
4	0.855	0.792	0.735	0.683
5	0.822	0.747	0.681	0.621

Such a table can be used to estimate the amount of investment required in order to achieve a specified amount within a given time period. For instance, if a sum of £500 is required in five years' time on an investment gaining 6% interest, then the amount required to be invested is found from the table as follows: An investment over five years at an interest rate of 6% has a discount factor of 0.747 as shown in the table. Therefore, the amount needed to be invested now to obtain £500 is $0.747 * 500 = £373.50$.

4.6 Exercises: APR and present value

1.(E) Calculate the annual percentage rate (APR) based on the following information where the interest rates are quoted per year. In each case, find the amount accrued in the investment at the end of the year.

(i) Invest £100 at a nominal interest rate of 6% paid monthly.
(ii) Invest £500 at a nominal interest rate of 10% paid quarterly.
(iii) Invest £1000 at a nominal interest rate of 7% paid every six months.

2.(I) Estimate the amount of investment required now in order to accrue the following lump sums at the end of the specified periods assuming that any interest is added to the investment at the end of each year:
(i) $2000 after two years at 10% per year,
(ii) $5000 after three years at 6% per year.

3.(I) Find the amount of investment required now in order to accrue a sum of £1000 after the given periods:

(i) five years at 4% per year,
(ii) two years at 7% per year,
(iii) six years at 10% per year.

4.(I) Find the NPV for each of the following investments and comment on which investment seems to provide the best yield:

(i) Current investment of £1000 yielding £1600 in two years assuming a discount rate of 6%.
(ii) Current investment of £3000 yielding £6000 after four years assuming a discount factor of 10%.
(iii) Current investment of £10 000 yielding £24 000 after six years assuming a discount factor of 8%.

4.7	**Depreciation**

The depreciation of an item can be evaluated in a similar way to compound interest methods. If the value of an item (or asset) reduces by a fixed percentage rate (denoted by r) per period, then the value of the item after n periods is found by the following formula:

$$A_n = A_0(1 - r/100)^n$$

where A_0 is the current value and A_n is the value after n periods. The value r is known as the **depreciation rate**.

This formula can be rearranged to give an expression for the depreciation rate as shown below:

$$r = 100[1 - \sqrt[n]{(A_n/A_0)}]$$

The following examples illustrate these formulae involving depreciation.

EXAMPLE 1

An item of machinery for the preparation of dough for baking bread at the Thornberry bakery company is currently valued at $300 000. Assuming a depreciation rate of 10% per year, estimate the value of this machinery after four years.

In this example, we have the following:

The current value $= A_0 = 300\ 000$

Depreciation rate $= r = 10\%$

Number of years $= n = 4$

Using the depreciation formula we have:

$$A_n = A_0(1 - r/100)^n$$
$$= 300\ 000(1 - 10/100)^4$$
$$= 300\ 000(0.9)^4$$
$$= 300\ 000 * 0.6561$$
$$= \$196\ 830$$

Thus, the value of this item of machinery after four years will be $196 830, giving a total reduction of $103 170 during this period.

EXAMPLE 2

An item that was purchased two years ago for £2000 is now valued at £1200. Evaluate the annual depreciation rate for this item.

The depreciation rate can be calculated by the following formula:

$$r = 100[1 - \sqrt[n]{(A_n/A_0)}]$$
$$= 100[1 - \sqrt[2]{(1200/2000)}]$$
$$= 100[1 - \sqrt[2]{0.6}]$$
$$= 100[1 - 0.775]$$
$$= 100 * 0.225$$
$$= 22.5$$

The value of the item given has depreciated at an annual rate of 22.5%.

4.8 Annuities and sinking funds

An annuity is a scheme in which a fixed lump sum of money is paid, and in return a lump sum or a number of regular payments are received for a specified length of time. For instance, a self-employed individual may wish to pay a lump sum into an annuity in order to obtain a monthly pension payable over a given period.

A sinking fund is an alternative version of the annuity, where a fixed sum of money is paid in at regular intervals in order to achieve a specified goal at a given point in time.

Some of the formulae relating to these areas can be complicated. However, it is useful to refer to one specific formula in this context as summarised below.

Consider a lump sum of A invested at the beginning of a period. If I is an amount added or subtracted from this investment at the end of each year, then the amount accrued at the end of n years is shown by the following formula:

$$S = A(1 + r/100)^n + \frac{I(1 + r/100)^n - I}{r/100}$$

The first element in this expression calculates the accumulated value from the initial investment (A) and the second element calculates the amount accrued from the regular payments.

This formula can be rearranged to give an expression for the regular payments. If an initial amount (A) is invested, at an interest rate of r per year, then in order to achieve a sum of S after n years, a regular payment (I) at the end of each year is required, where I is given by the formula:

$$I = \frac{r/100[S - A(1 + r/100)^n]}{(1 + r/100)^n - 1}$$

This formula can be simplified slightly by using the alternative expression for the interest rate $R = r/100$. The expression for the regular investment amount I is then given by:

$$I = \frac{R[S - A(1 + R)^n]}{(1 + R)^n - 1}$$

The following examples illustrate these annuity formulae.

EXAMPLE 1

Consider an initial investment of £1000 followed by regular payments at the end of each year of £500 for the next four years. Assuming an annual interest rate of 10% the value of the investment at the end of this period is found by the formula:

$$S = A(1 + r/100)^n + \frac{I(1 + r/100)^n - I}{r/100}$$

where

A = initial amount = £1000
I = regular annual payments = £500
r = annual rate of interest = 10%
n = number of years = 4

Substituting these values into the expression we obtain:

$$S = 1000(1 + 10/100)^4 + \frac{500(1 + 10/100)^4 - 500}{10/100}$$

$$= 1000(1.4641) + \frac{500(1.4641) - 500}{0.1}$$

$$= 1464.1 + 2320.5$$

$$= £3784.60$$

Note that the two elements of the formula evaluate the amount accrued for each element of the investment. For instance, in this example, the original payment of £1000 accumulates to £1464.10 after the four years. Similarly, the annual payments of £500 achieve a final amount of £2320.50. (This includes a final payment of £500 at the end of the fourth year.) Therefore, the total value of the investment is the combined total of these two values.

EXAMPLE 2

If an initial sum of £10 000 is placed into an account yielding an annual interest rate of 6% and £1500 is taken out at the end of each year, how much is left at the end of five years?

In this case we have $A = 10\ 000$, $r = 6\%$, $n = 5$, and the regular payment is a negative value since it is a withdrawal from the account. Thus, $I = -1500$, and the remaining investment after the period specified is found as follows:

$$S = A(1 + r/100)^n + \frac{I(1 + r/100)^n - I}{r/100}$$

$$= 10\ 000(1 + 6/100)^5 + \frac{-1500(1 + 6/100)^5 - (-1500)}{6/100}$$

$$= 10\ 000(1.33823) + \frac{-1500(1.33823) + 1500}{0.06}$$

$$= 13\ 382.30 - 8455.75$$

$$= 4926.55$$

Therefore, after the period specified there remains £4926.55 in the account. Note that the two elements of this answer are as follows: The value £13 382.30 is the amount that the initial investment of £10 000 would be worth after five years. The value £8455.75 includes the amounts withdrawn during this period (five lots of £1500) and any interest that has been lost because of these withdrawals.

EXAMPLE 3

An investor wishes to invest $5000 now, followed by a regular sum of money at the end of each year over the next six years. Assuming an interest rate of 8% how much would need to be invested at the end of each year in order to obtain $20 000 in six years' time?

Now in this case we need to use the formula giving an expression for the regular payment (I) as shown below:

$$I = \frac{r/100[S - A(1 + r/100)^n]}{(1 + r/100)^n - 1}$$

where, in this example, $r=8\%$ and S is the required sum $= £20\ 000$,

$A =$ initial investment $= \$5000$ and $n=6$ years.

The value of

$$\begin{aligned} I &= \frac{8/100[20\ 000 - 5000(1 + 8/100)^6]}{(1 + 8/100)^6 - 1} \\ &= \frac{0.08[20\ 000 - 5000(1.58687)]}{1.58687 - 1} \\ &= \frac{0.08(20\ 000 - 7934.35)}{0.58687} \\ &= 1644.75 \end{aligned}$$

Therefore, an annual payment of $1644.75 is required in order to build up the investment to a value of $20 000 after six years.

EXAMPLE 4

An annuity is available from a particular investment company where an initial lump sum payment of £12 000 will provide £2000 at the end of each year for the next ten years. Investigate whether this is a sound investment, assuming a nominal interest rate of 7%.

At first sight we see that the investment looks reasonable. For an investment of £12 000 we receive £20 000 in instalments. However, owing to the interest rates involved, the problem is more complex than this. In order to consider this let us evaluate what an initial investment should be in order to receive ten instalments of £2000.

In this case we have the following values:

The regular payment (i.e. withdrawal) is $I = -2000$
Interest rate $r = 7\%$

The final value of the investment is $S = 0$ since after ten years the investment will be finished. The number of years $n = 10$.

These values can be substituted into the annuity formula:

$$S = A(1 + r/100)^n + \frac{I(1 + r/100)^n - I}{r/100}$$

Thus, we have:

$$0 = A(1 + 7/100)^{10} + \frac{-2000(1 + 7/100)^{10} - (-2000)}{7/100}$$

$$0 = A(1.96715) + \frac{-2000(1.96715) + 2000}{0.07}$$

$$0 = A(1.96715) - 27\,632.86$$

Thus, rearranging this equation we have:

$$A(1.96715) = 27\,632.86$$

Therefore, $A = £14\,047.15$

Consequently, this annuity is worth a lump sum payment of £14 047.15, assuming that the interest rate is constant as given. Therefore, the annuity offered in which an initial payment of £12 000 is required seems to be a good investment.

Clearly, the final decision in determining whether a specific investment opportunity is reasonable will depend on other factors, including inflationary measures, and comparison with alternative schemes offered by different companies.

EXAMPLE 5

Calculate the annual repayment paid at the end of each year required to pay off a mortgage of £60 000 over 15 years, assuming an interest rate of 5%.

In this example, we have the initial sum $A = £60\,000$, and the sum at the end of the period is $S = 0$. The required repayment period is $n = 15$ years, and the interest rate $r = 5\%$. Therefore we have:

$$S = A(1 + r/100)^n + \frac{I(1 + r/100)^n - I}{r/100}$$

$$0 = 60\,000(1 + 5/100)^{15} + \frac{I(1 + 5/100)^{15} - I}{5/100}$$

$$0 = 60\,000(2.078928) + \frac{I(2.078928) - I}{0.05}$$

$$0 = 124\,735.68 + I(21.57856)$$

Therefore,

$$I = \frac{-124\,735.68}{21.57856} = -5780.54$$

The mortgage will be paid off by payments of £5780.54 at the end of each year over fifteen years. The total cost of this mortgage is $15 * £5780.54 = £86\,708.10$.

4.9   Exercises: depreciation and annuities

1.(E)   An item costing £5000 depreciates at the rate of 6% per year. Find the value of this item at the end of years 2, 3 and 4.

2.(I)   A machine that cost $10 000 when purchased three years ago is now valued at only $4000. Find the annual rate of depreciation for this item.

3.(I)   Find the value of an investment at the end of a given period based on the following information:

  (i) An initial invesment of £1000 followed by annual payments of £400 for three years at an interest rate of 8% per year.

  (ii) No initial payment, with £1000 paid in at the end of each year for five years at 4% per year.

  (iii) An initial investment of £5000 with £1000 taken out at the end of each year for four years at 6% annual interest rate.

4.(I)   After an initial investment of £2000, find the amount required to pay in at the end of each year in order to accumulate the given sum after a number of years:

  (i) £5000 after four years, assuming an annual interest rate of 8%,

  (ii) £10 000 after six years at 10% per year,

  (iii) £10 000 after six years at 4% per year.

5.(I)   Calculate the annual repayments required in order to pay off an outstanding loan over the given period:

  (i) £50 000 over 20 years at 8% per year,

  (ii) £40 000 over ten years at 6% per year,

  (iii) £25 000 over four years at 10% per year.

4.10   Investment appraisal

We can use the techniques involving compounding, depreciation and present values introduced in earlier sections of this chapter in order to investigate the viability of specific investments, or to compare a range of alternative investment options.

    An additional technique used in investment appraisal is the idea of an **internal rate of return (IRR)**. This is the percentage return on an investment calculated from the net present value and is often referred to as the **yield**. More technically, this can be described as the discount rate for a project which gives the net present value of zero. This seems rather a strange definition however, the following examples will illustrate the application of this value. In general, if A_0 is the amount invested now, and A_n denotes the value of the investment after n years, then we have the formula:

$$A_0 = A_n * \frac{1}{(1 + r/100)^n} = \frac{A_n}{(1 + r/100)^n}$$

This formula is given as the present value formula in an earlier section. If A_0 and A_n are known, then we can determine the value of r which denotes the internal rate of return.

This formula can be generalised by consideration of returns on the investment at various periods. For instance, if an initial investment of A_0 gives a return of A_1 at the end of the first year, A_2 at the end of the second, and so on, the general formula used to evaluate r would be:

$$A_0 = \frac{A_1}{(1 + r/100)^1} + \frac{A_2}{(1 + r/100)^2} + \frac{A_3}{(1 + r/100)^3} + \cdots$$

The evaluation of r from this complex formula becomes extremely difficult, and usually estimation methods need to be adopted. In practice, we consider a range of rates of yield, and find the NPV by comparing the present value with the initial investment. To obtain the best estimate of the internal rate of return (r) we consider one value of r that gives a small positive NPV and a second value of r that gives a small negative NPV. Then we can use graphical methods to estimate the rate of return between these two figures that gives a zero NPV.

EXAMPLE 1

Consider an initial investment of $1000 on machinery that is expected to yield $1600 at the end of the second year. The internal rate of return (r) on this investment can be evaluated from the following:

$$A_0 = \frac{A_n}{(1 + r/100)^n}$$

where $A_0 = 1000$, $A_n = 1600$ and $n = 2$. Therefore we have

$$1000 = \frac{1600}{(1 + r/100)^2}$$

Rearranging this equation we can solve for r and obtain $r = 26.5$. Therefore, the internal rate of return from this investment is 26.5% per annum.

EXAMPLE 2

Consider an initial investment of £2400 that yields £1200 at the end of year 1, £800 at the end of year 2, and £500 at the end of year 3. The internal rate of return (r) can be found from the equation:

$$A_0 = \frac{A_1}{(1+r/100)^1} + \frac{A_2}{(1+r/100)^2} + \frac{A_3}{(1+r/100)^3}$$

where $A_0 = 2400$, $A_1 = 1200$, $A_2 = 800$ and $A_3 = 500$ as shown below:

$$2400 = \frac{1200}{(1+r/100)^1} + \frac{800}{(1+r/100)^2} + \frac{500}{(1+r/100)^3}$$

This equation is difficult to solve for r and a graphical method could be used. We have that the NPV is:

$$NPV = \frac{1200}{(1+r/100)^1} + \frac{800}{(1+r/100)^2} + \frac{500}{(1+r/100)^3} - 2400$$

Consider values of r that make the NPV close to zero. (This is an ideal application of computers and will be demonstrated later in the chapter.) For instance, by trial and error we find that if $r=4\%$ then the NPV $=-62.01$, whereas for $r=2\%$ the NPV $= +16.57$. Therefore, the IRR lies between 2% and 4%. A simple graphical method can be used to obtain an estimate of the IRR as shown in Figure 4.1. Values of r between 2% and 10% have been plotted using the calculations similar to those introduced above. From the graph shown in Figure 4.1 we see that an estimate of the

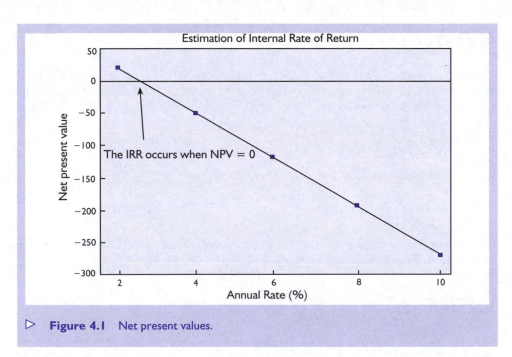

▷   **Figure 4.1**   Net present values.

IRR is just over 2%, at approximately 2.5%. In other words, the yield on this investment is very small and it is likely that other areas will need to be investigated in order to determine a preferred investment plan. A more accurate estimate could be obtained by estimating the NPV for values of r at closer intervals. For instance, if the NPV is evaluated for values of $r = 2\%, 2.2\%, 2.4\%, 2.6\%, 2.8\%$ and 3%, then an improved solution can be obtained. However, in practice, accuracy of this degree may not be required unless there are two or more options which produce very similar yields.

EXAMPLE 3

A consultant at the Parker & Jameson group is assisting a company to compare a range of investment opportunities. One of the factors that can be used is to compare the IRR of the various options. Consider the two options described below. Two projects are under consideration, each involving an initial capital expenditure of £1 million. Estimates of the contribution to profit each year over the next four years are shown in

| Projects | Contribution to profit at year end (£1000s) | | | |
	1997	1998	1999	2000
A	200	400	600	250
B	450	500	250	150

the following table:

A simple comparison of these projects could involve looking at the total expected profit over the four-year period. In this case, project A yields a total of £1 450 000, whereas project B yields £1 350 000. Consequently, it looks as though project A is a better investment. However, of course this does not take into account the value of money over time. Project B generates a larger profit in the early years, whereas a significant proportion of the profits from project A is achieved later. The method of evaluating the IRR could provide a useful comparison of these two options.

For project A, the NPV is calculated as shown below. The figures shown are given in £1000s. Thus, the initial investment of £1 million is shown as 1000 in the calculation.

$$\text{NPV} = \frac{200}{(1+r/100)} + \frac{400}{(1+r/100)^2} + \frac{600}{(1+r/100)^3} + \frac{250}{(1+r/100)^4} - 1000$$

The value of the NPV can be found for a variety of values of r. For example, when $r = 12\%$ the NPV $= 83.4$, $r = 14\%$ gives NPV $= 36.2$, and $r = 16\%$ gives NPV $= -7.9$. An estimate of IRR using these values will be approximately 15.6%.

Similarly, in project B, the NPV is as follows:

$$\text{NPV} = \frac{450}{(1+r/100)} + \frac{500}{(1+r/100)^2} + \frac{250}{(1+r/100)^3} + \frac{150}{(1+r/100)^4} - 1000$$

Calculations of the NPV for different values of r give the following: NPV = 37.0 at $r = 14\%$, NPV = 2.5 at $r = 16\%$, and NPV = -30.0 at $r = 18\%$. This shows that the IRR is approximately 16.2%.

Therefore, a simple comparison of the internal rate of return from these projects shows that project B has a higher projected yield. The company would be advised to consider this project in preference to project A.

4.11   Exercises: investment appraisal

1.(E) Find the IRR for each of the three projects described, assuming that the initial investment is £10 000. The details given below show the estimated yields from these investments at the end of specified years (note that the three parts should be treated as different investments):

  (i) Year 1: £12 000
 (ii) Year 2: £11 000
(iii) Year 3: £14 000

2.(I) Using a graphical method, or otherwise, estimate the IRR for each of the following investments:

  (i) Investment = £5000
       Yield at end of each year is: Year 1: £4000 and Year 2: £3000.
 (ii) Investment = £20 000
       Yield at end of each year is: Year 1: £12 000, Year 2: £8000 and Year 3: £4000.

3.(I) The Production Director at the Thornberry bakery company needs to make a decision on the acquisition of new technology in baking systems. Two potential systems are being considered, and the Financial Director at Thornberry has recommended that the company should base the decision on a range of factors, including the internal rate of return. The table below shows the cost of each of the systems being considered together with the expected return on investment for each system.

Project		A ($)	B($)
Initial investment		250 000	180 000
	Year 1	80 000	120 000
	Year 2	120 000	100 000
Yield at year	Year 3	100 000	90 000
end	Year 4	100 000	70 000
	Year 5	60 000	50 000

As can be seen, system A initially costs more than system B. However, this may be offset by an increased return due to the improved efficiency of the system A.

(i) Find the IRR for each project and advise the Production Director on the best option based on this information.
(ii) Comment on the use of the IRR as a measure of investment appraisal. What other factors should the Production Director consider?

4.12   Computer applications

The examples shown in this chapter involve a range of complex calculations ideally suited for the use of computer software. Applications such as the calculation of compound interest, NPV, annuities and investment appraisal can be analysed using the standard spreadsheet packages such as Lotus or Excel. The following examples illustrate a range of such applications.

EXAMPLE I

A spreadsheet package can be used to evaluate the mortgage repayments required to pay off a mortgage over a given number of periods. This type of problem is illustrated in Example 5 in Section 4.8. The basic formula used to evaluate the repayments is as follows:

$$S = A(1 + r/100)^n + \frac{I(1 + r/100)^n - I}{r/100}$$

where

A = initial value of mortgage
S = value of mortgage at end of period (= 0 for a repayment loan)
r = interest rate per period
I = regular payment per period

Substituting $S = 0$ in this equation and rearranging we have the following expression for the regular payment I as follows:

$$I = \frac{-A(1 + r/100)^n(r/100)}{(1 + r/100)^n - 1}$$

 Using the disk   Load the file called MORTGAGE.WK3 from the disk. The spreadsheet shown is displayed in Figure 4.2. The spreadsheet shown in Figure 4.2 enables the user to enter the amount of loan, the required loan period, and the annual nominal interest rate into the cells C3 to C5. The results giving the required monthly (and alternatively annual) repayments are given in the cells B9 and B10. The corresponding cells in C9 and C10 show the total amount of repayments over the full term of the loan.

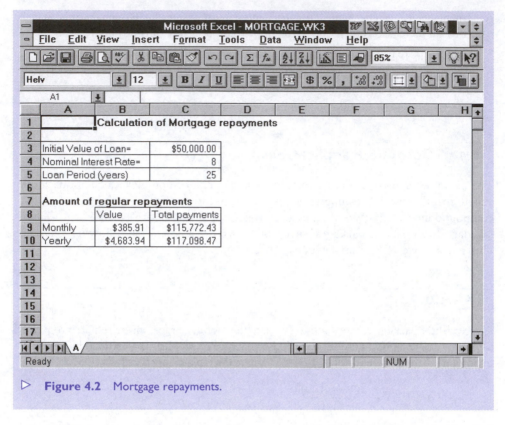

It should be noted that these repayments are calculated on the basis of a full repayment mortgage. In other words, at the end of the term specified the loan will have been fully paid. This is in contrast to an 'endowment' mortgage, in which only the interest is paid on the loan, and an endowment insurance policy is also paid which on maturity will enable the borrower to fully repay the outstanding loan.

EXAMPLE 2

The basic calculations involved in annuities and sinking funds can be complicated. Indeed, without the use of computer packages, or reference to financial tables, the calculations become impossible for anything other than those involving a small number of periods.

For example, consider the annuity formula shown below, giving the amount accrued (S) at the end of n periods, with A as the initial lump sum and I the regular payment at the end of each period.

$$S = A(1 + r/100)^n + \frac{I(1 + r/100)^n - I}{r/100}$$

Clearly, the expression $(1 + r/100)^n$ becomes difficult to calculate for large values of n without the aid of tables, sophisticated calculators or computer systems.

 Using the disk   Load the file called ANNUITY.WK3 from the disk. The spreadsheet shown is displayed in Figure 4.3. This spreadsheet enables the user to calculate the total amount accrued at the end of a specified period based on the initial sum invested, any regular repayments and interest rate used. The cells C3 to C6 contain values that can be entered by the user. The protected cells C9 to C11 contain the resulting amounts at the end of the investment period.

The user can try to enter different values in the cells C3 to C6 in order to find the resulting totals. For example, try to change the interest rate to 8%, or 6%, or 4% and look at the effect on the final values. Furthermore, consider a new annuity with the following values:

Initial sum invested = $20 000

Regular payments = $1000

Interest rate per month = 2%

Number of monthly payments = 36.

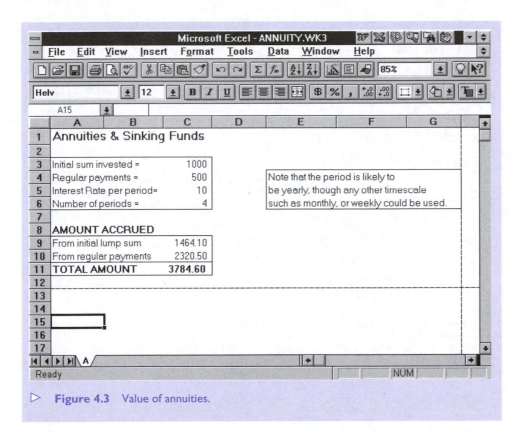

▷ **Figure 4.3**   Value of annuities.

Look at the results of this investment, and compare with the same figures paid in monthly over four or five years.

EXAMPLE 3

The calculation of the IRR involves the evaluation of the NPV, assuming a variety of discount rates. These complex calculations can best be achieved by the use of a spreadsheet package as shown in this example. Essentially, the IRR indicates the yield from an investment and is found where the NPV is zero as shown earlier in this chapter. Thus, for complex decisions, this involves the calculation of the NPV for a range of percentage rates, and an estimation of the IRR based on these values. This type of application is illustrated in the following spreadsheet.

Using the disk   Load the file called NPV1.WK3 from the disk. The spreadsheet shown on your screen is displayed in Figure 4.4. This spreadsheet evaluates the NPV for an investment based on the initial sum invested and the estimates of the likely returns over the first five years. The initial investment figure is entered in cell C3, with

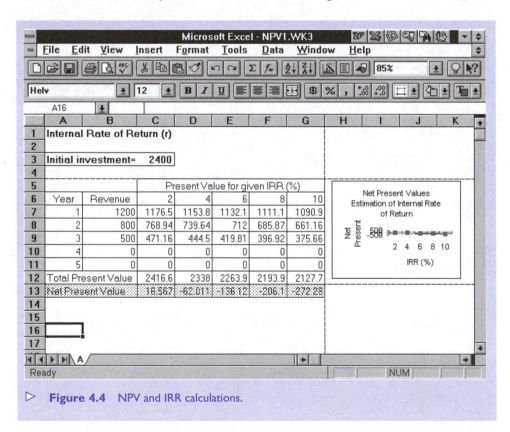

▷ **Figure 4.4**   NPV and IRR calculations.

the expected annual returns in cells B7 to B11. The discount percentage rates are entered in cells C6 to G6. These are currently the values 2% to 10%. However, these can be changed, depending on the resulting NPVs displayed in the cells C13 to G13. The aim is to look at the range of percentage rates that gives the NPV near zero. At the crossover between a positive NPV and a negative NPV (as shown between 2% and 4% in this table) the zero value will lie. This can be estimated graphically as shown in the spreadsheet.

The reader may wish to consider an initial investment of $5000, giving expected annual returns of:

Year 1: $2000,   Year 2: $2000,
Year 3: $1500,   Year 4: $1000,
Year 5: $1000.

Enter these values in the appropriate cells in the spreadsheet and use this to estimate the IRR.

4.13   Chapter summary

This chapter has considered some basic techniques involving the value of money over a period of time. Methods include those to calculate the total interest to be paid on loans using simple and compound interest formulae. The annual percentage rate (APR) is a standard method of specifying the 'real' annual interest rate to be paid. Compound interest formulae can also be modified to analyse the costs of depreciation of an asset over time. The calculation of the net present value (NPV) is used to determine the value of an investment at current prices taking into account the likely return over an extended period.

These methods can be adapted to estimate the total value of annuities in which a fixed sum is paid in and in return a lump sum or payments at regular intervals are received. A sinking fund is an alternative to this, where a regular payment is made over a given period of time in order to accumulate a specified investment at the end of a time period.

Further ideas, including the internal rate of return (IRR), to measure the yield of a given investment have been considered. The IRR is obtained by finding the discount rate for an investment which gives a NPV of zero. These complex techniques lead to the use of computer applications in order to ease calculations.

These techniques have a range of business applications including the following:

▶ Investment appraisal involving consideration of whether capital expenditure can be justified for a specific project, or providing an objective comparison of two or more projects.
▶ Financial decisions involving the costs and benefits of lending and borrowing money.
▶ Consideration of a range of accounting problems such as the valuation of assets and the use of depreciation.

4.14	**Further exercises**

1.(E) Calculate the total amount of interest earned on the following investments assuming that in each case the interest rate is quoted per annum:

(i) £1000 at a simple interest of 6% over ten years,
(ii) £500 at a simple interest of 8% over six years,
(iii) £700 at a simple interest of 9% over 30 months,
(iv) £2000 at a compound interest of 4% over three years payable yearly,
(v) £400 at a compound interest of 7.5% over four years payable yearly,
(vi) £10 000 at a compound interest of 12% over two years payable monthly.

2.(E) Calculate the APR for investments based on the following information:

(i) 6% per year payable quarterly,
(ii) 6% per year payable monthly,
(iii) 10% per year payable yearly,
(iv) 10% per year payable half yearly,
(v) 10% per year payable monthly.

3.(I) Calculate the net present value for each of the following investments and decide on which investment gives the best return assuming an annual discount rate of 8%:

(i) Invest $5000 with a return of $4000 at the end of year 1 and $2000 at the end of year 2.
(ii) Invest $10 000 with a return of $4000 at the end of the first three years.
(iii) Invest $8000 with a return of $10 000 at the end of year 2.

4.(I) (i) Use the discount factor tables given in section 4.5 of this chapter to evaluate the amount of investment required to achieve the specified amount after a given time period:

   (a) $2000 required in four years at 8% per year,
   (b) $6000 required in five years at 10% per year.

(ii) Find appropriate discount factors for the following interest rates over the specified years, and hence find the amount of investment required in order to achieve a final amount of £20 000 in each case:

   (a) 5% over three years,
   (b) 9% over four years,
   (c) 11% over six years.

5.(E) (i) Estimate the value of an asset after the specified number of years given the following annual depreciation rate:

   (a) Initial cost = £5000 after four years at 6% depreciation,

(b) initial cost = $2400 after three years at 3% depreciation,
(c) initial cost = £6400 after five years at 10% depreciation.
  (ii) Find the annual depreciation rate of an item given the following information:
    (a) initial cost = £1000, value after four years = £500,
    (b) initial cost = £4000, value after three years = £3000.

6.(I) Find the value of an investment at the end of the specified period given the following values:

  (i) Initial lump sum = £2000. £500 extra invested at the end of each year, over three years at 10% per year.
  (ii) No initial sum. £1000 invested at the end of each year for four years at 8% per year.
  (iii) Initial lump sum = £15 000. At the end of each year, £1000 is withdrawn for five years assuming 7% interest per year.
  (iv) Initial lump sum = £30 000. £500 per month is withdrawn for three years assuming 10% per year interest earned.

7.(I) Estimate the amount of each repayment required in order to pay off the following loans:

  (i) $50 000 at 6% per year paid annually over ten years,
  (ii) $100 000 at 8% per year paid half-yearly over six years,
  (iii) $40 000 at 9% per year paid monthly over four years,
  (iv) $60 000 at 8% per year paid quarterly over five years.

8.(D) A financial adviser at the Parker & Jameson consultancy group has been asked to compare a number of alternative loan schemes for capital projects. For an initial loan of £100 000 there are a number of possible alternative loan schemes available, spreading the repayments over a five year period. The repayments for this loan are summarised below:

Scheme 1: Monthly repayments. 'Low cost' initially at 4% per annum over two years, then 9% per annum for the remaining three years.

Scheme 2: Monthly repayments. A fixed nominal interest rate of 8% per year over five years.

Scheme 3: Half yearly repayments. A fixed nominal interest rate of 8.2% per year over five years.

  (i) Calculate the total amount of the repayments in each scheme. Does a comparison of these values give an indication of the best scheme?
  (ii) Calculate the NPV of each of these schemes in order to provide a comparison and comment on your preferred choice.

9.(1)   Using the disk   Load the file named NPV1.WK3 from the disk into a Lotus or Excel spreadsheet. Use this file to evaluate the net present value of the following investments:

(i) Invest £4000 with expected yields at the end of each year of £2500 in year 1 and £3000 in year 2, assuming a discount rate of 8%.

(ii) Invest $30 000 with expected yields of $10 000 at the end of the next four years assuming a discount rate of

  (a) 4% per year,
  (b) 6% per year,
  (c) 8% per year.

Comment on how the value of the NPV can be used in determining the advisability of an investment option.

Index Numbers

CHAPTER OBJECTIVES

At the end of this chapter you will be able to:

▶ understand the applications of index numbers in business

▶ use a variety of methods to calculate indices

▶ compare methods of weighting in index number construction

▶ consider methods of calculation of price and quantity indices

▶ use indices in the comparison of data

▶ describe a range of published economic indices

Introduction

In recent years index numbers have been increasingly used for business and management applications. Primarily, an index number is calculated to show the level of change in a specific value. For instance, index numbers are commonly used to indicate the change in the cost of living, share prices, industrial production output, exchange rates, in addition to many other economic and financial data. Essentially, an index number shows the percentage change in a given value over a period of time. The index obtained is a percentage of a value in a specified (base) period. This information can be very useful when comparing the changes in a number of different financial factors, or when attempting to analyse the performance of a specific factor as illustrated in the following case studies.

CASE STUDY   The British-American Parts Company Ltd

The British-American Parts Company Ltd (BAPC Ltd) is a multinational engineering organisation primarily involved in the production and sale of steel and alloy parts used in the assembly of a range of mechanical and electrical devices. BAPC has its headquarters in Chicago, with regional headquarters in Singapore for the Far East operations, and Toulouse for the Euro-African sector.

The costs of raw materials such as steel, oil and coal are important indicators for the company's profitability. The management in this company uses a variety of indices as measures of these costs in order to determine pricing strategies and long-term investment opportunities. Other indices such as those indicating the manufacturing output of the major industrial countries are closely monitored. Such indices can indicate a potential shortfall or glut in specific markets, which BAPC may be able to exploit.

The company's major production centres are located in the UK, USA, Indonesia and Nigeria. Subsidiary manufacturing sites include those in Germany, Holland, Poland and Brazil. The management in the specific countries uses indices, such as those showing changes in the national cost of living and wages, in order to back up negotiations on pay and conditions for its workforces. New pay and benefits strategies are also developed on the basis of such statistics.

CASE STUDY   The UK government statistics

In line with all of the major industrial countries around the globe, the UK government publishes a wide range of statistics indicating the growth, changes and performance of a variety of economic, financial and sociological data. Many of the statistics produced are converted into the form of indices. Such statistics are published by the Central Statistical Office (CSO) in a range of publications including the *Annual Abstract of Statistics*, *Monthly Digest of Statistics*, *Employment Gazette* and *Economic Trends*.

There is a tremendous range of data reproduced in the index number format. Common statistics are the Retail Price Index (RPI), showing changes in the cost of living, and the FT Share Index for stocks and shares prices. Other indices are calculated to show changes in factors such as manufacturing output, balance of trade, retail and wholesale trade, commodity prices and lending rates.

In addition to providing excellent information on the performance of different sectors in the country, this information can be used for political purposes by both the party in power and the opposition. Each party would stress different aspects of the indices in order to demonstrate the effectiveness or otherwise of the current government policies. Indices can be powerful tools for these purposes since they can be easily understood by the majority of people. An index number can be simply interpreted without necessarily having detailed knowledge on the actual mechanics of the calculations involved. Thus such statistics are important political tools for relaying a particular message because they can have high, immediate impact to a diverse audience. Further details on published indices in the UK and US are given in Sections 5.14 and 5.15.

5.1   Simple index numbers

An index number shows the change in a given value as a percentage of the value in a specific period. This initial period is known as the **base period**. Thus, the index number for a value in the base period would equal 100 (i.e. 100%). Other indices for different periods would indicate comparisons with the base period. For instance, an index for the price of a given commodity in 1999 is 120 compared with the base period of 1997. This shows that the price of this commodity has increased by 20% over the period 1997 to 1999. Similarly, an index over the same period for a second commodity is found to be 95. This shows that the commodity has decreased in value by 5% over this period. Thus, the index provides a simple method of illustrating the change in a given value such as price.

In general, when calculating a price index, if p_0 is the price in the base period and p_i is the price in the current period, then an index showing the change of price between the base period and the current period is as follows:

$$\text{Simple price index} = \frac{p_i}{p_0} * 100$$

The formula shows that the current price is divided by the base price, and this ratio is then converted into a percentage by multiplying by 100.

Definition: *An index number shows the change in value between the current period and a base period as a percentage. The index in the base period is usually set to 100.*

EXAMPLE 1

The table below shows the prices of crude oil per barrel over each year between 1995 and 2000.

Year:	1995	1996	1997	1998	1999	2000
Price per barrel ($):	20	22	21	18	23	25

Using 1995 as the base year, we can calculate the price indices for each subsequent year as shown below:

In 1995 (the base period) the price index is assumed to be 100.

In 1996 the price index is calculated as follows:

$$\frac{p_i}{p_0} * 100 = \frac{\text{price in 1996}}{\text{price in 1995}} * 100 = \frac{22}{20} * 100 = 110$$

This index for 1996 shows that the price of crude oil has increased by 10% since the base period (1995).

$$\text{Similarly, in 1997 the index} = \frac{\text{price in 1997}}{\text{price in 1995}} * 100 = \frac{21}{20} * 100 = 105$$

$$\text{In 1998, the price index} = \frac{\text{price in 1998}}{\text{price in 1995}} * 100 = \frac{18}{20} * 100 = 90$$

This index shows that the price in 1998 has dropped by 10% since the base period of 1995.

In 1999 the price index is $= \frac{23}{20} * 100 = 115$
Finally, in the year 2000 the price index $= \frac{25}{20} * 100 = 125$

Thus, we have a sequence of price indices for crude oil using 1995 as the base year as shown below:

Year:	1995	1996	1997	1998	1999	2000
Price index:	100	110	105	90	115	125

EXAMPLE 2

The table below shows the index of industrial production in the UK during the period 1996 to 1999, with 1996 as the base year.

Year:	1996	1997	1998	1999
Production index:	100	104	110	108

All the values shown are percentages using 1996 as the base. For instance, the industrial production has increased by 10% over the two years 1996 to 1998.

These indices can be converted to show the year by year changes in production. For example, consider the period 1997 to 1998, with indices of 104 and 110 respectively. The actual percentage change over this one-year period can be calculated as follows:

Index for 1998 based on 1997 $= \frac{110}{104} * 100 = 105.8$

This shows that the production output has increased by 5.8% between 1997 and 1998.

Similarly, comparing the indices in 1998 and 1999 we have

$$\frac{108}{110} * 100 = 98.2$$

This shows that during the period 1998 to 1999, production fell by 1.8%.

5.2 Chain base indices

In the previous section the examples used showed indices calculated in relation to a **fixed base** period. As shown in the second example it is possible to consider different base periods in the calculation of index numbers. The following examples explore this approach further, and compare two methods in index number construction. The two approaches considered are:

Fixed base index: each value is compared with a value in the same base period.

Chain base index: each value is compared with a value in the preceding period.

Again, using the chain based approach the resulting index is shown as a percentage.

EXAMPLE 1

Consider the following table showing average weekly wages for employees in the manufacturing sector in the USA:

Year:	1995	1996	1997	1998
Average weekly wage ($):	420	438	446	450

Using 1995 as the base period, the fixed base indices would be calculated as follows:

1996: $\frac{438}{420} * 100 = 104.3$

1997: $\frac{446}{420} * 100 = 106.2$

1998: $\frac{450}{420} * 100 = 107.1$

Alternatively, the chain base indices are calculated on the basis of the preceding period as shown below:

1996: $\frac{438}{420} * 100 = 104.3$

1997: $\frac{446}{438} * 100 = 101.8$

1998: $\frac{450}{446} * 100 = 100.9$

The chain base indices calculated here show the percentage changes year on year. These values give a much clearer indication of the annual changes in the weekly earnings. For instance, the chain base index in 1998 of 100.9 shows clearly that wages have not changed significantly over the year since 1997. The fixed base index for 1998 of 107.1

does not show this, and reference must be made to the index in the previous year (=106.2) to indicate that no real change has taken place.

However, chain base indices are poor at indicating real differences between a sequence of years. For example, the years 1997 and 1998 have chain base indices of 101.8 and 100.9 respectively. Such values can easily be misinterpreted as showing that the wages in 1998 are less than in 1997, which is clearly not the case. Thus, care must be taken in the analysis of such values and, in general, the fixed base index is the preferred method in most practical applications.

> **Definition:** *A fixed base index is calculated by comparing each successive value with a fixed figure in the base period. An alternative approach is the chain base index, which compares each value with its predecessor.*

5.3   Indices for grouped data

The previous sections have shown how to calculate indices of single values over a time period. One of the major problems with the evaluation of indices occurs when there are groups of data to compare. For instance, to compare the cost of living between two years it is necessary to consider the change in prices of many different items such as food and drink, housing, electricity, clothing and transportation. The changes in each of these items will affect the overall cost of living, and therefore a method of combining these changes into a single indicator must be found.

Consider the calculation of a price index for a combination of goods. Two simple approaches to the calculation of a single index combining all the changes for individual items are the **simple mean** and **simple aggregate** methods. These methods are briefly described below.

Using the same notation, the current price of an item is p_i, with the base price for the item equal to p_0.

The **simple mean index** is calculated by finding the average of all the individual price relatives. In other words, the ratio of the current price to the base price for each item is calculated. These ratios (or so-called 'relatives') are summed and the result is divided by the number of values (denoted by n). The following formula can be used:

$$\text{Simple mean index} = \frac{\sum (p_i/p_0)}{n} * 100$$

Alternatively, the **simple aggregate index** can be calculated. This is found by comparing the sum of the current prices with the sum of the base prices. These summations are divided and the result multiplied by 100 to convert to a percentage. The following formula is used:

$$\text{Simple aggregate index} = \frac{\sum p_i}{\sum p_0} * 100$$

These are demonstrated in the following example.

EXAMPLE 1

The management team at the British-American Parts Company Ltd (BAPC Ltd) closely monitors the price changes for a range of commodities, including iron, steel and copper. The average prices in 1998 and 1999 for this group of commodities are shown in the following table.

Commodity	Commodity price per tonne ($)	
	1998	1999
Iron	25	24
Steel	34	38
Copper	64	80

The combined index for prices of the three commodities in 1999 based on 1998 is calculated as follows:

$$\text{Simple mean index} = \frac{\sum (p_i/p_0)}{n} * 100$$

$$= \frac{(24/25 + 38/34 + 80/64)}{3} * 100$$

$$= \frac{(0.96 + 1.118 + 1.25)}{3} * 100$$

$$= \frac{3.328}{3} * 100$$

$$= 110.9$$

This method indicates that commodity prices have increased by an average of 10.9% during the period indicated.

Alternatively, the

$$\text{Simple aggregate index} = \frac{\sum p_i}{\sum p_0} * 100$$

$$= \frac{(24 + 38 + 80)}{(25 + 34 + 64)} * 100$$

$$= \frac{142}{123} * 100$$

$$= 115.4$$

Using this approach, the combined index indicates that commodity prices have increased by 15.4%.

As seen in this example, there can be a significant difference between the results obtained using the two alternative methods. Consequently, it is difficult for the management team at BAPC to interpret such results. Generally, care must be taken in using the most appropriate method in the calculation of combined indices. Improved methods will be considered in the following sections.

Definition: *One method of evaluating an index for a combined set of items is the simple aggregate index found by the formula:*

$$\text{Simple aggregate index} = \frac{\sum p_i}{\sum p_0} * 100$$

where p_i is the current price and p_0 is the base price for each item.
   An alternative is the simple mean index found as follows:

$$\text{Simple mean index} = \frac{\sum (p_i/p_0)}{n} * 100$$

5.4   Weighted aggregates

The basic methods of calculating indices for a combined set of prices involve a significant drawback. Both the simple mean and the simple aggregate methods assume that each item in the group is equally important. In general, of course, this is unlikely to be the case. A change in the price of some items will be much more significant than variations in others. The problem in calculating a combined index is to determine a reasonable weighting for each item. The weightings used will indicate the importance of each item in the calculation. The weighted aggregate index method uses this approach and is found using the following formula:

$$\text{Weighted aggregate index} = \frac{\sum wp_i}{\sum wp_0} * 100$$

where w = weight for each item in the calculation.
   The following examples will illustrate this improved method.

EXAMPLE 1

Consider the problem of analysing changes in commodity prices for BAPC Ltd. The table shown below gives the prices of commodities over a two-year period together with appropriate weightings for each item.

Commodity	Weighting	Commodity price per tonne ($)	
		1998	1999
Iron	7	25	24
Steel	12	34	38
Copper	1	64	80

The weightings given in the table show the relative importance for each commodity. For instance, the table shows that the price of copper is the least significant in this group, and that the price of steel is regarded as being twelve times as important.

The calculations involved in the weighted aggregate index method are shown in the table below. The weightings are denoted by w, the current prices by p_i and the base prices by p_0.

Commodity	w	p_0 (1998)	p_i (1999)	$w*p_0$	$w*p_i$
Iron	7	25	24	175	168
Steel	12	34	38	408	456
Copper	1	64	80	64	80
Totals	20			647	704

This table gives the following summations:

$$\Sigma\, w = 10, \qquad \Sigma\, wp_0 = 647, \qquad \Sigma\, wp_i = 704$$

Thus, the combined index for commodity prices can be calculated as follows:

$$\text{Weighted aggregate index} = \frac{\Sigma\, wp_i}{\Sigma\, wp_0} * 100$$

$$= \frac{704}{647} * 100$$

$$= 108.8$$

This indicates that the group of commodity prices has increased by 8.8% between 1998 and 1999. This gives a much more realistic picture of the changes in commodity prices as they have affected BAPC. The weightings for each individual item are likely to be estimated from the quantity of each product used in the company. Clearly, the weightings for this group of commodities would be different for a second company, and may possibly change over different periods of time within the same company. These ideas will be explored in the following sections in this chapter.

Definition: *An alternative method of evaluating an index for a combined set of items using weightings for each item is found by the formula:*

$$\text{Weighted aggregate index} = \frac{\sum w p_i}{\sum w p_0} * 100$$

where w is the weighting for each item.

5.5	**Exercises: simple and weighted indices**

1.(E) The table below shows the average price of steel (given in £ per tonne) over a five-year period, 1994 to 1998.

Year: 1994   1995   1996   1997   1998
Steel price: 250   255   260   236   224

(i) Calculate an index for steel prices on each year based on the average price in 1994.
(ii) Calculate a chain base index for the steel prices in each year.
(iii) Interpret what these two sets of indices represent.

2.(I) The values of imports into the UK from EC countries during the years 1995 to 1999 are shown below. (The figures are given in millions ECUs.)

Year: 1995   1996   1997   1998   1999
Imports: 1210   1135   1278   1340   1434

(i) Calculate a chain base and a fixed base index for each year between 1995 and 1999.
(ii) Comment on these values and interpret the differences between the two indices in each year.

3.(I) Evaluate the index for the combined commodity prices in 1998 based on 1996 prices based on the data shown below:

	Prices ($ per unit)	
Commodity	1996	1998
A	3.00	3.60
B	2.34	2.20
C	1.98	2.70

4.(I) (i) Assuming that the weightings for the three commodities A, B and C are 5, 1 and 14 respectively, calculate the weighted aggregate index for prices in 1998 based on 1996 figures.

(ii) What if the respective weightings were 10, 3, and 2? How would this affect your results? Explain why there are differences between the two sets of results.

5.6   The Laspeyre index

As shown in the previous sections, when calculating indices for a combined range of items it is much more realistic to use appropriate weightings for each item. When considering price indices these weightings are often based on the quantities involved. Thus, if q denotes the quantity for each item, then this could replace the more general weighting (w) in the weighted aggregate formula. The amended formula for a combined index would be:

$$\text{Index} = \frac{\sum qp_i}{\sum qp_0} * 100$$

The problem with this formula is that the quantities for specific items are likely to change over the period that the index is calculated. Consequently, we need to ask which quantity should we use? The **Laspeyre index** uses quantities from the base period in the calculation of the index. The following formula gives the combined index:

$$\text{Laspeyre index} = \frac{\sum q_0 p_i}{\sum q_0 p_0} * 100$$

where q_0 represents the quantities in the base period. The Laspeyre index is often referred to as the **base weighted index**. The calculation for this index will be illustrated in the following example.

EXAMPLE 1

Consider the problem of measuring the change in the 'cost of living'. Such a cost would involve changes in many items such as food, transport and clothing. In order to

Item	Weekly quantity in 1996	Unit price (£) 1996	1997
Bread	5	0.80	0.98
Butter	4	0.52	0.50
Milk	8	0.42	0.37
Meat	3	1.80	1.85

consider changes in food costs, a typical 'basket' of items is considered. The table above shows the prices of some items over the period 1996 to 1997, together with the average weekly quantity of items purchased in 1996 for each household.

Using the notation p_0 = base price, q_0 = base quantity and p_i = current price, the required calculations for the Laspeyre index are shown in the following table:

Item	q_0	p_0	p_i	$q_0 p_0$	$q_0 p_i$
Bread	5	0.80	0.98	4	4.9
Butter	4	0.52	0.50	2.08	2
Milk	8	0.42	0.37	3.36	2.96
Meat	3	1.80	1.85	5.4	5.55
Totals				14.84	15.41

The table shows the following totals:

$$\sum q_0 p_0 = 14.84 \quad \text{and} \quad \sum q_0 p_i = 15.41.$$

Therefore, the combined index for this selection of goods can be calculated as:

$$\text{Laspeyre index} = \frac{\sum q_0 p_i}{\sum q_0 p_0} * 100$$

$$= \frac{15.41}{14.84} * 100$$

$$= 103.8$$

This shows that the 'basket' of food items has increased by 3.8% over the one-year period.

Definition: *The Laspeyre index of prices is found using the base quantities as weightings as shown in the following formula:*

$$\text{Laspeyre price index} = \frac{\sum q_0 p_i}{\sum q_0 p_0} * 100$$

where p_i is the current price, p_0 is the base price and q_0 is the base quantity for each item.

5.7 The Paasche index

An alternative approach to using quantities in the base period as in the Laspeyre index is to incorporate the current quantities. This method is called the Paasche index and is found by the amended formula below:

$$\text{Paasche index} = \frac{\sum q_i p_i}{\sum q_i p_0} * 100$$

where q_i = quantities for each item in the current period.

This method of calculation is often referred to as the **current weighted index** and the following example illustrates the approach.

Consider the problem of determining an index of wages for a group of employees as introduced in an earlier example. The table below shows the average weekly wages for three groups of employees during 1997 and 1998, together with the average number of employees in each group during 1998.

Sector	Number of employees	Weekly wage (£s)	
		1997	1998
Technical	180	450	470
Operatives	270	340	355
Non-skilled	450	260	275

The table below shows the required calculations for producing the Paasche index. In this example, the wages can be regarded as 'prices' for the purposes of the index calculations.

Sector	q_i	p_0	p_i	$q_i p_0$	$q_i p_i$
Technical	180	450	470	81 000	84 600
Operatives	270	340	355	91 800	95 850
Non-skilled	450	260	275	117 000	123 750
Totals				289 800	304 200

The Paasche index $= \dfrac{\sum q_i p_i}{\sum q_i p_0} * 100$

$= \dfrac{304\,200}{289\,800} * 100$

$= 105.0$

This index shows that wages have increased by an 'average' of 5% over the period of calculation.

Definition: *The Paasche index of prices is found using the current quantities as weightings as given in the following formula:*

$$\text{Paasche price index} = \frac{\sum q_i p_i}{\sum q_i p_0} * 100$$

where p_i is the current price, p_0 is the base price and q_i is the current quantity for each item.

5.8   Comparison of Laspeyre and Paasche indices

The Laspeyre and Paasche methods are two common approaches to the calculation of combined index numbers. Essentially, the Laspeyre index looks at the change in price of a 'basket' of goods, assuming that the quantities purchased in the base period have not changed over the current period. Conversely, in the Paasche method the assumption is that the current quantities are also relevant for the base period.

Each method of index number calculation has its advantages and drawbacks, which will be discussed here. At first glance, we may conclude that the Paasche index is more appropriate since it uses 'up to date' information. The Laspeyre index incorporates quantities in the base period and as time goes on these may become less and less relevant. However, in many practical examples the changes in quantities over time are minor, and do not drastically affect the resulting index.

There are a number of practical advantages of the Laspeyre index. In particular, the Laspeyre index involves a simplified method of calculation leading to easier interpretation. For instance, consider the method of calculation for the two indices. The Laspeyre method requires knowledge of the quantities in the base period only. Subsequently, any index can be calculated on the basis of current prices. Conversely, the Paasche index requires information on current quantities. Therefore, such an index cannot be evaluated unless the current quantities are known. Imagine the tremendous amount of work this could entail when calculating a string of indices. For instance, if we require monthly price indices for a group of commodities then not only do we need the current prices of each quantity but also the current month's quantities purchased. Now the current prices may be known at the beginning of the month, whereas the quantities used in a given month will not be available until the end of the month at the earliest. Thus, the Laspeyre index could be calculated much earlier than the Paasche index. Furthermore, the collection and collation of information on the quantities for each item may not be an easy task and may result in lengthy delays in the Paasche calculations.

An additional advantage of the Laspeyre index is that individual indices in a string of values can be directly compared since they relate to the same 'basket' of goods. However, a sequence of Paasche indices is not easily comparable since each index is calculated based on a different set of quantities. This can have a major impact on the index values obtained.

The table below summarises the advantages of each method of index number construction.

Calculation method	Advantages	Drawbacks
Laspeyre index (base weighted)	▶ Easier to obtain data ▶ Simpler to compare a string of indices	▶ Can be regarded as being out-of-date ▶ Poor when quantities are changing significantly
Paasche index (current weighted)	▶ Uses up-to-date information	▶ Difficult to calculate ▶ Problems with evaluation of new quantities for each index calculated

Generally, the Laspeyre index is used in most practical examples. The only exception is when the quantities change significantly between successive periods, when it may be more realistic to consider the Paasche index.

EXAMPLE 1

Consider an earlier example on calculating the index for a 'basket' of food items. The table below shows the prices of these items in each year together with the average weekly quantities purchased each year.

Item	Weekly quantity 1996	Weekly quantity 1997	Unit price (£) 1996	Unit price (£) 1997
Bread	5	4	0.80	1.08
Butter	4	3	0.52	0.54
Milk	7	10	0.42	0.35
Meat	3	2	1.80	1.95

This information is shown in the following table with the required calculations for the Laspeyre and Paasche indices.

Items	q_0	q_1	p_0	p_1	$q_0 p_0$	$q_0 p_1$	$q_1 p_0$	$q_1 p_1$
Bread	5	4	0.80	1.08	4	5.4	3.2	4.32
Butter	4	3	0.52	0.54	2.08	2.16	1.56	1.62
Milk	7	10	0.42	0.35	2.94	2.45	4.2	3.5
Meat	3	2	1.80	1.95	5.4	5.85	3.6	3.9
Totals					14.42	15.86	12.56	13.34

The two indices are calculated as follows:

$$\text{Laspeyre index} = \frac{\sum q_0 p_1}{\sum q_0 p_0} * 100 = \frac{15.86}{14.42} * 100 = 110.0$$

$$\text{Paasche index} = \frac{\sum q_1 p_1}{\sum q_1 p_0} * 100 = \frac{13.34}{12.56} * 100 = 106.2$$

As can be seen, in this example there is a clear difference between the two values of the combined price index. One of the problems with using either the base quantities or the current quantities in the calculation is that these values can be affected by the prices themselves. For instance, if the price of an item increases, then there is a tendency for the quantity to decrease. Similarly, a reduction in price for an item may result in increasing demand.

Consequently, those items that have the highest price rises will tend to have lower current quantities. This means that the Paasche index (using current quantities) is likely to underplay these effects. Conversely, a price reduction on a given item may increase the current quantity. This means that the Laspeyre index (using base quantities) may suppress the effect of these reductions. The example given above demonstrates these differences. Note that the highest price rises occur in bread and meat, and in each case there is a reduction in the quantities consumed. Also one item (milk) has had a price reduction over the period, resulting in an increased demand. These effects have contributed to the two results where the Paasche index of 106.2 is significantly lower than the Laspeyre index for the same period.

5.9   Exercises: Laspeyre and Paasche indices

1.(I)   The table below shows the share prices at the end April in 1997 and 1998 for a group of four companies. The table also gives the average daily volume of sales traded in each company's shares.

Company	Share price (£) 1997	Share price (£) 1998	Number of shares sold 1997	Number of shares sold 1998
Adams Co.	2.54	2.80	2000	2400
Bartlett Ltd	1.15	2.34	1200	3400
Crain & Partners	3.60	3.88	3000	2900
Downbrooks	2.10	2.35	1800	2050

(i) Calculate an index for the share prices of the combined companies in 1998 based on the previous year's prices using each of the following methods:
  (a) Laspeyre index, and
  (b) Paasche index.

(ii) Comment on the differences between these two indices calculated. What would you suggest is the most appropriate index in order to illustrate the changes in share prices over this period?

2.(D) The table below shows the retail prices for a selection of motor cars over the period 1997–9 together with the volume of sales in the UK for each year.

Model	Retail price (excluding taxes)			Number sold (10 thousands)		
	1997	1998	1999	1997	1998	1999
Altro	6000	6080	6110	6.5	8.0	8.8
Bistro	7450	8090	8990	5.4	5.8	5.7
Castro	10 350	11 950	12 675	4.0	3.7	2.8

(i) Calculate the combined index for these car prices in each year based on 1997 using the Laspeyre method.
(ii) What other method could you use for these estimates? Without calculation, would the alternative method produce different values? If so, explain whether they will be higher or lower, giving reasons.

5.10 Further index methods

Despite the problems described in using the Laspeyre and Paasche indices, these remain the most popular methods of index number construction. In fact, the Laspeyre index is generally used because of the ease of construction. However, because of the limitations of these methods as outlined in the previous section there are a number of alternative methods available for the calculation of indices. These methods attempt to combine the advantages present in the Laspeyre and Paasche calculations, and will usually involve some form of 'average' of these indices. The two alternative methods outlined in this section are the Marshall–Edgeworth and Fisher's indices.

The **Marshall–Edgeworth index** uses a combination of the current and base quantities in the calculation. In fact, the total quantity $(q_0 + q_i)$ over the two periods is used as the weighting in the index calculation. Thus, the formula for this index is as follows:

$$\text{Marshall–Edgeworth index} = \frac{\sum (q_0 + q_i) p_i}{\sum (q_0 + q_i) p_0} * 100$$

An alternative to this is **Fisher's ideal index**, which involves the product of the Laspeyre and Paasche calculations as shown in the formula below.

$$\text{Fisher's ideal index} = \sqrt{\left(\frac{\sum q_0 p_1}{\sum q_0 p_0} \right) \left(\frac{\sum q_1 p_1}{\sum q_1 p_0} \right)} * 100$$

Both of these indices are considered to be better measures of the change in prices for a combined group of items. However, both methods require knowledge of the current quantities, and therefore suffer from the same drawbacks as the Paasche index. Both indices require a significant amount of work to construct and because of the constant change in quantities it is difficult to compare a sequence of these values.

EXAMPLE 1

Consider the index of wages for different groups of employees as shown in the following table. Owing to a reorganisation there have been significant changes in the workforce profile in the company, as shown by the numbers of employees in each sector. Owing to this 'downsizing' the total number of employees has been reduced and the resulting changes in wages of the three employees' groups are notably different.

Sector	Number of employees		Weekly wages (£)	
	1998	1999	1998	1999
Technical	180	210	470	505
Operatives	270	230	355	360
Non-skilled	450	340	275	255

Calculations required for the combined indices are shown in the following table.

Sector	q_0	q_1	p_0	p_1	$q_0 p_0$	$q_0 p_1$	$q_1 p_0$	$q_1 p_1$	$(q_0 + q_1)p_0$	$(q_0 + q_1)p_1$
Tech.	180	210	470	505	84 600	90 900	98 700	106 050	183 300	196 950
Ops	270	230	355	360	95 850	97 200	81 650	82 800	177 500	180 000
Non-s.	450	340	275	255	123 750	114 750	93 500	86 700	217 250	201 450
Totals					304 200	302 850	273 850	275 550	578 050	578 400

The following indices can be calculated from these summations:

$$\text{Laspeyre index} = \frac{\sum q_0 p_1}{\sum q_0 p_0} * 100 = \frac{302\ 850}{304\ 200} * 100 = 99.6$$

$$\text{Paasche index} = \frac{\sum q_1 p_1}{\sum q_1 p_0} * 100 = \frac{275\ 550}{273\ 850} * 100 = 100.6$$

$$\text{Marshall–Edgeworth index} = \frac{\sum (q_0 + q_1)p_1}{\sum (q_0 + q_1)p_0} * 100$$

$$= \frac{578\,400}{578\,050} * 100$$

$$= 100.1$$

$$\text{Fisher's ideal index} = \sqrt{\left(\frac{\sum q_0 p_1}{\sum q_0 p_0}\right)\left(\frac{\sum q_1 p_1}{\sum q_1 p_0}\right)} * 100$$

$$= \sqrt{\left(\frac{302\,850}{304\,200}\right)\left(\frac{275\,550}{273\,850}\right)} * 100$$

$$= \sqrt{(0.9956)(1.0062)} * 100$$

$$= 100.1$$

It can be seen from these calculations that the two modified indices – Marshall–Edgeworth and Fisher's – both provide indices that are between the Laspeyre and Paasche ranges. These values indicate that there has been very little movement in the wages between 1998 and 1999, taking all the employee groups as a whole.

5.11 | Exercises: further indices

1.(D) The table below shows the average tuition fees charged to students at the Blundells University for the years 1996 and 1998.

Attendance mode	Tuition fees ($)		Numbers of students (hundreds)	
	1996	1998	1996	1998
Full-time	2200	2800	35	41
One day per week	950	1050	12	10
Evening only	550	650	9	15
Short course	225	325	12	25

(i) Calculate each of the following indices showing the tuition fees in 1998 based on the 1996 prices:
(a) Marshall–Edgeworth index,
(b) Fisher's ideal index.
(ii) Comment on any differences you find between these two indices and specify which of these estimates, if any, you would use for the calculation of such an index.

5.12	**Quantity indices**

The previous sections have concentrated on the calculation of price indices using the quantities as weightings. There are many practical examples in which the changes in quantities need to be measured. In the evaluation of such indices the weightings used can be the unit price for each item. In these circumstances, the prices and quantities are simply interchanged in the specification of appropriate formulae.

For instance, a simple aggregate index of quantities would be:

$$\text{Quantity index} = \frac{\sum q_i}{\sum q_0} * 100$$

Using weightings for each item we have the amended formula:

$$\text{Weighted aggregate index} = \frac{\sum wq_i}{\sum wq_0} * 100$$

The weights in this formula can be replaced by the current or base prices, giving the two indices below.

$$\text{Laspeyre quantity index} = \frac{\sum p_0 q_i}{\sum p_0 q_0} * 100$$

$$\text{Paasche quantity index} = \frac{\sum p_i q_i}{\sum p_i q_0} * 100$$

The following examples show applications of these formulae.

EXAMPLE I

The table below shows the volume of a range of commodities used by BAPC Ltd over the two years 1997 and 1998.

	Volume (1000 tonnes)	
Commodity	1997	1998
Iron	60	70
Steel	108	120
Copper	8	10

A simple combined index of the quantity used in 1998 based on 1997 is found as follows:

$$\text{Quantity index} = \frac{\sum q_i}{\sum q_0} * 100$$

$$= \frac{70 + 120 + 10}{60 + 108 + 8} * 100$$

$$= \frac{200}{176} * 100$$

$$= 113.6$$

Thus, this index shows that the volume of these commodities has increased by 13.6%.

EXAMPLE 2

The management of BAPC has realised that the simple index calculated above does not give a true representation of the volume used since the usage of some of the commodities is more significant because of the costs involved. The table below shows the volume of commodities used over two years, together with the price per tonne of each commodity.

Commodity	Price ($ per tonne)	Volume (1000 tonnes) 1997	1998
Iron	20	60	70
Steel	29	108	120
Copper	68	8	10

As shown in the table, the change in volume for copper is more significant since it is an expensive commodity. The commodity prices can be used as weightings in the formula:

$$\text{Weighted aggregate index} = \frac{\sum wq_i}{\sum wq_0} * 100$$

$$= \frac{(20 * 70 + 29 * 120 + 68 * 10)}{20 * 60 + 29 * 108 + 68 * 8} * 100$$

$$= \frac{5560}{4876} * 100$$

$$= 114.0$$

EXAMPLE 3

The table below shows the prices and volumes of commodities over a two-year period.

Commodity	Price ($ per tonne)		Volume (1000 tonnes)	
	1997	1998	1997	1998
Iron	20	25	60	70
Steel	29	34	108	120
Copper	68	64	8	10

The Laspeyre and Paasche indices can be calculated from this set of data. The following table shows the calculations required in order to obtain these indices.

Comm.	p_0	p_1	q_0	q_1	$p_0 q_0$	$p_0 q_1$	$p_1 q_0$	$p_1 q_1$
Iron	20	25	60	70	1200	1400	1500	1750
Steel	29	34	108	120	3132	3480	3672	4080
Copper	68	64	8	10	544	680	512	640
Totals					4876	5560	5684	6470

The totals displayed in the above table are used in the following calculations.

$$\text{Laspeyre quantity index} = \frac{\sum p_0 q_1}{\sum p_0 q_0} * 100$$

$$= \frac{5560}{4876} * 100 = 114.0$$

$$\text{Paasche quantity index} = \frac{\sum p_1 q_1}{\sum p_1 q_0} * 100$$

$$= \frac{6470}{5684} * 100 = 113.8$$

Definition: *A quantity index measures changes in quantities (or volumes) between the current periods and base period. Two important quantity indices use the Laspeyre and Paasche methods where the prices are considered as the weightings for each item.*

$$\text{Laspeyre quantity index} = \frac{\sum p_0 q_i}{\sum p_0 q_0} * 100$$

$$\text{Paasche price index} = \frac{\sum p_i q_i}{\sum p_i q_0} * 100$$

where q_i is the current quantity, q_0 is the base quantity, p_i is the current price and p_0 is the base price for each item.

| 5.13 | **Exercises: quantity indices** |

1.(E) The following table shows the average daily output for a company during 1997 and 1998 for a range of products.

Product code	Output (number of units)	
	1997	1998
A3045	240	300
B2074	45	120
A1790	330	260

 (i) Calculate the combined index for the production output in 1998 based on the 1997 figures.
 (ii) If the selling prices for the three products listed are £30, £220 and £100 respectively, find the weighted aggregate index for the combined products.

2.(I) Calculate the Laspeyre and Paasche quantity indices for the production output shown in question 1 using the following prices:

Product code	Price (£ per unit)	
	1997	1998
A3045	30	40
B2074	220	194
A1790	100	140

3.(D) The table below shows the retail prices for a selection of motor cars over the period 1997–9 together with the volume of sales in the UK for each year.

	Retail price (excluding taxes)			Number sold (10 thousands)		
Model	1997	1998	1999	1997	1998	1999
Altro	6000	6080	6110	6.5	8.0	8.8
Bistro	7450	8090	8990	5.4	5.8	5.7
Castro	10 350	11 950	12 675	4.0	3.7	2.8

(i) Calculate the combined index for the volume of cars sold in each year based on 1997 using the Laspeyre method.

(ii) Calculate the Paasche index of volume in each year using the same data and comment on the differences between the values obtained.

5.14   Cost of living indices

A 'cost of living' index provides important information for a range of business applications. Knowledge of such changes can assist in establishing new wage rates, salaries and benefits for employees, and retail and wholesale prices for customers. All of the major industrialised nations regularly publish their own indices giving this information. The standard 'cost of living' index in the UK is the Retail Price Index (RPI) and in the US it is referred to as the Consumer Price Index (CPI). Both these indices are evaluated in similar ways as described below.

Consider the Retail Price Index giving information on the change in prices in the UK. This index has been evaluated since 1914 and measures changes in a 'basket' of goods bought by an 'average' family. A range of different goods is considered including the following:

▶ Food
▶ Alcoholic drink
▶ Tobacco
▶ Clothing and footwear
▶ Housing
▶ Transport and vehicles
▶ Fuel and light
▶ Services

The amount of spending on each of these categories is determined by the annual Family Expenditure Survey. The results from this ongoing survey are used as the weightings in the calculation of a combined index. Effectively, the RPI is calculated using the Laspeyre (base weighted) method, and is published on a monthly basis by the Central Statistical Office in the UK. The weightings are changed every year as a result of the Family Expenditure survey.

Similarly, in the US the Consumer Price Index (CPI) is calculated using changes in the prices of over 400 goods and services. The major categories in this group are:

▶ Food and beverages
▶ Housing
▶ Apparel and upkeep
▶ Transportation
▶ Medical care
▶ Entertainment

The CPI has been calculated since 1919 to measure the cost of living in the US. It was calculated primarily to measure inflation as a basis for wage negotiations. Since 1940 this statistic has been published in the '*Monthly Labor Review*' by the Federal Bureau of Labor Statistics. The weightings used in this calculation are established from a survey of consumer expenditure. These weightings are amended regularly on the basis of the survey results.

One of the criticisms of indices such as the RPI or CPI is that they do not accurately measure changes in the cost of living. Both indices actually measure changes in prices for the consumer. Although these changes can indicate aspects of the cost of living there are other factors which need to be taken into consideration. For instance, these indices do not take into account changes in income taxes, and National Insurance or Social Security contributions. Clearly, these will be important factors in the spending power of the population. To overcome this limitation, indices are also produced that incorporate tax and benefit changes with the retail price variations.

Other criticisms of these indices include the following:

▶ Such an index is a measure of the price rises for a 'typical' family. The question is what is typical? Most households would actually not conform to this model, and therefore for the majority such an index can be misleading.
▶ The index lacks information on the quality of goods purchased. For instance, it is misleading to incorporate the reduction in costs of an item of food (e.g. potatoes) if the quality of such an item has deteriorated from the previous year. It is necessary to compare like with like to obtain an unbiased picture of the overall price changes.
▶ Some sectors of the population are totally excluded from the determination of appropriate weightings for each item. For instance, in the calculations for the RPI, households in the top 3% of earnings and those households only containing pensioners are not included.

Thus, for these sections of the population, the RPI may not be a good indicator of price changes. For this reason other indices measuring price rises are calculated. For example, in the UK there are two 'pensioner indices' compiled for one-person and two-person pensioner households. These indices will have significantly different weightings for individual items than the general RPI. Furthermore, in the US there are two versions of the CPI produced. These are the Index for Urban Wage Earners and Clerical Workers (referred to as the CPI-W) and the Index for the Urban Consumers (CPI-U). The CPI-U covers a larger percentage of the population and is therefore more commonly used.

EXAMPLE I

Consider the analysis of earnings in the British-American Parts Company Ltd. In the UK, an index of the average earnings over the six years 1994 to 1999 is as follows:

Year:	1994	1995	1996	1997	1998	1999
Earnings index:	100	106	108	112	115	122

This shows a steady increase in the average earnings of the BAPC employees. Such information could be used by the management of BAPC in future wage negotiations, or simply as a piece of information for existing employees to demonstrate the continuing improvement in earnings within the company. Such information may also be useful for external publication for public relations purposes, for example, to show the apparent generosity of the company towards its employees.

However, analysis of this information with reference to the cost of living may present a different picture. For instance, the RPI may be used to provide a much better guide as to the 'real' improvement in earnings for employees in the company. The table below shows the RPI for the years 1994 to 1999 using 1994 as the base year.

Year:	1994	1995	1996	1997	1998	1999
Retail Price Index:	100	104	109	115	121	130

A comparison of the RPI and the earnings index for this company shows that the 'real' earnings for employees over the period 1994 to 1999 has declined. A more realistic index of the earnings would be obtained by extracting the rises due to inflation. For instance, consider the 1995 earnings index of 106. The corresponding RPI for this year is 104, and the effect of these increases can be combined with the earnings as follows:

$$\text{Index of 'real' earnings} = \frac{106}{104} * 100 = 101.9$$

This shows that the employees' 'buying power' has only increased by 1.9% over the year. Similarly, the earnings index for 1996, eliminating the effect of inflation, is as follows:

$$\text{Index} = \frac{108}{109} * 100 = 99.1$$

Showing that the employees' buying power has dropped by 0.9% over the two-year period 1994 to 1996. The remaining indices comparing the earnings index against the RPI can be similarly calculated and are shown in the following table.

Year:	1994	1995	1996	1997	1998	1999
'Real' earnings index:	100	101.9	99.1	97.4	95.0	93.8

These indices show a steady decline in the 'real' earnings of the BAPC employees. Clearly, such information can be used by the negotiation team on behalf of the workforce to illustrate how there has been a consistent decline over the period 1994 to 1999. Conversely, of course, the management team will attempt to emphasise the earnings in relation to other changes such as production output, working hours, together with national figures on earnings, prices and employment.

5.15 Further business indices

One of the common indices used for business data is the measurement of the change in the values of stocks and shares. In the UK the FT 100 share index is one of the popular indicators of changes in the prices of shares. This index, produced by the *Financial Times*, measures changes in the top 100 shares on the London Stock Exchange. The resulting FT 100 index is a weighted mean of the price indices for the individual shares. The weightings for this index need to be changed regularly to allow for new companies to be included and others to be discarded as and when appropriate. The *Financial Times*' Index of Industrial Ordinary Shares is an alternative measure of the changes in share prices on the London Exchange. This index is calculated from a representative selection of thirty market leaders in British industry.

A similar index is the Dow-Jones index, which measures price changes on the New York stock market. Indices such as the FT 100 and Dow-Jones differ from the standard methods outlined in this chapter in that they have a base value equal to 1000 rather than the usual 100. Thus, an FT 100 index of 3500 indicates that share prices have increased on average by 250% since the base period.

Other important indices of business activities include the following:

Index of Industrial Output – based on the production output of selected companies in different sectors. The weightings for this index are based on the contribution of each industry to the Gross Domestic Product (GDP) for the UK in any given year. For instance, the 1990 weightings for the primary production sectors were:

▶ Mining and quarrying 85
▶ Electricity, gas and water supply 79
▶ Manufacturing industries 836

There are also related indices published such as the index of Gross Domestic Product and index of the 'Real National Disposable Income'.

A similar index in the US published monthly in the *Federal Reserve Bulletin* is the Index of Industrial Production (IIP). This is calculated using a formula similar to that used in the Laspeyre method, and is based on the output in manufacturing, mining and utilities. This index is used as a measure of the growth or decline in the US economy.

Index of Producer Prices – calculated on the basis of changes in around 11 000 materials and products used and manufactured in the UK. Currently with a base period of 1995 the weightings are based on the volume of transactions in each sector of goods and services. The base is intended to change every 5 years, reflecting the changing requirements and output of UK industries.

Similarly, in the US the Producer Price Index (PPI) is published monthly by the Bureau of Labor Statistics and is based on the prices of approximately 10 000 items. The index is broken down into various categories, including raw materials, semi-finished goods, and completed goods, and also into a variety of different types of industries.

Tax & Price Index – this UK index is calculated to overcome some of the problems associated with the RPI for measuring changes in the real purchasing power of individuals. This index measures the changes required in employees' gross income in order to maintain their purchasing power, taking into account variations in retail prices.

Index of Average Earnings – this index provides information on the changes in average weekly earnings of all employees in Britain. The calculations are obtained by considering changes in earnings for the main sectors, including manufacturing, production industries and service industries. There is a similar index calculated monthly for wages and salaries per unit of output, which compares the earnings of employees together with the contribution to GDP.

Such indices can be useful for a business in monitoring results, comparing figures with national performance indicators, and to develop strategies on the basis of national and international statistics.

These indices can be obtained from a variety of sources including the following:

▶ *Economic Trends*, published monthly with an annual supplement by the Central Statistical Office (CSO) – a UK Government organisation.
▶ *Employment Gazette*, produced monthly jointly by the CSO and the Department of Education & Employment.
▶ *Monthly Digest of Statistics*, published by the CSO.
▶ *Main Economic Indicators*, published monthly by the Organisation of Economic Cooperation and Development (OECD).
▶ *New Earnings Survey*, published annually by the CSO.
▶ *International Yearbook of Industrial Statistics*, formerly the *Industrial Statistics Handbook*, produced by the United Nations Industrial Development Organisation (UNIDO).

| 5.16 | **Computer applications** |

The complexity of calculations involved in the evaluation of index numbers means that computer systems can be extremely useful in this process. As shown in previous examples on the calculations of indices, the tabulation format of results lends itself to the use of spreadsheet packages. Software such as Excel or Lotus can be valuable in performing these calculations. The following examples illustrate a range of problems in which indices have been evaluated using these spreadsheets.

EXAMPLE I

The British-American Parts Company keeps records of the average weekly wages of selected grades of employees. Information on these wages together with the corresponding weightings can be displayed in a spreadsheet. This information can be used to obtain an index of the combined wages.

Using the disk   Load the file called INDEX1.WK3 from the disk accompanying this book. The spreadsheet displayed is shown in Figure 5.1. The table shown gives the average weekly wages for the various sectors over a five-year period from 1994 to 1999. The spreadsheet displayed in Figure 5.1 shows the results of the combined index of wages for each year using 1994 as the base period. The method used for these indices is the weighted aggregate formula, as shown below:

$$\text{Weighted aggregate index} = \frac{\sum w p_i}{\sum w p_0} * 100$$

where p_i denotes the current wage and p_0 the base wage for each group of employees. The weightings (w) for the various groups are shown in the cells B6 to B10. The

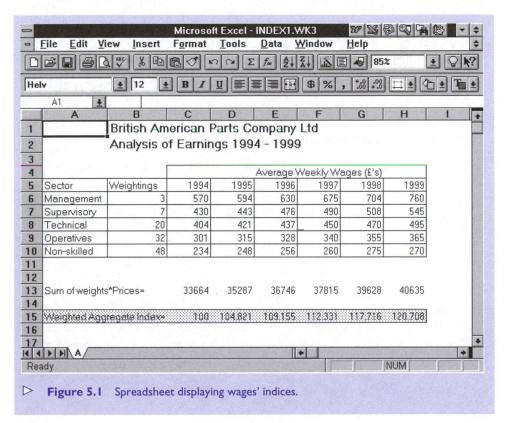

Sector	Weightings	1994	1995	1996	1997	1998	1999
Management	3	570	594	630	675	704	760
Supervisory	7	430	443	476	490	508	545
Technical	20	404	421	437	450	470	495
Operatives	32	301	315	328	340	355	365
Non-skilled	48	234	248	256	260	275	270
Sum of weights*Prices=		33664	35287	36746	37815	39628	40635
Weighted Aggregate Index=		100	104.821	109.155	112.331	117.716	120.708

(British American Parts Company Ltd — Analysis of Earnings 1994 – 1999; Average Weekly Wages (£'s))

▷ **Figure 5.1**   Spreadsheet displaying wages' indices.

appropriate summations required for the calculation of the combined indices are shown in C13 to H13. The resulting indices for earnings are calculated in the cells C15 to H15. The index for 1994 is 100 since this is the fixed base period used.

You may wish to change the wages for selected groups and/or years and look at the effect on the resulting indices. Alternatively, try to change the relative weightings for each group of employees and investigate the results.

EXAMPLE 2

As shown in earlier sections there are a range of alternative methods for calculating combined indices. The two most common approaches are the Laspeyre (base weighted) and Paasche (current weighted) indices. In terms of the previous example, these indices will be obtained using the numbers of employees in each sector either in the base period (Laspeyre) or in the current period (Paasche).

Using the disk Load the file INDEX2.WK3 from the disk. The spreadsheet displayed shows the average weekly wages and the corresponding numbers of

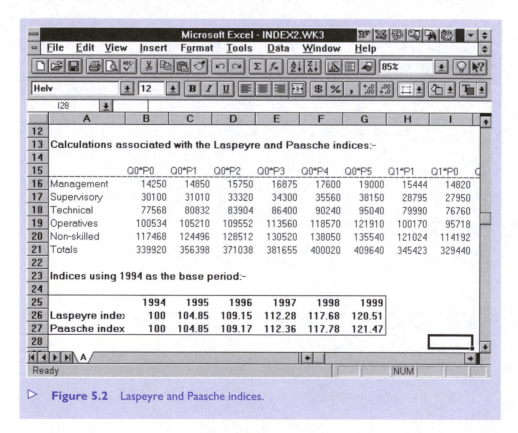

▷   **Figure 5.2** Laspeyre and Paasche indices.

employees in each sector for BAPC. Figure 5.2 shows the results of using these figures in the calculation of the Laspeyre and Paasche indices for each year based on the 1995 wages. The required calculations are shown in the rows 15 to 20, with the resulting totals evaluated in row 21. The cells B26 to G27 show the values for the Laspeyre and Paasche indices for each year between 1994 and 1999. It can be seen that the values of the two indices on any given year are very close. This is the case because the relative numbers of employees in the various sectors are similar in the years shown. Conversely, with significant changes in the proportion of employees in specific groups it is likely that the Laspeyre and Paasche indices could be very different.

Again, it may be interesting for the reader to investigate the effect of changes in the numbers of employees in each sector on the resulting indices in this spreadsheet. For example, enter the following numbers of employees into the spreadsheet for the years 1998 and 1999 and compare the resulting indices with the existing values:

	Number of employees	
Sector	1998	1999
Management	50	60
Supervisory	120	130
Technical	240	230
Operatives	280	260
Non-skilled	360	340

The combined wage indices for the years 1998 and 1999 using these quantities should show a higher increase than those displayed in the spreadsheet in INDEX2.WK3. This is because the proportions of those in management and supervisory grades have increased dramatically, and these are the sectors that have shown a much higher increase in earnings over the period under consideration. Of course this will only be displayed in the Paasche indices, using current quantities. The Laspeyre indices will remain as shown, and therefore we can easily see a comparison of the two sets of indices by only looking at the cells F26 to G27. This highlights a limitation of the Laspeyre method, namely that the quantities (or weightings) used may be out of date and irrelevant for the current situation.

5.17   Chapter summary

Index numbers are used to measure the changes in a given series of values. The most common indices involve consideration of the change in prices such as the 'cost of living' and share price indices. An index is an expression of the current value as a percentage of a value in the base period. A simple price index would compare the current price (denoted by p_i) with the base price (p_0) and would be calculated as follows:

$$\text{Simple price index} = \frac{p_i}{p_0} * 100$$

An index of prices involving a group of items would be calculated using appropriate weightings for each item. One method of calculating the combined index is as follows:

$$\text{Weighted aggregate index} = \frac{\sum wp_i}{\sum wp_0} * 100$$

where w denotes the weighting for each item.

A common method of obtaining the weightings is to consider the quantities involved with each item. Two common indices using the quantities as weights are shown below.

$$\text{Laspeyre (base weighted) index} = \frac{\sum q_0 p_i}{\sum q_0 p_0} * 100$$

$$\text{Paasche (current weighted) index} = \frac{\sum q_i p_i}{\sum q_i p_0} * 100$$

Quantity indices can be obtained by using prices as weightings. For instance, the combined quantity indices can be obtained as follows:

$$\text{Laspeyre quantity index} = \frac{\sum p_0 q_i}{\sum p_0 q_0} * 100$$

$$\text{Paasche quantity index} = \frac{\sum p_i q_i}{\sum p_0 q_0} * 100$$

Many of today's business indices use the Laspeyre method of calculation, with the base period being updated at regular intervals. Such indices include those illustrating the changes in retail and wholesale prices, stocks and shares prices, production output and average earnings.

5.18   Further exercises

1.(E)   (i) Calculate an index for the salaries in each year based on the values in 1993 from the following data:

Year:	1993	1994	1995	1996	1997	1998
Average annual salaries (£1000s):	16	17.2	18.5	18.7	19.0	20.2

  (ii) An alternative approach is to calculate the chain base indices for these data. Evaluate these indices and comment on the advantages and limitations of the two methods.

2.(I) Find a combined index of prices for 1997 based on 1996 for each of the following groups of commodities:

(i)

Commodity	Unit prices (£)	
	1996	1997
A	22	26
B	14	19
C	6	6
D	20	16

(ii)

Commodity	Weighting	Unit prices (£)	
		1996	1997
A	15	22	26
B	7	14	19
C	10	6	6
D	4	20	16

3.(I) (i) Calculate the Laspeyre and Paasche price indices for the group of commodities given below.

Commodity	Number of units sold		Unit prices (£)	
	1996	1997	1996	1997
A	10	20	22	26
B	40	20	14	19
C	15	30	6	6
D	8	22	20	16

(ii) Comment on the differences between the two values obtained in part (i).

(iii) Discuss the advantages and drawbacks of each of the two methods of index number calculation used.

4.(I) The following table gives details of the hourly rates of pay earned by different groups of employees in a company.

Employee grade	Hourly rate of pay ($)		Number of employees	
	1995	1997	1995	1997
I	4.50	4.75	240	220
II	5.00	5.30	170	130
III	6.25	7.75	50	85

(i) Calculate the Laspeyre and Paasche indices for the wage rates in 1997 based on 1995.

(ii) Calculate the Laspeyre and Paasche indices of the number of employees in 1997 based on the 1995 figures.

(iii) Comment on the differences between the two indices in each case.

5.(D) (i) Define what is meant by (a) fixed base and (b) chain base indices. Comment on the differences between these two approaches and give examples of where each type is likely to be used.

(ii) Calculate the Laspeyre price index for 1997 and 1998 based on 1996 from the following data.

Item	Quantity purchased			Selling price (£)		
	1996	1997	1998	1996	1997	1998
1	120	130	150	4.50	4.60	4.60
2	60	50	30	3.60	4.10	4.55
3	90	120	100	2.20	2.05	2.30

(iii) Alternatively, calculate the chain base Laspeyre index for each year, 1997 and 1998. Comment on any differences you find.

6.(D) The table given below shows two sets of indices calculated over the period 1994 to 1999. The indices are obtained from the total value of output (given in £ millions) for a particular industrial sector in the UK, and the change in retail prices.

Year:	1994	1995	1996	1997	1998	1999
Output index:	100	107	112	116	119	126
RPI:	100	104	109	115	121	130

(i) Comment on the actual growth in production output for this sector by comparing these two indices.

(ii) Calculate a new index of the volume of production output excluding the inflationary effects.

7.(I)   **(Using the disk)**   Load a file from the disk called INDEX.WK3 into a Lotus or Excel spreadsheet. The spreadsheet displayed gives the hourly rates of pay and numbers of employees in different sectors as introduced in question 4 in this section.

   (i) By using an appropriate formula, calculate additional columns corresponding to the manual calculations required, and therefore use the spreadsheet to evaluate the Laspeyre and Paasche indices for 1997 based on 1995.

   (ii) Now by changing the values for the number of employees in the three grades I, II and III to 250, 150 and 40 respectively, use the spreadsheet to recalculate the wage indices. Comment on the differences between these values and the original figures, and explain why they occur.

Forecasting

CHAPTER OBJECTIVES

At the end of this chapter you will be able to:

▶ understand the basic techniques of business forecasting
▶ analyse a range of possible forecasting models
▶ evaluate the applications of forecasting in a business context
▶ determine the validity and reliability of the methods used
▶ contrast the performance and accuracy of different models

Introduction

The application of business forecasting techniques provides an important tool in the decision making process. The generation of reliable estimates of future values such as sales demand, price of materials, labour and production costs will provide a clear competitive advantage for many businesses. Such forecasts could be used in strategic and tactical decision making. A previous chapter has outlined one approach to forecasting by the use of regression techniques. These methods are appropriate when considering causal relationships between variables. Thus, for example, sales could be forecasted by reference to changes in prices, or advertising expenditure. However, there are alternative methods of forecasting using time series analysis techniques. The forecasting methods outlined in this chapter involve consideration of historical data, and obtaining estimates based on past values.

CASE STUDY   The Associated Petroleum Inc (API)

Associated Petroleum Inc is a multinational company dealing primarily in chemical and fuel products. The company controls a worldwide network of production and distribution centres, and franchises over 12 000 petrol stations in forty countries around the globe. The company is split into a number of separate Divisions including Petroleum Sales & Distribution, Marketing, Production, and Exploration.

The Sales & Distribution Division of API, headed by Peter Halligan, had an annual turnover in excess of $1 billion during 1997. The senior management in the Sales & Distribution Division has become increasingly concerned over the lack of detailed information on future estimates in areas such as potential growth in demand, US dollar exchange rates, oil production and exploration costs. The Noeken Consultancy Group has been hired to produce a report including estimates of a range of values based on past data. Business analysts employed by Noeken have used a range of time series forecasting techniques, in addition to qualitative methods, in order to gain an insight into the range of variables under consideration at API.

This case study will be used as a basis for a range of forecasting examples introduced in this chapter.

CASE STUDY   St. Joseph's general hospital

St. Joseph's hospital, introduced in the case study in Chapter 2, will be used to illustrate a range of forecasting examples. In order to assist in the strategic and operational decisions made by the senior management team at St. Joseph's, a number of estimates are of significant interest. For example, short-term decisions on staffing of wards and other facilities at the hospital rely on predictions of the demand such as the number of admissions, and likely volume of outpatient visits. Furthermore, the senior management team at St. Joseph's is currently considering an expansion of a range of facilities to incorporate additional wards and new services. Such decisions will be partly based on long-term forecasts of potential demand and likely associated revenues. Such examples will be considered in this chapter.

6.1   Elements of a time series

A series of values taken over a time period is referred to as a **time series**. In order to consider the behaviour of such a series it is useful to separate the values into a number of components. These components will be briefly described in this section, and then methods for evaluating them will be explored in later sections. Generally, a specific value in a time series may incorporate the following components – trend, cyclical, seasonal, and irregular movements. These components can be described as follows:

Trend – This component can be considered as the overall pattern of changes in specific values viewed over a long period of time. For example, the volume of petroleum sales in Europe by Associated Petroleum Inc (API) shows an overall increase over the period 1981–96. The graph shown in Figure 6.1 gives the sales volumes during this period together with a line indicating the overall trend of sales. Clearly, although there are fluctuations in the sales from one year to the next, the overall trend in these values is increasing.

Cyclical – In addition to a trend in the series of values, it is often apparent that a cyclical component exists. These components indicate variations above or below the trend line for periods of longer than one year. The graph in Figure 6.1 shows a likely cyclical component to the series of sales figures. Between the years 1983 and 1988 the figures are consistently below the trend line, whereas after 1990 the sales figures are generally higher. The cyclical movements for financial and economic data would often conform to the business cycle of slump, recovery, boom and recession.

Seasonal – Many series of values show regular patterns of variation over one year or

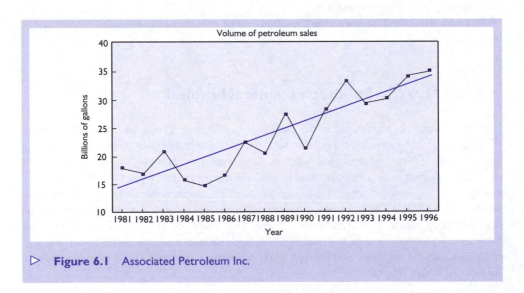

▷ **Figure 6.1**   Associated Petroleum Inc.

less. These seasonal variations can be identified after the trend and cyclical movements have been analysed. For example, the monthly sales figures of heating oil for API in Europe over the period 1994–7 are illustrated in the graph shown in Figure 6.2. The sales figures show clearly identifiable seasonal variations. For example, sales figures over the winter months are generally high, whereas there is a decline in sales during the summer months, before improving again in the autumn. Such seasonal variations are typical of a range of business data such as sales volumes, unemployment figures, prices of some commodities, transport and distribution costs. Many seasonal variations occur over an annual period although such patterns of variation can be evident over shorter periods of time. For instance, the hourly production output for a manufacturing company may consist of 'seasonal' factors each day. The first hour's production each day may be consistently lower because of setup times, and other variations in the output during the day may be due to regular breaks, shift changeover, and end of day maintenance checks.

Irregular – These components are the random elements that generally cannot be predicted. For example, irregular variations in production output could be caused by unscheduled stoppages, breakdowns in machinery, poor quality materials or industrial unrest. Such irregular variations are found by removing the trend, cyclical and seasonal elements from a given value. The remaining value is the irregular variation. Although such a value cannot be predicted beforehand, it can be useful in determining the likely accuracy of the forecasting model adopted. This process will be explored in later sections of this chapter.

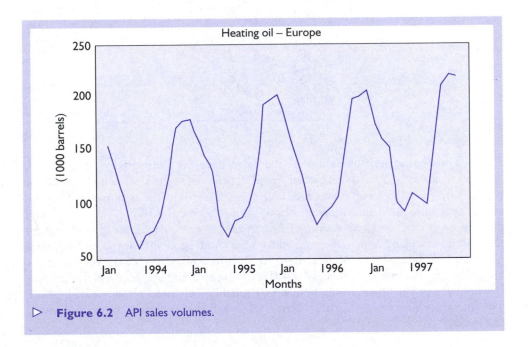

▷ **Figure 6.2**   API sales volumes.

| 6.2 | **Isolating the trend: regression methods** |

The ways in which regression can be used to obtain estimates of values based on given data have been outlined in Chapter 3. The following examples illustrate the regression method used in time series forecasting.

EXAMPLE 1

The table below shows the annual sales figures of motor oil by API in the North American sector.

Year	Annual sales ($ millions)
1984	170
1985	120
1986	105
1987	156
1988	189
1989	107
1990	167
1991	205
1992	178
1993	156
1994	189
1995	235
1996	203
1997	267
1998	239

There is a significant fluctuation in the sales data, as illustrated in Figure 6.3. However, there is a visible upward trend in the sales figures, which could be isolated by the use of regression methods. The regression line is illustrated on the graph in Figure 6.3. The diagram shows that the relationship is not as clearly defined as in the previous example. For instance, the correlation coefficient for these data would be much less, and indeed may not be significant. The long-term trend may be linear or non-linear. It is difficult to analyse the data because of the large fluctuations between successive values. Given such data, it is often necessary to smooth out the fluctuations before any meaningful forecasts can be obtained. The methods of smoothing time series data will be explored in the following sections.

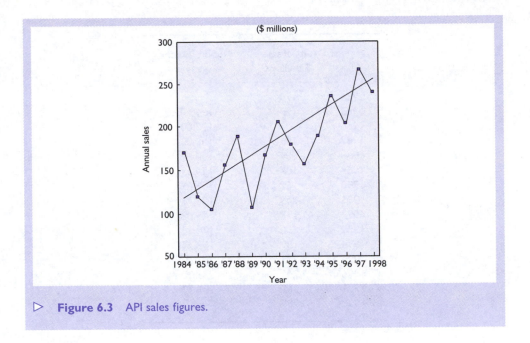

▷ **Figure 6.3**   API sales figures.

<table>
</table>

6.3	**Isolating the trend: moving averages**

The method of moving averages enables a series of values to be 'smoothed out' in order to isolate the trend. Using this method, an average (usually the arithmetic mean) of a fixed number of values is taken. This calculation is then repeated over the complete series of values. The resulting moving averages will then indicate the overall trend in the time series. The number of values used to calculate the average will determine the effectiveness of smoothing. In general, an increase in the number of points used will smooth out the data further.

Consider the data given in the previous example and illustrated in Figure 6.4. The fluctuations in sales figures between the years can be smoothed out using moving averages. For example, the table on p. 226 shows the original sales figures together with moving averages taken over every three values (so-called 3-point moving averages).

The moving averages displayed are calculated in the following way:

The first three sales values (representing 1984 to 1986) are added and divided by three to obtain the first moving average value. Thus,

$$\text{First moving average} = \frac{170 + 120 + 105}{3} = \frac{395}{3} = 131.67$$

Year	Annual sales ($ millions)	3-point moving averages
1984	170	
1985	120	131.67
1986	105	127.00
1987	156	150.00
1988	189	150.67
1989	107	154.33
1990	167	159.67
1991	205	183.33
1992	178	179.67
1993	156	174.33
1994	189	193.33
1995	235	209.00
1996	203	235.00
1997	267	236.33
1998	239	

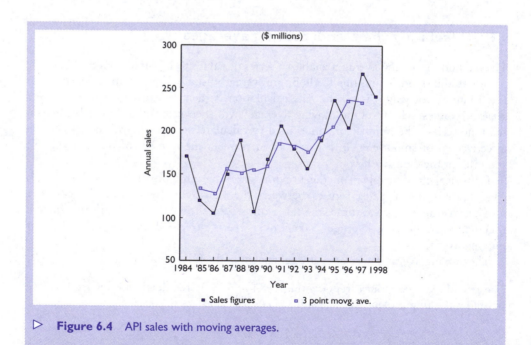

▷   **Figure 6.4**   API sales with moving averages.

This value is written in the **centre** of the values averaged, and therefore it is placed alongside the 1985 figure. The next moving average value is calculated as follows:

$$\text{Second moving average} = \frac{120 + 105 + 156}{3} = \frac{381}{3} = 127$$

This value is placed in the centre of the range and thus appears on the 1986 line.

Further calculations are performed for all sets of three values down to the final figures for 1996 to 1998, where the moving average is found to be 236.33. Note that again, this value is written in the centre of the range and thus corresponds to the 1997 figure.

Figure 6.4 shows how the 3-point moving averages have smoothed out the graph considerably. Many of the fluctuations indicated in the original set of sales figures have been removed, and the resulting set of values indicates more clearly the trend of the data. Thus forecasts could be obtained based on regression line estimates from the moving average values. However, the 3-point moving averages still show some fluctuations. The series could be further smoothed by increasing the number of points used for calculation of the moving averages. Thus, for example, the table below shows the 7-point moving averages calculated for the same set of figures.

Year	Annual sales ($ millions)	7-point moving averages
1984	170	
1985	120	
1986	105	
1987	156	144.86
1988	189	149.86
1989	107	158.14
1990	167	165.43
1991	205	170.14
1992	178	176.71
1993	156	190.43
1994	189	204.71
1995	235	209.57
1996	203	
1997	267	
1998	239	

The 7-point moving averages indicate a consistent trend for this series of data. The diagram shown in Figure 6.5 illustrates the 3-point and 7-point moving averages. It can be seen that the 7-point moving averages show a smoother line with fewer fluctuations than the 3-point values.

From this introduction it should be understood that an increase in the number of points used for the moving average calculations will tend to produce a smoother trend

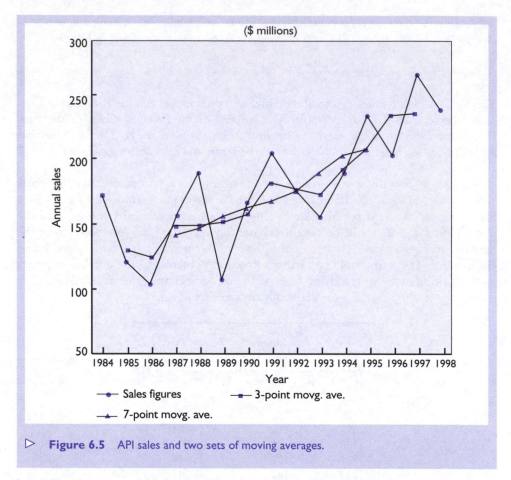

($ millions)

Annual sales

300

250

200

150

100

50

1984 1985 1986 1987 1988 1989 1990 1991 1992 1993 1994 1995 1996 1997 1998

Year

→ Sales figures   ■ 3-point movg. ave.

▲ 7-point movg. ave.

▷ **Figure 6.5**   API sales and two sets of moving averages.

line. Therefore, it could be argued that a 'better' trend line will be obtained by using a large number of points for the moving averages. So the question could be asked: why not take averages over 10 points, or 11 points, or even 15 points? The problem is that an increase in the number of points used in the moving average calculations results in a corresponding decrease in the number of values obtained. For instance, compare the two sets of moving averages calculated in this example. There are thirteen 3-point moving averages shown, and only nine 7-point moving averages obtained. The reader may wish to try to find 9-point or 11-point moving averages to illustrate the corresponding decline in the number of values obtained. Therefore, when deciding on the number of points to calculate moving averages, there needs to be a compromise between using a large number of points (to ensure that a relatively smooth graph is obtained), and a small number of points (to ensure that sufficient values are found).

The problem of deciding on the number of points to use in the moving average calculations is simplified in a situation where there is an obvious regular pattern for the data. For instance, consider data where there is a cycle of values repeated every five points; for example, if sales of a product reach a peak in the 5th, 10th and 15th years. In such a case the data would be smoothed out by using a 5-point moving average.

6.4   Isolating the trend: centred moving averages

When calculating the moving averages over an even number of points there can be problems concerning the placing of the results. As shown in the previous examples, the moving average is placed in the centre of the range of values used. With an even number of values, this would actually correspond to midway between the lines. For example, consider annual sales figures used in the previous section. The 4-point moving averages are calculated and given in the following table. To simplify this example, only the first few sales figures are given.

Year	Annual sales ($ millions)	4-point moving averages
1984	170	
1985	120	
		137.75
1986	105	
		142.50
1987	156	
		139.25
1988	189	
		154.75
1989	107	
		167.00
1990	167	
1991	205	

Note that the moving average figures are displayed in the middle of the appropriate range of values. For instance, the first moving average of the 1984–7 values is written halfway between 1985 and 1986. Similarly, the remaining 4-point moving averages are displayed in this way. The last moving average calculated from the 1988–91 figures is displayed in the centre of this range between 1989 and 1990.

In further analyses of these data it will be necessary to consider moving averages and the corresponding actual values. In order to achieve this **centred moving averages** can be calculated. These values are calculated by finding the average of every pair of moving average values. This equates to a 2-point moving average of the moving averages. These values are shown in the table below.

The centred moving averages could now be used to forecast the trend. These values when plotted on a graph would coincide with the horizontal position of the original data. It is left to the reader to calculate the 4-point moving averages and then the centred moving averages for the complete table of annual sales figures used in the previous section.

Year	Annual sales ($ millions)	4-point moving averages	Centred moving averages
1984	170		
1985	120		
1986	105	137.75	140.13
1987	156	142.50	140.88
1988	189	139.25	147.00
1989	107	154.75	160.88
1990	167	167.00	
1991	205		

6.5   Isolating the trend: exponential smoothing

An alternative approach to eliminating the fluctuations in a series of values is to use the technique of exponential smoothing. Each smoothed value is calculated by a combination of the previous smoothed value and the current time series value. In this calculation the current time series value is weighted using a **smoothing constant** usually denoted by a. The actual calculation can be shown by the following expression:

$$S_t = aX_t + (1 - a)S_{t-1}$$

where

S_t = current smoothed value
X_t = current time series value
S_{t-1} = previous smoothed value
a = smoothing constant

The value of a will always lie between 0 and 1, and a decision will need to be made on the most appropriate value to use in specific examples.

The reader should not be deterred by this seemingly complex mathematical formula. The actual mechanics of calculating the smoothed values using exponential smoothing are no more difficult than the moving averages described in the previous section. This will be illustrated by again considering the annual sales figures at API. The table below shows these sales figures together with the smoothed values assuming a smoothing constant $a = 0.1$

The smoothed values shown in the third column of this table are each based on the current sales figure and previous smoothed value. The first smoothed value (in 1984) is simply a copy of the sales figure, since no previous value is available. The general smoothing formula is used in this table to calculate each of the values as shown below.

$$S_t = aX_t + (1 - a)S_{t-1}$$

Year	Annual sales ($ millions)	Exponential smoothed value ($\alpha = 0.1$)
1984	170	170.00
1985	120	165.00
1986	105	159.00
1987	156	158.70
1988	189	161.73
1989	107	156.26
1990	167	157.33
1991	205	162.10
1992	178	163.69
1993	156	162.92
1994	189	165.53
1995	235	172.47
1996	203	175.53
1997	267	184.67
1998	239	190.11

The value of $\alpha = 0.1$, and therefore this expression becomes:

$$S_t = 0.1X_t + (1 - 0.1)S_{t-1}$$
$$S_t = 0.1X_t + 0.9S_{t-1}$$

Thus, the smoothed value in 1985 is found as follows:

$$S_{1985} = 0.1X_{1985} + 0.9S_{1984}$$

Now, the smoothed value in 1984 is $S_{1984} = 170$. Also, the sales value in 1985 is $X_{1985} = 120$. Therefore, the smoothed value in 1985 is

$$S_{1985} = 0.1 * 120 + 0.9 * 170$$
$$= 12 + 153$$
$$= 165$$

Similarly, the smoothed value in 1986 is found by:

$$S_{1986} = 0.1X_{1986} + 0.9S_{1985}$$
$$= 0.1 * 105 + 0.9 * 165$$
$$= 10.5 + 148.5$$
$$= 159$$

Similarly, the remaining smoothed values displayed in the table are calculated in this way.

Figure 6.6 shows the original sales figures together with the exponentially smoothed figures using $\alpha = 0.1$. The graph in Figure 6.6 shows that the exponential smoothing method does significantly smooth out the series of values. It would be straightforward to use these points to estimate the trend in subsequent years. However, using a value of α as low as 0.1 presents some problems. The main drawback is that there tends to be a lag (or delay) between changes in the original series of values and corresponding changes in the smoothed values. For instance, it can be seen that there is an increasing trend in sales for the data analysed. However, the moving averages are slow to identify this trend. Notice on the graph in Figure 6.6 how over the last five years the smoothed values are all lower than the actual sales figures. In general, a lower value of α is less likely to be sensitive to changes in the trend in a given time series. To solve this problem we could try using a higher value of α. For instance, consider the smoothing constant $\alpha = 0.3$. The table below shows the smoothed values calculated based on this constant.

Year	Annual sales ($ millions)	Exponential smoothed value ($\alpha = 0.3$)
1984	170	170.00
1985	120	155.00
1986	105	140.00
1987	156	144.80
1988	189	158.06
1989	107	142.74
1990	167	150.02
1991	205	166.51
1992	178	169.96
1993	156	165.77
1994	189	172.74
1995	235	191.42
1996	203	194.89
1997	267	216.52
1998	239	223.27

These values are calculated using the same approach. Thus, the first smoothed value in 1984 is simply a copy of the sales figure. After this, the smoothed values are calculated using the formula introduced earlier. For example, the smoothed value for 1985 is found by the following expression:

$$S_{1985} = 0.3 X_{1985} + (1 - 0.3) S_{1984}$$

$$= 0.3 * 120 + 0.7 * 170$$

$$= 36 + 119$$

Thus, $S_{1985} = 155$

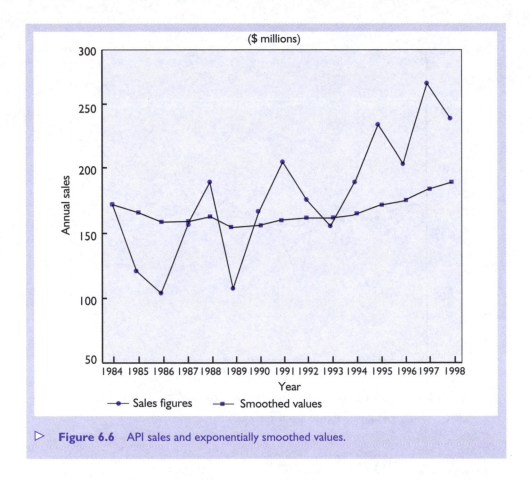

($ millions)

—●— Sales figures   —■— Smoothed values

▷   **Figure 6.6**   API sales and exponentially smoothed values.

The remaining smoothed values are calculated in a similar way. Figure 6.7 gives a comparison of using the two different smoothing constants in order to isolate the trend.

Two points should be noted in considering the differences between the performance of the two smoothing constants in isolating the trend. Firstly, the time lag apparent when using $\alpha = 0.1$ is much less marked for the smoothed values using $\alpha = 0.3$. Generally, higher values of α produce smoothed values which are more sensitive to changes in recent values of a time series. Thus, these smoothed values do not lag behind the time series to the same degree as when using lower values of the smoothing constant. This factor is not important when there is no notable change in the overall trend of the time series. However, this does present serious problems in forecasting when there is a significant increase or decrease in the overall trend of the time series. The values obtained in this example using $\alpha = 0.3$ provide a better indication of the overall trend than those using $\alpha = 0.1$ as shown in Figure 6.7.

The second point that should be considered is that lower values of α tend to produce a smoother set of figures, which enables the isolation of trend to be more

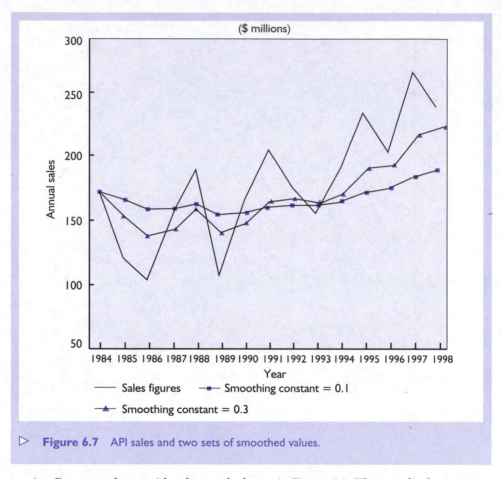

▷ **Figure 6.7**   API sales and two sets of smoothed values.

precise. For example, consider the graph shown in Figure 6.8. The set of values using a smoothing constant of $\alpha = 0.3$, whilst being relatively smooth, has considerably more variation than the series obtained using $\alpha = 0.1$.

Consequently, a compromise is needed when deciding on the most appropriate value of the smoothing constant to be used in a given problem. A low value of α produces a much smoother set of trend elements. However, a high value of α is more sensitive to changes in the trend. In most practical examples, the value of the smoothing constant α will lie between 0.1 and 0.3, though in exceptional circumstances values outside this range can be considered.

6.6   Exercises: isolating the trend

1.(E)   The number of patients treated each day in the Radiology Department at St. Joseph's hospital is shown below over a period of 20 days:

Day:	1	2	3	4	5	6	7	8	9	10
Patients:	35	29	40	30	52	22	19	30	47	28
Day:	11	12	13	14	15	16	17	18	19	20
Patients:	22	16	51	40	35	57	28	33	42	39

(i) Illustrate this series of values over the 20-day period. Allow additional space for day 21 on the horizontal axis in your graph.

(ii) Calculate the 5-point moving averages for these data, and plot these values onto the graph.

(iii) By drawing a line of 'best fit' through these moving average points, extend the line and estimate the number of patients treated in day 21. Consider how accurate this estimate is likely to be.

2.(I) Using the set of data on patients in the previous example, carry out the following analyses:

(i) Use exponential smoothing with $\alpha = 0.2$ to calculate smoothed values over the 20-day period.

(ii) Plot these smoothed values onto a graph and use this graph to estimate the number of patients treated in day 21. How does this estimate compare with the value obtained using moving averages?

(iii) Repeat parts (i) and (ii) using a smoothing constant of 0.1. Compare the results obtained.

3.(I) The annual car sales in the UK during the period 1986–97 are given in the table below:

Year	Car sales (100 thousands)
1986	3.8
1987	4.7
1988	3.9
1989	2.7
1990	2.9
1991	2.3
1992	3.0
1993	3.6
1994	2.9
1995	3.7
1996	4.5
1997	4.2

(i) Isolate the trend using 3-point moving averages, and plot these values on a graph together with the original sales figures.

(ii) By extending the trend line, forecast the car sales during 1998 and 1999. (Note that the trend may **not** be linear.)

(iii) Use exponential smoothing with $\alpha = 0.1$ to smooth out the car sales figures, and apply these figures to graphically obtain an estimate of the sales during 1998 and 1999. In this example, which method of isolating the trend would you consider is more appropriate, and why?

6.7   Seasonal variations

In many business examples involving financial and economic data, a seasonal element may be apparent. The following examples illustrate two models that are often used in estimating seasonal variations. These are the additive and multiplicative models. The two models can be briefly described as follows:

Additive model – used when the seasonal elements are relatively constant over the complete time period being analysed. In such a case the time series value can be expressed as the sum of a trend and seasonal component. The standard expression describing this type of model would be:

$$X_i = T_i + S_i$$

where

X_i = actual figure in period i
T_i = trend in period i
S_i = seasonal variation in period i

Multiplicative model – this type of model is used when the seasonal elements change in proportion to the trend values over the complete time period being analysed. In this case, the time series value can be expressed as the product of a trend and seasonal component. This can be formally expressed as:

$$X_i = T_i * S_i$$

The graphs shown in Figure 6.8 illustrate two time series together with the corresponding trend lines. In Figure 6.8(i) the variations from this trend are relatively constant, whereas in Figure 6.8(ii) the variations increase as the trend increases. This simple illustration suggests that an additive model would be used to represent the data in 6.8(i) and a multiplicative model used for Figure 6.8(ii).

It should be noted that the seasonal elements (S_i) indicated in the two expressions above are obtained in different ways, depending on the model used. The following sections illustrate the methods of estimating the seasonal components using each type of model. The examples given will use moving averages to isolate the trend values. However, the same approach could be adopted by using other methods of estimating the trend such as exponential smoothing.

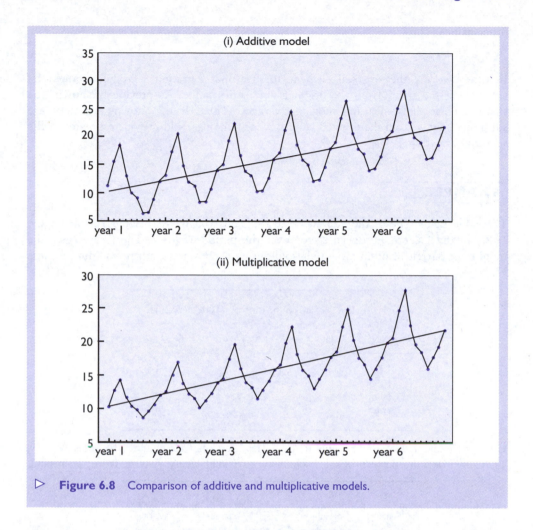

> **Figure 6.8** Comparison of additive and multiplicative models.

6.8 Seasonal variations: additive model

In this section we will consider how seasonal variations are calculated assuming that the additive model is appropriate. Thus we will use the model:

$$X_i = T_i + S_i$$

where

X_i = actual figure in period i
T_i = trend in period i
S_i = seasonal variation in period i

Rearranging this equation enables us to find the seasonal element in terms of the other values. Thus,

$$S_i = X_i - T_i$$

In other words, the seasonal element (or **seasonal variation**) can be obtained by subtracting the trend from the original time series value. As previously shown, the trend can be isolated using moving averages. Thus, if the moving averages are subtracted away from the original values, what remains could provide estimates of the seasonal variation.

EXAMPLE 1

The table below shows the volume of heating oil sold by Associated Petroleum Inc (API) in the Eastern European sector over the period 1994–7. The figures give the number of barrels of oil in thousands sold during each four-month period during these years.

	Sales of heating oil (1000 barrels)		
Year	Jan–Apr	May–Aug	Sep–Dec
1994	35	15	42
1995	36	19	44
1996	41	22	47
1997	45	26	52

Given this set of data there seems to be a clear seasonal element to the sales figures. There is a definite pattern in sales which repeats itself every year. It is not surprising

Year	Period	Sales (1000 barrels)	3-point averages
1994	Jan–Apr	35	
	May–Aug	15	30.67
	Sep–Dec	42	31.00
1995	Jan–Apr	36	32.33
	May–Aug	19	33.00
	Sep–Dec	44	34.67
1996	Jan–Apr	41	35.67
	May–Aug	22	36.67
	Sep–Dec	47	38.00
1997	Jan–Apr	45	39.33
	May–Aug	26	41.00
	Sep–Dec	52	

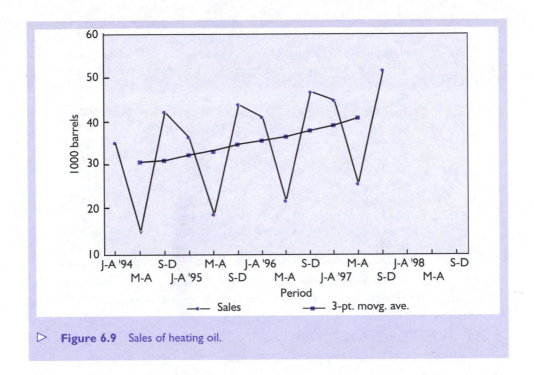

▷ **Figure 6.9** Sales of heating oil.

that the sales in heating oil tend to decline in the summer period and reach a peak at the start of the winter season. This fluctuation between successive values can be smoothed out using moving averages as shown in the table on p. 238. Three-point moving averages are used since there is a regular annual pattern in the sales figures (involving three values each year).

The graph in Figure 6.9 shows the sales figures together with the 3-point moving averages. The moving averages could be used to estimate the trend after 1997. The graph shows that there is a reasonably regular pattern of sales recurring each year. Now consider the seasonal component in this series of sales values. The variations above and below the trend line are relatively constant. Thus, the additive model seems to be the most suitable in this case. The seasonal element can be isolated by subtracting the moving average values from the original figures as described earlier in this section. The differences, usually referred to as the **deviations**, are shown in the table on p. 240.

There is no moving average figure for Jan–Apr in 1994, and therefore the first deviation is calculated for the following period. During May–Aug 1994 the actual sales figure was 15 and the corresponding moving average equalled 30.67. The deviation was then calculated as $15 - 30.67 = -15.67$.

Similarly, in Sep–Dec of 1994, the deviation was calculated by sales minus the moving average, which gave $42 - 31 = 11$. The remaining deviations in the above table were calculated using the same approach.

Year	Period	Sales (1000 barrels)	3-point moving averages	Deviations
1994	Jan–Apr	35		
	May–Aug	15	30.67	−15.67
	Sep–Dec	42	31.00	11.00
1995	Jan–Apr	36	32.33	3.67
	May–Aug	19	33.00	−14.00
	Sep–Dec	44	34.67	9.33
1996	Jan–Apr	41	35.67	5.33
	May–Aug	22	36.67	−14.67
	Sep–Dec	47	38.00	9.00
1997	Jan–Apr	45	39.33	5.67
	May–Aug	26	41.00	−15.00
	Sep–Dec	52		

The 'seasons' (or periods) during the year are considered separately in order to analyse the seasonal variations. For instance, during the period Jan–Apr the following deviations were obtained:

1995: 3.67;   1996: 5.33;   1997: 5.67

Note that no deviation for 1994 has been obtained. These values show the difference between the actual sales figures and the moving average values in the given periods. The average of these values would provide a simple estimate of the seasonal variation for Jan–Apr in other years. Thus, the seasonal variation for Jan–Apr would be estimated as:

$$\frac{3.67 + 5.33 + 5.67}{3} = \frac{14.67}{3} = 4.89$$

Similarly, the other seasonal variations can be estimated as follows:

$$\text{May–Aug:} \quad \frac{-15.67 - 14.00 - 14.67 - 15.00}{4} = \frac{-59.34}{4} = -14.83$$

Note that four deviations have been calculated in the table for the May–Aug period.

Finally, the seasonal variation in Sep–Dec can be estimated as follows:

$$\text{Sep–Dec:} \quad \frac{11.00 + 9.33 + 9.00}{3} = \frac{29.33}{3} = 9.78$$

These estimates of the seasonal variations can be combined with the trend estimates to obtain forecasts for later sales figures. For instance, in order to forecast the sales during each period in 1998 we can estimate the trend from the moving averages, and add to the seasonal variation estimates.

Figure 6.10 shows the graph of sales and moving averages. A trend line is drawn as the line of 'best fit' through the moving average values. This line has been extended to obtain estimates of the trend during each period in 1998.

Alternatively, a regression equation method could be used to obtain these estimates mathematically. From the graph shown in Figure 6.10, the trend estimates for each period in 1998 are as follows:

Jan–Apr: 43;   May–Aug: 44;   Sep–Dec: 45

Combining these trend estimates with the seasonal variations previously calculated using the additive model, $X_i = T_i + S_i$, we can obtain forecasts of the sales figures in each period of 1998 as follows:

Jan–Apr: $43 + 4.89 = 47.89$ (=48)

May–Aug: $44 - 14.83 = 29.17$ (=29)

Sep–Dec: $45 + 9.78 = 54.78$ (=55)

Clearly, such forecasts cannot be given to a greater accuracy than the original data provided. Thus, the values should be rounded to the nearest whole numbers. The forecasts of sales of heating oil during 1998 are:

Jan–Apr: 48 000 barrels

May–Aug: 29 000 barrels

Sep–Dec: 55 000 barrels

Thus, total sales during 1998 are estimated to be 132 000 barrels.

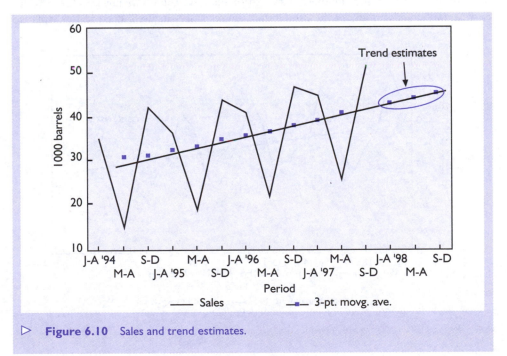

▷ **Figure 6.10** Sales and trend estimates.

EXAMPLE 2

In this example we will consider a situation requiring the calculation of moving averages over an even number of values. This will then involve the use of centred moving averages in order to determine the trend of the time series. The table below shows the bimonthly production figures of a medium-sized manufacturing company based in Dublin. The figures given in the table show the total production output for every two months given in tonnes.

Period	Production output (tonnes)			
	1995	1996	1997	1998
Jan–Feb	120	119	110	107
Mar–Apr	132	125	119	114
May–Jun	106	99	102	92
Jul–Aug	98	98	89	88
Sep–Oct	88	86	79	75
Nov–Dec	94	90	88	80

The production output given displays a regular annual pattern. Thus, moving averages taken over the annual period will enable the trend to be isolated. Thus, a 6-point moving average is found for these data. Unfortunately, these moving averages do not correspond exactly to any of the production figures since they will need to be displayed

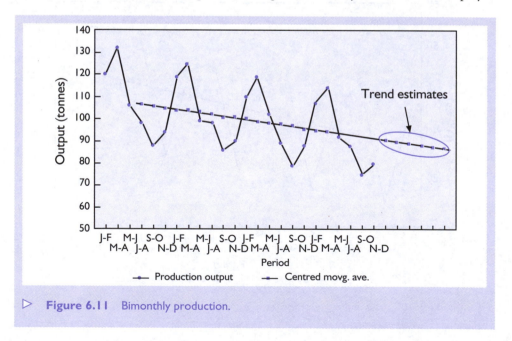

▷ **Figure 6.11** Bimonthly production.

Year	Period	Output	6-point moving ave.	Centred moving ave.	Deviations
1995	Jan–Feb	120			
	Mar–Apr	132			
	May–Jun	106			
			106.33		
	Jul–Aug	98		106.25	−8.25
			106.17		
	Sep–Oct	88		105.58	−17.58
			105.00		
	Nov–Dec	94		104.42	−10.42
			103.83		
1996	Jan–Feb	119		103.83	15.17
			103.83		
	Mar–Apr	125		103.67	21.33
			103.50		
	May–Jun	99		103.17	−4.17
			102.83		
	Jul–Aug	98		102.08	−4.08
			101.33		
	Sep–Oct	86		100.83	−14.83
			100.33		
	Nov–Dec	90		100.58	−10.58
			100.83		
1997	Jan–Feb	110		100.08	9.92
			99.33		
	Mar–Apr	119		98.75	20.25
			98.17		
	May–Jun	102		98.00	4.00
			97.83		
	Jul–Aug	89		97.58	−8.58
			97.33		
	Sep–Oct	79		96.92	−17.92
			96.50		
	Nov–Dec	88		95.67	−7.67
			94.83		
1998	Jan–Feb	107		94.75	12.25
			94.67		
	Mar–Apr	114		94.33	19.67
			94.00		
	May–Jun	92		93.33	−1.33
			92.67		
	Jul–Aug	88			
	Sep–Oct	75			
	Nov–Dec	80			

halfway between the lines. Thus, the centred moving averages are found as shown in the table on p. 243. The deviations are then obtained by subtracting these centred moving averages from the production data as shown in the table.

The production output figures together with the centred moving averages are displayed in the graph in Figure 6.11. The graph shows how the centred moving averages are used to obtain estimates of the trend during the next year (1999). From the graph the trend estimates during each period in 1999 are as follows:

Jan–Feb: 90.6   Mar–Apr: 89.8   May–Jun: 89.1

Jul–Aug: 88.3   Sep–Oct: 87.5   Nov–Dec: 86.8

The seasonal variations are estimated as the average deviations in each period as shown in the following table:

Year	Jan–Feb	Mar–Apr	May–Jun	Jul–Aug	Sep–Oct	Nov–Dec
1995				−8.25	−17.58	−10.42
1996	15.17	21.33	−4.17	−4.08	−14.83	−10.58
1997	9.92	20.25	4.00	−8.58	−17.92	−7.67
1998	12.25	19.67	−1.33			
Average	12.45	20.42	−0.50	−6.97	−16.78	−9.56

These estimates for the seasonal variations can be combined with the trend estimates to obtain forecasts of the production output during each period in 1999 as shown below:

Jan–Feb: 90.6 + 12.45 = 103.05 = 103 tonnes

Mar–Apr: 89.8 + 20.42 = 110.22 = 110 tonnes

May–Jun: 89.1 − 0.5 = 88.6 = 89 tonnes

Jul–Aug: 88.3 − 6.97 = 81.33 = 81 tonnes

Sep–Oct: 87.5 − 16.78 = 70.72 = 71 tonnes

Nov–Dec: 86.8 − 9.56 = 77.24 = 77 tonnes

The accuracy and reliability of these forecasts will be discussed in a later section. However, it should be noted that the forecast model is totally based on past data. It is assumed that all other factors are constant, and that the trend and seasonal patterns continue as displayed in the historical data provided.

EXAMPLE 3

In this example we will consider in more detail the process of evaluating seasonal variations. The actual values of the seasonal variations obtained in the previous two examples should be amended because of the slight bias that has been introduced. Consider example 1 again. In this example the following deviations were obtained:

Year	Jan–Apr	May–Aug	Sep–Dec
1994		−15.67	11.00
1995	3.67	−14.00	9.33
1996	5.33	−14.67	9.00
1997	5.67	−15.00	
Average	4.89	−14.84	9.78
Overall average deviation			−0.06

The table shows the deviations obtained and the average deviations in each period. The overall mean of the three averages 6.89, −14.84 and 9.78 is found to be −0.06. Strictly, the overall average should be zero if no bias is to be introduced into the forecasts. Thus, the average deviation for each period should be adjusted in order to achieve this. This can be done by adding 0.06 to each value. Thus the true estimates of the seasonal variations should be

Jan–Apr: $4.89 + 0.06 = 4.95$

May–Aug: $-14.84 + 0.06 = -14.78$

Sep–Dec: $9.78 + 0.06 = 9.84$

These values could then be combined with the trend estimates to obtain the most reliable forecasts. In many examples, this adjustment of the seasonal variations will not drastically affect the overall estimates. However, in order to avoid bias in the forecasts, this process should be performed.

6.9 Seasonal variations: multiplicative model

In this section we will consider how seasonal variations are calculated assuming that the multiplicative model is appropriate. Thus we will use the model:

$$X_i = T_i * S_i$$

where

X_i = actual figure in period i
T_i = trend in period i
S_i = seasonal variation in period i

Rearranging this equation enables us to find the seasonal element in terms of the other values. Thus,

$$S_i = X_i / T_i$$

In other words, the seasonal element can be obtained by dividing the trend into the original time series value. One approach to isolating the trend is to use moving averages. Thus, if the moving averages are divided into the original values, the results provide estimates of the seasonal variation. This process is illustrated in the following examples.

EXAMPLE 1

A property management organisation is considering a long-term strategy on the acquisition of commercial buildings. The company has employed business consultants to produce forecasts of the commercial rentals likely to be charged over the next five years. The data below show the average advertised annual rents charged for office space in central London over the years 1993–7. The information has been collected every four months over this period. The figures shown in the following table give the average annual rental per square metre of office space.

Year	Annual office rental (£ per sq. m.)		
	Jan–Apr	May–Aug	Sep–Dec
1993	120	100	121
1994	138	120.	142
1995	160	138	163
1996	184	162	182
1997	208	175	206

Again this example illustrates a strong seasonal element. In many practical examples, it is difficult to decide whether to use an additive or multiplicative model. Essentially, if the variations remain constant then an additive model is appropriate. In this example, the variations tend to increase as the trend increases. For instance, consider the spread of values in 1993 (100 in May–Aug and 121 in Sep–Dec), compared to the corresponding spread in 1997 (175 in May–Aug and 206 in Sep–Dec). This shows that the spread seems to be increasing, and therefore a multiplicative model may be more appropriate.

The trend can be isolated by calculating the 3-point moving averages. The seasonal element in a multiplicative model can be isolated by dividing the original data by the trend values. Thus, the table on p. 247 shows the rental data, with the next column displaying the 3-point moving averages. The final column gives the **ratios** obtained by dividing the rentals by the moving averages.

The ratios in the last column are calculated by dividing the rental values by the corresponding moving averages. The first available moving average figure corresponds to May–Aug 1993. In this period the rental is £100 and the moving average is £113.67. Thus, the ratio is obtained by $100/113.67 = 0.88$. Similarly, the remaining ratios are calculated in this column.

Year	Period	Office rentals	3-point moving averages	Ratios
1993	Jan–Apr	120		
	May–Aug	100	113.67	0.88
	Sep–Dec	121	119.67	1.01
1994	Jan–Apr	138	126.33	1.09
	May–Aug	120	133.33	0.90
	Sep–Dec	142	140.67	1.01
1995	Jan–Apr	160	146.67	1.09
	May–Aug	138	153.67	0.90
	Sep–Dec	163	161.67	1.01
1996	Jan–Apr	184	169.67	1.08
	May–Aug	162	176.00	0.92
	Sep–Dec	182	184.00	0.99
1997	Jan–Apr	208	188.33	1.10
	May–Aug	175	196.33	0.89
	Sep–Dec	206		

These ratios can be used to estimate the seasonal element in the time series. This can be simply achieved by finding the average ratio in each 'season' separately. Estimates of the seasonal variations are shown in the following table:

Year	Jan–Apr	May–Aug	Sep–Dec
1993		0.88	1.01
1994	1.09	0.90	1.01
1995	1.09	0.90	1.01
1996	1.08	0.92	0.99
1997	1.10	0.89	
Average	1.090	0.898	1.005

As in the previous examples using the additive model, the trend can be estimated graphically from the moving averages. The graph shown in Figure 6.12 illustrates the rental data together with the 3-point moving averages. A trend line is drawn through the moving averages and is extended in order to obtain forecasts for each period in 1998. From the graph, the estimates of trend in each period in 1998 are as follows:

Jan–Apr: 203   May–Aug: 210   Sep–Dec: 217

Combining these values with the seasonal elements using the multiplicative model we can obtain estimates of the likely office rental charges during 1998:

Jan–Apr: $203 * 1.090 = £221$

May–Aug: $210 * 0.898 = £189$

Sep–Dec: $217 * 1.005 = £218$

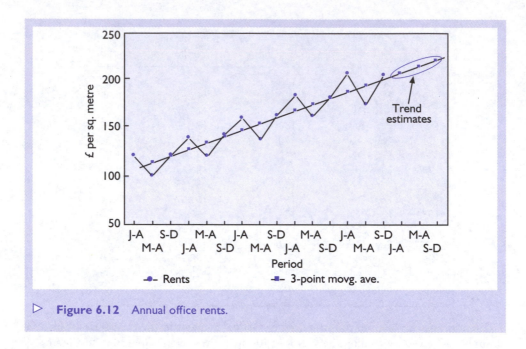

Figure 6.12   Annual office rents.

Further estimates could be obtained for future years by extending the trend line to obtain new trend estimates and combining these figures with the seasonal variations already estimated.

EXAMPLE 2

The actual estimates of the seasonal variations should be adjusted for any bias that is inherent as introduced when considering the additive model. Consider the previous example in this section. The table below shows the ratios and average ratios that have been obtained.

Year	Jan–Apr	May–Aug	Sep–Dec
1993		0.88	1.01
1994	1.09	0.90	1.01
1995	1.09	0.90	1.01
1996	1.08	0.92	0.99
1997	1.10	0.89	
Average	1.090	0.898	1.005
Overall average ratio			0.998

The average ratios for each 'season' have been calculated as 1.090, 0.898 and 1.005. An unbiased estimate would be obtained if the overall average of these deviations is 1. In this example, the overall average is 0.998. Thus an adjustment is made to all the averages by dividing by 0.998 in order to correct the seasonal estimates. Thus, the seasonal variations in this example are estimated to be:

Jan–Apr: 1.090/0.998 = 1.092

May–Aug: 0.898/0.998 = 0.900

Sep–Dec: 1.005/0.998 = 1.007

These corrected values of the seasonal variations can be combined with the trend estimates to obtain an improved forecast.

6.10 Exercises: additive and multiplicative models

1.(E) The table below shows the total export orders for a company during 1993–6. The figures are given in £ millions.

	Total exports (£ millions)		
Year	Jan–Apr	May–Aug	Sep–Dec
1993	4.5	5.6	4.9
1994	5.1	5.9	5.2
1995	5.4	6.8	5.8
1996	6.0	6.8	6.1

(i) Using three-point moving averages, isolate the trend.

(ii) Estimate the seasonal variations, and thus forecast the value of exports for the company during the three periods in 1997.

2.(I) The figures shown below give the total newspaper sales of a company based in Canada in each quarter during the years 1994–7. The figures show the average daily circulation over each quarter in 100 000s.

	Daily newspaper sales			
Period	1994	1995	1996	1997
1st Quarter	2.2	2.6	2.9	3.2
2nd Quarter	2.9	3.2	3.4	3.6
3rd Quarter	3.3	3.6	3.9	4.2
4th Quarter	2.4	2.7	2.8	3.1

(i) Plot these values onto a graph.

(ii) Using trend and seasonal variations, estimate the circulation figures in each quarter during 1998 by using an additive model.

(iii) Would an additive or multiplicative model be appropriate in this example? Forecast the same range of figures using the multiplicative model and compare your results from the two methods.

3.(I) The following table shows the number of new car registrations in the UK during the period 1994–7. The figures are given in thousands.

	Number of new car registrations (thousands)		
Year	Jan–Apr	May–Aug	Sep–Dec
1994	–	220	431
1995	225	264	530
1996	282	352	650
1997	334	410	770

(i) Draw a graph of these figures together with the moving averages to isolate the trend.

(ii) What would be the most appropriate model to use for forecasting this time series?

(iii) Use this model to estimate the number of new car registrations in the three periods in 1998.

(iv) How would you forecast the number of registrations in the first period Jan–Apr of 1999?

6.11 Cyclical variation

The identification of a cyclical element in the time series can be extremely difficult. It is usually only possible when there are data available over a long period of time. The method of smoothing out the series of values using moving averages or exponential smoothing removes the seasonal and irregular variation from the data and the remaining values contain both the trend and the cyclical elements. It is beyond the scope of this text to consider cyclical variation in isolation. Most techniques involve the analysis of the trend and cyclical elements together as one entity. However, it is useful to consider an example where a cyclical variation is evident from the data. The graph shown in Figure 6.13 gives the sale of automobiles in the UK during the years 1966–96. The graph shows the number of cars sold each year together with the 5-year moving averages. The graph shown in Figure 6.13 indicates the cyclical element in this series of values. The overall trend in car sales is increasing during this period. However, there are a number of peaks and troughs corresponding to the

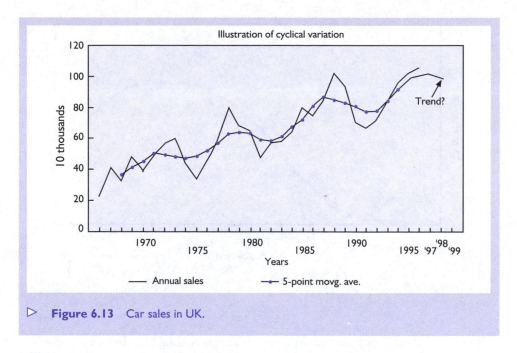

▷ **Figure 6.13**   Car sales in UK.

business cycle periods of economic boom and slump. For instance, the moving averages show peak periods in 1971, 1979 and 1987. The bottom of each cycle corresponds to the slump periods of 1974–5, 1982 and 1991–2. The moving averages help to highlight these elements, particularly when there are considerable irregular movements inherent in the data. These cyclical movements are typical of a range of data which in some way follow the business cycle indicating the general state of the economy.

Figure 6.13 illustrates a plausible forecast of the trend incorporating the cyclical element. The illustration shows the trend increasing for another two years and then starting to decline again. Such estimates of the trend could be incorporated with seasonal elements to forecast the volume of car sales in each quarter or each month as shown in earlier sections. Forecasting models incorporating distinct cyclical elements can be expressed as follows:

Additive model: $X_i = T_i + S_i + C_i$

Multiplicative model: $X_i = T_i * S_i * C_i$

where C_i is the cyclical element in period i.

Other cyclical variations can occur in sales/demand forecasting corresponding to the life-cycle of specific products. For instance, the standard life-cycle of a single product includes the stages of introduction, growth, maturity and decline. Consider the introduction of a new product such as the mobile phone. Initially, sales of such a product are slow, when only the 'innovators' or technical enthusiasts would be

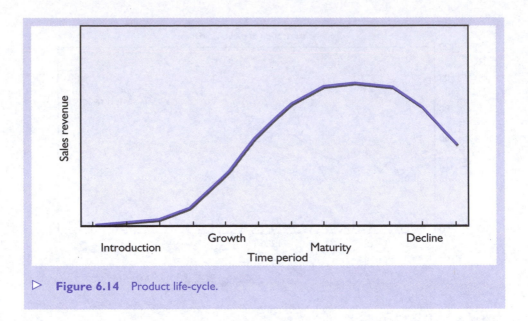

willing to purchase. In the growth stage, an increasing number of people are interested in the product, with unit prices falling and services improving. The maturity stage is reached when the vast majority of potential customers have already bought a mobile phone. Following this there is a decline in sales, which can only be reversed by the introduction of new improved products to replace the existing range. This life-cycle is illustrated in Figure 6.14, which shows the volume of sales at each stage in the product life-cycle. Such a cycle can be incorporated in the forecast model used and can be considered as part of the trend or as a separate cyclical element.

6.12   Irregular variations: errors in forecasting

Irregular (or random) movements are present in most practical time series. A measurement of the magnitude and spread of these random fluctuations can assist us in determining the accuracy of the forecasting model used. These irregular variations can be considered as the errors in the forecast. Such errors can be determined by using the forecast model on data already collected. Thus, the model is used to predict total sales in the first quarter and the result is compared with the actual sales figure obtained. The difference between the forecasted value and the actual figure is the error (or irregular variation) that has occurred.

The **average error** and the **root mean square** of errors are two useful statistics in evaluating the performance of the forecast model. The following examples will illustrate the use of these two values.

EXAMPLE I

A forecast has been obtained on the number of patients each day requiring treatment in the Radiology Department of St. Joseph's hospital. The table below shows the estimated number of patients requiring treatment using the forecasting model compared to the actual number of patients arriving. The data have been collected over an eight-day period.

Day:	1	2	3	4	5	6	7	8
Forecast (F_i):	28	30	35	29	27	24	30	31
Actual (X_i):	35	28	40	28	31	19	33	32

Denoting the forecast values by F_i and the actual figures by X_i, we can calculate the forecasting error by finding the difference between them, i.e. calculating $X_i - F_i$ as shown below:

$$X_i - F_i: \quad 7 \quad -2 \quad 5 \quad -1 \quad 4 \quad -5 \quad 3 \quad 1$$

The average (arithmetic mean) of these errors is found by the general formula:

$$\text{Average error} = \frac{\Sigma(X_i - F_i)}{n}$$

where n is the number of values under consideration.

In this example, the

$$\text{Average error} = \frac{\Sigma(X_i - F_i)}{8} = \frac{12}{8} = 1.5$$

This indicates that, on average, the actual number of patients is 1.5 above the forecast value. This implies that the forecast model being used generally underestimates the number of patients arriving. In such a case it may be that the model needs to be investigated and amended. Ideally, the average error is zero, and is obtained when the positive and negative errors tend to balance each other. However, it should be stated that the average has been obtained over a very small sample. A larger sample, such as the data for a complete year, would enable us to determine the likely accuracy of the forecasting method with a greater degree of confidence.

The root mean square (RMS) of these errors is obtained by the following formula:

$$\text{Root mean square} = \sqrt{\frac{\Sigma(X_i - F_i)^2}{n}}$$

In this example we have:

$$(X_i - F_i)^2: \quad 49 \quad 4 \quad 25 \quad 1 \quad 16 \quad 25 \quad 9 \quad 1$$

These data give $\Sigma (X_i - F_i)^2 = 130$. Therefore the

$$\text{RMS} = \sqrt{130/8} = \sqrt{16.25} = 4.03$$

This value gives some indication of the accuracy of the forecast model used. A low value of the RMS indicates a more reliable forecasting model. The RMS can be used to provide an estimate of the confidence intervals in any forecast. The value can be used as an estimate of the standard deviation, and assuming that the errors are normally distributed, the 95% confidence limits for the actual value based on a forecast F are obtained by:

$$F \pm 1.96\text{RMS}$$

This is obtained by using the normal distribution confidence limits formula described in Chapter 2. This formula also assumes that there is no bias in the forecast method. Thus, over a large sample, the average error is found to be zero. If this is not the case, then this error term should also be included in the formula to obtain confidence intervals.

Thus, in this example, let us assume that the forecast model gives an estimate that the number of patients arriving on a given day will be 40. Therefore, we know that the 95% confidence limits for the number of patients arriving are:

$$
\begin{aligned}
F \pm 1.96\text{RMS} &= 40 \pm 1.96 * 4.03 \\
&= 40 \pm 7.9 \\
&= 32.1 \text{ to } 47.9
\end{aligned}
$$

Thus, we can be 95% sure that the number of patients arriving on this day will be between 32 and 48.

EXAMPLE 2

In an earlier example, forecasts have been obtained for the bi-monthly production output for a company in Dublin. The estimates were obtained for 1999 by using linear trend and an additive model. The forecasted values given in tonnes were as follows:

Jan–Feb: 103	Mar–Apr: 110	May–Jun: 89
Jul–Aug: 81	Sep–Oct: 71	Nov–Dec: 77

In fact during 1999, the actual production output values were found to be:

Jan–Feb: 110	Mar–Apr: 107	May–Jun: 79
Jul–Aug: 90	Sep–Oct: 72	Nov–Dec: 75

The table on p. 255 shows the actual values (X_i) together with the forecasted figures (F_i) with columns for the calculation of the required summations.

From the table we find that $\Sigma (X_i - F_i) = 2$ and $\Sigma (X_i - F_i)^2 = 244$. Thus, the average error from these data

$$\frac{\Sigma (X_i - F_i)}{6} = \frac{2}{6} = 0.33$$

X_i	F_i	$X_i - F_i$	$(X_i - F_i)^2$
110	103	7	49
107	110	−3	9
79	89	−10	100
90	81	9	81
72	71	1	1
75	77	−2	4
533	531	2	244

The RMS is

$$\sqrt{\frac{\Sigma (X_i - F_i)^2}{6}} = \sqrt{\frac{244}{6}} = \sqrt{40.67} = 6.38$$

Therefore, consider a forecast of 90 tonnes for the production output in the next period. Assuming that the errors are normally distributed with an average of zero, the 95% confidence limits for the actual production figure are found as follows:

$$F \pm 1.96\,\text{RMS} = 90 \pm 1.96 * 6.38$$
$$= 90 \pm 12.5$$
$$= 77.5 \text{ to } 102.5$$

Thus, with such a forecast, the actual production figure is likely to be in the range 77 to 103 tonnes. This demonstrates that the forecast model does not produce very reliable results. A likely error of up to 12.5 on an estimate of 90 tonnes (or 14% error) may be unacceptable in many applications.

6.13   Performance of forecasting models

The performance of the model used for forecasting can be measured using the techniques introduced in the previous section. Essentially, we are concerned with the accuracy of the forecasted values. The forecast error is the difference between the predicted value and the actual value. Whichever model is applied, it is important to examine its effectiveness in relation to this accuracy, and ideally forecast errors should be kept to a minimum. The performance of a specific model relies on a number of factors as described below:

Available data

The historical data available for use in developing the forecasting model are a vital ingredient. Ideally, there should be a large amount of data available over a wide time-span. For instance, in order to forecast the sales demand during 1998, it would not generally be sufficient to use data obtained just from the previous year. A span of at least four or five years of available sales data may be enough to produce a reliable model. Furthermore, the data used must be 'typical' of the situation. For instance, during October 1986 the global financial markets suffered a crash in share prices. Thus, data taken from this untypical period would not be useful in predicting the share prices for the same period in the following years. Specific data that are not typical of the overall time series should be removed before formulating a forecasting model.

Forecasting model used

The accuracy of a forecast clearly depends on the model that is being used. However, this does not imply that only one model would be appropriate in a given forecasting problem. It may be that in certain circumstances, a number of different models would produce relatively reliable estimates. The trend would be a primary element in any forecasting model. In most of the examples given in this chapter it is assumed that the trend is linear. In general, this may not be the case, and many business and financial time series will conform to non-linear trend. Other elements in the forecasting model include seasonal and cyclical variations in addition to irregular variation, which at specific points in time cannot be predicted.

The combination of these elements is also an important part of the model. For instance, the application of the additive or multiplicative model may be crucial and can be determined from past data.

Further models are developed by the consideration of relationships with other variables using regression techniques described in the previous chapter. For instance, a variable such as sales demand for oil products may depend on other variables such as advertising, pricing, interest rates and exchange rates. These so-called **causal relationships** are often more important than the time series forecasting models in producing accurate and reliable estimates.

Validation of the model

Before using the model to produce real forecasts, it should be validated to ensure that accurate forecasts are obtained. This can be achieved in a number of ways:

(i) By using all available historical data, a model is developed. Now actual data are compared with the corresponding estimates obtained from the model. The difference between the two values will give an indication of how the model will perform on future values. However, this process may not give a true reflection of forecasting accuracy since the model is likely to perform better within the range of data used than it would on time periods outside the range.

(ii) The results of the model can be compared with the actual values when they occur. Thus, we can use the model to forecast demand in January 1998. When the actual January results are available then the accuracy of the model can be tested. The problem with this approach is that validation of the model can take a long time. Essentially, the model can only be tested over a long time period. Clearly, this approach to validation is frequently used, though there needs to be an initial validation process based only the existing data in order to reduce the time required.

(iii) To attempt to rectify the problems highlighted in (i) and (ii) we can develop the forecasting model based on a subset of the historical data available. For instance, if we have sales figures for the period 1990–7, then the model can be developed only using the values from 1990–6. The remaining sales values in 1997 can then be used to compare with the predicted values obtained from the model. This validation check is more realistic since it actually simulates the forecasting situation. The problem with this method is that the most up-to-date, and therefore most relevant, figures are excluded from the initial model development.

Modification of the model

In the light of the validation processes described above the model will be changed in an attempt to reduce the expected errors. This modification will continue as the model is used in real-life. Invariably the model will need to be updated owing to changing circumstances. Changes can be made on an ongoing basis relating to the trend, seasonal and cyclical elements, and to any causal relationships that are being used. Such changes are then validated using the same approaches as described here. The

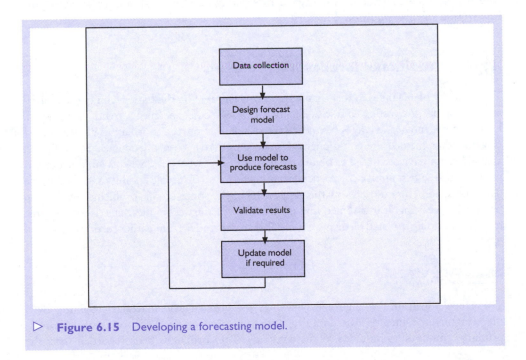

▷   **Figure 6.15**   Developing a forecasting model.

model formulation follows a development life-cycle as illustrated in Figure 6.15. The diagram shows the primary elements of building and maintaining a forecasting model including the stages of data collection, initial model design, testing and validation, updating, and repeating the process of continually collecting more data to ensure that the model remains a reliable source of forecasted information.

External factors

Using the techniques described in this chapter forecasting models are developed largely based on historical data. For such models to be reliable it is assumed that the future situation does not vary significantly from the present. Thus, all relevant factors are either incorporated into the forecasting model or assumed to remain unchanged for the lifetime of its application. In practical situations a range of external factors and unforeseen circumstances can affect the accuracy of the forecasted values. For example, sales performance for a range of products could be affected by factors such as:

▶ Industrial action resulting in stock being unavailable.
▶ Competitors introducing new products, changing promotional campaigns, and pricing structures.
▶ Natural disasters such as fire, earthquake or flooding.
▶ Changes in national taxation, interest rates and currency exchange rates.

Often these factors cannot be predicted and thus will not be incorporated into the forecasting model. However, the user of forecasting techniques should be aware of the importance of these additional factors.

6.14   Additional forecasting problems

The majority of examples in this chapter have concentrated on the basic techniques involved in developing forecasting models. Firstly, in most cases a linear trend is assumed. Furthermore, moving averages have been the standard approach to isolating the trend even though other methods (e.g. exponential smoothing) have been introduced. Secondly, all available data have been used to obtain the forecast of future values, whereas in practice this may not be the best approach, particularly if there are some atypical values included in the data collected. The examples in this section highlight some of the problems involved in practical forecasting. It is assumed that the basic forecasting techniques such as isolating the trend and finding seasonal elements are familiar to the reader from earlier sections.

EXAMPLE 1

The graph illustrated in Figure 6.16 shows the cost of raw materials required by a manufacturing company. The data illustrated give the cost in £ per tonne of one of the primary commodities required by the company. The costs have been recorded from the

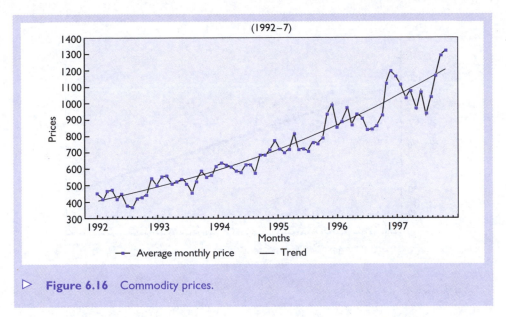

▷ **Figure 6.16** Commodity prices.

commodity markets on a monthly basis over the six-year period. The graph illustrates the average monthly price for each month during 1992–7. The horizontal scale states the year at January of each annual period. A trend line has also been drawn based on annual moving averages. The trend shows an ever-increasing growth in prices over the six years. An assumption of linear trend during this period would have produced inaccurate results. There is a seasonal element to the commodity prices which is often overshadowed by a significant irregular variation. However, it can be seen that there is a dip in prices at the middle of each year. The prices generally reach a peak during December – January before falling back again for the summer months. Furthermore, the variations tend to increase as the trend increases. For instance, in particular, the figures for 1996–7 include large variations around the trend line compared to earlier years. Therefore, a multiplicative model is likely to be appropriate.

Thus, any forecast for the next year would be based on the following elements:

▶ non-linear trend
   (there seems to be 'exponential' growth during the period shown)
▶ multiplicative model
▶ high irregular variation.

However, because of the large irregular variation in this time series the commodity prices are shown to be unpredictable. In particular, the values during late 1996 and 1997 show a higher than expected variation, and this may lead to a revision of the seasonal variation estimates. Furthermore, the cyclical element has not been considered. It is often the case that commodity prices will conform to the standard business cycle from boom to slump. The stage reached in the data illustrated could represent the growth stage in the cycle and a downward trend could evolve in the near future.

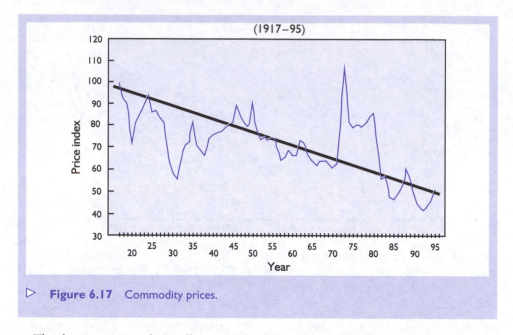

(1917–95)

▷ **Figure 6.17**   Commodity prices.

The long-term trend in all commodity prices tends to be downward. This is illustrated by the graph in Figure 6.17, showing an index of all non-oil commodity prices since 1920. The overall trend in this series is linear. However, clearly the trend cannot continue to be linear since eventually the price index will go below zero, indicating zero prices for the commodities. The areas where the commodity values differ significantly from the trend include a period in the early 1930s corresponding to a global depression. During this time, commodity prices were extremely low compared to the trend. Another outstanding feature of the graph is the period in the 1970s and early 1980s in which commodity prices were very high corresponding to general financial stability and improving growth in the world economy. The trend illustrated in Figure 6.17 would need to be taken into account when forecasting the particular commodity prices introduced earlier in this example. Using regression techniques, other factors may be used to help in the forecast such as interest rates, exchange rates, share prices, production and volume indices.

EXAMPLE 2

Consider the change in share prices as shown in Figure 6.18. The graph illustrates the change in a group of share prices between 1977 and 1994. The prices are recorded and graphed at the end of each quarter during this period. The share index at the beginning of 1977 is assumed to be 100. As can be seen, by 1994 the index had increased to a value approaching 1000. This indicates that during the eighteen years shares had increased nearly tenfold. The graph shows a steady increase in the share prices between 1977 and the early part of 1987, with increasing growth during the latter years. Thus,

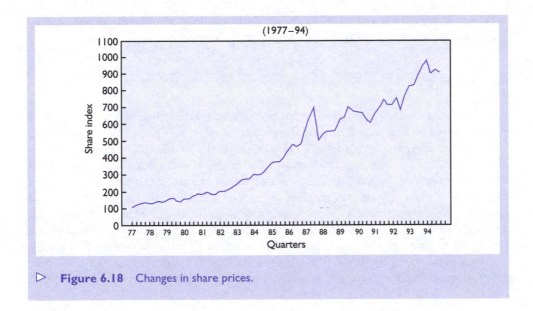

(1977–94)

overall the trend seems to conform to a curve similar to that shown in the previous example and illustrated in Figure 6.16. The pattern of growth in share prices was very smooth until the collapse during the late 1980s. In October 1987, share prices on the London Stock Exchange dropped by an average of around 30%. This is reflected in the graph illustrated in Figure 6.18. The graph shows that within three years the share prices had recovered to their former values. Another mini-collapse in prices occurred during 1991, but by 1992 share prices were again quickly increasing.

In establishing the long-term trend it may be useful to discard some of the details available from these data. For example, the rapid increase and following decline in prices during 1987 can be excluded from the data. This would give a better indication of the long-term trend for the series of values. However, such violent fluctuations must be incorporated into the final analysis in terms of the projected irregular variations that can occur. The periods of 1987 and 1991 are significant in giving an indication of the likely accuracy of long-term forecasts using this approach. In general, share prices cannot be considered in isolation. There are other economic indicators that can be used to obtain short-term and medium-term forecasts of the value of shares. Indicators such as the amount of new orders, consumer goods, orders for plant and machinery, and industrial confidence may enable more accurate forecasts to be obtained.

6.15   Computer applications

In this section we will consider the application of computer software in time series analysis and business forecasting. There is a range of general statistical packages which incorporates time series analysis techniques such as SPSS, MiniTab, Genstat, UNISTAT and P-STAT. Again, as with other areas of statistical analysis, the popular spreadsheet packages such as Lotus and Excel can be used in a number of forecasting applications. The following examples illustrate some applications of these packages.

EXAMPLE 1

In an earlier example, a multiplicative model has been used to forecast automobile sales in 1998 based on quarterly data over the previous four years. These sales figures have been entered using the SPSS package in order to obtain an analysis of the time series. The screen shown in Figure 6.19 illustrates the results of some basic analysis on these data. Using the SPSS package the initial sales data are entered into a single column in a spreadsheet format. The package enables the user to define the dates for these data. For example, this shows quarterly data commencing at the first quarter in 1994. The SPSS package can then automatically create the date columns such as those displayed in the first three columns of the main window in the screen. The specification of quarterly data will define the 'periodicity' of the time series, and the package can then determine the most appropriate moving averages (e.g. 4-point) to use in order to isolate the trend.

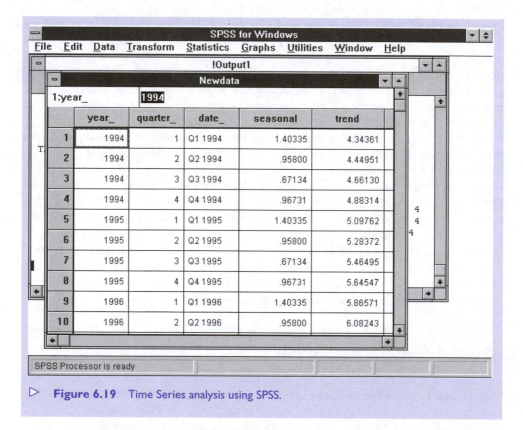

▷ **Figure 6.19** Time Series analysis using SPSS.

The user can also define whether to use an additive or multiplicative model. In this example, a multiplicative model has been used, and the remaining two columns displayed in the window show estimates of the seasonal variations and trend for the corresponding periods. Clearly, as discussed in earlier sections of this chapter, these values can then be used to forecast future automobile sales figures. The package also calculates the errors of such estimates based on existing data, which would assist in determining the reliability of future estimates.

EXAMPLE 2

Consider the use of a spreadsheet package in the analysis of time series. A spreadsheet is ideally suited for this purpose. For instance, the basic manual analysis of such data involves the creation of a table containing a number of columns including the actual data, moving averages and seasonal variation estimates. These values can be set up into a spreadsheet. The screen shown in Figure 6.20 shows an analysis of data considered earlier in this chapter. Current annual office rentals being charged are recorded every

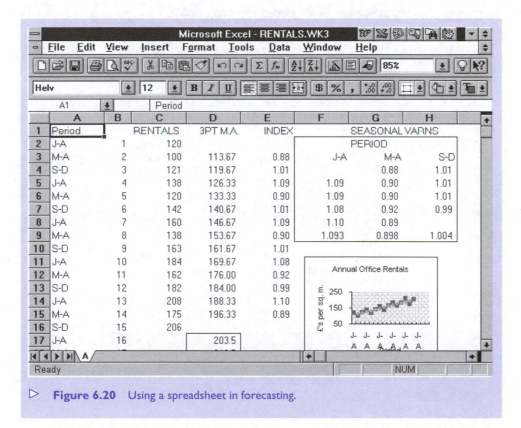

▷ **Figure 6.20**   Using a spreadsheet in forecasting.

four months over a five-year period 1993–7. The table displayed in the screen gives the corresponding fifteen rental values over this period. A 3-point moving average has been calculated and, assuming a multiplicative model, the ratios between the actual data and moving averages have been found.

Further analysis shown in the spreadsheet includes a calculation of the average ratios in order to estimate the seasonal variations. A graph of the actual figures is displayed. Furthermore, using regression methods within the package, estimates of the trend for the next three periods (16, 17 and 18) corresponding to 1998 are displayed at the bottom of the moving average column. A combination of these estimates and the seasonal variations will enable the user to obtain forecasts of the rental values during subsequent periods.

EXAMPLE 3

Consider another set of data introduced earlier in this chapter. The production output of a company recorded every two months over the years 1995 to 1998 is displayed on

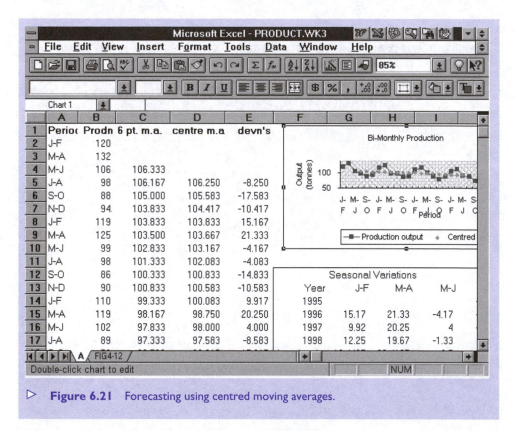

▷ **Figure 6.21** Forecasting using centred moving averages.

the screen shown in Figure 6.21. This screen contains the production figures in the second column. The third column contains the 6-point moving averages. The display of these values is misleading since they should be presented in between successive rows of the production figures. For this reason, the centred moving averages are calculated and displayed in the correct location. An additive model is assumed in this analysis, and thus the deviations are calculated in the fifth column. A graph in this screen shows the actual data and the centred moving averages displayed. Further analysis includes a calculation of the average deviations in each season. The overall mean of these averages is calculated and subsequent adjustments made to the estimates of the seasonal variations.

 Using the disk The spreadsheet displayed in Figure 6.21 has been saved in the file named PRODUCT.WK3. Load this file from the disk provided. The display should be similar to that shown in Figure 6.21. Note that the screen does not show all the production figures. Scroll down to view the remaining values in column B and corresponding calculations in the additional columns. The user may wish to insert new data into this spreadsheet and investigate the changes to the resulting calculations. For example, enter the following production figures into column B of the spreadsheet:

Period	Production output (tonnes)			
	1995	1996	1997	1998
Jan–Feb	100	110	111	118
Mar–Apr	90	90	98	102
May–Jun	84	92	100	100
Jul–Aug	90	98	104	110
Sep–Oct	94	101	105	112
Nov–Dec	102	108	116	117

It is interesting to note how the graph changes on entering new values. Look at how the trend line evolves as new data is entered. The spreadsheet is currently set to automatically recalculate and thus all formulae and graphs are amended after each data entry. Unfortunately this can slow down processing and you may wish to change the spreadsheet settings so that the recalculation is only performed when required. This can be done in Lotus using the / **Worksheet Global Recalc Manual** options. Following this, recalculation is performed when required by pressing the <F9> key. Similarly, in Excel this can be achieved using the **Tools Options** and selecting **Calculation**. The data given above show an increasing trend with a strong seasonal element. Note the seasonal variations have been recalculated in the spreadsheet based on this new data.

Try to enter a new set of data as shown below:

Period	Production output (tonnes)			
	1995	1996	1997	1998
Jan–Feb	85	75	81	91
Mar–Apr	67	65	66	77
May–Jun	87	86	92	105
Jul–Aug	86	85	93	108
Sep–Oct	90	87	96	108
Nov–Dec	94	98	103	124

The data given in this table exhibit a non-linear trend. There is a slight dip in the trend in the early periods before a steady increase in the latter half of the time-scale. However, a reasonable estimate of the trend may be obtained by assuming a linear relationship based only on the last ten moving average values. Visually, the user may wish to confirm whether this is valid. Try to use the regression facility in the spreadsheet package to estimate the trend for each period in 1999 based on this approach. An additive or multiplicative model could be used to determine the seasonal variations. Finally, combine these values with the trend estimates to produce forecasts of the output.

6.16   Chapter summary

In this chapter we have considered a range of basic forecasting techniques involved in analysing a series of data given over a time period. Such techniques involve reducing the actual historical figures into a number of constituent elements. Common elements in many time series include the following:

▶ **Trend.** Shows the overall pattern of changes in the historical data.
▶ **Seasonal variations.** These are the fluctuations around the trend which occur on a regular basis. Usually such regular variations occur over periods of one year or less.
▶ **Cyclical movements.** These variations occur over periods of more than one year. They can often be seen in financial data conforming to the standard economic business cycle of slump, growth, boom and recession.
▶ **Irregular variations.** These include the unpredictable random fluctuations present in most practical time series. An analysis of these can be used to calculate the likely errors and evaluate the reliability of the forecasting model used.

A range of techniques for the decomposition of the time series into these components have been introduced, including:

▶ **Smoothing the graph,** using moving averages, centred moving averages or exponential smoothing.

▶ **Trend estimation,** using linear and non-linear regression estimates.
▶ **Seasonality,** assuming additive or multiplicative models.
▶ **Error analysis,** to compare the forecasts obtained from the model with any actual data obtained in order to investigate the model's validity and reliability.

In addition to the statistical methods described here, it is important to consider any external factors that may affect the variables being analysed. For example, the demand for a product may be affected by external influences such as the competitors' performance, pricing and promotional campaigns. In many practical examples, these external factors have a greater influence on the reliability of the forecast than do the statistical factors described earlier. Often such factors can be incorporated into a forecasting model by using regression techniques as described in the previous chapter. The use of these techniques can provide vital information to assist in tactical and strategic management decision making.

6.17	**Further exercises**

1.(E) The number of patients admitted to the Microbiology Unit at St. Joseph's hospital each day over a four-week period are shown in the following table:

Week	1	2	3	4
Monday	15	17	17	16
Tuesday	14	15	18	17
Wednesday	17	20	19	22
Thursday	20	19	22	21
Friday	28	25	30	29
Saturday	14	15	14	13
Sunday	7	8	10	9

  (i) Using 7-point moving averages, isolate the trend for this time series. Using a graphical method or otherwise, estimate the trend during each day in week 5.
 (ii) Assuming an additive model, estimate the 'seasonal variations' for these data and hence forecast the number of admissions on each day in week 5.
(iii) Comment on the accuracy of this forecast, and on how the hospital management can use this type of information.

2.(I) Based on the series of values given above, obtain an alternative forecast of the number of admissions in week 5 using a multiplicative model. Would you say that this model is more appropriate? Give your reasons.

3.(I) The annual research funding obtained by the Neurological Centre at St. Joseph's hospital is shown in the following table. The figures are given in $100 000s.

Year:	1985	1986	1987	1988	1989	1990	1991	1992
Funding:	4.3	3.2	5.7	7.0	9.2	6.7	7.5	8.9
Year:	1993	1994	1995	1996	1997			
Funding:	10.5	12.6	15.0	12.5	14.6			

(i) Using 5-point moving averages, smooth out this time series and hence estimate graphically the trend values in 1998 and 1999.

(ii) Compare these estimates from those obtained using exponential smoothing using a smoothing constant of 0.2.

(iii) Comment on the differences between the two estimates obtained and state with reasons which is likely to be more reliable.

4.(D) The number of package tours booked through a local travel agent in each quarter over a four-year period is as follows:

	Number of package tour bookings			
Year	1st Qtr	2nd Qtr	3rd Qtr	4th Qtr
1993	234	410	296	140
1994	250	438	310	150
1995	276	452	334	164
1996	274	460	336	178

(i) Draw a graph of this series of values. From your graph, determine whether an additive or multiplicative model is likely to provide the best estimates of future package tour bookings.

(ii) Using moving averages, estimate the trend in each quarter in 1997.

(iii) Find the seasonal variations using the model specified in part (i), and hence estimate the number of bookings received during each quarter in 1997.

(iv) Comment on the likely accuracy of your estimates. State how such estimates could be used by the travel industry.

(v) Describe any other factors which may influence the number of bookings received. How could these factors be incorporated into the forecasting model?

5.(D) The actual quarterly bookings in 1997 were as follows:

1st Qtr: 260   2nd Qtr: 470   3rd Qtr: 360   4th Qtr: 110

(i) Compare these values with the estimates obtained in the previous question and find the average forecasting error.

(ii) Using the same values, calculate the root mean square of these errors.

(iii) Assuming that the errors are normally distributed, find the 95% confidence limits for the estimates in 1997 based on the previous data.

(iv) Comment on the reliability of the forecast based on these calculations. Without further calculations, how would you modify your forecasting model in the light of the 1997 values?

6.(I) **(Using the disk)**   The file named DEMAND.WK3 on the disk contains data relating to the demand of a product in each quarter over a period of five years. Load this file from the disk. The spreadsheet displays the years, quarters and total demand figures in 1000s of units. Furthermore, in column D the 4-point moving averages have been calculated. Notice that the moving averages are displayed coinciding with the demand figures, whereas in the examples shown in this chapter, these values are displayed in between lines. Thus, it is still necessary to 'centre' the moving averages as shown in column E of the spreadsheet.

 (i) Use the regression facility in Lotus or Excel to obtain estimates of the trend during the four quarters of 1998.

 (ii) Set up an additional column to calculate the deviations between the demand figures and the centred moving averages. Use these figures to evaluate the seasonal variations assuming an additive model for the data.

(iii) Combine the trend estimates with the seasonal elements in order to obtain estimates of the demand in each quarter of 1998.

(iv) Experiment with a multiplicative model for these data, by setting up an extra column to calculate the ratios of demand over the centred moving averages. Use these values to produce a similar forecast to that required in part (iii).

 (v) Comment on the validity of the additive or multiplicative models with reference to the data given.

Inventory Control

CHAPTER OBJECTIVES

At the end of this chapter you will be able to:

▶ describe the main attributes of inventory control models

▶ evaluate the optimum batch size using appropriate formula

▶ analyse appropriate order quantities subject to discounted prices

▶ consider batch quantities when the user is also the producer

▶ analyse more complex models such as those involving uncertain demand

▶ compare fixed and periodic review methods

▶ understand the practical issues involved in determining inventory policies

Introduction

This chapter covers the basic techniques used in the process of controlling inventory (or stock) levels. This is an important area involving the application of quantitative methods, particularly in the manufacturing and supply sectors. However, other business sectors such as sales, distribution and maintenance also depend on the efficient use of available stock. The level of stock held at any given moment can be a critical factor. The cost of holding too much stock can make the difference between profitability and failure. Alternatively, there are inherent dangers involved in holding too little stock. The obvious problems are that stock will run out and consequently customers' and clients' orders will not be satisfied. Thus, a compromise must be reached where the risks of running out of stock are minimised at the same time as keeping inventory costs under control. Optimum solutions to these problems can be explored using analytical techniques, and these will be described in the following sections.

CASE STUDY   The CMG car company

CMG is a small car producer based in Kingston, near Toronto, Canada. The company manufactures low-volume sports cars, and has an annual turnover of over $10 million. The company assembles three different sports car models largely from components purchased from external companies. The only components that CMG produces itself are some of the specially designed body parts. There are around 180 production workers at CMG in addition to twenty administration and managerial staff.

CMG sells the range of cars direct to customers. Thus, there are no external sales staff, and no distribution network of sales centres. Customers can order cars from CMG by phone or in person, and the company has built a reputation on being able to deliver any model to the customer's specification within a six-week period. Models with standard specifications, such as the common bodywork colours and basic internal trimmings, can be delivered in significantly less time.

The company has encountered problems with stocking some of the components required. In the past the company has run out of critical components, resulting in delays in production and in delivery times to customers. The Inventory Manager, Ralph Prentice, commented 'We have over 2000 different components used in the production. The engines, gearboxes and electronic components are the only items purchased already assembled. All other items of stock need to be assembled, and any problems with stock levels can cause major disruptions to the production schedules. It's my job to ensure that the raw materials and sub-assemblies are available when required. One problem we have is that the limited capacity of our warehouse means that we are restricted in the amount of stock we can keep, particularly for the bulkier items.'

CMG will be used to illustrate a range of inventory control problems and potential solutions throughout this chapter.

CASE STUDY   The Littlewoods pharmacy group

The Littlewoods group manages over twenty retail outlets in southern England. All the Littlewoods shops include a pharmacy where customers can obtain medicines prescribed by their doctors. Customers can also purchase non-prescription drugs, and a range of other goods including cosmetics, beauty treatments, vitamins and toiletries.

A central warehouse, located in Southampton, is used to stock all items for these stores. Stock is requested from each store at the end of every day, and is forwarded as soon as it is available. The Managing Director of Littlewoods, Myrtle Ahmad, has stated that individual stores should not be expected to wait for any drug or non-drug goods for more than two working days. In the past this has been difficult to achieve. In particular, there are some prescription items that require a two-week gap between ordering from suppliers and receiving to the central warehouse. The demand for some of these items is not consistent, and there have been occasions when an unusually high demand for these products has caused problems for the company.

The problems of stock control are not restricted to the central warehouse at Littlewoods. Each store has a limited amount of stock, and it is particularly important that all the common prescription drugs are immediately available for customers on demand. It has been found that with the increasing competition in this market sector, there is little customer loyalty, and if a customer's order cannot be satisfied immediately then it is likely to be lost. A two-day delay before satisfying the customer's request is not satisfactory, and the customer is likely to try to obtain the goods elsewhere. This can cause long-term problems because the customer's first choice will then shift to a competitor pharmacy.

7.1   Attributes of inventory control

Inventory control involves the ordering, storage and delivery of a range of goods or items. The type of stock being held will include raw materials, work in progress and finished goods. The primary reasons for holding stock are as follows:

Ensuring stock is available. Holding inventory ensures that demand can be satisfied immediately. The stock acts as a buffer against abnormally high usage and fluctuations in supply. Thus, if there is excessive demand or an extended delay in deliveries, the items in stock will help to satisfy most of the requirements. Furthermore, if existing stock is used, there should be no delay between the customer's demand and delivery of goods.

Economic quantities. In order to produce or order items in the most economic quantities it is usually necessary to store items that are not immediately required. The production or ordering of single items as required may in practice not be an option because of the excessive costs involved. Often, discounts can be obtained when bulk orders are requested, and these will require stockholding facilities when received.

Recent techniques such as just-in-time (JIT) methods have been developed to avoid holding large amounts of stock. These approaches will be discussed later in the chapter. However, in many examples, the holding of a limited amount of stock is essential, and the basic techniques for ensuring that this process is cost-effective will be illustrated in the following sections.

Inventory control techniques can assist in answering the following questions:

(i) When should new stock be ordered?

and

(ii) How many items should be ordered?

In order to answer questions of this type, a range of inventory control models have been developed. The standard inventory control models described in later sections assume knowledge of a number of attributes including the following:

Demand. The requirements of customers may, in practice, be difficult to estimate. Simple models assume that the demand is constant, though in general, probabilistic estimates of demand may need to be used. The demand for some items may depend on orders for other goods. For example, the demands for components at CMG are interrelated. Each model of car requires a fixed range of items. Therefore, a demand for one stock item will automatically correspond to requirement for a range of other items. Conversely the demand of a specific item may preclude other items in the range. For instance, the requirement of a 2-litre engine excludes any other engine type for a particular vehicle, and also defines a range of associated components.

Lead time. The time taken for the supplier to deliver the goods following placement of an order is called the lead time. For instance, the lead time for some items of drug ordered by Littlewoods is two weeks. Often, this time is not constant. For instance, a supplier may promise to deliver within a given time period, e.g. three days from receiving the order. Thus, in practice the actual lead time may be one, two or three days.

Stockouts. A stockout occurs when demand exceeds the available stock. In this situation the demands of customers cannot be immediately satisfied. Stockouts are treated in different ways, depending on the application. For example, in some critical circumstances stockouts are simply not allowed. For instance, in a production environment, a stockout on any one of a number of important items will result in a total stoppage. This would prove to be inefficient and totally unacceptable in most production environments. Other stockouts will result in immediate loss of sales. For instance, in the Littlewoods shops, if a request for a prescription item cannot be met, then the customer is likely to go elsewhere. Alternatively, a stockout may simply result in a delay in the delivery of the item required.

Holding costs. Costs involved in the storage of goods include the costs of staffing, rental, lighting and heating of storage facilities. Such costs can often be stated in terms of the cost per item of goods over a given time period. For instance, it is estimated that it costs $1 per week for each gearbox kept in store at CMG. Other factors such as depreciation can be incorporated into the estimation of holding costs.

Ordering costs. These costs are the costs of placing an order for goods and are considered to be independent of the size of order. For example, the administrative costs involved in producing and sending an order may be fixed regardless of the number of items being ordered. Similarly, the supplier may charge a fixed fee for the packaging, transportation and delivery of goods regardless of the quantity required. The ordering costs would be expressed as a fixed cost per order. Thus, for example, it costs £15 for every order placed to Beechams, one of the Littlewoods suppliers, regardless of the size of order sent.

Purchase costs. These are costs incurred relating to the individual items being ordered. These costs are stated per unit item. For instance, the cost price of a headlight fitting used in one of the models at CMG is $18 per item.

Stockout costs. If a stockout occurs for a given item, additional costs may be incurred. For example, the company may need to pay in excess of the normal purchase cost in order to speed up delivery of the item, or there could be a long-term reduction of revenue because of loss of customer good will. Stockout costs can sometimes be expressed as the cost per item of unavailable stock. However, estimates of these costs can be subjective, particularly when estimating the cost of reduced customer good will and potential future loss of earnings.

The characteristics outlined here will be described and used in the range of inventory control models discussed in this chapter.

7.2   The economic order quantity model

One of the simplest models in inventory control is the economic order quantity (EOQ) model. This is sometimes referred to as the economic batch quantity (EBQ) model. This approach is used to estimate the size of order for a specified item that will minimise the overall inventory costs for that item. This model assumes the following:

Constant demand. The demand of the item is known and is equal to D per time period, e.g. demand could equal 500 per year for a given item.

Zero lead time. There is assumed to be no delay in the delivery of items. Thus, an order placed is immediately replenished.

No stock-outs. Items must never run out of stock. Thus, all demands from customers can be satisfied immediately.

Purchase price. There is a fixed cost of each item denoted by P.

Holding costs. The costs of holding stock (denoted by H) can be expressed as a given amount per item. This is often expressed as a proportion (i) of the purchase price of the item. Thus, the holding cost $H = iP$ for each item per time period.

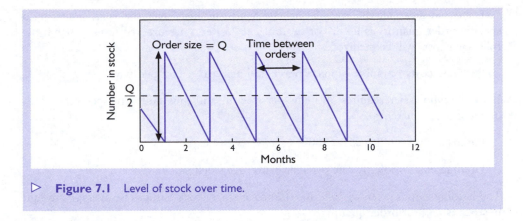

Order costs. The cost of placing an order (denoted by C) is fixed and independent of the order size.

The level of stock for a given item using this simple model can be illustrated as shown in Figure 7.1. The graph illustrates the time period along the horizontal axis. The amount of stock at the beginning of the period (Month 0) is shown. Following this, the level of stock gradually declines at a constant rate until no stock remains. At this point a new batch of stock arrives and thus the stock level increases immediately to its maximum level. The size of increase is equal to the batch size ordered. Again, the stock level constantly reduces and the cycle repeats itself again. This simple illustration is useful when considering the different variables used in the EOQ model. The graph shows the two variables that need to be evaluated, namely the size of order and the time between successive orders. The graph also highlights the average stock level for this item, which is half the order quantity. Thus, if the order quantity is denoted by Q, then the average stock is $Q/2$.

With the inventory information described in this section, it is possible to estimate the most economic order quantity for a given item as shown in the following examples.

Definition: *The economic order quantity (EOQ) or economic batch quantity (EBQ) is the number of items that should be included in a single order so that the total inventory costs are minimised.*

EXAMPLE 1

A wholesaler has a steady demand for 50 items of a given product each month. The purchase cost of each item is £6, and the holding cost for this item is estimated to be 20% of the stock value per annum. Every order placed by the wholesaler costs £10 in administration charges regardless of the number ordered.

Given this information we will evaluate all the relevant costs, and attempt to determine the most economic order quantity for this item of goods.

Let us consider all the costs associated with this item over the year, assuming a specific order quantity is used. For example, if 25 items are ordered in each batch the following costs will be incurred:

Purchase costs = number of items purchased per year * cost per item

Now the wholesaler requires 50 items per month, and thus 600 items per year. Each item costs £6. Therefore,

Purchase costs = 600 * £6 = **£3600**

Holding costs = holding rate per year * average stock value

The holding rate is given as 20% (or 0.2) of average stock value. The average amount in stock is half the order quantity.

Thus, the average number of items in stock = 25/2 = 12.5

It follows that the average stock value = 12.5 * £6 = £75

Therefore, holding costs = 0.2 * £75 = **£15**

Order costs = Number of orders per year * cost per order

Now, 600 items are required each year, and the order quantity is 25. Therefore, the number of orders that need to be placed each year is = 600/25 = 24

Each order costs £10. Therefore,

Order costs = 24 * £10 = **£240**

It follows that the total costs to the wholesaler are as follows:

Total costs = purchase costs + holding costs + order costs
            = 3600 + 15 + 240

Total costs = **£3855** based on an order quantity of 25.

Now, we are attempting to discover the order quantity that minimises the overall costs to the wholesaler. The calculations shown above can be made for alternative order quantities, and a comparison of the costs involved can then be made. For instance, let us consider an order quantity of 50 in this example. The following annual costs are incurred:

Purchase costs = number of items purchased per year * cost per item
               = 600 * £6
               = £3600

Holding costs = holding rate per year * average stock value

Now, the average stock value $= \dfrac{Q}{2} * £6$

$$= \dfrac{50}{2} * £6$$

$$= 25 * £6$$

$$= £150$$

Therefore, holding costs $= 0.2 * £150$

$$= £30$$

Finally, order costs = number of orders per year $*$ cost per order

The number of orders per year $= 600/50 = 12$

Therefore, order costs $= 12 * £10 = £120$

The sum of these costs gives

Total costs $= 3600 + 30 + 120$

Total costs $= £3750$ based on an order quantity of 50.

These calculations can be repeated for a range of order quantities until an optimum value can be estimated. The table below gives a summary of these calculations for a selection of values of the order quantity Q. D represents the annual demand, P is the unit price ($£6$) and i is the stock holding rate (0.2).

Order quantity (Q)	Average stock ($Q/2$)	Purchase costs (PD)	Holding costs ($Q/2)iP$	Order costs $O(D/Q)$	Total costs
25	12.5	3600	15	240	3855
50	25	3600	30	120	3750
100	50	3600	60	60	3720
200	100	3600	120	30	3750

Note that the purchase costs remain constant for all values of the order quantity (Q). This is because over the year there is a fixed demand and, therefore, independent of the order size, a fixed number of items need to be purchased during that period. Assuming that there are no discounts for bulk purchase, then the annual purchase cost must remain the same. Therefore, in order to determine the optimum order quantity it is only necessary to consider the two costs associated with holding and ordering. These costs are plotted and illustrated in Figure 7.2. It can be seen that the two cost components (order costs and holding costs) change in relation to the order quantity. As the order quantity increases, the holding cost increases in direct proportion. This is the case because a higher order quantity will involve a higher average stock level, and using this model, the holding costs are directly dependent on this amount. Conversely, the

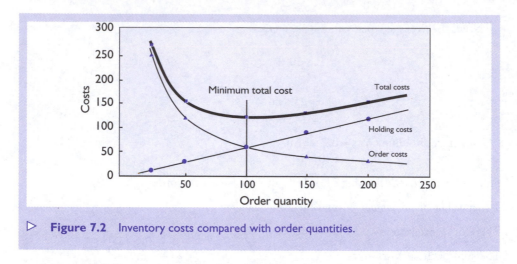

▷   **Figure 7.2**   Inventory costs compared with order quantities.

order costs decrease as the order quantity increases. Clearly, if the number of items in each order is increased then fewer orders are required over a given period. Thus, the annual costs involved in preparing and transmitting the orders are reduced.

The minimum total cost occurs at the intersection of the graphs of holding costs and order costs, as shown in the graph in Figure 7.2 corresponding to an economic order quantity (EOQ) of 100. The result obtained from the graph can be summarised as the EOQ = 100.

From this analysis, we would recommend an order quantity of 100 items. Since the demand for these items is running at 50 per month, this would require one order every two months. The order frequency over a given period can be calculated by the expression: order frequency = D/Q. In this example, D = annual demand = 600, and we have just determined the optimum value of Q = order quantity = 100.

Therefore, the order frequency = $600/100$ = 6 orders per year (or once every two months).

EXAMPLE 2

The Managing Director at Littlewoods, Myrtle Ahmad, has asked you to devise ordering policies at the central warehouse for all the major drug items required by their stores. Consider a single item of stock: the Becotide inhaler for asthma sufferers. Assume that there is a constant demand for this item of 400 per week. Each inhaler costs £3 to purchase. It is estimated that it costs an average of £2 per week to store 100 inhalers in the warehouse. Each order placed to the suppliers costs Littlewoods £12 in administration fees. Using this information, what is the optimum order quantity and order frequency for this product?

Let us consider the total weekly costs involved in holding and ordering this product. Remember that the cost of purchase of the product is constant, and therefore will not affect the optimum order quantity. However, it should be noted that the purchase costs are likely to be the most significant when evaluating the overall costs and, therefore, they should not be ignored in the final analysis of inventory expenditure.

Consider an order quantity of 100 inhalers. This means that the average stock level for this product would be 50.

Now, in this example, the holding costs = £2 per 100 items per week.

Therefore, the holding costs = £2 * $\frac{50}{100}$ = £1.00 per week

Furthermore, the order costs = number of orders per week * Cost per order

With a demand of 400 per week, the number of orders required = $\frac{400}{100}$ = 4 per week

Therefore, the order costs = 4 * £12 = £48.

Combining these two costs we obtain the total costs for the week as follows:

Total costs = 1 + 48 = £49.00

Similarly, other values of the order quantity can be investigated. The table below shows the order and holding costs for a range of values of the order quantity (Q) over each weekly period.

Order quantity (Q)	Average stock ($Q/2$)	Holding costs ($Q/2)H$	Order costs $C(D/Q)$	Total costs
100	50	1	48	49
200	100	2	24	26
400	200	4	12	16
600	300	6	8	14
800	400	8	6	14
1000	500	10	4.8	14.8
1200	600	12	4	16

The graph shown in Figure 7.3 illustrates these data. The illustration shows the same pattern of costs, with holding costs increasing and order costs reducing as the order quantity increases. The minimum total cost occurs at the intersection of the two components, which corresponds to an order quantity of around 700 items. Therefore, the EOQ is 700. With a demand of 400 per week, this order size will involve placing orders every 700/400 = 1.75 weeks. So the time between placing successive orders is less than two weeks.

This illustrates one limitation of such an analysis. The order quantity obtained based on this approach may not be a convenient amount in terms of the frequency of orders. Perhaps in this example it would be better to order once every two weeks using a batch size of 800. These issues will be discussed more fully later in this chapter. In practice the EOQ is used as a guide to the optimum order size and other factors may mean that a modified order quantity is applied.

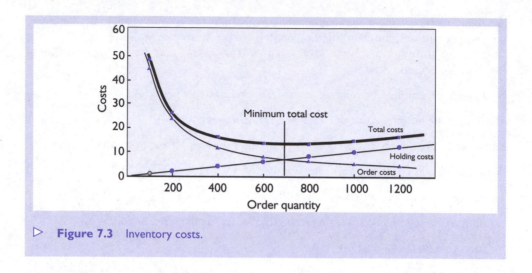

▷ **Figure 7.3**   Inventory costs.

7.3   The economic order quantity formula

The value of the EOQ found by a graphical method in the previous examples can be obtained using a mathematical formula. The formula is based on locating the minimum point on the graph of the function of total costs. The EOQ formula will be described in this section; however, it is outside the scope of this book to derive the expression stated.

The following notation will be used:

D = constant demand for given time period
P = cost price per item
C = cost of a single order
H = cost of holding one item of stock over the time period

Given these variables it can be shown that the EOQ is obtained by:

$$EOQ = \sqrt{\frac{2CD}{H}}$$

Now, the holding cost is often expressed in terms of:

i = holding cost rate as a proportion of cost price per given time period

In this situation, the holding cost $H = iP$ and the EOQ formula becomes:

$$EOQ = \sqrt{\frac{2CD}{iP}}$$

Given the EOQ (denoted by Q) we can determine the order frequency as follows:

Order frequency = D/Q per given time period

To illustrate these formulae the previous problems solved using graphical methods will be reconsidered.

EXAMPLE 1

In an earlier example a wholesaler has a steady demand for 50 items of a given product each month. The purchase cost of each item is £6, and the holding cost for this item is estimated to be 20% of the stock value per annum. Every order placed by the wholesaler costs £10 in administration charges regardless of the number ordered.

Assuming a standard time period of one year, we are given:

D = annual demand = 50 * 12 = 600
P = unit price = £6
C = order cost = £10
H = holding cost of one item per year
= iP

where i = 20% or 0.2.

Thus we can use the EOQ formula as follows:

$$\text{EOQ} = \sqrt{\frac{2CD}{iP}}$$
$$= \sqrt{\frac{2*10*600}{0.2*6}}$$
$$= \sqrt{10\,000}$$
$$= 100$$

We see that the EOQ formula produces the same result as the earlier graphical method. This result shows that to minimise costs, an order size of 100 is used at an order frequency of 600/100 = 6 times per year.

EXAMPLE 2

In Example 2 in the previous section the following information was given:

D = demand per week = 400
P = purchase price = £3
H = holding cost = £2 per 100 items per week
= £0.02 per item per week
C = order costs = £12 per order

Thus the EOQ can be found by the formula:

$$EOQ = \sqrt{\frac{2CD}{H}}$$

$$= \sqrt{\frac{2*12*400}{0.02}}$$

$$= \sqrt{480\ 000}$$

$$= 692.8$$

Therefore, in order to minimise costs, an order size of 693 items is recommended. The previous example, showing the graphical approach to this problem, produced an answer of approximately 700. The EOQ formula confirms that this value is reasonable. However, clearly it is very unlikely that an order quantity of 693 will be used. In practice, rounding this value to 700 will provide a more realistic figure. As already stated it may be that an order size of 800 would be preferred so that the order frequency is more realistic and practical, i.e. every two weeks.

7.4 Exercises: economic order quantity

1(E) Demand for a particular type of fridge from the ABS Discount Mart is constant at 100 per month. Each fridge costs $200, and stockholding costs are 5% of the total stock value over the year. It is estimated that each order processed by ABS involves $40 in administrative and fixed transportation costs.

(i) Using a graphical method, sketch the costs involved for order quantities between 40 and 160 fridges.
(ii) Using your graph, estimate the order quantity that minimises the total costs.
(iii) Using a suitable formula, find the EOQ for this product.
(iv) How often should ABS send orders for this product?
(v) Evaluate the total annual costs involved in purchasing and holding this product assuming that the EOQ is used.

2(I) An engineering company based in Melbourne, Australia, uses $21 000 worth of a specific item of stock every year. Ordering costs total $30 per order, and warehouse costs are approximately 9% of the average stock value over the year.
   If the unit cost for this stock item is $3, find the EOQ by:

(i) graphical methods, and
(ii) using a formula.

Compare the results obtained using these methods.

7.5	## Quantity discounts

It is often the case that the price of any single item of stock is not constant. The cost price of the item may depend on the size of order placed, and many suppliers will offer attractive discounts for large orders. Therefore, the simple EOQ approach assuming a fixed unit price (P) may not be appropriate in many applications. The graph shown in Figure 7.4 illustrates the total cost curve, incorporating order and holding costs, for a situation where the cost of an item changes depending on the order size. In the graph shown, the supplier is offering discounts on the cost price for orders of 5 items or more, and an even larger discount for orders of 12 items or over. The graph shows that at these critical points, where the order size is 5 or 12, the total costs are reduced. Whether or not this changes the EOQ needs to be investigated for specific examples. The graph illustrates that the EOQ is approximately 8. The discount available for orders of 12 or more does not sufficiently reduce the overall costs and, therefore, in general would not be utilised.

When considering whether or not to take advantage of any discounts being offered it is necessary to evaluate the additional costs and potential savings involved. For instance, ordering in bulk would normally involve increased holding costs incurred owing to the additional requirements for storage space. Conversely, additional savings will be made on reduced ordering costs.

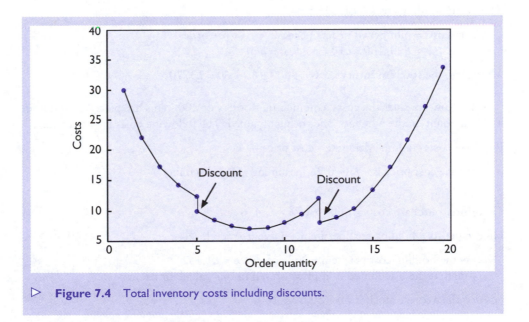

▷ **Figure 7.4**   Total inventory costs including discounts.

EXAMPLE I

An earlier example evaluated the EOQ based on the following information:

$D = 600$ items per year $P = £6$ per item
$\quad i = 20\%$ per item per year $C = £10$ per order

From this information the EOQ = 100.

Let us assume that the supplier is offering two discounts for bulk purchases as described below:

(a) a 4% discount is offered on orders of 200 or over,
(b) an 8% discount is available for orders of 1000 or over.

The question is whether to take advantage of either of these discount offers.

Consider the total costs involved when using the various order quantities.

(1) Firstly, if the standard EOQ value of 100 is used then the following costs are incurred on average each year:

Purchase costs = annual demand * cost price
$$= 600 * £6 = £3,600$$

Holding costs = holding cost per item * average stock level

Now the holding cost per item = 20% of £6 = £1.20

and the average stock level = 100/2 = 50

Therefore, holding costs = £1.20 * 50 = £60

Order costs = number of orders per year * cost per order
$$= 600/100 * £10 = 6 * £10 = £60$$

Therefore, the **total inventory costs** = 3600 + 60 + 60 = **£3720**

(2) Now consider the costs assuming that orders of 200 items are placed resulting in a 4% discount on the purchase price being obtained. The following costs are obtained:

Purchase costs = annual demand * cost price

Now the cost price is = £6 * 0.96 (assuming a 4% discount)
$$= £5.76$$

Therefore, purchase costs = 600 * £5.76 = £3456

Holding costs = holding cost per item * average stock level

Now the holding cost per item = 20% of £5.76 = £1.152
(Note that the discounted unit price is used in this calculation)

Also the average stock level = 200/2 = 100

Therefore, holding costs = £1.152 * 100 = £115.20

Order costs = Number of orders per year * cost per order
= 600/200 * £10 = 3 * £10 = £30

Therefore, based on an order quantity of 200

the **total inventory costs** = 3456 + 115.2 + 30 = **£3601.20**

(3)   Similarly, consider the costs assuming that orders of 1000 items are placed resulting in an 8% discount on the purchase price being obtained. The following costs are obtained:

Purchase costs = annual demand * cost price

Now the cost price is = £6 * 0.92 (assuming an 8% discount)
= £5.52

Therefore, annual purchase costs = 600 * £5.52 = £3312

Holding costs = holding cost per item * average stock level

Now the holding cost per item = 20% of £5.52 = £1.104

Also the average stock level = 1000/2 = 500

Therefore, holding costs = £1.104 * 500 = £552

Order costs = number of orders per year * cost per order
= 600/1000 * £10 = 0.6 * £10 = £6

Note that in this case there is an **average** of 0.6 orders per year.

Therefore, based on an order quantity of 1000

the **total inventory costs** = 3312 + 552 + 6 = **£3870**

To summarise, the following table gives the total costs associated with the three order quantities considered:

Order quantity	Purchase costs	Holding costs	Order costs	Total costs
100	3600	60	60	£3720.00
200	3456	115.2	30	£3601.20
1000	3312	552	6	£3870.00

The table shows that costs are minimised when orders of 200 items are placed resulting in a 4% discount being obtained. The 8% discount on orders of at least 1000 items is not worth while purely on cost terms. It can be seen from the table that the discount obtained when purchasing 1000 items is outweighed by the additional holding costs incurred in storing the high volume of stock.

Based on costs, the recommendation in this case would be to place orders in batches of 200 items.

7.6   Lead time for deliveries

In the earlier sections there has been no reference to the possible delay in delivery of goods ordered. This delay, referred to as the **lead time**, is the time taken between sending the order and delivery of the requested goods. Knowledge of the lead time will enable us to determine the most appropriate time to place orders. For example, consider a situation where the demand for an item is constant at 10 per day, and the lead time for delivery of this item is three days. During this lead time the demand will be $3 * 10 = 30$ items. Therefore, there need to be at least 30 items in stock when the order is placed to avoid a stockout. This level of stock is called the **reorder level** for the item. In general, assuming that demand is constant at D and the lead time is denoted by L, then the level at which orders must be placed in order to avoid stockouts is:

Reorder level $= LD$

The reorder level (ROL) and lead time are illustrated in Figure 7.5. It should be noted that the level of stock in this illustration follows the same pattern as in an earlier diagram. It follows that the EOQ formula used in previous sections is still valid. A knowledge of the lead time can affect the way in which an ordering policy is specified. For instance, in previous examples, the order frequency, or time between orders, has been specified, e.g. place an order for 30 items every 2 months. Alternatively, using knowledge of the lead time, the reorder level can be explicit, e.g. order 30 items when the level of stock reaches 12 items. In this simple model, where the demand is constant, there is no difference in the actual result. However, in later, more complex models the definition of ordering policies in a company may prove significant in determining the effectiveness of its stock control procedures.

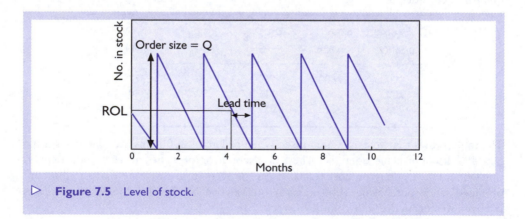

▷   **Figure 7.5**   Level of stock.

Definition: *The lead time for stock is the amount of time between placing the order and receiving the goods.*

Definition: *The reorder level is the minimum amount of stock in hand when a new order should be placed so that no stockouts should occur.*

7.7 | Running out of stock

In the earlier sections it has been assumed that there is always enough stock to satisfy demand. If there is insufficient stock to satisfy all demands, then a **stockout** takes place. This situation can be dealt with in a number of ways, depending on the given application. For instance, it may be assumed that if there is a stockout then all customers' demands are lost. The customer will simply go to an alternative supplier to obtain the required goods. Clearly, if this is the case then the chance of a stockout should be minimised whenever possible. However, it may be that for a number of reasons the risk of stockouts cannot be avoided. For instance, there may not be enough storage space to hold the required amount of stock if the EOQ is used. Therefore, the order quantity may need to be reduced accordingly, and thus stockouts may occur more frequently than is desirable.

Another scenario is that the demands during a stockout need not be lost. For example, the customers may be prepared to wait a short period before delivery of goods, or they may be persuaded to do so with an incentive such as a price reduction. In such a case, back orders can be satisfied, and need not be squandered. The diagram in Figure 7.6 illustrates a situation where stockouts are allowed. The diagram shows stockouts occurring at regular intervals. The stockout is shown by a negative stock level during the given period. When a new batch is received, then all back orders are satisfied. Thus, the maximum stock level is below the EOQ. Such a situation may be something that the company would aim to achieve. The ability to satisfy back orders may mean a reduction in overall costs for the company. For instance, as shown in Figure 7.6, the average stock level is reduced, resulting in reduced holding costs.

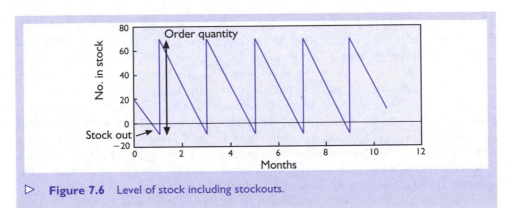

▷ **Figure 7.6**   Level of stock including stockouts.

However, there may be additional costs incurred in the use of stockouts in this way. For example, tangible costs would include any discounts given to the customer to compensate for the delay in delivery. Intangible costs would include loss of good will and deteriorating public relations because of the inability to satisfy demand immediately.

7.8   Exercises: quantity discounts and lead times

1.(I)   The Littlewoods pharmacy group purchases around 3000 boxes of the 'Purity' perfume range every year. Each box costs £5 and ordering costs are £20 per order regardless of the order quantity. The costs of holding this product in stock are estimated to be 5% of the average stock value per year.

(i) Find the EOQ for this product.
(ii) Assuming that there is a one-month lead time for deliveries of this product, estimate the reorder level.
(iii) The supplier of the 'Purity' range offers bulk discounts at the following rates:
(a) 5% discount for orders of 1,000 boxes or over,
(b) 8% discount for orders of 2,000 boxes or over.

On the basis of cost, what order quantity would you recommend for this product?

2.(I)   The Badger chain of supermarkets purchases 60 000 boxes of a brand of washing powder each year. Each box costs £2 and every order costs £16 to process. Holding costs for this product average £25 per 100 boxes per year.
Badger has used the EOQ model to determine the most appropriate order quantity for this product. However, the supplier offers a 4% discount on orders of at least 6000 boxes. Should the company take advantage of this offer?

7.9   The production order quantity model

In previous examples it has been assumed that the stock required is ordered from an external source. In these cases, the stock is received in a single batch and the stock level increases immediately from a low point to the required maximum, as illustrated in Figure 7.1. In practice, there are instances where the stockholder is also the supplier. For example, the CMG car manufacturer uses specially designed body parts in the car assembly line. These body parts are produced on site at CMG. Thus, when an order is placed, the parts can be produced and the stock levels rise gradually over a period of time until the order is satisfied. The diagram in Figure 7.7 shows the level of stock in this situation. This diagram illustrates the situation where the stockholder is also the producer. The problem is to determine the optimum order level or **production order quantity (POQ)**. The diagram shows the buildup of stocks until the production order has been fulfilled. At this point, production of the item ceases. Subsequently, the stock

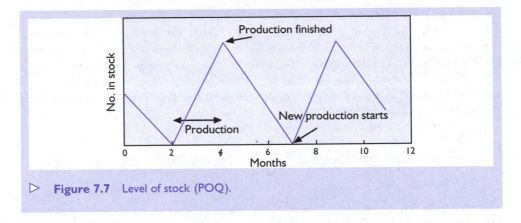

▷ **Figure 7.7**   Level of stock (POQ).

runs down at the same rate as in the basic EOQ model. The diagram shows an ideal situation where the stock is allowed to run down to zero, before a new production cycle starts to replenish the stock levels.

The following notation will be used:

D = demand per time period
P = cost price per item
C = setup costs for production run
i = stock holding rate per time period
R = production rate per time period

Given these variables, the most economic batch size for the production is found as follows:

$$POQ = \sqrt{\frac{2CD}{iP(1 - D/R)}} \quad \text{or} \quad \sqrt{\frac{2CD}{H(1 - D/R)}}$$

The average stock level in this situation is:

$$\text{Average stock} = \frac{Q}{2}\left(1 - \frac{D}{R}\right)$$

Also, in practice, it is important to estimate the maximum storage capacity required. The maximum stock level in this model is simply double the average level.

Therefore

$$\text{maximum stock level} = Q\left(1 - \frac{D}{R}\right)$$

The reorder level in the production model needs to be considered more closely. In most cases the reorder level is simply DL. However, if the lead time is large so that a new order should be placed whilst the current order is still being produced, then an amended formula for the reorder level needs to be given. The diagram shown in Figure 7.8 illustrates this type of situation. The graph shows the level of stock increasing through the production period and then reducing down to zero when a new production cycle commences. The lead time for setting up the new production is such that a production order must be placed whilst production is being carried out. The total time between the start of a production and the commencement of the next production is denoted by T and can be found by:

$$T = Q/D$$

The time taken to complete one production run is denoted by t, and can be found by:

$$t = Q/R$$

Therefore, the time period where the existing items are being used and no production is taking place is $T - t$. If the lead time is less than this, then as we have already shown, the reorder level is DL. However, if the lead time is greater than this value, then the reorder level is found by the formula $(R - D) * (T - L)$. To summarise, the reorder level is found as follows:

$$\text{ROL} = D * L \qquad \text{if } L \leqslant T - t$$

or

$$\text{ROL} = (R - D)(T - L) \qquad \text{if } L > T - t$$

Note that these formulae assume that the production rate (R) exceeds the demand (D). If the demand exceeds the production rate then the production will always be insufficient to satisfy the requirements, and additional stock will need to be obtained from external sources. This situation is indicated by obtaining negative values from the formulae given. Furthermore, if the production rate (R) equals the demand (D) then the average stock level formula reduces to zero, which illustrates the 'just-in-time' situation described later in this chapter.

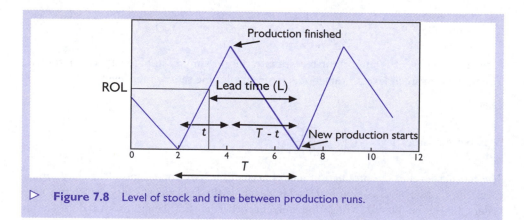

▷ **Figure 7.8**   Level of stock and time between production runs.

The following examples will illustrate the application of these formulae using the production order quantity model.

EXAMPLE 1

Consider the stock control problem at the CMG company. The company requires ten items of a particular body panel per week for the assembly line. These panels can be produced at the rate of three per day, and production can be continued every day, seven days a week. The setup costs for a production run of this body panel are $1000, and the unit production costs are $120 per panel. The company estimates that the annual holding cost of this item is 20% of the stock value. This estimate includes the cost of storing and maintaining these items to a high production quality standard.

Estimate the production order quantity which will minimise the total inventory costs.

In this example, we are given the following information:

D = demand per year = $10 * 52 = 520$

(Assuming that production utilising this particular item continues at a steady rate over all 52 weeks of the year.)

P = cost per body panel = $120
C = setup costs = $1000
i = stock holding rate per year = 20% (or 0.2)
R = production rate = 3 per day = 21 per week = $21 * 52 = 1092$ per year

Using the POQ formula we obtain:

$$POQ = \sqrt{\frac{2CD}{iP(1 - D/R)}}$$

$$= \sqrt{\frac{2 * 1000 * 520}{0.2 * 120 * (1 - 520/1092)}}$$

$$= \sqrt{\frac{2 * 1000 * 520}{0.2 * 120 * (1 - 0.4762)}}$$

$$= \sqrt{82\,728.8} = 287.6$$

Thus, rounding off this value we would recommend a production order quantity of 290 body panels. In fact, it may be better to consider the production over a given number of weeks. For instance, production of these body panels over a 14-week period would produce $14 * 21 = 294$ panels. If the Production Manager wishes to avoid splitting weeks, then this may be the recommended economic batch size.

Consider using a POQ of 290 panels. Production of this batch would take just under 14 weeks to complete. The 290 panels would be enough for 29 weeks of car assembly.

Consequently, for the first 14 weeks the panel would be produced and used in the assembly line. After this period, for the next 15 weeks, production of the body panel would not be necessary, and the car assembly would continue using existing stock. At the end of the 29-week period, production of the body panel would need to restart in order to replenish stocks.

The average stock level would be as follows:

$$\text{Average stock} = \frac{Q}{2}\left(1 - \frac{D}{R}\right)$$

$$= \frac{290}{2} * \left(1 - \frac{520}{1092}\right)$$

$$= 145 * (1 - 0.4762)$$

$$= 76.0$$

Thus, the average stock level is approximately 76 body panels. Also, the maximum stock level for this body panel would be $2 * 76 = 152$ parts.

This maximum stock level may indicate that such a production order quantity is not feasible. For instance, if the amount of storage space is such that no more than 100 body parts can be stored, then the production batch size will need to be reconsidered. Additional factors such as this will be discussed in a later section in this chapter.

EXAMPLE 2

Consider the example shown above with additional information on the lead time. The time taken to set up production of the body panel is 4 weeks. This means that the Production Department will require 4 weeks' notice before starting production of the stock item. Thus, a request for the production of a new batch of panels will need to be initiated four weeks before the stock runs out. During four weeks the number of body panels used is $4 * 10 = 40$. Thus, when the level of stock reaches 40 body panels, a new production batch is requested (i.e. an order is placed).

This can be expressed as the reorder level = 40 items.

Let us consider this problem by using the formula on reorder levels previously introduced. We know that the time between successive production runs is

$T = Q/D = 290/520 = 29/52$ year $= 29$ weeks

Furthermore, the time taken to complete a production run is:

$t = Q/R = 290/1092 = 0.266$ year $= 13.8$ weeks.

Therefore, $T - t = 29 - 13.8 = 15.2$ weeks. (These values can be expressed in terms of years if required.) Consequently we see that L (=4) is less than $T - t$. So the formula for the reorder level is ROL $= DL = 10 * 4 = 40$. The diagram in Figure 7.9 shows the level of stock and reorder level (ROL) for this product.

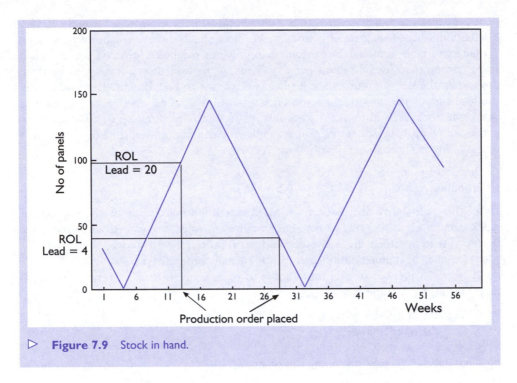

Production order placed

▷ **Figure 7.9**   Stock in hand.

Alternatively, consider a situation where the lead time is 20 weeks. In this case, the lead time (L) is greater than the value of $T - t$, and so the alternative formula for the ROL should be used:

$$\text{ROL} = (R - D)(T - L)$$
$$= (1092 - 520)(29/52 - 20/52)$$

(Note that the same time periods must be used for all units in the formula. In this case, the production rate (R) and demand (D) are given per year and, therefore, the time periods T and L must be given in years, i.e a. 20-week lead time equates to $20/52$ years.)

So we find that $\text{ROL} = (572)(9/52) = 99$

In this case, a new production cycle would be ordered when the stock reaches 99 during the previous production phase. This is also illustrated in Figure 7.9.

7.10   Uncertain demand

In many practical situations, the demand of a given item is unlikely to be constant as assumed in the previous examples. Generally, there will be uncertainty as to the exact requirements for a given item. In this section we will consider situations where the demand conforms to known probability distributions. In other words, we will consider a situation where the demand is not known precisely, but the probability of a given demand can be determined. For instance, in previous examples, demand was assumed to be constant, such as 30 items per day. Thus, if the lead time is known to be three days, then the demand during the lead time is known to be 90 items. Demand during the lead time is the important factor since this will determine whether or not there is sufficient stock in hand to avoid stockouts. In an uncertain situation demand could be expressed in probabilistic terms. For example, the demand during lead time conforms to the following probability distribution:

Demand (no. of items):	10	20	30
Probability:	0.2	0.5	0.3

Using this probability distribution we could determine the chance of running out of stock using a given ordering policy. For instance, if orders are placed when the stock reaches 20 items, then given the demand distribution shown above, there is a 0.3 (30%) chance of running out of stock before the new order arrives.

There are a number of decisions that need to be made in basic inventory management, including the following:

▶ What is the best order quantity?
▶ What is the reorder level?
▶ What are the costs involved?
▶ What are the chances of running out of stock?

Often these values are based on initial requirements which can be expressed in terms of probability. For instance, it is useful to consider the **service level**, which is the proportion of orders that should be satisfied during the lead time. For example, if the required service level is 95%, this implies that we wish to be 95% sure that demand during the lead time will be satisfied. We can write

Service level = Prob(satisfying demand during lead time)

It should be noted that this relates to the probability of a stockout:

Prob(satisfying demand during lead time) = 1 − Prob(stockout during lead time)

Now given a required service level it is possible to determine the necessary reorder level. These problems will be considered in relation to demand conforming to two common probability distributions:

▶ the uniform distribution
▶ the normal distribution

EXAMPLE 1   (the uniform distribution)

The uniform probability distribution is such that every value within a given range is equally likely to occur. For example, consider a situation at the CMG company where the demand of an engine part during the lead time conforms to the uniform distribution given below:

Demand (no. of parts):	5	6	7	8	9
Probability:	0.2	0.2	0.2	0.2	0.2

It is required that the chance of meeting the demand during the lead time for an order must be at least 90%. What should the reorder level be to satisfy this circumstance?

In this problem, the required service level is 90%.

This means that the probability of meeting the demand during lead time must be at least 0.9. Alternatively, this can be expressed as

Prob(stockout during lead time) ⩽ 0.1

Now it can be seen that during the lead time for an order, the probability of demand equalling 9 is 0.2. Therefore, if the reorder level is only 8 then the probability of a stockout will be 0.2. This is not acceptable in the given conditions. Therefore, the reorder level will need to be set at 9. This will actually ensure that all demand is met, i.e. Prob(stockout during lead time) = 0 and consequently the service level is 100%.

EXAMPLE 2   (normal distribution)

The lead time for receiving orders of a specific drug required by the Littlewoods pharmacy group is three days. The demand of this drug during the three-day period is normally distributed with a mean of 220 grams and a standard deviation of 50 grams. What is the reorder level for this drug to ensure that the probability of a stockout is less than 2%?

Now the diagram in Figure 7.10 shows the distribution of demand during the lead time. The distribution is normal, with mean $\mu = 220$, and standard deviation $\sigma = 50$. Figure 7.10 shows the point (x) which will be exceeded by only 2% of demand. The area shaded in the diagram shows the probability (2%) above the value of x. This

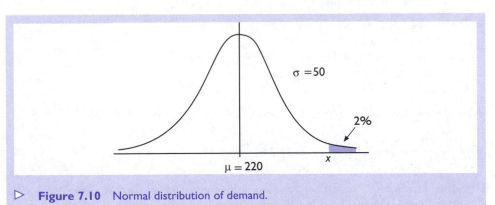

▷ **Figure 7.10**   Normal distribution of demand.

value would be the ideal reorder level since the demand will only exceed this on 2% of occasions.

Using normal tables we find that

$$z = \frac{x - \mu}{\sigma} = \frac{x - 220}{50} = 2.05$$

Thus, rearranging the equation we find that $x = 2.05 * 50 + 220 = 322.5$. Therefore, using a reorder level of 323 grams for this drug will ensure that the probability of a stockout is less than 2%. The reorder level is one of the elements required in determining the best ordering policy for this item of goods. Other elements will include finding the optimum order quantity as shown in the following example.

EXAMPLE 3   **(normal distribution)**

A computer manufacturer needs to give four days' notice in order to receive orders of the 586 processor microchip. Each chip costs the manufacturer £17, and it is estimated that every order costs the manufacturer £30 in administration fees. Storage of this 586 processor costs an estimated £10 per microchip per year because of the dust-free, temperature-controlled environment required. The actual number of microchips required by the company varies from day to day, but tends to conform to the normal distribution with an average over the four-day period of 700 and a standard deviation of 200 items.

The manufacturer wishes to determine the EOQ for this product and find the reorder level required so that the probability of running out of stock before an order is received is no more than 1%.

Now the EOQ is found as before using the given values of demand, order costs, holding costs and unit price. In this example, the average demand figure will need to be used. Also, we will consider the standard time period as being 4 days. Thus, the holding cost expressed per year will need to be converted before inserting into the EOQ formula.

We are given the following:

D = average demand per 4 days = 700
P = unit price = £17
H = holding costs per 4 days = £10 * 4/365 = £0.1096
   (assuming an average of 365 days per year)
C = order costs = £30

Using these values we can obtain the economic order quantity as follows:

$$\text{EOQ} = \sqrt{\frac{2CD}{H}} = \sqrt{\frac{2 * 30 * 700}{0.10959}} = \sqrt{383\ 246.65} = 619$$

Therefore, from this calculation we would recommend an order quantity of 620 microchips per batch.

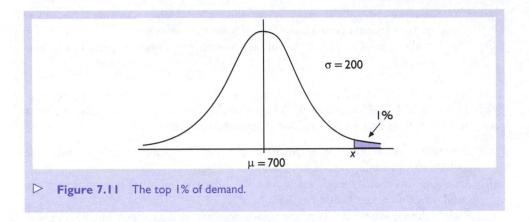

▷ **Figure 7.11**   The top 1% of demand.

Now, the next problem is to decide when such an order should be placed. This is based on the fact that the probability of a stockout is required to be at most 1%. The demand during the lead time is known to be normally distributed with a mean of 700 and a standard deviation of 200. The diagram shown in Figure 7.11 illustrates this demand distribution. The diagram also shows an area shaded equal to 1% of the total area. The value of x shown on this diagram will be equal to the reorder level required in order to ensure that Prob(stockout during lead time) ≤ 0.01 (1%).

From normal tables we have that

$$z = \frac{x - \mu}{\sigma} = \frac{x - 700}{200} = 2.33$$

Rearranging this equation we have $x = 2.33 * 200 + 700 = 1166$. So, we conclude that the most appropriate ordering policy would be to order 620 microchips when the level of stock reaches 1166 or less.

Care should be taken when utilising this policy. When we state the level of stock as 1166 we have previously considered this to be simply the stock-in-hand. In general, the level of stock referred to is the sum of the stock-in-hand plus outstanding orders. This is particularly important when, as in this case, the demand over the lead time is likely to exceed the order quantity. In such a case, there will occasionally be two orders in progress simultaneously.

7.11   Exercises: POQ and probabilistic demand

1.(E)   An engineering company requires 120 sub-assemblies per month to manufacture the finished product. The sub-assemblies can be produced on site at a rate of 200 per month. Each sub-assembly costs $60, and it is estimated that the company spends $30 per 10 sub-assemblies per year on holding costs. Setup costs for every new production run of the sub-assemblies amount to $220.

(i) Find the production order quantity for this sub-assembly. On this basis, what would be your recommended order quantity for this product?

(ii) Illustrate the level of stock for the sub-assembly over a two-year period using this order quantity.

2.(I) The AMG service station needs to give 48 hours' notice before receiving new deliveries of diesel fuel. Demand over 48 hours tends to be normally distributed with a mean of 3000 gallons and a standard deviation of 800 gallons.

(i) Determine the reorder level for this product in order to ensure that the probability of running out of stock is at most 2%.

(ii) Assuming this reorder level, draw a graph of the level of stock assuming that the standard delivery size is 6000 gallons.

(iii) Each delivery costs £50 for transportation costs regardless of the delivery quantity. The diesel fuel costs £1.80 per gallon and it is estimated that the holding cost for this product is £12 per 1000 gallons per day. Estimate the optimum order quantity for this product.

7.12 The periodic review model

In the previous examples we have considered a situation where a fixed quantity of stock is ordered at variable time intervals. These models assume that the level of stock under consideration is monitored constantly, and when the reorder level is reached, a new order is placed immediately. In practice, such monitoring may be impossible to achieve. The procedure requires continuous stock checking, which is likely to involve unnecessary expense and a considerable amount of wasted staff time. Furthermore, when a range of items is considered, it may be that the use of variable time intervals will result in staggering orders for individual items, rather than ordering quantities of many items at the same time. Again, this would involve additional administrative time, which may not be advisable, or even possible, in many circumstances.

An alternative model to be considered is the **periodic review model**, where the level of stock is checked at specified intervals, and the required number of items are ordered at these times. A comparison can be made between the two inventory models as shown below:

Continuous review — Fixed order quantity, variable time between orders.

Periodic review — Variable order quantity, fixed time between orders.

Using the periodic review model, the following questions need to be considered:

▶ What is the time between orders?
▶ How much should be ordered?
▶ What is the chance of a stockout?
▶ What are the costs involved?

As with the continuous review model previously considered, these factors are interrelated. For instance, given a specified time between orders, and a required service level (or probability of satisfying demand), then the order quantity in a given situation can be evaluated.

The following examples use knowledge of the distribution of demand. In general, if a variable X is distributed with a mean $= \mu$ and standard deviation $= \sigma$, then any multiple of this variable such as aX would be distributed with a mean of $a\mu$ and a standard deviation of $\sqrt{a}\sigma$. So, for example, if the daily demand of an item has a mean of 340 items and a standard deviation of 50 items, then the demand over a two-day period would be distributed with:

Mean $= 2 * 340 = 680$

and

Standard deviation $= \sqrt{2} * 50 = 70.7$

EXAMPLE 1

Consider the Littlewoods ordering problem introduced in the previous section. The following information relating to a specific drug stocked by Littlewoods was analysed:

Lead time = 3 days

Demand during lead time is normally distributed with mean = 220 grams, and standard deviation = 50 grams.

Required service level = 98% (i.e. probability of stockout $\leqslant 2\%$)

Let us assume that the level of stock is reviewed every six days. We need to decide on the amount of stock to be ordered, depending on the level of stock found. For instance, consider a situation where at a given review there are 400 grams of the drug remaining in stock.

Enough drug must be ordered so that there is sufficient stock to cover the demand over the next nine days. This is because the quantity must last not only up to the next review period, but through until the next order arrives. The next review period is in six days, and the next order will arrive three days after that. The amount of stock required to cover the review period plus the lead time is called the **replenishment stock level**. The diagram in Figure 7.12 illustrates the level of stock over two review periods. Note that the first order needs to be sufficient until the second order arrives in day 9.

Now, on average, the demand for this drug over 3 days is 220 grams. Therefore, over 9 days the demand will average $220 * 9/3 = 660$ grams. Thus, the replenishment stock level is 660 grams. With the existing 400 grams, we only need to order 260 grams in order to be able to satisfy the average demand. However, this would not be a satisfactory ordering method since we would only be able to satisfy 50% of orders. This is because in a normal distribution there is a 50% chance of obtaining a value

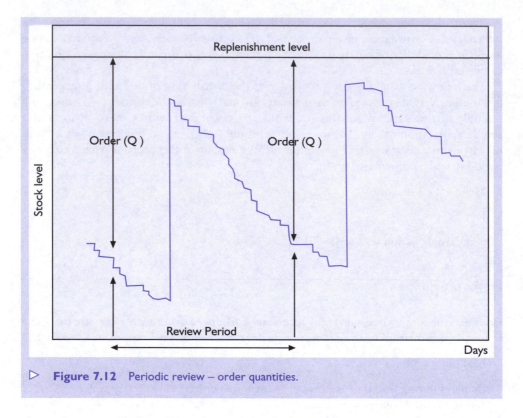

▷   **Figure 7.12**   Periodic review – order quantities.

above the mean. With a required service level of 98% it is necessary to reconsider the order quantity required in this case.

We know that the demand over a three-day period is normally distributed with:

Mean = 220 grams, Standard deviation = 50 grams.

Therefore, over nine days the demand is normal with:

Mean = 220 * 9/3 = 660 days
Standard deviation = 50 * $\sqrt{9/3}$ = 50 * 1.732 = 86.6

The diagram shown in Figure 7.13 shows the required replenishment stock level to ensure that the required service level is reached. The value of R indicated in the diagram can be obtained using normal tables as follows:

We have $z = \dfrac{R - \mu}{\sigma} = \dfrac{R - 660}{86.6} = 2.05$ from normal tables

Therefore, rearranging this equation we can obtain the value of R as follows:

$R = 2.05 * 86.6 + 660 = 837.5$

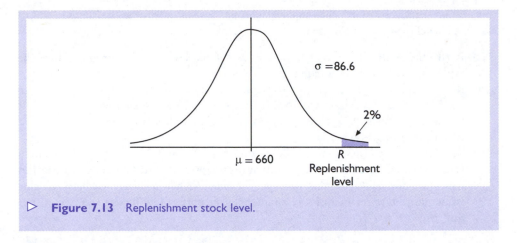

Figure 7.13   Replenishment stock level.

Rounding this value up we find that the replenishment level is 838 grams. Since there is already 400 grams in stock, we only need to order 438 grams more. This will ensure that the probability of running out of stock during the required period is under 2%. In practice, an appropriate order size would be used, e.g. 400 or 500 grams.

It is left to the reader to determine an appropriate replenishment level if the required service level is 99%.

7.13   Exercises: periodic review model

1.(I)   The daily demand for tobacco leaf in a cigarette manufacturer is uniformly distributed as shown in the table below:

Demand (tonnes):	12	13	14	15	16	17	18	19
Probability:	0.125	0.125	0.125	0.125	0.125	0.125	0.125	0.125

(i)   If tobacco leaf can be obtained from the local wholesaler given one day's notice, and stock is checked at the end of each day, find the replenishment level required in order to achieve a service level of at least 98%.

(ii)   If stock is checked every two days, how would this affect the replenishment level?

(iii)   Assuming the lead time is 2 days, recalculate the replenishment level based on a periodic review every 2 days.

(iv)   It has been discovered that the demand is not uniform but conforms to a normal distribution with a daily average of 15.5 tonnes and a standard deviation of 2 tonnes. Recalculate the replenishment levels obtained in parts (i)–(iii) on this basis.

2.(D)   Adams-Kimber (AK) Ltd supply a wide range of doors and door furnishings. The weekly demand for a de-luxe brass door handle assembly is known to be normally distributed with an average of 38 and a standard deviation of 8 fittings. AK Ltd obtain this de-luxe fitting from a local supplier, who promises a lead time of 5 days. AK Ltd check the level of stock on this item every two weeks.

(i) If AK Ltd wish to attain at least a 96% service level on this product, find the replenishment stock level required.

(ii) If the supplier can be persuaded to reduce the lead time for deliveries of this item down to three days, how would this affect the replenishment level necessary? If the level of stock at a review period is 20 assemblies, how many would you recommend should be ordered?

(iii) The price of the brass door handle assembly is £24, and depreciation on this item is estimated to be 10% per year. If each order costs AK Ltd £20 in administration fees, find the EOQ for this product. Comment on the difference between this value and the order quantity recommended in part (ii). Why are the two values different?

<h2>7.14   Further inventory management models</h2>

The inventory models introduced in this chapter involve basic assumptions about the level of stock required and the likely demand of a single product. These models are primarily appropriate for the control of 'finished goods', i.e. items that are sold directly to customers or clients. Recent developments and techniques in inventory control involve the analysis of more complex situations as described below.

Materials requirements planning (MRP)

The techniques of MRP can be utilised in the manufacture of goods involving a number of stages in the production process. The stock levels of raw materials, single components, sub-assemblies and finished goods are all analysed in the MRP approach. Essentially, much of the demand can be accurately predicted when the demand of the finished product is known. For instance, an order for a specific customised model of sports car received by CMG, results in exact requirements of the sub-assembled components such as body panels, which determine the raw materials requirements such as steel and types of paint. The control of stock where the demand of one item depends on the demand of a higher order item and all relevant links are employed can be achieved using **materials requirements planning** (MRP). Using MRP the production schedule for a company will define the inventory requirements for the various components. Actual ordering of these components can be achieved using a variety of methods including those described in previous sections such as periodic review or economic order quantities. However, an MRP system will incorporate knowledge of when such orders should be placed based on demand for the finished products.

Consider the Adams-Kimber Ltd manufacturing company based in Barnsley, England. AK Ltd produces a range of door furniture for the building and retail markets. The items produced by AK Ltd include door handles, locks, push plates, and hinges. These are produced in a variety of specifications using aluminium, steel, stainless steel, and brass. The diagram shown in Figure 7.14 shows the requirements for items generated by an order for a complete door handle assembly (referred to as CDA). An order for a specific CDA as shown in the diagram generates requirements for stock items in the hierarchy.

In order to produce the item shown, some of the components will be required immediately, whilst others will only be needed later in the process in order to complete the assembly. Thus, demand for the finished product not only generates demand for the components, but also determines the time each component will be required. These ideas form the basis of MRP.

The application of MRP would involve a sophisticated information system incorporating knowledge of links between individual stock items and complete assemblies. The MRP system would automatically generate orders for given items based on the demand of finished goods.

Just-in-time methods

The **just-in-time (JIT)** approach to inventory control involves the elimination of any unnecessary stock. In theory there need be no spare stock in hand at any given time. The only stock available at a particular moment is that which is necessary to complete the manufacture of a given item. If a producer can achieve or get close to the ideal of 'zero' stock, then significant savings can be made in inventory costs. For instance, less stock means that there are reduced holding costs, little wastage and improved cash flow.

A common method of implementing the JIT approach is the so-called 'Kanban' system introduced by Toyota in the 1980s. The Kanban system is used to start the production of a component when it is required by the next point in the assembly line.

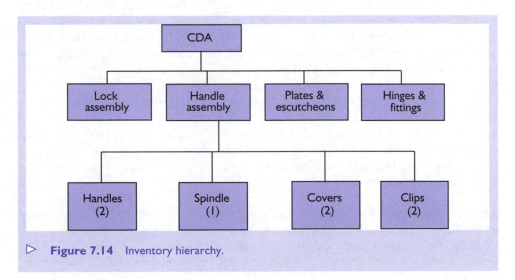

▷ **Figure 7.14** Inventory hierarchy.

The complete system works from the input of raw materials to production of components, then sub-assemblies through to the finished product. At each stage the Kanban system initiates production or assembly further down the line, and the complete production process from start to finish is coordinated, with no large amounts of stock remaining unutilised.

The Kanban system of JIT uses three basic items in the stock control process:

Containers. These contain a specific number of parts for use in the next stage of the production. The actual number of parts would correspond to an order quantity in the simple inventory control systems.

Move cards. The cards (or 'Kanbans') are used to authorise the movement of containers from one production section to the next. These will determine the number and positioning of containers in the production line.

Production cards. These are used to authorise the production of a container of parts (or sub-assemblies).

The combination of containers, move and production cards enables the stock to be used in the most efficient way and minimum stock levels to be achieved. It should be noted that in order to implement JIT methods satisfactorily, it is necessary to closely integrate any external suppliers into the product chain. The system relies on supplies of raw materials and stock items being available when required. Consequently, short lead times and total quality are expected from the suppliers.

7.15   Practical issues

The models introduced in this chapter will enable the practitioner in inventory management to gain an insight into the many problems and range of potential solutions in stock control and effective ordering policies. However, it should be stressed that in many circumstances, these solutions at best give a first attempt at the optimum. The ordering policies obtained using these analytical techniques will often need to be developed in the light of practical experience. The complexity of most real-life situations dictates that refinements will almost certainly need to be made before practical, optimum solutions are attained. Models such as EOQ and periodic review are based on initial assumptions that are often much too simplistic. In particular the assumptions relating to constant or probabilistic demand may be misleading. The following give an indication of the many factors which will affect the validity of the stock control techniques described in this chapter.

Analysis of demand. The models have assumed constant demand or demand expressed in probabilistic terms. The practical situation may be much more complex. For example, the demand may be split into the bulk orders from regular clients and the *ad hoc* orders from other customers. For instance, AK Ltd, producers of door furnishings, has a range of customers. There are the bulk orders received from large DIY retailers which tend to be regular, though not totally predictable. Other minor orders are received from individuals or small traders. These tend to be unpredictable even though they account for over 30% of the total orders received by AK Ltd.

Furthermore, there is often a seasonal element to the demand for specific items. Sports car sales by the Canadian company CMG tend to be higher in the spring and summer, with little activity during the winter period. Similarly, sales of certain drugs, such as those for combating asthma and hay-fever, tend to increase during the summer months. Any ordering policies will obviously need to take such seasonal elements into account.

Monitoring stock levels. The control of stock usage and the monitoring of the amount of stock available are important aspects in stock control. For instance, they are key components in the periodic review model, where the level of stock at a given point in time determines the order quantity. In practice, it is extremely difficult to produce accurate, up-to-date information on inventory. The use of computerised stock control and ordering systems has assisted in this process, though such systems do not solve all the problems. For instance, no system will be able to keep track of unauthorised usage such as from stealing and undeclared breakages. At best, an estimate of these additional losses will be included. Thus, at regular intervals a manual check needs to be performed on the current inventory and this can be compared with the 'official' inventory figures, resulting in updated information being available. In many circumstances, such an inventory check may only happen once or twice a year. Thus, it is important to realise that for most of the time the inventory records may be inaccurate and there should be sufficient slack in the system to cater for hidden usage as described.

Practical batch sizes. In many situations there may not be a complete choice on the order quantity for a given item. For instance, products may be available in specific batch sizes. The Littlewoods pharmacy company purchases some medicines in liquid form in 2-litre (2000 ml) bottles. Thus, if it is found that the EOQ for this product is 2740 ml there will need to be a rounding up (to 4000 mls) or down (to 2000 mls) of this figure, with consequent possible changes in holding costs, order frequency and total inventory costs. Similarly, the AMG service station receives fuel to sell on to customers by the tanker load. Each tanker holds a maximum of 8000 gallons and so an economic order quantity found to be 12 000 gallons may be impractical.

Shelf life. This is an important attribute when considering the quantity of stocks that should be retained. For instance, there is a short shelf life on many of the drugs stored at Littlewoods pharmacies. Thus, the total inventory at any given time should not exceed that which will be required within the product's lifetime. Consider the storage of bread at a large distribution centre. The bread must be consumed within 5 days and demand for the product is currently running at 1000 loaves per day. Thus, the maximum stock level for this item should be 5000. In practice it is likely that the level of stock will be considerably less than this figure. However, using an EOQ formula we may find that purely in relation to cost an optimum of 6000 loaves is obtained. Other factors such as wastage will need to be taken into account to evaluate the real inventory cost for this product.

Lead time. In most of the examples in this chapter it has been assumed that there is a fixed known lead time for receiving orders. In practice, this is usually a variable amount. Suppliers may try to guarantee delivery of given products within a certain timescale. However, in these circumstances there may still be problems in predicting the lead time due to unforeseen occurrences such as freak weather conditions, industrial disputes, transportation problems. The variability of lead time should be incorporated into any model that is being used. It may be that this can be combined with the variability in demand in the models previously considered. For instance, in some of the later examples in this chapter we considered the demand over the lead time period. If demand and lead time both vary, then these can be expressed as a single variable 'Demand during lead time', which can then be analysed in the ways previously described. For instance, the demand during lead time could be normally distributed and be used to analyse the likely service levels for given ordering policies.

Capacity. An obvious factor when deciding on the order quantity to be used is to consider the storage capacity available for a given item. The order quantity cannot usually be greater than the amount of storage available. The exception to this rule is when planned stockouts are used as part of the inventory strategy. Thus, when a batch arrives, the unsatisfied demands of customers are then processed, and the remainder of the order is stored. For instance, a retailer dealing in televisions can use this approach to a limited extent. Customers may be willing to wait for one or two days before receiving their goods. In such a case, orders can be placed with suppliers for direct delivery to the customer. Conversely, where stockouts are not allowable the storage capacity defines the maximum limit for an order quantity. This situation is clearly illustrated in the case of a service station serving fuel to its customers. The AMG service station has a capacity of 5000 gallons for unleaded fuel. Thus, this automatically limits the order quantity for the product.

Interrelated items. The inventory systems illustrated in this chapter have concentrated on single stock items. In practice, it is likely that a company will obtain a range of goods from a given supplier. Therefore, it is more efficient to place a number of items on a single order to the supplier. Consequently, the order frequency of these items should coincide, and cannot be considered in isolation for each product. Furthermore, as described in the MRP and JIT systems, the demands of many items particularly in a production situation will be interrelated. Thus, a customer's demand for a finished product will generate a string of demands for sub-assemblies, components and raw materials. In this situation, estimates of the EOQ or POQ on single items become meaningless, and the relationship between items must be taken into account.

Costs. In many circumstances the unit costs for a given item cannot be defined precisely. In addition to discounts on bulk orders as previously described there may be other factors that affect the unit costs. These could include additional inducements from suppliers such as free transportation/delivery, delayed or staggered payments, and discounts on orders of 'bundles' of several items. Furthermore, consideration of inflationary factors may affect the overall costing, particularly on items involving a long lead time or extended shelf life.

Other costs incorporated in earlier inventory models include order costs and holding costs. In practice, these costs are difficult to estimate and are likely to vary as the order strategy changes. For instance, many of the simple models assume a fixed cost for ordering a batch of items. In practice, the cost is likely to include a variable element as well as a fixed component. There may be fixed administration costs independent of the number of items ordered, but packaging and delivery costs are likely to increase for larger orders. Similarly, the holding costs will contain fixed and variable elements. For example, the rental, lighting and heating of a warehouse facility, and the staffing cost can remain relatively constant regardless of the quantity of goods stored. Conversely, other holding costs such as depreciation and maintenance will be related to the size of inventory stored.

7.16   Computer applications

There is a range of inventory control packages currently available. Most of these systems keep a track of the level of inventory, and automate the orders of predefined quantities. The systems tend to be most appropriate in an industrial/manufacturing environment though they can also be utilised in a range of service and supply industries. Inventory management software currently available includes Axis, GEMpack, Global 2000, TABS and Pegasus. Other inventory facilities are often available in accounting systems, where the stock control and purchase order control are integrated to provide additional monitoring of a company's budget. Accounting packages such as Pegasus and Sage incorporate these facilities.

The use of spreadsheets can provide additional information on a range of inventory models. In particular, the spreadsheet can be used to consider the costings associated with alternative ordering policies in order to provide an analysis of the optimum solutions. Using a spreadsheet, questions can be posed such as: What if the order quantity is increased, how will this affect costs, and service levels? Alternatively, the spreadsheet can be used to evaluate a range of formulae as described in this chapter. Applications of this type will be considered in the following examples.

EXAMPLE 1

Consider an example introduced earlier in this chapter of the car manufacturer, CMG, using a number of electronic fuel components. Basic details in this application gave the following:

Demand = 10 per month
Unit cost = $115
Stock holding rate = 10%
Order costs = $30

These values can be entered into a spreadsheet in order to obtain a variety of inventory management statistics such as the optimum order quantity, maximum stock level, average stock level, and a breakdown of the relevant costs. This application is illustrated in a file contained on the computer disk provided with this text.

Using the disk Load a file called STOCK1.WK3 from the disk provided. The spreadsheet displayed is illustrated in Figure 7.15 and is based on the assumption of a constant, known demand. The spreadsheet contains a range of calculations based on user input for the two models: economic order quantity (EOQ) and production order quantity (POQ). The user can insert values as follows: demand in cell B5, unit price in B6, order costs in B7, holding rate in B8, and lead time in B9. Notice that these values

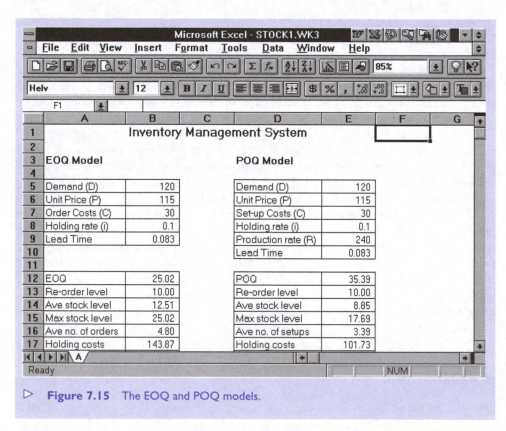

▷   **Figure 7.15**   The EOQ and POQ models.

are automatically transferred to the corresponding cells in the POQ model. The only additional requirement in the POQ model is a value for the production rate entered in cell E9. Other cells in the spreadsheet are protected and cannot be changed to ensure that the appropriate formulae are not deleted.

The resulting analyses provide information on the optimum order quantity, reorder level, average and maximum stock levels, and the holding and ordering costs incurred. It is important to note that a standard time period must be used throughout the spreadsheet. For instance, if the demand is given per year, then all other variables are referenced to a one-year period. Thus, in the spreadsheet shown, the holding rate is 10% (0.1) of the stock value per year, and the lead time is 1/12 (0.083) of a year (i.e. lead time is one month).

Insert new values into the spreadsheet in order to consider a problem where: demand = 300 per month, unit price = £100, order costs = £50 per order, holding rate = 12% per year, lead time = 2 weeks.

Furthermore, if the production rate is 1000 per year, what is the optimum POQ?

Now insert a new set of values into the spreadsheet and consider the resulting changes.

EXAMPLE 2

The previous example has illustrated the use of a spreadsheet in calculating formulae from the EOQ and POQ models based on constant demand. In this example, we will consider a situation where the demand conforms to the normal distribution, and the two basic model; EOQ and periodic review, will be considered. Given information on demand, and required service levels, the values for reorder level or replenishment level can be obtained.

 Using the disk   Load the file called STOCK2.WK3 from the disk. The screen displayed is illustrated in Figure 7.16. The standard time period used in this spread- sheet is the lead time. Thus, the demand is given in terms of the mean and standard deviation over lead time. Similarly, the holding costs are specified as costs over the lead time. For example, the spreadsheet shows that over the lead time of four days the demand is normally distributed with a mean of 700 items, and a standard deviation of 200 items. The unit price is £17, and the order costs are £30 per order.

The holding costs of £10 per year (365 days) have been converted to costs over a four-day period using the expression £10 * 4/365 = £0.1096. Using these details, the spreadsheet calculates the EOQ displayed in cell E8. Finally, a service level of 99% enables the estimation of the reorder level shown in cell E9 using a lookup table located in cells I1 . . . J16.

In the periodic review model the period between orders shown in cell E13 is stated in terms of the lead time. For instance, in this example, the period between orders is twice the lead time. Thus, for instance, the lead time could be 3 days and the period between orders 6 days. Alternatively, if the period between orders was only one day

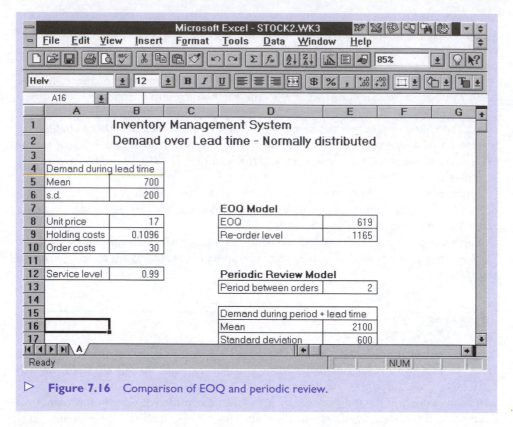

▷ **Figure 7.16**   Comparison of EOQ and periodic review.

then the value inserted into cell E13 would be 1/3 (0.333). The periodic review model analyses the demand over a period including the lead time plus the ordering period. Thus, a new mean and standard deviation have been calculated and displayed in cells E16 and E17. These figures are used together with the required service level to obtain the replenishment level necessary.

   Try to change the data in the spreadsheet as shown below:

Consider a lead time of 10 days, with a demand over this period which is normally distributed with a mean of 300 items and a standard deviation of 100 items. The unit price is $40 and the holding costs are $1 per day per item. Each order costs $25 to process.

(1) Find the EOQ if the service level required is 97%.
(2) What if the service level is different, e.g., 98%, 99%, 95%, . . . ? Investigate these new values.
(3) Assume that in a periodic review, the stock is checked every 50 days, what would the replenishment level be in order to achieve a service level of 95%?
(4) Finally, check the replenishment level required in order to obtain different service levels such as 96%, 97%, 98%, ...

Try to experiment with different values for the demand, costs and service level requirements using the spreadsheet loaded. It is advisable to save your new file, if you wish, using a different filename so that, if required, you can retrieve the original file STOCK2.WK3 at a later time.

7.17	**Chapter summary**

This chapter has introduced a range of inventory control techniques in order to answer practical questions such as:

▶ How many items should be ordered?
▶ When should the order be placed?
▶ What are the costs?
▶ What are the risks of running out of stock?

Some of the important inventory models have been described including:

The EOQ model, based on constant demand (D), fixed unit price (P), holding costs (H) which can sometimes be expressed as a proportion (i) of the stock value, and order costs (C). Using this model the economic order quantity is obtained by minimising the order and holding costs, and is found by the formula:

$$\text{EOQ } (Q) = \sqrt{\frac{2CD}{H}} \quad \text{or} \quad \sqrt{\frac{2CD}{iP}}$$

In this case, the average stock level $= Q/2$ and the order frequency $= D/Q$. Knowledge of the lead time (L) for delivery of orders will enable the reorder level (ROL) to be found.

The POQ model, uses the same assumptions as the EOQ but in addition the user is also the producer with a known production rate (R). In this situation the optimum production order quantity is:

$$\text{POQ } (Q) = \sqrt{\frac{2CD}{H(1 - D/R)}} \quad \text{or} \quad \sqrt{\frac{2CD}{iP(1 - D/R)}}$$

Using the POQ,

$$\text{the average stock level} = \frac{Q}{2}\left(1 - \frac{D}{R}\right)$$

Given the demand expressed in probabilistic terms then the following factors are important:

$$\text{Service level} = \text{Prob(satisfying demand during lead time)}$$
$$= 1 - \text{Prob(stockout during lead time)}$$

The reorder level can then be determined in order to ensure the required service level.

Another important model used in stock control is the **periodic review model**. In this case, stock is checked at regular intervals and an appropriate amount of stock is ordered based on existing stock levels. In this case, given a probabilistic demand, and a required service level, the order quantity can be found with reference to the **replenishment stock level**, which is the required level of stock to cover the demand during a review period plus the lead time for orders.

It should be emphasised that such models consider the questions of order quantity, order frequency and service levels largely in probabilistic and financial terms. In practice, a range of factors will determine the optimum ordering strategies including: product shelf life, stock holding capacity, market volatility, and the relationship between individual stock items. New techniques in inventory management such as MRP and JIT methods have been explored.

7.18   Further exercises

1.(E)   Assuming that the demand for a product is constant, find the economic order quantity and the total annual inventory costs, given the following:

(i) demand = 330 per month, order costs = £30 per order,
stock holding costs = £10 per item per year,
unit price = £150.

(ii) demand = 200 per week, order costs = £25 per order,
holding costs = 10% of average stock value per year,
unit price = £36.

(iii) demand = 400 per day, order costs = £50 per order,
holding costs = £45 per 100 items per month (30 days),
unit price = £99.

2.(I)   If in question 1, the stock holder is also the producer, then estimate the production order quantity for each of the items assuming a production rate for the items as shown below:

(i) 1000 per month,
(ii) 15 000 per year (assume production is over 52 weeks each year),
(iii) 5000 per week (assume production is 7 days per week).

3.(I)   The Thomas-Matthews (T-M) discount store stocks a range of televisions, hi-fi units and computer systems. A new computer system costs the T-M stores $1100. The annual holding costs at T-M are calculated to be 8% of the stock value. Ordering costs are approximately $65 per order, and the expected demand for this product is 40 systems per month.

(i) Estimate the EOQ and calculate the annual holding costs associated with this order quantity.

(ii) If there is only sufficient storage space to hold a maximum of 50 systems, how will this affect the total annual costs?

(iii) The supplier of the computer systems has offered T-M a discount of 5% on orders of at least 250 systems. Assuming that holding capacity is not a problem, would you recommend that T-M take up this offer?

(iv) If the lead time on orders of this product is two months, what is the reorder level assuming that the EOQ is used?

4.(I) A local hypermarket sells an average of 1200 pints of semi-skimmed milk every day. Demand tends to be normally distributed with a standard deviation of 300 pints per day. It is estimated that 5% of this product is lost each day owing to damage and wastage. The order costs are £20 per order, and each pint costs the hypermarket £0.25.

(i) Find the EOQ for this product. What order quantity would you recommend based on your findings? What is the reorder level using this order quantity to ensure that a service level of 95% is achieved assuming that there is a one-day lead time on the orders?

(ii) The level of stock is checked at the beginning of each day and then an order for an appropriate quantity is placed which arrives one day later. Find the replenishment level in order to ensure that at least 95% of customers' demands can be satisfied.

(iii) Assuming that the shelf life of this product is 2 days after which it must be removed and discarded, do you think that the replenishment level obtained in part (ii) is reasonable? Assuming that there are 1500 pints of milk at a given stock check, how many pints would you order for the following day? What is the chance that stock held today will still be unsold tomorrow?

(iv) If there is a lead time of two days, and stock is checked every two days, find the replenishment level required to provide a 95% service level.

5.(D) The 'Toys-U-R' chain of toy shops stocks an exclusive playhouse costing $345. Weekly demand for this product in California is estimated to be normally distributed with a mean of 130 units and a standard deviation of 40 units. Ordering costs for this product are $95 per order, and the annual holding rate is 13% of the average stock value.

(i) Determine the economic order quantity and total annual costs for this product.

(ii) If the lead time for this playhouse is 6 weeks, find the reorder level required to ensure a service level of at least 90%.

(iii) The 'Toys-U-R' company wishes to modify its ordering procedures, and a periodic review model has been considered. If stock for the playhouse can be checked every 8 weeks, with a lead time of 6 weeks for delivery of orders, find the replenishment level required to guarantee the same service level as in part (ii).

(iv) If the stock can be checked every four weeks, how will this affect your answer in part (iii)?

6.(I)   Adams-Kimber (A-K) Ltd manufactures a range of door furnishings. Demand for a specific door assembly is constant at 2000 per year. The door assembly includes a number of components which are produced on site. For instance, A-K Ltd can produce the unique door plate for this assembly at a rate of 50 per day. There are 300 production days per year at A-K Ltd. The cost of the door plate is £3.50 and stock holding costs are 17% of the stock value per year. Setup costs for a new production of the door plate are £320.

(i)   Find the production order quantity that will minimise the company's costs.
(ii) What is the length of the production run of the door plate, and what is the gap between successive production runs?
(iii) If a new production run takes two weeks to set up, find the stock level at which the production should be ordered.

7.(D)   The CMG car company uses a standard gearbox on all sports car models. The demand for CMG cars tends to be constant at around 70 cars per month. The gearbox costs $295 and there is a 25% annual depreciation cost on holding this product. Each new order to the overseas supplier costs $400 regardless of the order quantity.

(i)   The company currently regularly orders enough gearboxes for two months supply. Estimate the cost of this policy for CMG over a year.
(ii) How do these costs compare with those using the economic order quantity?
(iii) If a new supplier offers CMG the same product at a cost of $300 with only $50 order costs, would this offer be cost-effective?
(iv) Assuming that CMG stays with the original supplier, and that a 3% reduction is being offered on orders of at least 200 gearboxes, would you advise the company to take advantage of this offer?

8.(I)   Using the disk   Load the file STOCK1.WK3 from the disk. The spreadsheet displayed shows the calculations for the EOQ and the POQ based on values including the demand, unit price and order costs.

(i)   Edit this spreadsheet by changing the following values of the variables: demand = 200 per week, unit price = £25, order costs = £35, holding costs = 5% and lead time = 5 days.
(ii) Now consider how changes in the lead time and/or the unit price will affect the EOQ.
(iii) If the production rate is 400 per week, use the spreadsheet to obtain the POQ.

CHAPTER

8

Linear Programming

SUMMARY OF CHAPTER CONTENTS

▷ Formulation of linear programming problem

▷ Graphical solution

▷ Summary of graphical methods

▷ Maximising and minimising

▷ Special cases

▷ Simplex method: maximisation with ⩽ constraints

▷ Simplex method: minimisation with ⩾ constraints

▷ Transportation problem

▷ Unbalanced transportation problem

▷ Maximisation problem

▷ Interpretation of results – management issues

▷ Computer applications

CHAPTER OBJECTIVES

At the end of this chapter you will be able to:

► understand the use of linear programming techniques in optimisation

► formulate the objective function and constraints from a given problem

► use graphical methods and simplex to solve linear programming problems

► use transportation methods in appropriate problems

► interpret results obtained and understand the limitations of such approaches

Introduction

The application of linear programming techniques enables the manager to solve a range of optimising problems subject to constraints. For example, the Production Manager makes decisions on production quotas for a number of finished goods in order to maximise company profits. Such quotas will be subject to conditions such as the availability of resources and customer demand. The same manager may need to decide on the assignment of staff to specific jobs subject to constraints on availability, hours and expertise in order to minimise the costs. Furthermore, the market researcher may need to decide on the ways of collecting information in the shortest time possible. Decisions such as how many interviews should be conducted, and how many questionnaires sent, will be subject to conditions on the required accuracy of results, timescales and staff availability. In addition, the Distribution Manager in a large supply company will make decisions on the most efficient method of transporting goods between the distribution centres, in order to minimise costs, subject to conditions on availability, and requirements of goods.

Situations of this type involving maximising or minimising a given linear expression subject to a range of linear constraints or restrictions can be solved by **linear programming**. This chapter introduces the basic processes involved in solving linear programming problems by using graphical and other analytical means.

CASE STUDY   The Stenlux Refrigeration Company

Stenlux is a multinational production and distribution company with headquarters in Stockholm, Sweden. The company manufactures a range of refrigeration equipment, from small domestic fridges and freezers, up to large commercial refrigeration units for the retail and wholesale trade. Stenlux has recently introduced a range of air-conditioning equipment for the European market.

Production is divided into three sectors catering for: domestic, commercial, and air-conditioning systems. Ralph Sternberg, the Production Manager in the Domestic Division, with the help of his logistics team, reviews the production schedule in the company every six months. The setup costs involved in changing production to a new product are high, and therefore careful consideration must be given to the planned production mix. The Domestic Division contains six production work teams, and each team can, if required, manufacture a separate product. The use of linear programming provides Ralph Sternberg with an important objective tool in order to make the correct decisions based on the limitations on staff hours, availability of raw materials, product demand and machine schedules, whilst attempting to maximise the Division's profitability.

The Stenlux company has a number of distribution centres throughout Europe, including major sites at Leipzig in Germany, Lyons in France, and Birmingham in the UK. The Distribution Manager, Bjorn Sholer, has been asked to reduce overall transportation costs. More efficient ways have been considered of transporting finished products to the distribution centres in order to minimise costs and carrying times, subject to constraints on availability and requirements. Linear programming methods have been adapted for this type of transportation problem, and will be discussed later in this chapter.

CASE STUDY   Wiley-Macken Financial & Investment Analysts

The Wiley-Macken financial consultancy group has its headquarters in London, with subsidiary offices in Bonn and Milan. The group provides expertise and financial advice on a range of areas such as investment decisions, taxable benefits, insurance and employment benefits, as well as legal implications in the financial sector. A standard problem posed by clients is to reconsider their investment portfolios in order to maximise the likely return on investment, whilst minimising the risks involved. These two objectives are often incompatible, and therefore a compromise needs to be reached and agreed with the clients on the level of risk required. Simple problems can involve the consideration of a small number of potential share options. The client needs advice on whether (and how much) to invest in particular shares. Information on each share is available such as the likely annual return (based on current performance) and the risks of losses (in probability terms) being incurred. The client may have an existing portfolio or an investment sum in mind. In either case, Wiley-Macken will advise on the quantity of each share to purchase in order to optimise the chosen objective. The use of linear programming can be applied in this area to consider such optimisation problems.

8.1 Formulation of a linear programming problem

A linear programming problem is one in which a specific expression (called the objective function) needs to be optimised (maximised or minimised), subject to a number of constraints. Both the objective function and the constraints can be written as linear (straight line) expressions. Such problems occur frequently in practical situations and it is therefore useful to concentrate on their solution. The formulation of such problems can be summarised in the following steps:

(1) Identify the variables used.
(2) Find an expression for the objective function in terms of these variables.
(3) Find the constraints.

After the formulation stage, a number of methods can be used to obtain optimum solutions. In this section we will consider the initial formulation stage of the problem in relation to some practical applications.

> **Definition:** *A linear programming problem involves the optimisation of an expression called the objective function, subject to a number of constraints.*

EXAMPLE I

Consider the production problems at the Stenlux company. The company produces a wide range of domestic fridges, though there are specific problems with decisions on the required mix of two fridges coded as the A470 and A370 models. Both these models are profitable for Stenlux, with the A470 making $70 profit each and the A370 making $60 each. The company wishes to maximise profits.

There are restrictions on the number of each of these models that can be produced. For instance, the number of staff-hours required to produce each fridge is estimated to be: 3 hours for the A470 and 2 hours for the A370. In any given week the Stenlux Domestic Division only has 3000 staff-hours available for the production of these two models. Furthermore, the value of raw materials used in the two models is: $50 for the A470, and $60 for the A370. A maximum weekly budget for the raw materials for these two models has been set at $75 000.

This information can be used to formulate a linear programming problem as follows:

(1) Identify the variables used

The company needs to decide on the number of each type of fridge to produce in order to maximise profits. The number of each type of fridge defines the variables under consideration. In this case, we could define the variables as:

x = number of model A470 fridges made per week,

and

y = number of model A370 fridges made per week.

The company wishes to find the values of x and y in order to maximise profits.

(2) Find the objective function

The objective function is the expression that we require to be optimised. In this example, we wish to maximise the profit, which we should be able to express in terms of the variables outlined in part (1) above.

We know that each model of fridge makes the following profit:

A470: $70;   A370: $60

Thus, if in each week the company produces x of the A470 fridges and y of the A370 fridges, then the total profit from these fridges is found by the expression:

Profit $= 70x + 60y$

This is the objective function that should be maximised.

(3) Find the constraints

We must now define all the restrictions on the production output of this company expressed in terms of the two variables x and y.

There are two main restrictions as defined in the statement above. Firstly, there is a restriction on the number of staff hours available. There are a maximum of 3000 hours available, whilst every A470 fridge requires 3 hours and every A370 fridge requires 2 hours for production.

Consider the number of hours required by producing x of the A470 fridges and y of the A370 models. Each A470 fridge takes 3 hours to produce, and therefore to manufacture x of these fridges will require $3x$ hours. Similarly, to produce y of the A370 model will require $2y$ hours. Consequently, the total hours required for production of the two models are:

Total hours $= 3x + 2y$

The total cannot exceed 3000 hours, and therefore we can write this as the inequality:

$3x + 2y \leqslant 3000$

This defines one of the constraints on the production mix. The second constraint involves the payment for raw materials. The A470 fridge requires raw materials to the value of $50, whereas the A370 fridge requires $60 worth. With x of the A470 fridges and y of the A370 fridges being produced, this gives a total expenditure on raw materials of:

Total costs $= 50x + 60y$

The maximum weekly budget for this production is $75 000, and therefore this gives another condition as shown:

$50x + 60y \leqslant 75\ 000$

The constraints on total hours and total costs define the major conditions for the solution of this problem. It should be noted that there are two other obvious conditions which should be included, namely, the variables x and y, giving the number of the types of fridge being produced, cannot be negative. Thus, two additional 'non-negativity' constraints for this problem can be expressed as follows:

$x \geqslant 0$ and $y \geqslant 0.$

This concludes the formulation of the linear programming problem. In summary we have the following:

(1) $x =$ number of A470 fridges produced

   $y =$ number of A370 fridges produced

(2) We wish to maximise the objective function:

   Profit $= 70x + 60y$

(3) Subject to the following constraints:

   $3x + 2y \leqslant 3000$

   $50x + 60y \leqslant 75\ 000$

   $x \geqslant 0,$ $y \geqslant 0.$

The solution of this type of problem will be considered in the next section.

EXAMPLE 2

A financial adviser at Wiley-Macken is advising a client on the optimum investment portfolio. The client wishes to invest in two major share options in the Hanson group, a multinational conglomerate of companies in mining, tobacco, chemicals and minerals. The two shares that are being considered are the Hanson-Equity and Far-East options.

The share prices for these two options are as follows:

Hanson-Equity: £6.00 per share   Far-East: £4.00 per share

A total of £30 000 is available for investment in these two options.

The client has specified that he wishes to purchase a maximum of 6000 shares spread between the two options, with no more than 5000 shares of any single option being bought.

Finally, Wiley-Macken has estimated the return on investment of these two shares over the next year. It has been forecasted that the profit from each share over the next twelve months is likely to be:

Hanson-Equity: £1.20   Far-East: £1.00

The problem for the financial adviser is to advise the client in order to maximise the estimated profit from the client's investment.

This is an optimisation problem which can be solved using the linear programming formulation as shown below:

(1) Identify the variables used

The problem is to decide on how many of each share option should be purchased. The two variables are:

x = number of Hanson-Equity shares purchased,

and

y = number of Far-East shares purchased.

(2) What is the objective function?

The objective is to maximise the forecasted return on investment from these shares. We are given that the forecasted profit on the Hanson-Equity share is £1.20. Therefore, if x of these shares are purchased then the estimated profit will be £1.20x. Similarly, the estimated profit for each Far-East share is £1.00, and if y of these shares are bought then the profit will be £1.00y.

Thus, the total estimated profit from investment in the two shares will be:

Return on investment (ROI) = £1.20x + £1.00y

More simply this can be written as

Return on investment = $1.2x + 1y = 1.2x + y$

This is the objective function which we would wish to maximise.

(3) What are the constraints?

There are a number of conditions which must be satisfied in this problem. These relate to the amount of money available for shares and also the number of shares the client wishes to purchase.

Consider the amount of money available for investment. The client has a maximum of £30 000 to invest. Now, each Hanson-Equity share costs £6 and if x of these shares are purchased, then this will cost £$6x$. Similarly, each Far-East share costs £4, and thus the purchase of y such shares will cost £$4y$. Consequently, the total amount of money invested in the two shares is:

Total investment $= 6x + 4y$

Since this amount cannot exceed £30 000 we have the following constraint:

$6x + 4y \leqslant 30\ 000$

Secondly, there is a condition relating to the number of shares in the investment portfolio. The client wishes to purchase a maximum of 6000 shares. Now, the total number of shares purchased is simply $x + y$. Thus, this expression must be less than or equal to 6000. So the second condition is:

$x + y \leqslant 6000$

Thirdly, the client has expressed that no more than 5000 shares should be purchased of any option. Thus this gives two more conditions:

$x \leqslant 5000$ and $y \leqslant 5000$

Finally, it should be stated that the number of shares purchased of either option cannot be negative, and so the other relevant conditions for this problem are:

$x \geqslant 0,$ $y \geqslant 0$

To summarise we have the following:

(1) $x =$ number of Hanson-Equity shares purchased

   $y =$ number of Far-East shares purchased

(2) We wish to maximise the objective function:

   Return on investment $= 1.2x + y$

(3) Subject to the following constraints:

   $6x + 4y \leqslant 30\ 000$

   $x + y \leqslant 6000$

   $x \leqslant 5000,$ $y \leqslant 5000$

   $x \geqslant 0,$ $y \geqslant 0.$

Again, the solution of this problem will be considered later.

8.2 Graphical solution

In this section we will consider the solution of a linear programming problem by graphical methods. It should be noted that such a method is only practicable when considering two unknown variables (e.g. x and y), and that it is not appropriate for problems involving more than two unknowns. For instance, if the Production Manager at Stenlux needs to decide on the quantity of three or more different models of fridges to produce, then a graphical solution cannot be considered. Similarly, the investment analyst at Wiley-Macken could not use a graphical method when determining the optimum portfolio of more than two shares. As can be seen, the graphical method is extremely limited. However, it does provide a useful insight into the search for optimum solutions which can assist in the interpretation of more complex problems involving many variables.

The graphical solution of linear programming problems will be illustrated using the two problems formulated in the previous section. Essentially, the method involves two steps:

(1) illustrate the **feasible region** from the constraints given, and
(2) find the optimum value of the objective function within this region.

EXAMPLE I

Consider the problem of the Production Manager at Stenlux. A decision must be made on the quantity of two products to be manufactured. The formulation of the problem is summarised below:

(1) $x =$ number of A470 fridges produced

   $y =$ number of A370 fridges produced

(2) We wish to maximise the objective function:

   Profit $= 70x + 60y$

(3) Subject to the following constraints:

   $3x + 2y \leqslant 3000$

   $50x + 60y \leqslant 75\,000$

   $x \geqslant 0, \qquad y \geqslant 0.$

Let us consider the solution of this problem in two parts:

(1) Illustrate the feasible region
The first step in solving this problem graphically is to illustrate the constraints.

Consider the first inequality $3x + 2y \leqslant 3000$

The region satisfying this condition will be one side of the straight line:

$3x + 2y = 3000$

To draw this straight line it is only necessary to plot two points. Generally, $x = 0$ and $y = 0$ will provide the simplest plots to obtain.

For instance, when $x = 0$, we have $3 * 0 + 2y = 3000$

Therefore, $2y = 3000$, giving $y = 1500$.

Similarly, when $y = 0$, we have $3x + 2 * 0 = 3000$

Therefore, $3x = 3000$, and so $x = 1000$.

Thus, the equation $3x + 2y = 3000$ includes the points:

$x = 0, \ y = 1500;$ and $x = 1000, \ y = 0$

These points can be plotted on the graph as shown in Figure 8.1.

Now, the region satisfying the inequality $3x + 2y \leqslant 3000$ can be illustrated by shading the area on one side of the line $3x + 2y = 3000$.

To determine which side of the line, it is only necessary to consider a single point and find whether or not the point satisfies the inequality. For instance, when $x = 0$ and $y = 0$ we have $3 * 0 + 2 * 0 = 0$. This value is less than 3000 and therefore satisfies the inequality.

Therefore, the shaded region satisfying the inequality $3x + 2y \leqslant 3000$ includes the point $x = 0, \ y = 0$. The region is shown as the shaded area on the graph in Figure 8.1.

Similarly, we can sketch the region satisfying the second constraint:

$50x + 60y \leqslant 75\ 000$

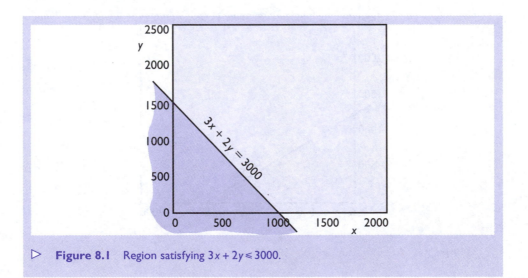

▷ **Figure 8.1** Region satisfying $3x + 2y \leqslant 3000$.

We do this initially by considering the equation $50x + 60y = 75\ 000$

Firstly, plot two points:

When $x = 0$: $50 * 0 + 60y = 75\ 000$
Therefore, $60y = 75\ 000$, and it follows that $y = 1250$

Also, when $y = 0$: $50x + 60 * 0 = 75\ 000$
Therefore, $50x = 75\ 000$, and so $x = 1500$

Therefore, the straight line $50x + 60y = 75\ 000$ can be drawn by plotting the points $x = 0$, $y = 1250$, and $x = 1500$, $y = 0$.
 Furthermore, the point when $x = 0$ and $y = 0$ satisfies the inequality and is therefore included in the region as shown by the diagram in Figure 8.2.
 The two remaining inequalities are $x \geqslant 0$ and $y \geqslant 0$. These can be illustrated by shading the positive values only on the graph. The shaded region in Figure 8.3 illustrates these two inequalities.
 Finally, the regions illustrated in the previous diagrams can be combined together to indicate the region satisfying all the constraints:

$3x + 2y \leqslant 3000$

$50x + 60y \leqslant 75\ 000$

$x \geqslant 0, \qquad y \geqslant 0$

The diagram shown in Figure 8.4 shows the region satisfying all the constraints. This region is known as the **feasible region** since it contains all the feasible solutions to the linear programming problem.

Definition: *The feasible region is an area obtained by graphing the constraints in a given problem and contains all the possible solutions to the optimisation.*

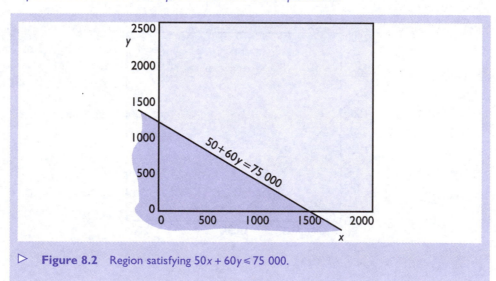

▷   **Figure 8.2**   Region satisfying $50x + 60y \leqslant 75\ 000$.

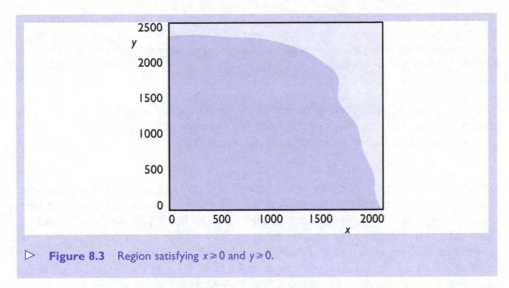

▷ **Figure 8.3**   Region satisfying $x \geq 0$ and $y \geq 0$.

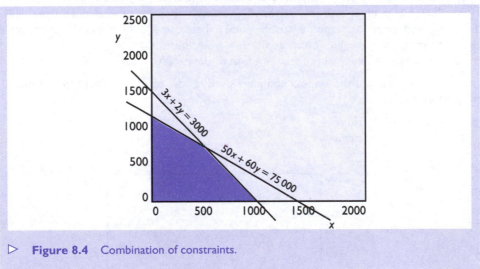

▷ **Figure 8.4**   Combination of constraints.

(2) Optimise the value for the objective function

Any point in the feasible region could be a potential solution to the problem of maximising the profit in this problem. It only remains for us to find the point which will maximise this function. The so-called objective function is:

Profit $= 70x + 60y$

We could look at any point in the feasible region and calculate the corresponding profit. For instance, the feasible region contains the point $x = 500$ and $y = 500$. These values yield a value for the profit $= 70 * 500 + 60 * 500 = \$65\,000$.

We need to investigate whether other values of x and y would give a higher value for the profit. Instead of considering individual points like this we can use an alternative, more efficient approach. Consider a specific value for the profit, e.g. $30 000. This gives an equation:

$$70x + 60y = 30\ 000$$

This straight line equation can be plotted on the graph containing the feasible region as shown in Figure 8.5. Any point on this line will yield a profit of $30 000.

Now, consider a higher value for the profit, e.g. $50 000. This gives the equation:

$$70x + 60y = 50\ 000$$

Again, this equation can be plotted on the graph as shown in Figure 8.6. As can be seen the resulting line is parallel to the original line. This can be shown again by plotting a third line representing another profit value, e.g. 70 000. The resulting equation, $70x + 60y = 70\ 000$, can be plotted on the graph as shown in Figure 8.7. It can be seen that the profit lines are parallel to each other, and as the profit increases, the lines get further away from the origin of the graph ($x = 0$, $y = 0$). Using this approach it can be seen that the maximum profit line will occur at the point indicated on the graph in Figure 8.8. The point shown in Figure 8.8 gives the optimum solution of this problem. The optimum point corresponds to the point where $x = 375$ and $y = 937$. Note that these are approximate values obtained directly from the graph.

Consequently, we have obtained a solution to the problem as follows:

It is recommended that the Stenlux company produce the two products in the following proportion each week:

Number of A470 fridges $= 375$
Number of A370 fridges $= 937$

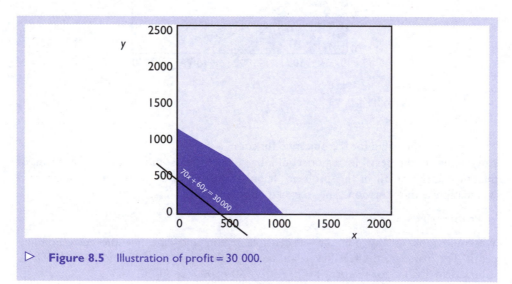

▷ **Figure 8.5**   Illustration of profit $= 30\ 000$.

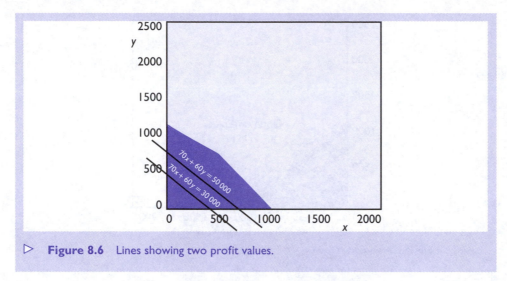

▷ **Figure 8.6**   Lines showing two profit values.

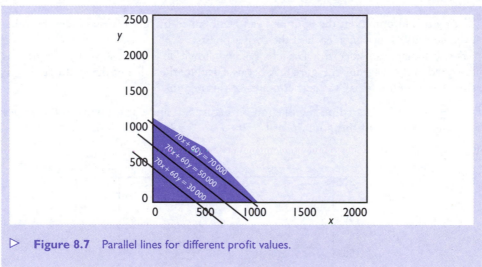

▷ **Figure 8.7**   Parallel lines for different profit values.

This will yield a maximum profit of:

Profit $= 70x + 60y = 70*375 + 60*937 = \$82\ 470$ per week.

(3) Alternative optimising method

An alternative method can be used to obtain the optimum value for the objective function based on a knowledge of the feasible region. It is known that the optimum value will occur at the boundary of the feasible region. In fact, an optimum value will always occur at a corner of the region. (Although other boundary points may also yield the same optimum value. An example of this situation will be considered later in the chapter.)

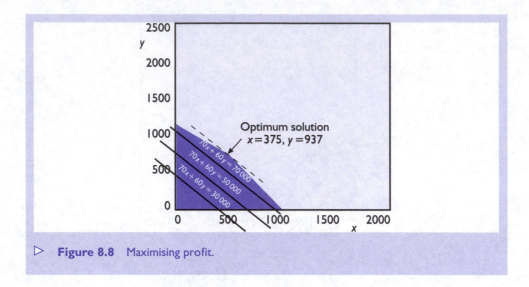

▷ **Figure 8.8**   Maximising profit.

Using this information, the optimum can be obtained by simply calculating the value of the objective function at each of the corner points.

For instance, consider the feasible region shown in Figure 8.4. This region is illustrated in the diagram in Figure 8.9. Let us calculate the value of the profit function: profit $= 70x + 60y$, for all the corner points of this region.

Point A: This is indicated on the diagram in Figure 8.9 and corresponds to the values $x = 0$ and $y = 1250$. At this point, profit $= 70 * 0 + 60 * 1250 = \$75\ 000$.

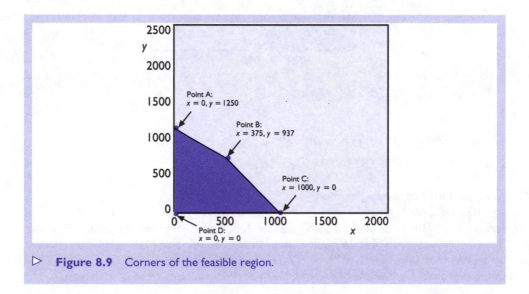

▷ **Figure 8.9**   Corners of the feasible region.

Point B: This point gives the values $x = 375$ and $y = 937$. Using these values for x and y we obtain: profit $= 70 * 375 + 60 * 937 = \$82\ 470$.

Point C: This corresponds to the values $x = 1000$ and $y = 0$. At this point the objective function is: profit $= 70 * 1000 + 60 * 0 = \$70\ 000$.

It should be noted that there is a fourth corner in the feasible region. This is indicated in Figure 8.9 as point D where $x = 0$ and $y = 0$. At this point the profit $= 70 * 0 + 60 * 0 = \$0$.

From these calculations we see that the maximum profit occurs at the point B corresponding to $x = 375$ and $y = 937$. This result confirms the values obtained using the previous method.

8.3   Summary of graphical methods

Using a graphical method we can locate the optimum value of an objective function subject to a number of constraints as follows:

(1) **Illustrate the feasible region.** This is done by shading the area satisfying all of the inequalities representing the constraints in the problem. The region which satisfies **all** the conditions is the feasible region.
(2) **Find the optimum value of the objective function.** This involves finding the point in the feasible region which optimises (maximises or minimises) the objective function. Two approaches can be used in order to find this point:

Either (a) Assume any specific value for the objective function. Using this value, plot the straight line on the graph. Now move this line in parallel until it reaches the edge of the feasible region. The point now reached will give the optimum for the objective function.

Or   (b) Calculate the value for the objective function for every corner point on the feasible region. The optimum value will correspond to one of these points.

8.4   Maximising and minimising

The following examples will illustrate the graphical method of solution for the linear programming problem. In the previous example, we have considered a maximisation problem where all the constraints were inequalities expressed in terms of '$\leqslant$'. In general, linear programming problems can involve a mixture of constraints including a combination of $\leqslant$, $\geqslant$ and $=$. Furthermore, minimising problems are also important. For instance, a company may wish to minimise costs, staff time or losses. The following examples will illustrate the graphical method in such cases.

In order to simplify the problems, it is assumed that the problem formulation has been achieved and the examples below indicate the resulting objective functions and constraints.

EXAMPLE 1

Given the following constraints:

$5x + 2y \leqslant 90$

$3x + 4y \geqslant 110$

and $x \geqslant 0, \qquad y \geqslant 0$

Find the values of x and y in order to find the optimum values of the functions:

(a) Maximise $P = 20x + 30y$
(b) Minimise $C = 2x + 20y$

This linear programming problem is solved as follows:

(1) Find the feasible region
We need to shade the region satisfying each of the conditions:

Consider $5x + 2y \leqslant 90$.

Given the equation $5x + 2y = 90$, we can plot two points as follows:

When $x = 0$, $5 * 0 + 2y = 90$, and so $y = 45$.
Similarly, when $y = 0$, $5x + 2 * 0 = 90$, giving $x = 18$.

The points $x = 0$, $y = 45$, and $x = 18$, $y = 0$ can be plotted on a graph in order to draw the straight line for $5x + 2y = 90$. The region satisfying the inequality is the area below this line.

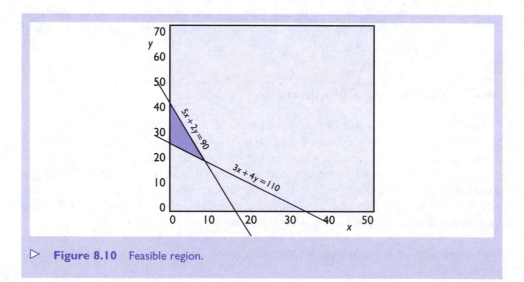

▷   **Figure 8.10**   Feasible region.

In the same way, we consider the other inequality, $3x + 4y \geqslant 110$.

The equation $3x + 4y = 110$ gives the points $x = 0$, $y = 27.5$, and $y = 0$, $x = 36.67$. These points can be plotted on the graph in order to draw the straight line representing this equation. In this case, the inequality involves a $\geqslant$, and therefore the appropriate shading is above the straight line.

These two constraints combined with the conditions that $x \geqslant 0$ and $y \geqslant 0$ will give the feasible region illustrated in Figure 8.10.

(2) Locate the optimum value

There are two objective functions to optimise in this problem.

(a) Consider the objective function $P = 20x + 30y$. We wish to maximise this function.

Consider the points at the corners of the feasible region. The diagram shown in Figure 8.11 indicates the corner points for the feasible region. These points yield the following values for the objective function:

Point A: $x = 0$ and $y = 45$, giving $P = 20 * 0 + 30 * 45 = 1350$.

Point B: $x = 10$ and $y = 20$, giving $P = 20 * 10 + 30 * 20 = 700$.

Point C: $x = 0$ and $y = 27.5$, giving $P = 20 * 0 + 30 * 27.5 = 825$.

Therefore, we see that the maximum value of $P = 1350$ occurs at $x = 0$ and $y = 45$.

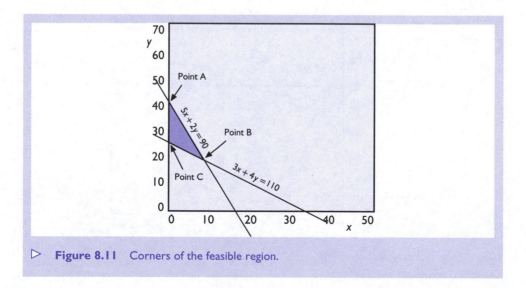

▷ **Figure 8.11** *Corners of the feasible region.*

(b) Similarly, consider minimising the objective function $C = 2x + 20y$.

Again, we can investigate the value of this function at the corner points of the feasible region:

Point A: $x = 0$ and $y = 45$, giving $C = 2*0 + 20*45 = 900$.

Point B: $x = 10$ and $y = 20$, giving $C = 2*10 + 20*20 = 420$.

Point C: $x = 0$ and $y = 27.5$, giving $C = 2*0 + 20*27.5 = 550$.

Therefore, the minimum value of $C = 420$ occurs at $x = 10$ and $y = 20$.

EXAMPLE 2

Minimise the expression $C = 120x + 100y$ subject to the following conditions:

$4x + 3y \geqslant 60$
$10x + 5y \geqslant 120$

$6x + 12y \geqslant 120$

$0 \leqslant x \leqslant 18$

$0 \leqslant y \leqslant 25$

(1) The feasible region is illustrated in Figure 8.12. Note that the three main conditions involve $\geqslant$ signs result in a shaded region **above** the lines. The condition on $x \leqslant 18$ gives an area to the left of the straight line $x = 18$. Similarly, the condition on $y \leqslant 25$ gives an area below the line $y = 25$ on the graph. A combination of all these areas gives the feasible region as shown.

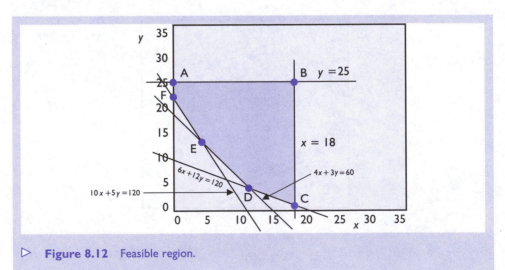

▷ **Figure 8.12**   Feasible region.

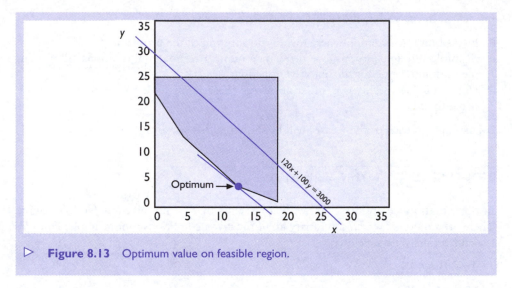

(2)   The corners of the region shown will provide the optimum value for the objective function C.

Point A: $x = 0$, $y = 25$: $C = 120 * 0 + 100 * 25 = 2500$

Point B: $x = 18$, $y = 25$: $C = 120 * 18 + 100 * 25 = 4660$

Point C: $x = 18$, $y = 1$: $C = 120 * 18 + 100 * 1 = 2260$

Point D: $x = 12$, $y = 4$: $C = 120 * 12 + 100 * 4 = 1840$

Point E: $x = 6$, $y = 12$: $C = 120 * 6 + 100 * 12 = 1920$

Point F: $x = 0$, $y = 24$: $C = 120 * 0 + 100 * 24 = 2400$.

This shows that a minimum value of $C = 1840$ occurs at $x = 12$ and $y = 4$.

It can be seen that sometimes the approach of calculating the values of the objective function at all the corners of the feasible region can be a clumsy method. The alternative of sketching the objective function for any specific value and then looking at a parallel line to minimise the expression may be preferred in this example. The diagram shown in Figure 8.13 illustrates the objective function where $C = 3000$, i.e. the straight line $120x + 100y = 3000$ is drawn. Now this line can be moved down in parallel until the minimum value is obtained at the point $x = 12$, $y = 4$. This confirms the values obtained using the previous method.

8.5   Special cases

There are a number of potential difficulties in solving linear programming problems. This section considers a range of special cases in obtaining the solutions to such problems. In particular, the following cases are shown:

▶ **Infeasibility.** A situation where there is no solution to the problem.
▶ **Multiple solutions.** In this case there are a number of potential solutions, all yielding the optimum value for the objective function.
▶ **Unboundedness.** This is a situation where there is no limit to the optimum value being found.

An example of each of these cases will be shown in this section.

| **EXAMPLE 1** | **(infeasibility)** |

In this situation we are presented with constraints that do not give any feasible region. There are no points which can satisfy all of the given conditions. For example, consider the constraints shown below:

$$4x + 5y \geqslant 40$$

$$10x + 2y \leqslant 30$$

$$y \leqslant 3, \qquad x \geqslant 0$$

These conditions are similar to Example 2 in the previous section except that some of the inequalities have been reversed.

The two main conditions give the region A as shown in Figure 8.14. The condition on $y \leqslant 3$ gives the region B on the graph. It can be seen that there are no points which lie in both of these regions, and thus there are no points which can satisfy all of the conditions. Thus this situation is **infeasible** and cannot provide any optimum solutions.

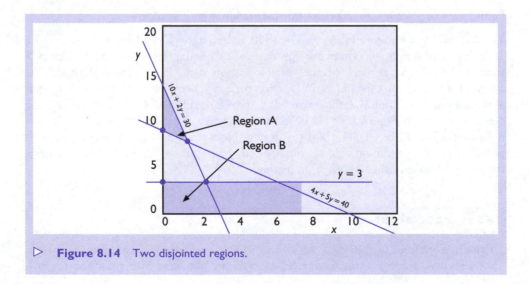

▷ **Figure 8.14**   Two disjointed regions.

In practice, this would be a situation where conditions on costs, staffing and resources make it impossible to produce any goods!

EXAMPLE 2 **(multiple solutions)**

Consider the problem of maximising the expression $P = 8x + 10y$ subject to the following constraints:

$$4x + 5y \leqslant 40, \qquad 10x + 2y \leqslant 30$$

$$y \geqslant 3, \qquad x \geqslant 0$$

The graph illustrated in Figure 8.15 shows the feasible region based on these constraints. The graph also shows the line $P = 8x + 10y = 40$. This line can be moved further in parallel towards the edge of the feasible region. It can be seen that this line is parallel to one of the lines at the limit of the region. Therefore, the maximum value of P will occur anywhere along this line.

Thus, we have multiple solutions to this optimisation problem. For instance, the following points all yield the maximum values of $P = 8x + 10y = 80$:

(i) $x = 0, y = 8$ (ii) $x = 0.125, y = 7.9$
(iii) $x = 0.5, y = 7.6$ (iv) $x = 1, y = 7.2$

There are, in fact, an infinite number of solutions for x and y which give the maximum value of $P = 80$. However, the end points in the line segment are considered to be the basic solutions to this problem.

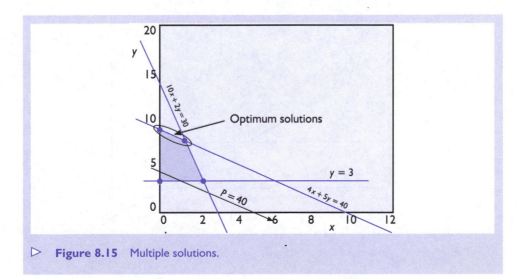

▷ **Figure 8.15** Multiple solutions.

| EXAMPLE 3 | (unboundedness) |

Consider the problem of maximising the value of $P = 8x + 6y$ subject to the following conditions:

$$4x + 5y \geqslant 40, \qquad 10x + 2y \geqslant 30$$

$$y \geqslant 3 \quad \text{and} \quad x \geqslant 0$$

The diagram in Figure 8.16 shows the feasible region satisfying all the constraints. It can be seen that this region is boundless in the top right hand corner and, therefore, there is no limit on the highest values of x and y. Thus, the solution to this is that x and y should be infinite. In practice, this situation is likely to occur if one or more conditions have been omitted from the problem formulation. For instance, if x and y are the number of two items being produced, then upper limits may need to be included because of constraints on the likely customer demand for these products, or on the availability of resources such as staff, raw materials, or budgets.

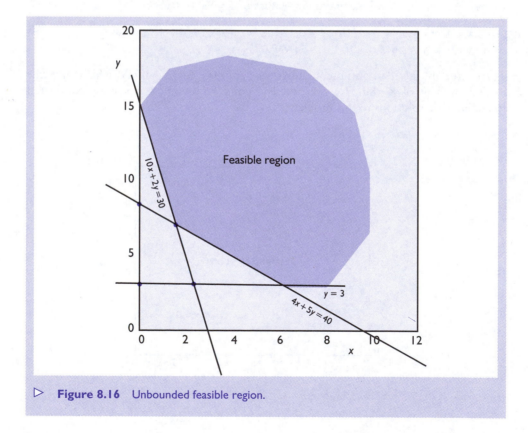

▷ **Figure 8.16** Unbounded feasible region.

| 8.6 | **Exercises: graphical methods** |

1.(E) Illustrate the feasible regions for each of the sets of conditions given below:

(i) $2x + y \leqslant 50$, $\quad x + 3y \leqslant 90$, $\quad x, y \geqslant 0$

(ii) $3x + 2y \leqslant 12$, $\quad 4x + 5y \geqslant 20$, $\quad x, y \geqslant 0$

(iii) $4x + y \leqslant 90$, $\quad 2x + y \leqslant 50$, $\quad x + y \leqslant 40$, $\quad x, y \geqslant 0$

(iv) $3x + 10y \geqslant 30$, $\quad 4x + 8y \geqslant 32$, $\quad 3x + 10y \leqslant 36$, $\quad x, y \geqslant 0$

2.(I) The following examples give a number of conditions in terms of x and y. In each case use these constraints to find the positive values of x and y in order to optimise the expression as stated:

(i) $x + y \leqslant 20$, $\quad 2x + y \leqslant 30$

Maximise $P = 4x + 3y$

(ii) $5x + 8y \leqslant 120$, $\quad 6x + 3y \leqslant 90$, $\quad 5x + 5y \leqslant 90$

Maximise $P = 10x + 11y$

(iii) $10x + 4y \leqslant 400$, $\quad 3x + 5y \geqslant 300$, $\quad x \leqslant 20$

Maximise $P = 2x + 3y$ and minimise $C = x + 4y$

(iv) $x + y \geqslant 50$, $\quad 3x + 2y \geqslant 120$, $\quad x \leqslant 60$, $\quad y \leqslant 70$

Minimise $C = 7x + 8y$ and maximise $P = x + 6y$

3.(I) A company manufactures two main products A and B. The products require major work in two processes, and the table below shows the number of hours spent on the two processes in order to produce a unit of each product.

	Staff hours per unit	
Product	Process I	Process 2
A	3	4
B	2	5

In any given week the total number of hours available for each of the processes is:

Process 1: 60 hours   Process 2: 100 hours

The company makes £50 profit from the sale of each unit of either product.

(i) How many units of each product should the company produce in order to maximise the total profit?

(ii) If the company makes £40 per unit for product A and £60 per unit for product B, would this change the number of units of each product you would recommend producing?

4.(I) A client is considering investing in a range of stocks. In particular, she has decided to invest up to a maximum of $10 000 in a combination of two stocks from the companies Arnold Inc and Bassett Company.
The present price of each share is:

  Arnold Inc: $5.00   Bassett Company: $7.50

The expected percentage return on each share is:

  Arnold Inc: 8%   Bassett Company: 10%

No more than $6000 should be spent on any one share.
Formulate this as a linear programming problem and find the number of each company's shares to be purchased in order to maximise the likely return on investment.

8.7   The simplex method: maximisation with ⩽ constraints

As already stated, the graphical methods introduced in the previous sections are only suitable for problems involving two unknowns (e.g. x and y). In the majority of practical situations it is likely that there are significantly more unknowns than this. The simplex method provides one of the best known approaches to the solution of linear programming problems using algebraic methods. The simplex method has been used in a wide range of computer application packages for the solution of these problems.
The simplex approach will be introduced using the following examples.

Definition: The simplex method is a mathematical approach to the solution of linear programming problems. It is the standard method of solution to problems involving more than two variables.

EXAMPLE I

Consider the problem, solved earlier in this chapter using a graphical method, of determining the number of two types of fridge to be produced in order to maximise profit.
The problem formulation was as follows:

(1) x = number of A470 fridges produced
    y = number of A370 fridges produced
(2) We wish to maximise the objective function:

  Profit = $70x + 60y$

(3) Subject to the following constraints:

$$3x + 2y \leqslant 3000$$

$$50x + 60y \leqslant 75\ 000$$

$$x \geqslant 0, \qquad y \geqslant 0$$

The simplex method of solution follows the following stages:

Stage 1: Include so-called 'slack variables' into the constraints in order to express them as equations. For instance, the inequality $3x + 2y \leqslant 3000$ can be made into an equation by adding the slack variable S_1 to the left hand side. We therefore have the equation:

$$3x + 2y + 1S_1 = 3000$$

Similarly, adding a slack variable S_2 to the second condition gives:

$$50x + 60y + 1S_2 = 75\ 000$$

The slack variables can also be incorporated into the objective function $P = 70x + 60y$ to give:

$$P = 70x + 60y + 0S_1 + 0S_2$$

This can be written as $0 = -P + 70x + 60y + 0S_1 + 0S_2$

Stage 2: The resulting equations can be placed in the simplex tableau as shown below:

Row	Basis	Value	x	y	S_1	S_2
1	S_1	3000	3	2	1	0
2	S_2	75 000	50	60	0	1
3	$-P$	0	70	60	0	0

The columns labelled x, y, S_1 and S_2 contain the coefficients of these variables in the equations given. For instance, the condition $3x + 2y + 1S_1 = 3000$ is given in row 1 of the table. In this equation the coefficient of x is 3, y is 2 and S_1 is 1. The coefficient of S_2 is zero in this equation.

Similarly, row 2 in the table represents the second condition and row 3 shows the equation containing the objective function P.

The basis column contains the variables that could provide a solution to the problem. In this initial 'solution' we see that $S_1 = 3000$ and $S_2 = 75\ 000$, giving a value of $P = 0$. The other variables (x and y) in this solution would be zero. Thus, if we produce no fridges of either model, then our total profit will be $0. In such a case, we would have 3000 staff-hours remaining unused, and $75 000 of the weekly budget still spare.

Stage 3: In this stage we need to transform the tableau in order to determine whether there is a better solution to the problem.

In order to do this we proceed as follows:

(i) **Identify the pivotal column.** This is the column with the largest positive value in the last row as shown in the table below. The pivotal column is indicated by ***.

Row	Basis	Value	x	y	S_1	S_2
1	S_1	3000	3	2	1	0
2	S_2	75 000	50	60	0	1
3	$-P$	0	70	60	0	0

$$***$$
$$\uparrow$$
Pivotal column

(ii) **Identify the pivotal row.** To achieve this we divide each number in the value column by the corresponding number in the pivotal column. This is shown in the following table:

Row	Basis	Value	x	y	S_1	S_2	Value/pivot
1	S_1	3000	3	2	1	0	3000/3 = 1000 *
2	S_2	75 000	50	60	0	1	75000/50 = 1500
3	$-P$	0	70	60	0	0	

The row with the smallest non-negative value (shown by *) is the pivotal row.

(iii) **Identify the pivot.** This is the value at the intersection of the pivotal row and pivotal column. The pivot is shown in bold type in the next tableau

Row	Basis	Value	x	y	S_1	S_2
1	S_1	3000	**3**	2	1	0
2	S_2	75 000	50	60	0	1
3	$-P$	0	70	60	0	0

(iv) **Divide each number in the pivotal row by the pivot.** The pivotal row is row 1. All numbers in this row are divided by the pivot (3) as shown in the next table:

	Row	Basis	Value	x	y	S_1	S_2
Row 1/3	1	S_1	1000	1	0.667	0.333	0
	2	S_2	75 000	50	60	0	1
	3	$-P$	0	70	60	0	0

(v) **Reduce each other number in the pivotal column to zero.** This is done by subtracting multiples of the pivotal row from the other rows. For instance, in row 2 in the pivotal column (the x column) we have the value 50. In order to reduce this to zero we can calculate the formula Row $2 - 50*(\text{Row } 1)$. This is abbreviated in the table as $R2 - 50*R1$. Similarly, the value in row 3 can be eliminated by calculating $R3 - 70*R1$. The results of these calculations are shown in the following table:

	Row	Basis	Value	x	y	S_1	S_2
	1	x	1000	1	0.667	0.333	0
$R2 - 50*R1$	2	S_2	25 000	0	26.667	−16.667	1
$R3 - 70*R1$	3	$-P$	−70 000	0	13.333	−23.333	0

It should be noted that in this table the basis in the pivotal row has been replaced by the variable in the pivotal column, i.e. S_1 has been replaced with x in the basis column.

We have now obtained an improved solution. Thus, if the value of $x = 1000$ then the profit has been increased to $70 000.

Stage 4: We ask whether the solution obtained can be improved.

If all the values in the last row in the table are negative or zero, then an optimum solution has been reached. If not, then there is room for improvement and we repeat the process from Stage 3 again.

In the above table we have 13.333 in the last row and therefore an improvement can be made to this solution. We therefore repeat the process as before:

(i) **Identify the pivotal column.** The pivotal column is the column with the largest positive number in the last row, i.e. in this table the pivotal column is the y column, where there is a value of 13.333.

(ii) **Identify the pivotal row.** This is identified by dividing the value by the number in the pivotal column. The smallest resulting number indicates the pivotal row as shown in the following table:

Row	Basis	Value	x	y	S_1	S_2	Value/pivot
1	x	1000	1	0.667	0.333	0	$1000/0.667 = 1500$
2	S_2	25 000	0	**26.667**	−16.667	1	$25\,000/26.667 = 937.5$
3	$-P$	−70 000	0	13.333	−23.333	0	

***
↑
Pivotal column

(iii) **Identify the pivot.** This is indicated in bold type in the previous table at the intersection of the pivotal row and pivotal column.

(iv) **Divide numbers in the pivotal row by the pivot.** Thus we obtain the table:

	Row	Basis	Value	x	y	S_1	S_2
	1	x	1000	1	0.667	0.333	0
R2/26.667	2	S_2	937.5	0	1	−0.625	0.0375
	3	−P	−70 000	0	13.333	−23.333	0

(v) **Reduce each of the other numbers in the pivotal column to zero.** The following table shows the required calculations to obtain this. Note that the basis variable S_2 in the pivotal row has been replaced with the variable y in the pivotal column.

	Row	Basis	Value	x	y	S_1	S_2
R1 − 0.667 * R2	1	x	375	1	0	0.75	−0.025
	2	y	937.5	0	1	−0.625	0.0375
R3 − 13.333 * R2	3	−P	−82 500	0	0	−15	−0.5

We have now reached Stage 4 again, where we ask whether a further improvement could be made. All the values in the bottom row of the table are negative or zero, and therefore no further improvement is possible.

The simplex tableau shows the solutions as:

$$x = 375, \qquad y = 937.5$$

giving a maximum profit $P = \$82\ 500$.

In this example, the values of x and y are the number of fridges of two different models to be produced per week. Thus, we would expect these values to be whole numbers. Consequently, rounding down the values obtained in the table we have:

$$x = \text{number of A470 fridges produced} = 375,$$

and

$$y = \text{number of A370 fridges produced} = 937.$$

This will change the maximum profit obtained, which can be found by substituting these values into the expression $P = 70x + 60y$, giving a maximum profit of \$82 470. These values confirm the results obtained using the graphical method in Section 8.2.

It should be noted that there are potential difficulties when solutions involve rounding. For example, there are cases where an optimum integer solution may not be close to the solution obtained from the standard linear programming approach. Further consideration of this is beyond the scope of this book and involves 'integer programming' methods.

EXAMPLE 2

Consider a linear programming problem involving more than two variables as outlined below. The problem described is a modification of the Stenlux example previously solved.

The Stenlux company needs to make a decision on the production mix for three models of fridge: the A470, A370 and B270. Estimated profit from the sale of each fridge is:

A470: $70,   A370: $60,   B270: $50

The number of staff-hours required to produce each fridge is estimated to be:

A470: 3 hours,   A370: 2 hours,   B270: 2.5 hours

The value of raw materials required in the production of these models is:

A470: $50,   A370: $60,   B270: $40

The company has 3000 staff-hours and a $75 000 budget for the production of these models. Furthermore, the demand for the A470 model is not likely to exceed 250.

The problem can be formulated as follows:

(i) The variables are:

x = number of A470 fridges produced

y = number of A370 fridges produced

z = number of B270 fridges produced

(ii) We require to maximise $P = 70x + 60y + 50z$

(iii) Subject to the following constraints:
- (a) staff-hours: $3x + 2y + 2.5z \leqslant 3000$
- (b) raw materials: $50x + 60y + 40z \leqslant 75\ 000$
- (c) demand: $x \leqslant 250$

Now to solve this problem using the simplex method we proceed as follows:

Stage 1. Introduce slack variables to reduce the constraints to equations:

$3x + 2y + 2.5z + S_1 = 3000$

$50x + 60y + 40z + S_2 = 75\ 000$

$x + S_3 = 250$

We wish to maximise $P = 70x + 60y + 50z + 0S_1 + 0S_2 + 0S_3$

This equation can be written as:

$0 = -P + 70x + 60y + 50z + 0S_1 + 0S_2 + 0S_3$

Stage 2. The equations can be placed into the simplex tableau as shown below:

Row	Basis	Value	x	y	z	S_1	S_2	S_3
1	S_1	3000	3	2	2.5	1	0	0
2	S_2	75 000	50	60	40	0	1	0
3	S_3	250	1	0	0	0	0	1
4	$-P$	0	70	60	50	0	0	0

The pivotal column can be identified as the column containing the largest positive value in the bottom row. The pivotal row is found by calculating the number in the value column divided by the number in the pivotal column as shown below:

Row	Basis	Value	x	y	z	S_1	S_2	S_3	Value/pivot
1	S_1	3000	3	2	2.5	1	0	0	3000/3 = 1000
2	S_2	75 000	50	60	40	0	1	0	75 000/50 = 1500
3	S_3	250	**1**	0	0	0	0	1	250/1 = 250 *
4	$-P$	0	70	60	50	0	0	0	
			**						

The smallest result of the value/pivot calculation indicates the pivotal row. Therefore, the pivot at the intersection of the pivotal row and pivotal column is identified and shown in bold type.

In general, at this stage, we reduce the pivot to 1. In this case the value is already 1, so no calculations are necessary. Finally, we set the other values in the pivotal column to zero by subtracting multiples of the pivotal row from each remaining row. These calculations are shown in the next table. Note that the basis variable (x) of the pivotal row is obtained from the pivotal column.

	Row	Basis	Value	x	y	z	S_1	S_2	S_3
R1 − 3 * R3	1	S_1	2250	0	2	2.5	1	0	−3
R2 − 50 * R3	2	S_2	62 500	0	60	40	0	1	−50
Pivot	3	x	250	1	0	0	0	0	1
R4 − 70 * R3	4	$-P$	−17 500	0	60	50	0	0	−70

An optimum solution has not yet been reached since there are still positive values in the bottom row. The new pivotal column is identified by the maximum value in this bottom row, and the ratio of the number in the value column by the number in the pivotal column is calculated in order to find the pivotal row:

Row	Basis	Value	x	y	z	S_1	S_2	S_3	Value/pivot
1	S_1	2250	0	2	2.5	1	0	−3	1125
2	S_2	62 500	0	60	40	0	1	−50	1041.67
3	x	250	1	0	0	0	0	1	−
4	−P	−17 500	0	60	50	0	0	−70	

**

Row 2 is found to be the pivotal row. The pivot of 60 is reduced to 1 by dividing all values in this row by 60. This amended row 2 (referred to as new row 2 or NR2) is used in the calculations to ensure that all other values in the Pivotal column are zero.

	Row	Basis	Value	x	y	z	S_1	S_2	S_3
R1 − 2 * NR2	1	S_1	166.67	0	0	1.167	1	−0.033	−1.333
R2/60	2	y	1041.67	0	1	0.667	0	0.0167	−0.833
R3	3	x	250	1	0	0	0	0	1
R4 − 60 * NR2	4	−P	−80 000	0	0	10	0	−1	−20

Again, there is still a positive value in the last row of this table and so we repeat the process. The z column is identified as the pivotal column, and the pivotal row is found by calculating the value/pivot as shown below:

	Row	Basis	Value	x	y	z	S_1	S_2	S_3	Value/pivot
Pivotal row	1	S_1	166.67	0	0	1.167	1	−0.033	−1.333	142.86 *
	2	y	1041.67	0	1	0.667	0	0.0167	−0.833	1562.5
	3	x	250	1	0	0	0	0	1	−
	4	−P	−80 000	0	0	10	0	−1	−20	

**

The pivot (1.167) is reduced by dividing every value in the first row (the pivotal row) by 1.167. Other numbers in the pivotal column are reduced to zero by subtracting multiples of the new row (NR1) from each row as shown:

	Row	Basis	Value	x	y	z	S_1	S_2	S_3
R1/1.167	1	z	142.86	0	0	1	0.857	−0.0286	−1.143
R2 − 0.667 * NR1	2	y	946.43	0	1	0	−0.571	0.0358	−0.071
R3	3	x	250	1	0	0	0	0	1
R4 − 10 * NR1	4	−P	−81 428	0	0	0	−8.57	−0.714	−8.57

An optimum solution has now been reached since there are no positive numbers displayed in the bottom row of the table.

Thus, the maximum profit $P = \$81\ 428$, by producing the following numbers of fridges:

x = number of A470 models = 250

y = number of A370 models = 946

z = number of B270 models = 142

Note that the values of x, y and z have been rounded down, and therefore this will have a slight effect on the overall profit obtained.

8.8   Simplex method: minimisation with ⩾ constraints

In the previous examples we considered the simplex method for problems of maximising the objective function subject to ⩽ constraints, such as $x \leqslant 250$ and $3x + 2y \leqslant 3000$. In this section we will consider the problem of minimising the objective function subject to ⩾ constraints. This would be applicable in situations where we are seeking to minimise the costs of production subject to lower limits on the amount of staff hours, raw materials and machine time used.

Examples of this type can be converted into maximisation problems with subsequent use of the methods described in the previous section. Given a minimisation problem, then the corresponding maximisation problem is called the **dual**. The process of finding the dual problem is shown in the following examples.

EXAMPLE 1

Consider the production problems of Stenlux. The company must decide on the weekly production numbers for two models of washing machine, the standard and de luxe models. The costs involved in the production of these washing machines are:

standard: $80,   de luxe: $110

The number of staff hours required to produce each model of washing machine are:

standard: 4 hours,   de luxe: 5 hours

At least 2000 staff-hours per week must be used.

The Standard washing machine requires one drive belt, whereas the de luxe uses two to improve reliability. The number of belts used each week must be at least 700 because of a long-term contract with the suppliers.

The welding time taken for each washing machine is:

standard: 20 minutes,   de luxe: 16 minutes

The automatic welding equipment must be utilised for at least 130 hours per week, otherwise significantly higher maintenance costs will be incurred.

The formulation of this problem is as follows:

(i) x = number of standard washing machines produced

     y = number of de luxe washing machines produced

(ii)   We wish to minimise the objective function:

$$C = 80x + 110y$$

(iii)   Subject to the following constraints:

     (a)   staff hours: $4x + 5y \geqslant 2000$

     (b)   drive belts: $1x + 2y \geqslant 700$

     (c)   welding time: $20x + 16y \geqslant 7800$

     (Note 130 hours = 7800 minutes)

To find the dual of this problem we interchange rows and columns, and at the same time reverse the $\leqslant$ and $\geqslant$ signs, i.e. reading down the coefficients of x will give us a dual condition $4X + 1Y + 20Z \leqslant 80$. Similarly, the coefficients of y give a second condition: $5X + 2Y + 16Z \leqslant 110$.

We wish to maximise $c = 2000X + 700Y + 7800Z$

Now the simplex method can be used to solve this problem as follows.

Stage 1. The slack variables are introduced to transform the constraints to equations as given below:

$$4X + 1Y + 20Z + 1S_1 = 80$$

$$5X + 2Y + 16Z + 1S_2 = 110$$

The equation involving the objective function can be written:

$$-c + 2000X + 700Y + 7800Z + 0S_1 + 0S_2 = 0$$

Stages 2 and 3. The equations can be displayed in the simplex tableau with the pivotal column shown and calculations to determine the pivotal row included:

Row	Basis	Value	X	Y	Z	S_1	S_2	Value/pivot
1	S_1	80	4	1	20	1	0	4 **
2	S_2	110	5	2	16	0	1	6.875
3	$-c$	0	2000	700	7800	0	0	

                                   **

These rows are transformed to first change the pivot to 1, and then to set the remaining values in the pivotal column to zero as shown in the next table.

	Row	Basis	Value	X	Y	Z	S_1	S_2	Value/pivot
R1/20	1	Z	4	0.2	0.05	1	0.05	0	20 **
R2 − 16 * NR1	2	S_2	46	1.8	1.2	0	−0.8	1	25.556
R3 − 7800 * NR1	3	− c	−31 200	440	310	0	−390	0	

**

The above table also shows the start of the next iteration in which a new pivotal column is identified and the value/pivot is calculated in order to find the pivotal row.

The pivotal column containing the largest positive value is the X column. Again the pivotal row is found to be row 1. This row is divided by 0.2 so that the pivot is 1, and the other values in other rows are transformed to zero as shown below.

	Row	Basis	Value	X	Y	Z	S_1	S_2	Value/pivot
R1/0.2	1	X	20	1	0.25	5	0.25	0	80
R2 − 1.8 * NR1	2	S_2	10	0	0.75	−9	−1.25	1	13.333 **
R3 − 440 * NR1	3	− c	−40 000	0	200	−2200	−500	0	

**

From the above table we see that the pivotal column is the Y column, and that row 2 has been identified as the pivotal row. Dividing row 2 by 0.75 we change the pivot into 1, and suitable row transformations are used to set the other values in the pivotal column to 0 as shown:

	Row	Basis	Value	X	Y	Z	S_1	S_2	Value/pivot
R1 − 0.25 * NR2	1	X	16.667	1	0	8	0.667	−0.333	2.083 **
R2/0.75	2	Y	13.333	0	1	−12	−1.667	1.333	−1.111
R3 − 200 * NR2	3	− c	−42 666.67	0	0	200	−166.67	−266.67	

**

It should be noted in the above table that only positive results of the ratio (value/pivot) should be considered. Thus, the pivotal row in this table is the first row. The pivot is found to be in row 1 and column Z, and the transformations are repeated as below:

	Row	Basis	Value	X	Y	Z	S_1	S_2
R1/8	1	Z	2.083	0.125	0	1	0.083	−0.042
R2 + 12 * NR1	2	Y	38.333	1.5	1	0	−0.667	0.833
R3 − 200NR1	3	− c	−43 083.33	−25	0	0	−183.33	−258.33

A solution has now been reached since there are no positive values in the bottom row.

Now to interpret the results of this final tableau, the final row shows -183.33 in the S_1 column and -258.33 in the S_2 column. These values define the solutions for the original minimisation problem as follows:

$$x = 183.33, \qquad y = 258.33 \qquad \text{and} \qquad C = 43\,083$$

Therefore, we would recommend that the company produce:

$x =$ number of standard washing machines $= 183$,

and

$y =$ number of de luxe washing machines $= 258$.

This minimises the costs as $C = 80x + 110y = 80 * 183 + 110 * 258$

i.e. costs $= \$43\,020$

Note the difference between the costs obtained here and those from the simplex tableau. The discrepancy results from rounding errors. However, as previously noted, non-optimal solutions can be obtained by rounding, and care must be taken when this is done. To avoid the need for rounding we could consider the solutions obtained to be average values. Thus, each week we would aim to produce an average of 183.33 standard and 258.33 de luxe washing machines. Consequently, over a period of three weeks the target output would be 550 standard and 775 de luxe models.

8.9 Exercises: simplex method

1.(E) Use the simplex method to obtain the values of the given variables which optimise the stated objective function:

(i) Given $x + y \leqslant 20$, $2x + y \leqslant 30$, $x \geqslant 0$ and $y \geqslant 0$,

     maximise $P = 4x + 3y$

(ii) Given $2x + 3y + 4z \leqslant 240$

              $x + 5y + 2z \leqslant 300$

              $2x + y + z \leqslant 150$

              x, y and $z \geqslant 0$

              maximise $P = 10x + 5y + 8z$

(iii) Given $4x + 2y + z \leqslant 400$

              $3x + 5y \leqslant 240$

              $y + 2z \leqslant 200$

              x, y and $z \geqslant 0$

     maximise $P = 15x + 10y + 8z$

2.(D) Consider the problem of deciding between a range of shares for investment. Wiley-Macken is advising a client on investment. Three different shares are being considered. The current prices of these shares are:

Hanson-Equity: £6.00 per share
Far-East: £4.00 per share
Maxwell Managed: £5.00 per share

A total of £30 000 is available for investment. The risks associated with these shares have been classified by Wiley-Macken on a scale of 1 to 10. A score of 1 would indicate a very secure, no-risk option, whereas a score of 10 involves an extremely high-risk venture. The client wants an investment that is relatively secure, and does not wish to consider a portfolio of shares with an average score of more than 5. The risk scores for the three options are:

Hanson-Equity: 3,   Far-East: 8,   Maxwell Managed: 6

Estimates of the likely return on investment per share over the next twelve months are as follows:

Hanson-Equity: £1.00,   Far-East: £2.00,   Maxwell Managed: £1.50

Furthermore, it has been decided that no more than 2000 Far-East shares should be purchased.

Use the simplex method to estimate the number of shares of each type the client should purchase in order to maximise the expected return on investment over the next year.

8.10   The transportation problem

Transportation problems usually involve consideration of the distribution of goods from various sources to a range of destinations. For instance, a company may have a number of warehouses holding goods for distribution to various sites throughout the country. A decision must be made concerning the best way of moving these goods in order to minimise costs, time or transportation resources. Such a problem is a special case of the linear programming problem. We are given a number of constraints (e.g. concerning the requirements of destinations and the availability of resources) and wish to minimise the costs. As such, it is possible to formulate the transportation example as a linear programming problem, and then use the simplex method to obtain a solution. However, transportation involves constraints in a particular format, and a simplified method of solution is appropriate.

The process of obtaining a solution to the transportation problem follows the same pattern as in using the simplex method. An initial 'solution' is found, and checked to see whether it provides the best or optimum solution. If not, then an improved solution is found. This process is repeated until the optimum solution is obtained. This iterative method is illustrated in the diagram in Figure 8.17.

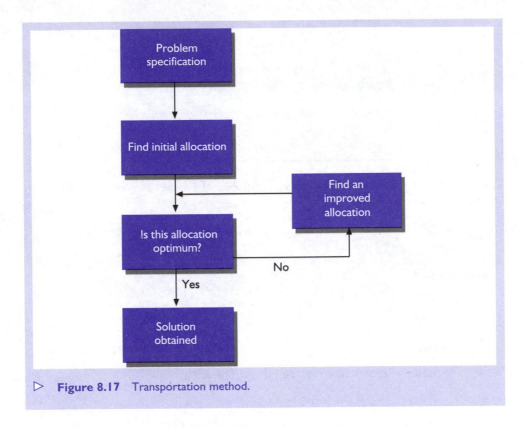

▷ **Figure 8.17** Transportation method.

The following examples illustrate the solution of this type of problem.

EXAMPLE 1

A manufacturing company has three main production lines and two primary storage areas. Items are stored in batches in the primary storage areas for later shipment to customers.

On each day the three production lines A, B and C produce 20, 50 and 20 batches of goods respectively. The capacity of each storage area is as follows: area 1 stores 60 batches and area 2 stores 30 batches.

The time taken to move the goods from each production line to the storage areas is shown in the following table. The times are shown in minutes per batch.

The table shows that it takes 7 minutes to move a batch of goods from line A to store 1. Similarly, it takes only 4 minutes to move a batch from line B to store 1.

The problem is to determine the optimum storage locations of the batches from each production line in order to minimise the total time involved. This can be formulated as a linear programming problem as shown below.

Time taken for moving goods (in minutes)			
	Production lines		
Storage areas	A	B	C
1	7	4	6
2	4	3	5

The following notation will be used: x_{A1} = number of batches moved from line A to store 1. The constraints are:

$$x_{A1} + x_{B1} + x_{C1} \leqslant 60$$

$$x_{A2} + x_{B2} + x_{C2} \leqslant 30$$

$$x_{A1} + x_{A2} \leqslant 20$$

$$x_{B1} + x_{B2} \leqslant 50$$

$$x_{C1} + x_{C2} \leqslant 20$$

$$x_{A1}, x_{A2}, x_{B1}, x_{B2}, x_{C1}, x_{C2} \geqslant 0$$

We wish to minimise the total time given by the expression:

$$T = 7x_{A1} + 4x_{A2} + 4x_{B1} + 3x_{B2} + 6x_{C1} + 5x_{C2}$$

This complex linear programming problem involving six variables can be more easily solved using the transportation method as follows. The information given on the times involved together with the production output and storage capacity are shown in the following table:

	A	B	C	Total
1	7	4	6	60
2	4	3	5	30
Total	20	50	20	90

Notice that the times are shown in the bottom right of each cell in the table. This will be the standard method of presenting information in the examples shown in this section. The objective is to determine the best way of sending the output from the production lines to the storage areas. For instance, how many of the 20 batches from production line A should be moved to each storage area? The following method can be used to obtain the optimum solution.

Step 1: obtain the initial allocation

In this first step a feasible allocation must be obtained. There are a number of approaches to obtaining this initial allocation. A sensible approach would be to consider the 'least cost' routes. In other words, look for the routes that cost the least (or as in this example, take the least amount of time) and place the maximum allocation through these routes.

In terms of this example, the shortest route is from line B to store 2, where it only takes 3 minutes to move each batch. Thus, as an initial allocation we would place the maximum amount (i.e. 30) through this route. Store 2 takes a maximum of 30 batches and therefore we cannot allocate more through this route. This then fills up the second row (store 2) as shown in the following table.

	A	B	C	Total
1	7	4	6	60
2	– 4	30 3	– 5	30
Total	20	50	20	90

Then consider the next shortest route of the remaining empty cells. In this example, the time taken from line B to store 1 is the shortest at 4 minutes. A further 20 batches can be allocated in this cell, in order to allocate all the batches from line B as shown below:

	A	B	C	Total
1	7	20 4	6	60
2	– 4	30 3	– 5	30
Total	20	50	20	90

The next shortest route is line C to store 1 (6 minutes) where 20 batches can be allocated. Finally, the remaining 20 batches are allocated to the last cell in the table (line A to store 1). The following initial allocation is then obtained:

	A	B	C	Total
1	20 7	20 4	20 6	60
2	– 4	30 3	– 5	30
Total	20	50	20	90

From this table we could calculate the time taken to move all the batches as follows:

$$\text{Total time} = 20*7 + 20*4 + 20*6 + 30*3$$
$$= 140 + 80 + 120 + 90$$
$$= 430 \text{ minutes.}$$

Thus using this approach it would take a total of 430 minutes to move all the batches to their storage areas.

Step 2: is this the optimum allocation?

It is likely that the initial allocation obtained does not minimise the total costs (times). In order to check whether the allocation is optimum we proceed with the following steps:

Step 2(a): evaluate shadow costs

The unit transportation cost specified for each route can be considered as two separate costs: the cost (time) of moving from a given production line (column cost) and the cost (time) of receiving into a specified store (row cost). Each row and column cost is called a **shadow cost**.

The shadow costs are evaluated using the **allocated cells only**. This is done by splitting the total cost displayed in each cell into the row cost and the column cost. In order to start this process it is necessary to make an assumption about a single cost. A common approach here is to assume that the cost in the first row is zero and proceed to calculate the other costs using this value. The zero shadow cost in row 1 is displayed in the following table:

	A	B	C	Total
1	20 $_7$	20 $_4$	20 $_6$	60 $_0$
2	– $_4$	30 $_3$	– $_5$	30
Total	20	50	20	90

Using the allocated cells we can calculate the remaining shadow costs. For instance, the cell A to 1 has a total 'cost' of 7. This is split between the row cost of 0 and the column cost of 7. This can be thought of as the cost of receiving into store 1 is zero, and the cost of sending from line A is 7. Similarly, the total cost for route B to 1 is 4. The row cost is 0 and therefore the column cost is 4. In the same way the column cost for line C is found to be 8. These costs are shown in the following table:

	A	B	C	Total
1	20 $_7$	20 $_4$	20 $_6$	60 $_0$
2	– $_4$	30 $_3$	– $_5$	30
Total	20 $_7$	50 $_4$	20 $_6$	90

Similarly, the total cost in the route B to 2 is 3 minutes. The column cost is 4 and therefore the row cost must be −1. (Note that the sum of the row cost and column cost should equal the cost in each cell.) Thus we have the shadow costs displayed in the following table:

	A	B	C	Total
1	20 _7	20 _4	20 _6	60 _0
2	− _4	30 _3	− _5	30 _{-1}
Total	20 _7	50 _4	20 _6	90

Step 2(b): comparison of shadow costs with totals

Now consider the **empty** (or **unallocated**) **cells** in the table. In each case, find the difference between the total cost and the sum of the two associated shadow costs. For instance, in the route from line C to store 2 the total cost in this route is 5. The shadow costs for this cell are −1 for the row and 6 for the column. Therefore, we calculate the following $5 - (-1 + 6) = 5 - 5 = 0$.

Similarly, the same calculation can be performed in the other empty cell (line A to store 2). The results of these calculations are shown in the following table in the top left hand corner of the appropriate cells.

	A	B	C	Total
1	20 _7	20 _4	20 _6	60 _0
2	-2 − _4	30 _3	0 − _5	30 _{-1}
Total	20 _7	50 _4	20 _6	90

In the empty cells, if there are any calculations found to be negative then this implies that the allocation is not optimum. These calculations are displayed in the top left hand corner of each of the empty cells. The route A to 2 shows a negative value here. Therefore, an improved allocation which further reduces the total costs can be found.

Step 3: obtain a better allocation

Step 3(a): add X into a cell

Look for the highest negative value in these cells as calculated in part 2(b). In this example, there is only one route (line A to store 2) which gives a negative value here. We therefore try to place as many additional allocations in this cell as possible. Thus, let us add X into this cell as shown below:

	A	B	C	Total
1	20 $_7$	20 $_4$	20 $_6$	60 $_0$
2	$^{-2}$ +X $_4$	30 $_3$	^{0} – $_5$	30 $_{-1}$
Total	20 $_7$	50 $_4$	20 $_6$	90

Step 3(b): adjust the other allocated cells

If X is added into the route A to 2, then other routes must be adjusted in order that the row and column totals remain unchanged. Thus, we must add and subtract X to other cells in order to achieve this. It should be noted that **other empty cells should not be used for this purpose.**

Thus, in order to preserve the column total of 20 in column A, the route from A to 1 will need to be reduced by X. Similarly, the route from B to 2 must be reduced by X in order to preserve the row total. Similarly, the route B to 1 will need increasing by X to preserve the other totals. These adjustments are shown in the following table:

	A	B	C	Total
1	$20-X$ $_7$	$20+X$ $_4$	20 $_6$	60 $_0$
2	$^{-2}$ +X $_4$	$30-X$ $_3$	^{0} – $_5$	30 $_{-1}$
Total	20 $_7$	50 $_4$	20 $_6$	90

Step 3(c): find the maximum value of X

Look at the cells that have been changed in the table, i.e. those including $+X$ or $-X$. We wish to make X as large as possible in order to maximise the savings made. The only restriction is that these cells cannot go negative. The cells in question in this case contain the following values: $20-X$, $20+X$, $+X$ and $30-X$.

The value of X can be up to 20 without any of these values being negative. (Any value of X over 20 will make at least one of the values negative.) Therefore, the maximum value of $X = 20$.

Step 3(d): obtain a new allocation

Substituting this value of $X = 20$ into the table we obtain a new improved allocation as shown on the next page.

It is worth considering the time taken to move all the batches using this allocation.

$$\text{The total time is} = 40*4 + 20*6 + 20*4 + 10*3 = 160 + 120 + 80 + 30$$
$$= 390 \text{ minutes.}$$

As can be seen, this is an improvement over the original allocation.

	A	B	C	Total
1	$-_7$	40_4	20_6	60
2	20_4	10_3	$-_5$	30
Total	20	50	20	90

Step 4: continue improving the allocations

Steps 2 and 3 are repeated until no improved allocation can be obtained.

Consider Step 2 again using the new allocations.

(a) The shadow costs are evaluated using only the **allocated cells** as shown in the following table. The first row is assumed to have a shadow cost of 0.

	A	B	C	Total
1	$-_7$	40_4	20_6	60_0
2	20_4	10_3	$-_5$	30_{-1}
Total	20_5	50_4	20_6	90

(b) In the **empty cells** the differences between the total cost and the two shadow costs are calculated:

	A	B	C	Total
1	$^2-_7$	40_4	20_6	60_0
2	20_4	10_3	$^0-_5$	30_{-1}
Total	20_5	50_4	20_6	90

(c) There are no negative values in the top left hand corner of the cells in this table. Thus, no further improvement to the allocations can be made. Therefore, we have obtained an optimum solution to this problem.

To summarise, the time taken to move batches from the production lines to storage areas is minimised if the following allocations are made:

From line A: 20 batches to store 2

From line B: 40 batches to store 1 and 10 batches to store 2

From line C: 20 batches to store 1

This gives a total time of 390 minutes.

Such an optimum allocation may not be unique, i.e. it is likely that there are a number of different ways of moving goods from the production lines to storage areas where the total time is 390 minutes.

It should be noted that this method of solution relies on having sufficient 'allocated' cells in the table in order to calculate shadow costs. For the 2×3 table (2 rows and 3 columns) in this example the four allocated cells were sufficient. In general, given an $m \times n$ table (m rows and n columns) we require $m + n - 1$ allocated cells. If this is not the case then the problem is said to be 'degenerate' and additional techniques are required in order to obtain a solution.

EXAMPLE 2   (transportation at the Stenlux Refrigeration Company)

The Distribution Manager at Stenlux has been asked to consider current transportation methods and suggest alternative strategies to minimise costs. There are three major distribution centres at Leipzig, Lyons and Birmingham. Commercial refrigeration units are produced in three main production sites at Stockholm, Trieste and Rouen. The costs of transporting each unit from the production site to distribution centre are shown in the following table:

Transportation costs (Figures given in £ per unit)		Distribution centres		
		Leipzig	Lyons	Birmingham
Production sites	Stockholm	30	14	16
	Trieste	18	8	22
	Rouen	12	6	14

In each month, the output from the production sites is as follows:

Stockholm: 120 units
Trieste: 40 units
Rouen: 90 units

The requirements for the distribution centres are as follows:

Leipzig: 100 units
Lyons: 80 units
Birmingham: 70 units

The information on the transportation costs between the production sites and the distribution centres together with the requirements and availabilities are shown in the following table. Note that the costs are shown in the bottom right hand corner of each cell.

	Leipzig	Lyons	Birmingham	Total output
Stockholm	30	14	16	120
Trieste	18	8	22	40
Rouen	12	6	14	90
Total	100	80	70	250

Now in order to find the optimum transportation scheme which will minimise the costs we proceed as shown in the previous example.

Step 1: The initial allocation is obtained by allocating as many units as possible to the least-cost routes. For instance, the route between Lyons and Rouen is the cheapest and therefore has a maximum allocation of 80. This then satisfies the requirements for Lyons as shown in the second column, and the next cheapest route is found to be Rouen to Leipzig. Thus, a further 10 units are sent using this route, which completes the production output from Rouen. Continuing using the least-cost routes we obtain the following initial allocation:

	Leipzig	Lyons	Birmingham	Total output
Stockholm	50 30	– 14	70 16	120
Trieste	40 18	– 8	– 22	40
Rouen	10 12	80 6	– 14	90
Total	100	80	70	250

Step 2: Now by calculating the shadow costs we will consider whether this is an optimum solution. Using the **allocated cells only** we split up the total cost displayed in each cell into the row and column cost. We start with a cost of zero in the first row. These shadow costs are displayed in the bottom right hand corner of each cell in the total column and total row:

	Leipzig	Lyons	Birmingham	Total output
Stockholm	50 30	– 14	70 16	120 0
Trieste	40 18	– 8	– 22	40 –12
Rouen	10 12	80 6	– 14	90 –18
Total	100 30	80 24	70 16	250

Now using the **empty cells only** we calculate the difference between the total cost displayed and the sum of the row and column shadow costs. For instance, in the cell representing the route from Stockholm to Lyons the cost is 14 and the two shadow costs are 0 (in the row) and 24 (in the column). Thus we calculate $14 - (0 + 24)$ obtaining a result of -10. This value and the values for the other empty cells are shown in the top left hand corner of these cells.

	Leipzig	Lyons	Birmingham	Total output
Stockholm	50 $_{30}$	$^{-10}$ — $_{14}$	70 $_{16}$	120 $_{0}$
Trieste	40 $_{18}$	$^{-4}$ — $_{8}$	^{18} — $_{22}$	40 $_{-12}$
Rouen	10 $_{12}$	80 $_{6}$	^{16} — $_{14}$	90 $_{-18}$
Total	100 $_{30}$	80 $_{24}$	70 $_{16}$	250

Now we look for the largest negative value in the top left hand corner to determine where extra units should be added. The route from Stockholm to Lyons has the value -10 and therefore we should add $+X$ into this cell. Other allocated cells must be adjusted so that we preserve the row and column totals as shown below:

	Leipzig	Lyons	Birmingham	Total output
Stockholm	50−X $_{30}$	$^{-10}$ +X $_{14}$	70 $_{16}$	120 $_{0}$
Trieste	40 $_{18}$	$^{-4}$ — $_{8}$	^{18} — $_{22}$	40 $_{-12}$
Rouen	10+X $_{12}$	80−X $_{6}$	^{16} — $_{14}$	90 $_{-18}$
Total	100 $_{30}$	80 $_{24}$	70 $_{16}$	250

From the table the maximum value of X is 50, since it can be seen that if X is greater than 50 then at least one allocation (the Stockholm to Leipzig route) becomes negative.

Therefore, we substitute $X = 50$ in order to obtain a new improved allocation as shown in the following table.

	Leipzig	Lyons	Birmingham	Total output
Stockholm	— $_{30}$	50 $_{14}$	70 $_{16}$	120
Trieste	40 $_{18}$	— $_{8}$	— $_{22}$	40
Rouen	60 $_{12}$	30 $_{6}$	— $_{14}$	90
Total	100	80	70	250 ·

This process is then repeated to examine whether the allocations can be further improved. The whole process of calculating shadow costs using the allocated cells and then considering differences for the empty cells is shown in the following table. The table also includes the addition of X in the cell that gives a negative value for these differences as displayed in the top left hand corner of each empty cell.

	Leipzig	Lyons	Birmingham	Total output
Stockholm	^{10} — $_{30}$	50 $_{14}$	70 $_{16}$	120 $_0$
Trieste	$40-X$ $_{18}$	$^{-4}$ $+X$ $_8$	^{8} — $_{22}$	40 $_{-2}$
Rouen	$60+X$ $_{12}$	$30-X$ $_6$	^{6} — $_{14}$	90 $_{-8}$
Total	100 $_{20}$	80 $_{14}$	70 $_{16}$	250

From this table we see that the maximum value of X is 30. Substituting this value of X into the allocations we obtain the following table. This table also includes the calculation of shadow costs in order to determine whether a further improvement can be made.

	Leipzig	Lyons	Birmingham	Total output
Stockholm	^{6} — $_{30}$	50 $_{14}$	70 $_{16}$	120 $_0$
Trieste	10 $_{18}$	30 $_8$	^{12} — $_{22}$	40 $_{-6}$
Rouen	90 $_{12}$	^{4} — $_6$	^{10} — $_{14}$	90 $_{-12}$
Total	100 $_{24}$	80 $_{14}$	70 $_{16}$	250

We see that there are no negative values in the top left hand corner of the cells in this table. Thus, no further improvement can be made and the table displays the optimum allocations. Therefore, the best transportation plan in order to minimise costs is to move the goods as follows:

50 units from Stockholm to Lyons

70 units from Stockholm to Birmingham

10 units from Trieste to Leipzig

30 units from Trieste to Lyons

90 units from Rouen to Leipzig

The total cost of this transportation strategy is:

$$= 50 * 14 + 70 * 16 + 10 * 18 + 30 * 8 + 90 * 12$$

$$= £3320 \text{ per month}$$

Exercises: transportation problem

1.(I) The table shown below gives the costs of transporting goods from four factories to three warehouses on different sites. The costs shown are given in $s per unit of goods.

	Factories			
Warehouses	A	B	C	D
X	15	10	45	30
Y	40	35	20	35
Z	25	15	9	15

The monthly output from the factories are as follows:

A: 8 units,   B: 17 units,   C: 11 units,   D: 10 units

The monthly requirements for the three warehouses are as follows:

X: 11 units,   Y: 13 units,   Z: 22 units

Use a suitable method to obtain the best strategy for transporting goods between the factories and warehouses in order to minimise the total costs.

2.(I) An electronics company has four distribution centres and four large retailing outlets based in California. The distances between the centres and outlets are shown in the following table together with the number of batches of computer systems available at each distribution centre and the number required at each retail outlet.

Retail outlets	Distribution centres				Requirements
	1	2	3	4	
A	90	60	450	300	6
B	350	130	300	450	7
C	300	200	350	500	10
D	40	300	110	250	17
Total availability	8	4	18	10	40

Using the transportation method, suggest routes for the batches of computer systems which will minimise the total distances travelled.

8.12   The unbalanced transportation problem

The transportation problems given in the previous section are considered to be balanced since the total requirements equal the total availability in each case. An unbalanced problem occurs where this is not the case as illustrated in the following example.

Consider an earlier problem relating to the movement of goods from production lines (A, B and C) to storage areas (1 and 2). The following table gives the times taken to move goods between the production lines and storage areas as well as the total output of the lines and total capacity of the stores. (The times are given in minutes and displayed at the bottom right of each cell in the table.)

	A	B	C	Total
1	7	4	6	45
2	4	3	5	30
Total	20	50	20	

This is an unbalanced problem, as the total capacity in the stores (75 units) is less than the total production output (90 units).

It is necessary to balance out the problem by inserting an extra line so that the row and column totals are the same. In this example, an extra row (called a dummy row) is required where the total is 15 as shown in the following table:

	A	B	C	Total capacity
1	7	4	6	45
2	4	3	5	30
Dummy	0	0	0	15
Total output	20	50	20	90

Note that the costs given in the dummy row are shown to be zero. The effect of adding an extra row into this table is that we now have a balanced problem to solve. The total output and total capacity are both now equal to 90.

This problem can now be solved in the same way as shown in the previous examples. Firstly, an initial allocation is found based on least-costs routes. Any of the zero-cost routes could be used as an initial allocation. For instance, the route from production site A to store 3 could have an allocation of 15 units. The remaining allocations are shown in the following table. The table is also used to calculate the shadow costs using the allocated routes, and then differences between the total costs and shadow costs for the empty cells:

	A	B	C	Total
I	$5-X$ $_7$	$20+X$ $_4$	20 $_6$	45 $_0$
2	$^{-2}$ $+X$ $_4$	$30-X$ $_3$	^{0} $-$ $_5$	30 $_{-1}$
Dummy	15 $_0$	^{3} $-$ $_0$	^{1} $-$ $_0$	15 $_{-7}$
Total output	20 $_7$	50 $_4$	20 $_6$	90

The value X is added into the cell in which there is the largest negative value in the top left hand corner. Thus, X is added in the cell representing the route A to 2. Other cells are then adjusted in order to preserve the overall row and column totals. The maximum value of X is 5, which will then produce the improved allocation as shown below. Again, the shadow costs are calculated in order to determine whether a better allocation can be made.

	A	B	C	Total
I	^{2} $-$ $_7$	$25+X$ $_4$	$20-X$ $_6$	45 $_0$
2	$5+X$ $_4$	$30-X$ $_3$	^{0} $-$ $_5$	30 $_{-1}$
Dummy	$15-X$ $_0$	^{1} $-$ $_0$	$^{-1}$ $+X$ $_0$	15 $_{-5}$
Total output	20 $_5$	50 $_4$	20 $_6$	90

From this table it can be seen that the route C to 3 can be used to further reduce the overall costs. The variable X is added to this cell and other cells are adjusted accordingly. Notice that only the allocated cells can be used to adjust the totals. In this example, we see that all the allocated cells need adjusting in order to preserve the correct totals. The maximum value of X from this table is 15, and the result of this is shown in the next table. Again, the shadow costs are recalculated to investigate whether a further improvement can be made.

	A	B	C	Total
I	^{2} $-$ $_7$	40 $_4$	5 $_6$	45 $_0$
2	20 $_4$	10 $_3$	^{0} $-$ $_5$	30 $_{-1}$
Dummy	^{1} $-$ $_0$	^{2} $-$ $_0$	15 $_0$	15 $_6$
Total output	20 $_5$	50 $_4$	20 $_6$	90

In this table we see that no negative values occur in the calculations in the empty cells. Therefore, the allocation cannot be improved further. Therefore the following routes would minimise the overall costs:

Production line A: 20 units to store 2

Production line B: 40 units to A and 10 units to B

Production line C: 5 units to store A

The remaining output from line C (15 units) will be unused (this is shown by the allocation in the dummy row)

8.13 Maximisation problem

In previous examples we have considered techniques of minimising resource requirements (such as time or costs) for given transportation problems. The methods outlined can also be used in situations involving the maximisation of values. For instance, we may wish to maximise the income, or profit, resulting from a transportation allocation. The process of maximisation requires a modification to the techniques outlined. In particular, a maximisation problem can be changed into a minimisation problem as shown in the following example.

Consider the table below showing the expected profit obtained from the sale of a commercial refrigeration unit dependent on the Production site and distribution centre used.

Gross profit (Figures given in £100s per unit)		Distribution centres		
		Leipzig	Lyons	Birmingham
Production sites	Stockholm	20	36	34
	Trieste	32	42	28
	Rouen	38	44	36

Thus, the table shows that a unit produced in Stockholm and transported to Leipzig will generate a profit of £2000 (note that the figures given in the table are in £100s).

The problem is to determine the optimum transportation routes in order to maximise the total gross profit.

In each month, the output from the production sites is as follows:

Stockholm: 120 units,   Trieste: 40 units,   Rouen: 90 units

The requirements for the distribution centres were as follows:

Leipzig: 100 units,   Lyons: 80 units,   Birmingham: 70 units

Instead of solving this as a maximisation problem, we convert the information to provide a minimisation example.

The profit figures in the first table are changed using the following technique:

1. Find the largest profit figure in the table.
2. Now subtract each value from this largest figure.

The resulting figures can be regarded as 'costs' and in order to maximise the profit, we can minimise these figures. For instance, in the above table, the maximum profit figure is 44. Now, every value can be subtracted from 44 to produce the following table.

'Costs' (Figures given in £100s per unit)		Distribution centres		
		Leipzig	Lyons	Birmingham
Production sites	Stockholm	24	8	10
	Trieste	12	2	16
	Rouen	6	0	8

Now we have changed this into a minimisation problem as indicated in the following table:

	Leipzig	Lyons	Birmingham	Total output
Stockholm	24	8	10	120
Trieste	12	2	16	40
Rouen	6	0	8	90
Total	100	80	70	250

Using the minimisation techniques described in the previous examples we obtain the following optimum solution:

	Leipzig	Lyons	Birmingham	Total output
Stockholm	– 24	50 8	70 10	120
Trieste	10 12	30 2	– 16	40
Rouen	90 6	– 0	– 8	90
Total	100	80	70	250

The same allocations will maximise the total profit as indicated in the following table. The cost figures are transformed back to the original profit values and displayed in the bottom right hand corner of each cell.

	Leipzig	Lyons	Birmingham	Total output
Stockholm	– 20	50 36	70 34	120
Trieste	10 32	30 42	– 28	40
Rouen	90 38	– 44	– 36	90
Total	100	80	70	250

The maximum profit using these allocations is:

$$\text{Total gross profit} = 10 * 32 + 90 * 38 + 50 * 36 + 30 * 42 + 70 * 34$$
$$= 9180$$

Since the figures given in the table are in £100s, this corresponds to a maximum gross profit of £918 000.

8.14	**Exercises: maximisation and unbalanced problems**

1.(I) For each of the following problems determine the optimum method of transporting goods from the warehouses to retail outlets. The tables shown give the costs of transportation per unit, the requirements of the retail outlets and the number of units available at the warehouses.

(i)

Retail outlet	Warehouse			Total required
	A	B	C	
1	£5	£7	£10	25
2	£4	£9	£9	25
3	£6	£10	£12	50
Total available	40	30	20	

(ii)

Retail outlet	Warehouse			Total required
	A	B	C	
1	£7	£6	£5	15
2	£4	£4	£6	30
3	£6	£3	£4	40
Total available	20	35	35	

2.(D)   The table below shows the amount of profit made from the transportation of each unit between a production site and a distribution centre. The figures are given in $ per unit.

Production site	Distribution centre			Total availability
	A	B	C	
I	$30	$40	$33	25
2	$25	$34	$26	25
3	$31	$20	$19	50
Total requirements	40	30	30	

Use a transportation method to ascertain the optimum routes for the required goods in order to maximise the expected profit.

8.15   Interpretation of results – management issues

In the optimisation solutions using the simplex and transportation techniques, care must be taken to interpret the results in a realistic and practical way. For instance, consider the problem considered earlier in this chapter on the production mix of fridges at the Stenlux company. The initial problem determined the number of two models of fridge to produce in order to maximise profits subject to constraints on the amount of raw materials and staff-hours available. The resulting solution gave the optimum number of each fridge to produce. In the example illustrated it was determined that 375 of the model A470 and 937 of the model A370 should be produced each week, resulting in a gross profit of $82 470. Such results must be considered in the light of a range of additional factors and should not always be taken at face value. Thus, the manager may need to balance these results with additional information before making a final decision on the best production mix. The following factors should be taken into account:

1. A range of additional constraints may need to be considered. For instance, in this production problem there are likely to be additional materials required which could be unique to the particular model. Such materials may be limited and therefore additional constraints would need to be incorporated into the simplex solution.
2. There may be factors outside the original problem which will affect the validity of the results. For example, sales and marketing issues will need to be considered in the production mix problem. For instance, the sales demand of each product may limit the number of fridges produced, or change the optimum mix of items. If it has

been found that demand for the model A370 will not exceed 600 items per week, then the current production quantities will not be appropriate. Information on potential demand can also be incorporated into the constraints before obtaining a solution.

3. The production mix will have implications on other areas such as the storage space available for these products. Again, the storage facilities will need to be incorporated into the specification of the problem.

4. The objective function may be more complex than has been considered. For instance, it has been assumed that there is a fixed profit figure per unit produced for each of the models. In practice, the actual profit may change as the production volume increases. For instance, there are a number of fixed costs associated with the production such as capital costs, e.g. costs for machinery, and storage facilities. In addition, the variable costs would include running costs for the machinery and additional staff costs. There are often savings associated with extra quantities. Thus, it is unlikely that the profit for the A470 model is always $70 per unit. If a small number of these fridges is produced, it is likely that the profit per unit will be considerably less. In fact, a loss will be incurred when production gets down to a specific level. These considerations will make the profit function considerably more complex, and in fact it may be that the linear programming methods outlined will not be appropriate in such cases.

5. A range of external factors will affect the appropriate production mix. For instance, the activities of competitors in this market, pricing, promotion and marketing plans, will all affect the final decisions made.

Similarly, in the solution of transportation problems the results need to be reconciled against any additional factors that may affect the final allocations. For example, consider the transportation problem at Stenlux Refrigeration Company involving the dispatch of commercial refrigeration units from three production sites to three distribution centres. The transportation techniques provide us with an allocation of units between production sites and distribution centres which will minimise the transportation costs. However, other factors need to be considered such as:

▶ Storage facilities: If there are limited storage facilities in the various sites then the transportation of the required number of goods as designated by the transportation technique may need to be phased over the given period.

▶ Transport costs: It is likely that a change in the number of units transported between sites will change the unit costs. For instance, the use of a larger transport vehicle may reduce the costs per unit.

▶ 'Batch' sizes: There are many circumstances where a particular number of units is appropriate for transporting in one batch. For example, if the transport vehicle is capable of holding a maximum of six units, then it is likely to be cost-effective to transport in multiples of that number.

The points raised in this section should indicate that, in general, the results obtained from the analytical techniques must be carefully used and modified according to additional factors. Clearly, it is not usually sufficient to minimise costs or maximise profits without reference to other issues.

8.16   Computer applications

As shown in the examples in this chapter, the process of solving linear programming problems involves a series of complex calculations. In particular, in practical situations the optimisation problems will involve a significant number of variables. For instance, in the production mix problems illustrated we have only considered the quantities of two or three different items. In reality, a manufacturer may have hundreds of different items to produce with complex constraints. The manual solution of such problems would be impossible, and the use of computer systems to analyse the problem is essential.

In this section, we will consider the use of spreadsheets to solve linear programming problems. The Lotus and Excel spreadsheets include a facility called 'Solver'. The Solver option is used to obtain optimum values to a specific function subject to a range of conditions. The following examples illustrate the output from such a function within the spreadsheet package.

EXAMPLE I

Consider the production decisions at Stenlux Refrigeration Company. The initial problem introduced in Section 8.1 involved a decision concerning the number of two different fridges to be produced. The two models, the A470 and the A370, were subject to a number of constraints including limitations on the number of staff-hours available, and the quantity of raw materials required.

 Using the disk   The information on these two products has been set up in a file named EX1.WK4. Load this file into Lotus or Excel. The spreadsheet should be displayed as shown in Figure 8.18.

The screen displayed in Figure 8.18 contains the following elements:

1. The objective function (i.e. the expression for profit to be optimised) is displayed in the cell E9. This is referred to as the 'Target Cell' in Excel and the 'Optimal Cell' in Lotus.
2. The answers (i.e. the values of x = number of A470 fridges produced and y = number of A370 fridges produced) are shown in cells B12 and C12. These are referred to as the 'Adjustable Cells' in Lotus and the 'Changing Cells' in Excel.
3. Information relating to the constraints is displayed in the cells A5 to E6. For instance, the condition relating to staff-hours is $3x + 2y \leqslant 3000$. The coefficients of x and y are displayed in the cells B5 and C5 respectively. The maximum value for the staff-hours (=3000) is shown in cell E5. Using Lotus, the actual constraint is entered into the cell G5. For instance, the expression entered in this cell is the inequality $B5 * B12 + C5 * C12 \leqslant E5$. Similarly, the constraint relating to raw

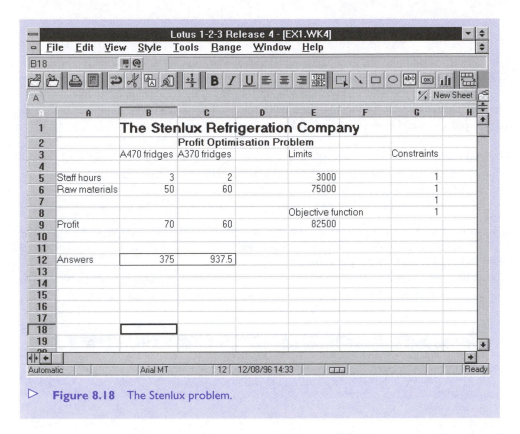

> **Figure 8.18** The Stenlux problem.

materials is entered into the cell G6. The other constraints, entered into the cells G7 and G8, involve the additional constraints $x \geqslant 0$ and $y \geqslant 0$. It should be noted that the values displayed in these cells indicate whether the constraints have been satisfied or not. A value of 1 indicates that the inequality is satisfied, whereas a value of 0 indicates that the inequality is false. In Excel, when using Solver we would need to specify that the constraints are either true or false.

Having entered all these values, the Solver facility is used to generate possible solutions to the problem. The screen shows the optimum solution obtained using Solver. The maximum value of the profit is displayed in cell E9 as 82 500 when the number of fridges produced is:

A470 models = 375 (in cell B12)

A370 models = 937.5 (in cell C12)

In practice, the number of A370 models must be a whole number. Thus, the value in cell C12 will need to be modified down to 937. This can be done manually, and it is left to the reader to do this in this spreadsheet. Following this, an amended value for the profit will be displayed as 82 470 in cell E9.

EXAMPLE 2

Section 8.7 introduced the use of the simplex method to solve linear programming problems. The Stenlux production problem relating to the production mix of three products was considered. This problem involved determining the most appropriate number of each of the following models: the A470, A370 and B270 fridges. Constraints on the number of fridges to be produced included limits on staff-hours, raw materials and demand.

 Using the disk   A spreadsheet file has been set up involving this problem. Load the file named EX2.WK4 into a Lotus or Excel spreadsheet. The screen displayed should be similar to that shown in Figure 8.19.

In the screen shown in Figure 8.19 the spreadsheet contains the following elements:

1. The objective function involving the profit is contained in the cell D16. The coefficients of the profit function expressed in terms of the numbers of each model to be produced are found in the cells B12 to D12.
2. The actual solutions for x = number of A470 models, y = number of A370 models and z = number of B270 models are displayed in the cells B14 to D14.

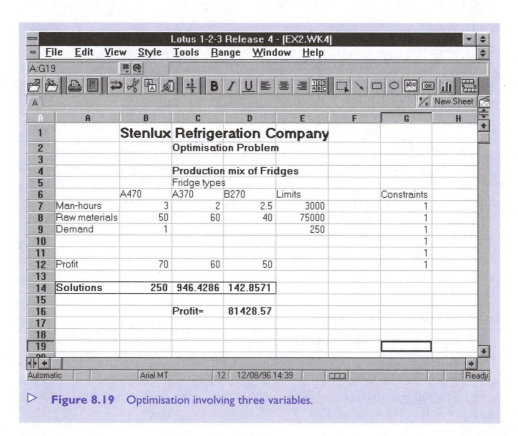

▷　**Figure 8.19**　Optimisation involving three variables.

3. Details on the constraints are given in the cells B7 to E9, and the actual expressions for each of the constraints are entered in the cells G7 to G12.

Using the Solver facility in the Lotus and Excel spreadsheet packages enables us to obtain the optimum value of the profit shown as 81 428.57 assuming the values of the production quantities are $x = 250$, $y = 946.42$ and $z = 142.86$. Rounding down these values we obtain the following optimum solution. The number of each model produced should be:

A470 model: 250

A370 model: 946

B270 model: 142

It is left to the reader to insert these values into the appropriate cells. When complete, the revised optimum profit is shown to be 81 360.

The reader could try to consider different constraints for this problem. For example, if you change the values in the cells B12 to D12, then a different profit function can be analysed. For instance, consider that the profit from the sale of each model is as follows:

A470: $50,   A370: $70,   B270: $80

Enter these new values into the cells B12 to D12 and then use the Solver facility to investigate a new optimum solution. Try different values in these cells and look at the effect on the profit function.

EXAMPLE 3

The Solver facility in Lotus or Excel can also be used to obtain optimum solutions to transportation problems. As stated in the introduction to transportation in Section 8.11, this is a particular form of the linear programming problem, and can thus be solved in the same way.

 Using the disk   Load the file named TRANSPT.WK4 into your spreadsheet package. The screen displayed should be similar to that shown in Figure 8.20. The spreadsheet displays the parameters in the transportation problem introduced at the beginning of Section 8.11. The problem involves determining the optimum routes for goods moved between storage areas and production lines in a factory. The 'costs' in this example are times, and are shown in cells B6 to D7 in the spreadsheet.

The potential answers to the problem are displayed in the cells B12 to D13, indicating the number of batches to be moved between production line and store. The total time shown in cell E19 is the expression to be optimised. The constraints are listed in the cells G10 to G20. These constraints will ensure that the row and column totals are as required. Additional constraints are that the number of batches on any route

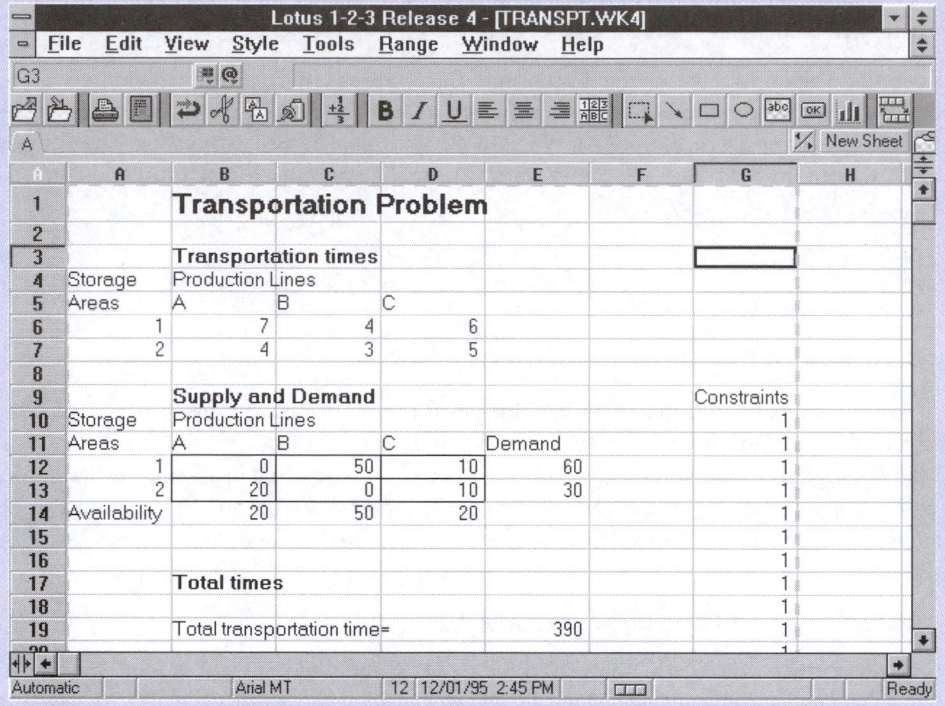

	A	B	C	D	E	F	G	H
1		**Transportation Problem**						
2								
3		**Transportation times**						
4	Storage	Production Lines						
5	Areas	A	B	C				
6	1	7	4	6				
7	2	4	3	5				
8								
9		**Supply and Demand**					Constraints	
10	Storage	Production Lines					1	
11	Areas	A	B	C	Demand		1	
12	1	0	50	10	60		1	
13	2	20	0	10	30		1	
14	Availability	20	50	20			1	
15							1	
16							1	
17		**Total times**					1	
18							1	
19		Total transportation time=			390		1	

Figure 8.20   Transportation solution using Solver.

cannot be negative. With these constraints, the optimum solution is obtained using Solver. It is left to the reader to compare this with the solution obtained in example 1 of Section 8.11. The suggested movement of goods shown in the spreadsheet differs from that obtained manually, although the total minimum time (equal to 390 minutes) is the same. This illustrates that there may not be a unique optimum solution to such problems.

The reader can experiment with this spreadsheet. For example, different transportation times (costs) can be entered in the cells B6 to D7, and Solver used to determine the revised optimum transportation method.

8.17   Chapter summary

In this chapter we have considered the linear programming techniques involved in optimisation problems. A typical example would be to maximise the profitability in a company by selecting the most appropriate product mix. Similarly, linear programming problems could involve the minimisation of a variable such as costs. The expression to be optimised is called the objective function. This function is evaluated subject to a number of constraints. One of the major difficulties with solving such problems is the initial stage of problem formulation involving interpreting constraints and writing in terms of inequalities, and producing an expression for the objective function. For simple problems involving only two variables such problems can be solved graphically. For more complex problems the simplex method can be used.

One specific linear programming problem is concerned with transportation. Such a problem can be solved by special techniques involving the tabulation of transportation costs and comparison with the requirements and availabilities of goods. The transportation method adopts an iterative approach where an initial allocation is obtained and checked to see whether an improvement can be made. If so, a new allocation is found and the method is repeated until no further improvement can be obtained.

Such optimisation problems are generally solved using computer packages because of the complexity of the calculations involved. Many spreadsheet packages include facilities to solve problems of this type.

8.18 Further exercises

1.(E) The following table shows the time required to manufacture two products in each of the three required processes.

Product	Number of minutes per process		
	Process A	Process B	Process C
1	20	10	40
2	30	20	30

The company earns $40 profit per product 1 and $50 profit per product 2.
The number of minutes available for each process is as follows:

process A: 1600 minutes,   process B: 1000 minutes,   process C: 2400 minutes

Use a graphical method to determine the number of each product to manufacture in order to maximise the total profit.

2.(I) An electronics retailer must decide on the number of a range of computer systems to stock. In particular, the retailer has decided to keep one or both of the two models:

model A: the TXB 486 DX

model B: the TXB 586 SX

Ordering of these computers is performed monthly and the orders arrive the following day. There is a maximum storage space available for 30 systems. Each model takes the same amount of storage space.

The cost price to the retailer for these computers is:

model A: £500,   model B: £800

The retailer has a maximum of £20 100 per month available for the purchase of these models. The retailer makes £200 profit on each model A sold and £300 profit on each model B.

From past experience it is known that monthly sales for model B will not exceed 20. Advise the retailer on the monthly quantity of each model that should be ordered to maximise the expected profit.

3.(I) The retailer described in question 2 must decide on the number of the two computer systems to purchase subject to a range of different constraints. In each of the following cases, find the most appropriate number of computers to purchase:

(i) There is enough storage space for 50 computers.

Purchase costs for each model are:

model A: £300,   model B: £500

The retailer has £21 000 available

The retailer earns a gross profit on each model of:

model A: £150,   model B: £200

Maximise the gross profit.

(ii) There is enough storage space for 100 computers.

The retailer must purchase at least 20 of each model.

Order costs per computer including administration and transportation costs are:

model A: £20,   model B: £24

Purchase costs for each computer are:

model A: £400,   model B: £500

The retailer wishes to spend a total of between £24 000 and £44 000 on the two models.

Minimise the order costs.

Why might this not be the most appropriate number of computers to purchase?

4.(I) An advertising agency is deciding on the number of advertisements to place in a range of media. The three media available are local radio, local newspaper and public posters. The estimated number of people who would see the adverts in the three media are:

   local radio: 3000   local newspaper: 6000   posters: 2500

The cost per advert is as follows:

   local radio: £800   local newspaper: £500   posters: £400

A total of £15 000 is available for advertising, and no more than 15 adverts can be placed in any single medium.

   Use the simplex method to determine the number of adverts to be placed in each of the three media in order to maximise a product's exposure.

5.(I) A manufacturer wishes to determine the optimum quantity of each of three items (products X, Y and Z) to produce per day in order to maximise profit.

The following constraints are placed on the manufacturer:

Product	No. of staff required per unit	Raw materials per unit	Machine hours
X	4	5	1
Y	3	8	1
Z	3	6	2
Number available	700	1200	300

It is estimated that the company earns a gross profit from each unit of:

   product X: $50,   product Y: $40,   product Z: $30

Use the simplex method to advise the manufacturer on the optimum daily production mix.

6.(I) A carpet producer manufactures carpets in 10 feet, 12 feet and 15 feet widths, and sells them to retailers in 200-feet rolls. The amount of wool used in the production of each roll of carpet is as follows:

   10-feet carpet: 40 kilograms,   12-feet carpet: 45 kilograms,

   15-feet carpet: 50 kilograms.

   Only 2750 kilograms of wool is available.

Total combined sales for the 12-feet and 10-feet rolls are unlikely to exceed 30 rolls. The producer has already received orders for 20 of the 15-feet rolls.

The following profit is made on each roll sold:

   10-feet carpet: £400,   12-feet carpet: £500,   15-feet carpet: £600

Find the number of rolls of each carpet that should be produced in order to maximise profit.

7.(I)   The table below shows the costs of transporting batches of goods from three factories (A, B and C) to four warehouses (S, T, U and V). The table also shows the number of batches available at the factories and the number required at each warehouse.

	Warehouses (cost per batch)				
Factory	S	T	U	V	Available
A	£20	£40	£15	£30	60
B	£10	£25	£25	£35	100
C	£15	£45	£30	£20	80
Required	70	50	90	30	240

Use the transportation method to determine the routes for the goods to be transported in order to minimise the total costs.

8.(D)   A detergent manufacturer produces three products, Fizz, Shoot and Zoom. A batch of each of these products makes a profit contribution to the company of:

   Fizz: £40,   Shoot: £30,   Zoom: £25

Production requirements for each batch of detergent are shown in the following table:

	Requirements per batch		
Product	Chemicals (mg)	Machine time (minutes)	Staff time (minutes)
Fizz	20	8	10
Shoot	16	7	10
Zoom	22	6	8
Total available per day	1000	400	400

   (i) Use the simplex method to obtain the number of batches of each detergent to be produced per day in order to maximise the total profit contribution.
  (ii) If the number of batches of the Zoom detergent should not exceed 25 in any one day, would this affect your solution?

9. (D) **(Using the disk)**   Load the Lotus or Excel spreadsheet package. Now load a file from the disk called INVEST.WK4. This spreadsheet shows the linear programming problem involving an analysis of the investment portfolio by Wiley-Macken. This application was introduced in example 3 at the end of Section 8.10. The information entered into the spreadsheet shows details of three different share options: Hanson, Far-East and Maxwell. The conditions relating to a limit on the investment capital, estimates of risk, and Far-East options are indicated in the cells B8 to E10.

The estimated return on investment (ROI) per share is indicated in cells B13 to D13, and the total ROI is calculated in cell E13.

Try to change the values in cells B8 to D9 and use Solver to obtain new advice on the best mix of shares to purchase. Furthermore, look at the effect of different estimates on the return on investment for each share in cells B13 to D13. Try to enter different values here and use Solver again to obtain new recommendations.

Simulation Techniques

CHAPTER OBJECTIVES

At the end of this chapter you will be able to:

► use random numbers to simulate variables

► apply simulation in analysing inventory control decisions

► apply simulation in solving queuing problems

► understand the role of simulation in a range of business problems

Introduction

Simulation techniques can be used to assist management decision making where purely analytical methods are either not available or inappropriate. Simulation involves the use of models to represent a real-life situation. Such a model can then be manipulated in order to consider possible alternative solutions to given problems. The process of simulation can involve relatively simple techniques in order to solve extremely complex problems. Often, simulation will provide an added insight into a given problem, and assist the manager to consider the advantages and disadvantages of alternative strategies and potential solutions. Furthermore, simulation methods provide a cost-effective, risk-free approach to experimentation that would not be feasible using 'real-life' experiments.

Simulation techniques will usually involve numerous, repetitive operations, and can be very time-consuming. Consequently, it is essential that computer systems are used in most practical situations. A number of simulation packages are now available to assist in the development of realistic models, and these will be described later in this chapter. Typical business problems where simulation could be effectively used to aid management decision making are:

- Stock control
- Queuing problems
- Production planning
- Risk analysis
- Resource utilisation

The following case studies provide practical examples where simulation could be used to aid the management decision making process.

CASE STUDY   Support services from the Rednall company

The Rednall company is a computer services supplier providing a range of services to a largely European client base. Services provided by the Rednall company include consultancy on computer installation, software purchase, and system development procedures. The company can provide initial consultancy in such areas through to completion by assisting in design, development and installation of systems, and providing long-term support in order to ensure that any problems are quickly and efficiently rectified.

The support service provided by Rednall is a significant element in customer relations, and assists in the generation of future business opportunities. Users of systems can telephone the Rednall support service in order to obtain advice and assistance in a range of areas including:

- help with usage of application packages
- technical assistance with hardware problems
- correction of 'bugs' in software systems
- advice on additional requirements

Some of these problems can be handled over the telephone, though many require more complex work, possibly involving a number of staff and visits to the client. Each category of problem is handled by a separate user support team within Rednall. The Rednall support service records each client enquiry and categorises the problems and requests. Specific action is then taken which will involve one or many staff from an appropriate user support team. The use of simulation here may help to establish a clearer picture of the workloads in each team, and determine the optimum number of staff required in each team in order to minimise the time taken to assist individual clients. Thus, simulation can be used by Rednall to improve the quality of customer service, and consequently enhance the company's external reputation.

In addition, the company is concerned that a range of hardware products is repeatedly out of stock, resulting in delays of deliveries to clients. The company needs to reconsider the stock level requirements for some of the major items, and simulation may assist in this process.

CASE STUDY   **A risky business – the Barings banking affair**

During the early part of 1995 the Baring Brothers Bank was effectively insolvent owing to dealings in derivatives in the Far East. Barings was a small bank with a long history. Founded in 1762 by Francis and John Baring, the bank quickly built an international reputation, described in 1818 by Duc de Richelieu, the French Foreign Minister, as one of the great powers of Europe alongside England, France, Prussia, Austria and Russia. In the 1990s the bank was still considered to be a solid, reliable institution.

During the 1980s the Barings Bank started trading in derivatives in the Far East markets. One of the most profitable arms of the Barings empire was involved in this area of 'proprietary trading'. The so-called 'derivatives' trade involves investing large sums of money on the basis of rises and falls in the world's financial markets. Essentially, such an investment is a gamble; with incredible profits, if successful, but the risk of huge losses, if not. A section managed by Nick Leeson in the Singapore office of Barings generated enormous profits for the bank during the early 1990s in this market.

Unfortunately, during the early part of 1995, there were heavy sums of money invested in the hope that the Japanese stock market (measured by the Nikkei index) would rise. The Nikkei was actually falling during this time, resulting in more and more funds being paid by Barings just to keep its investments afloat. Eventually, Barings were forced to go to the Bank of England for assistance in order to continue trading. With little information concerning the exact losses and indeterminate sums due for payment to creditors, the Bank of England together with other financial institutions was unable to assist Barings. The Barings Bank went into liquidation and was put into the hands of the Receivers. It was subsequently estimated that the Bank owed around £850 million on assets of only £400 million. Eventually the Dutch banking group ING stepped in to take over the company and the Barings Bank continued trading under its original name.

The risk associated with the derivatives trade can be illustrated by the use of simulation. Indeed, in hindsight, the use of such simulation methods could have deterred senior management in the Barings organisation from risking excessive sums of money in the derivatives market. At least the simulation results would have encouraged increased monitoring and improved controls on the derivatives trading activities.

However, it should be noted that in such a volatile, unpredictable market, the use of simulation models could only be one of many management tools used to evaluate the risks involved. Clearly, the rise and fall of financial markets is related to other economic factors. The use of correlation and regression analysis (as described in Chapter 3) in conjunction with simulation could provide realistic information to enable the testing of a variety of investment strategies. However, it should be stressed that the complexity of this area dictates the application of a wide range of decision making techniques in addition to simulation.

9.1 | Development of simulation models

The process of simulation involves the development and testing of appropriate models. This cycle starts with the identification of a 'business' problem as illustrated in Figure 9.1.

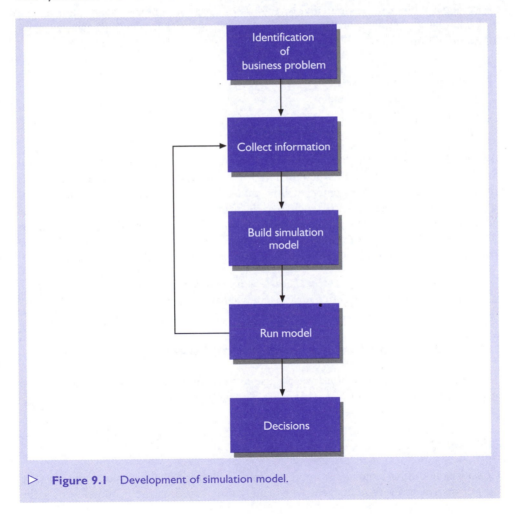

▷ **Figure 9.1** Development of simulation model.

The figure illustrates that the initial impetus for the development of a simulation model is a given business problem e.g. a consideration of the variations in customer orders or sales revenue. Data are collected in order to provide sufficient information to build a workable model. The model is then used and the subsequent results could provide further evidence to develop and improve the simulation. Finally, the results can be used to assist in the decision making process.

A range of modelling techniques can be used in this process. However, this chapter concentrates on the basic approaches using empirical and probabilistic information. These methods involve the use of random numbers introduced in the following section.

9.2   Random numbers

Specific variables can be simulated by the use of random numbers. Such numbers can be computer generated, and are often listed in published statistical tables. Below is a set of random numbers.

```
89  07  37  29  28  08  75  01  21  63
34  65  11  80  34  14  92  48  83  91
52  49  98  44  80  04  42  37  87  96
85  46  51  73  10  83  99  24  49  70
68  22  13  71  56  35  76  16  69  94
```

The random numbers are displayed as two-digit numbers in the range between 00 and 99. Every single digit (0 to 9) is equally likely to occur and there is no pattern, and thus no way of predicting what number will be next in the sequence. Thus in the set of two-digit random numbers shown, each two-digit number (ranging from 00 to 99) is equally likely to occur. The chance of getting a 16 is the same as getting a 34, or 02, or 87, or any other two-digit number. Each number has a 1% chance of occurring. The following section shows how these numbers can be used to simulate a given variable.

> **Definition:** *A random digit can take any value between 0 and 9, with an equal chance of any specific value occurring. Such a random digit is impossible to predict.*

9.3   Use of random numbers in simulation

The following examples demonstrate the use of random numbers in the simulation of a variety of business situations.

EXAMPLE 1

Consider the output from an assembly line in a medium-sized electronics company. The output of fridges every hour from an assembly line, based on the production over the past month, is summarised in the table below:

No. of fridges produced per hour:	3	4	5	6
Percentage frequency:	15	45	30	10

The output from such an assembly line can be simulated using random numbers as described below.

We wish to simulate the hourly output from the assembly line, on the basis of the output described in the table. Output in a specific hour is unpredictable. Although we do know that the number of fridges produced will range between 3 and 6. We also know the chance of a specific number of fridges being produced. For instance, there is a 15% chance of 3 fridges being produced, a 45% chance of 4 fridges, and so on. In order to simulate this, we could take a number at random and use the first 15% of these numbers to represent a production output of 3. Similarly, the next 45% of random numbers would represent an output of 4, and outputs 5 and 6 will be represented by the subsequent 30% and 10% respectively. There are 100 two-digit random numbers (00 to 99). Thus, the first 15 numbers (00 to 14) can represent an output of 3. The next 45 numbers (15 to 59) will represent an output of 4 fridges. This can be summarised in the table below, which shows the two-digit random numbers that will be used to represent the various production outputs.

Production output per hour:	3	4	5	6
Random numbers:	00–14	15–59	60–89	90–99

Thus, any random number between 00 and 14 will indicate a production figure of 3 fridges, between 15 and 59 will indicate 4 fridges, and so on. For instance, if a random number of 72 is obtained, then this will correspond to a production output of 5 fridges (since it is in the range 60 to 89).

In this way the production output can be simulated over a number of hours. The resulting values will, over a long period of time, conform to the original percentage distribution of production output. A complete simulation of the production over a ten-hour period is shown in the table below.

Hour	Random number	Production output
1	89	5
2	07	3
3	37	4
4	29	4
5	28	4
6	08	3
7	75	5
8	01	3
9	21	4
10	63	5

The random numbers used in this simulation are taken from the first line of the random number table given in the previous section. For each hour, a random number is taken, and the corresponding output values obtained. For instance, in the first hour, the random number 89 is selected. This value lies in the range 60–89, and therefore generates a production output value of 5 as shown in the third column of the table. Similarly, production values for subsequent hours are obtained as shown.

Having obtained the output figures in such a simulation, these could be used to consider variables such as output rates, storage requirements, packaging rates and transportation needs. Such examples will be considered later in this chapter.

EXAMPLE 2

Consider the case study on the Barings banking collapse in 1995. One of the main causes of the bank's demise was the risky dealing in derivatives. During this period, Barings had significant investments in the 'Nikkei 225 Futures' contract. This in effect represented a bet on whether the Nikkei index would rise or fall over a given period. A rise in the Nikkei would have resulted in large profits for Barings. Any stagnation or fall in the Japanese share index would signify a loss in this investment. The table below shows the weekly percentage change in the Nikkei index during a period in 1994.

Weekly change:	−3%	−2%	−1%	0%	+1%	+2%	+3%
Percentage of weeks:	10	10	20	20	25	10	5

Random numbers can be used to simulate the percentage change in the Nikkei index over a 15-week period based on this table of past performance.

The random numbers used to generate the various percentage changes in the Nikkei index are shown in the following table:

Weekly change:	−3%	−2%	−1%	0%	+1%	+2%	+3%
Random numbers:	00–09	10–19	20–39	40–59	60–84	85–94	95–99

Thus the table shows that a random number in the range 00 to 09 will indicate a 3% reduction in the value of the Nikkei index. Similarly, a random number between 10 and 24 implies a reduction of 2%, and so on for the remaining values. The table on the next page shows the percentage changes obtained using the indicated random numbers from the table of values shown earlier in this section.

The table shows the relative changes in the Nikkei index over the 15-week period. Based on this simulation it would not have been a good time to have significant capital invested in the Nikkei. The index rose on only five weeks during this period. Furthermore, the average percentage change over the fifteen weeks was −0.7%. However, it should be noted that in practice the past performance of the Nikkei would never be used as a sole indicator of future changes. Other factors, such as the fluctuations in global markets, exchange rates and balance of payments, may need to be considered in a realistic model.

Week	Random number	Percentage change
1	89	+2
2	07	−3
3	37	−1
4	29	−1
5	28	−1
6	08	−3
7	75	+1
8	01	−3
9	21	−1
10	63	+1
11	34	−1
12	65	+1
13	11	−2
14	80	+1
15	34	−1

The method of using random numbers to simulate a given situation (described in probabilistic terms) can be used in many different situations in order to analyse problems and consider alternative solutions. A variety of examples will be used in this Chapter to illustrate the simulation process.

9.4 Simulating demand

Consider the following example involving the storage of electrical goods in a warehouse. Demand for a particular television model is indicated in the table below:

Daily demand (No. of TVs):	0	1	2	3	4
Percentage frequency:	10	22	37	28	3

Using random numbers, we can simulate the daily demand of these televisions based on the percentage frequencies previously observed. As in the previous example, two-digit random numbers can be used. The first 10% of random numbers (00–09) will be used to represent a zero demand, the next 22% of numbers (10–31) will represent a demand of 1 television, and similarly for the other demand figures. The table below shows the random numbers that will be used to simulate the demand for televisions.

Daily demand: (No. of TVs)	0	1	2	3	4
Random nos.:	00–09	10–31	32–68	69–96	97–99

Using the random number table shown in the previous section, demand for televisions over a specified period can be simulated. The table below shows a simulation of demand over a 15-day period.

Day	Random number	Demand
1	89	3
2	07	0
3	37	2
4	29	1
5	28	1
6	08	0
7	75	3
8	01	0
9	21	1
10	63	2
11	34	2
12	65	2
13	11	1
14	80	3
15	34	2

The simulation of demand illustrated in this table can be used to determine appropriate stock holding facilities, and develop ordering strategies for selected items in order to optimise critical success factors such as costs, profitability or sales revenue.

9.5   Stock control

In the previous example, we simulated daily demand for televisions over a number of days. Consider additional information that may be relevant when considering stock control problems.

(i) The initial stock level is 12 televisions.
(ii) Stock levels are checked at the beginning of each day. When stock is 10 or below, a new batch of 8 televisions is ordered.
(iii) Delivery of the order takes 2 days.

By simulating the demand over 15 days, estimate:

(i) the average level of stock, and
(ii) the number of orders required over this period.

The table below shows the demand simulated over a 15-day period. (These demand figures have been generated in the previous section.) The table also shows the stock level at the start of each day, and when orders of new stock occur.

Day	Initial stock level	Demand	Orders placed	Deliveries received	Closing stock level
1	12	3			9
2	9	0	8 ordered		9
3	9	2			7
4	7	1		8 received	14
5	14	1			13
6	13	0			13
7	13	3			10
8	10	0	8 ordered		10
9	10	1			9
10	9	2		8 received	15
11	15	2			13
12	13	2			11
13	11	1			10
14	10	3	8 ordered		7
15	7	2			5

In this table, the columns have been calculated as follows:

(i) **Demand.** These figures have been simulated using random numbers as shown in the previous sections.

(ii) **Initial stock level.** On day 1, the initial stock level is known to be 12. On subsequent days the initial stock level equals the closing stock level of the previous day.

(iii) **Orders placed.** An order of 8 televisions is placed on the day that the initial stock level reaches 10 or below. It should be noted that no further orders are placed until the current order has been delivered.

(iv) **Deliveries received.** A delivery of 8 televisions occurs 2 days after the order has been placed.

(v) **Closing stock level.** The stock level at the end of each day is calculated as follows:

Closing stock = Initial stock − Demand + Deliveries received

Using this simulation enables us to estimate statistics such as:

(i) **Average stock level.** This can be obtained by using the initial daily stock levels. Simply add up the initial stock levels for the 15 days and divide by 15. Thus, the average stock level is $162/15 = 10.8$ televisions.

(ii) **Order frequency.** Over the 15-day period we see that only three orders have been placed. It should be noted that the third order is still in progress at the end of this period.

Definition: *A simulation approach can be used to consider stock control situations, where random numbers are used to simulate variables such as the demand and delivery time.*

| 9.6 | **Running out of stock** |

Using simulation, we are able to analyse a given ordering strategy in order to determine whether stockouts are likely to occur. A stockout is a situation where the demand for an item exceeds current stock levels. Stockouts can be a major cause of concern for suppliers, since unsatisfied demand may not only mean reduction of immediate sales, but also long-term loss of customers, increased costs, poor customer relations and revenue reduction.

> **Definition:** *A stockout occurs when demand at a particular point in time cannot be satisfied.*

In the previous example, there were no stockouts. The daily closing stock level never reached zero, and all demands could be satisfied. Thus, the simulation demonstrates that the reordering policy adopted by the company (i.e. order a batch of 8 televisions when stock level reaches 10 or below) is a conservative one, and ensures that no stockouts are experienced. This is achieved by having relatively high levels of stock at any point in time. In some circumstances, high stock levels are undesirable since they may be prohibitively expensive. In such a situation it may be that the company is prepared to risk occasional stockouts in exchange for lower levels of stock.

In the following example, a different ordering strategy is simulated. Consider the ordering policy in which a batch of 4 televisions is ordered when stock reaches 4 or below. Assuming that all other factors remain unchanged, and using the same simulated demand figures, the following table is obtained.

Day	Initial stock level	Demand	Orders placed	Deliveries received	Closing stock level	Unsatisfied demand
1	12	3			9	
2	9	0			9	
3	9	2			7	
4	7	1			6	
5	6	1			5	
6	5	0			5	
7	5	3			2	
8	2	0	4 ordered		2	
9	2	1			1	
10	1	2		4 received	3	
11	3	2	4 ordered		1	
12	1	2			0	1 lost sale
13	0	1		4 received	3	
14	3	3	4 ordered		0	
15	0	2			0	2 lost sales

This simulation illustrates a worsening situation as the initial high levels of stock are used up. It can be seen that adopting this alternative ordering strategy reduces the stock levels and increases the risk of stockouts and subsequent loss of sales.

It should be noted that the values in this table assume that any demand which cannot be met with existing stock results in a lost sale. The model does not allow for delays in satisfying demand, for instance, using a new delivery of stock to satisfy a previous day's demand. However, such a situation could be incorporated into a more realistic model of the situation if required.

9.7   Incorporation of costs

To continue with the simulation developed in the previous examples, let us consider the costs involved in the management of stock. The following information is known:

(i)   The sale price for each television is £100.
(ii) The stockout cost is £150 per lost sale. (This means that if there is a demand that cannot be satisfied, we subtract £150 from the income to indicate future loss of revenue.)
(iii) The stock holding cost is £5 per day per television (based on the initial stock level).

The simulation developed in the previous example can be used to find a range of statistics, including:

(i)   Total number of televisions sold.
(ii) Total sales income.
(iii) Total stock holding costs.
(iv) Total stockout costs.
(v)   Average daily profit.

Such statistics can be used to determine which ordering policy is best for this item of stock.

The table on the next page shows the relevant calculations.

From the table it can be seen that over the 15-day period simulated, the following values are obtained:

(i)   A total of 20 televisions were sold.
(ii) The total sales income is £2000.
(iii) The total stock holding costs are £325.
(iv) The total stockout costs are £450 (resulting from three lost sales during this period).
(v)   The total profit (obtained by subtracting the stockholding costs and stockout costs from the sales income) is £1225.
(vi) The average daily profit is 1225/15 = £81.67.

Day	Initial stock	Demand	No. sold	No. unsatisfied	Sales income	S/H costs	Stockout costs	Profit
1	12	3	3	–	300	60	–	240
2	9	0	0	–	0	45	–	–45
3	9	2	2	–	200	45	–	155
4	7	1	1	–	100	35	–	65
5	6	1	1	–	100	30	–	70
6	5	0	0	–	0	25	–	–25
7	5	3	3	–	300	25	–	275
8	2	0	0	–	0	10	–	–10
9	2	1	1	–	100	10	–	90
10	1 (+4)	2	2	–	200	5	–	195
11	3	2	2	–	200	15	–	185
12	1	2	1	1	100	5	150	–55
13	0 (+4)	1	1	–	100	0	–	100
14	3	3	3	–	300	15	–	285
15	0	2	0	2	0	0	300	–300
		Totals	20	3	£2000	£325	£450	£1225

Further investigation of the simulation may reveal other interesting facts. For instance, there seems to be a deteriorating situation following the high stock levels at day 1. In order to obtain a truer picture of the actual situation, the simulation should be performed over a longer period of time. It is only after the high stock levels have been diminished that a more realistic impression emerges. For instance, the stockouts (resulting in additional costs and loss of sales) do not occur until towards the end of the simulation (the first stockout occurs on day 12 of this 15-day simulation). Thus, it can be seen that a more realistic view will be obtained by extending the simulation for the given situation.

9.8   Comparison of stock control policies

A wholesaler wishes to compare the advantages and disadvantages of two reordering policies for an item of stock where demand is uncertain. The two ordering policies are:

(i) order batches of 10 units at a reorder level of 10,
(ii) order batches of 15 units at a reorder level of 15.

Stock levels are checked at the beginning of each day.

Daily demand for this item over the past year has conformed to the following distribution:

Demand per day:	4	5	6	7	8
Percentage:	10	15	25	30	20

Other details related to this stock holding situation are as follows:

   (i) Stock holding costs are estimated to be £15 per unit per day.
  (ii) Ordering costs are £50 per order for administration, transportation and packaging costs.
 (iii) Loss of good will for each item out of stock is estimated to be equivalent to a loss of £30 in revenue.
 (iv) Delivery occurs at the beginning of the third day from the day of ordering.
  (v) Opening stock on day 1 is 17 units.

Using simulation will enable us to determine which ordering policy is most effective and economical.

    Two-digit random numbers can be used to simulate the daily demand for this product. There is a 10% chance of a demand of 4 and this can be represented by using the first 10 random numbers (i.e. 00 to 09). Similarly other demand values can be simulated as shown in the following table.

Daily demand:	4	5	6	7	8
Percentage:	10	15	25	30	20
Random numbers:	00–09	10–24	25–49	50–79	80–99

Using the random numbers given in the table earlier in this chapter we will be able to simulate the demand for this item of stock. The table below shows the simulation over a 10-day period for the order quantity and reorder level of 10 units.

Day	Opening stock	Demand	Sales	Closing stock	Order costs	St. hld costs	Stockout costs	Total costs
1	17	8 (89)	8	9	–	255	–	255
2	9	4 (07)	4	5	50	135	–	185
3	5	6 (37)	5	0	–	75	30	105
4	0	6 (29)	0	0	–	–	180	180
5	0 (+10)	6 (28)	6	4	50	150	–	200
6	4	4 (08)	4	0	–	60	–	60
7	0	7 (75)	0	0	–	–	210	210
8	0 (+10)	4 (01)	4	6	50	150	–	200
9	6	5 (21)	5	1	–	90	–	90
10	1	7 (63)	1	0	–	15	180	195
	Totals	57	37		£150	£930	£600	£1680

The columns in this table have been evaluated as follows:

   (i) The opening stock level on day 1 has been given as 17 units. Following this, from day 2 onwards, the opening stock is equal to the closing stock level from the previous day. One exception to this is when a new batch order arrives. This batch

Quantitative methods for business studies

of 10 is added onto the opening stock and is included in the calculations for stock holding costs for that day.

(ii) Demand is simulated using the random numbers outlined in the previous table. The actual random numbers used are shown in brackets in this column.

(iii) The sales figures are the same as the demand, providing that there is sufficient opening stock. If the demand is greater than the opening stock, then the sales figure equals the opening stock level.

(iv) Closing stock equals opening stock minus sales.

(v) An order cost of £50 is incurred when an order is placed. Orders are placed in this example when the opening stock reaches 10 or below. The batch of 10 will then arrive three days later and will be added on to the opening stock level.

(vi) Stock holding costs are obtained by multiplying the opening stock value by £15. (The opening stock value includes any new orders that have just arrived.)

(vii) Each item demanded that cannot be satisfied costs the company £30. The number of lost sales on a given day are obtained by the difference between the demand and opening stock level when demand exceeds opening stock. Thus the figure in the stockout costs column are calculated by this difference multiplied by £30.

(viii) The total costs are calculated by adding the three previous columns – order costs, stock holding costs, and stock out costs.

As can be seen, the ordering policy simulated in this table is not effective. There seem to be a large number of lost sales. Only 37 sales took place over this period when the demand was for 57 items. This is likely to be unacceptable in most circumstances, regardless of other costs involved.

Now, consider the same simulation using a different ordering policy where the batch size is 15 on a reorder level of 15. The simulation is shown below using the same pattern of demand.

Day	Opening stock	Demand	Sales	Closing stock	Order costs	St. hld costs	Stockout costs	Total costs
1	17	8 (89)	8	9	–	255	–	255
2	9	4 (07)	4	5	50	135	–	185
3	5	6 (37)	5	0	–	75	30	105
4	0	6 (29)	0	0	–	–	180	180
5	0 (+15)	6 (28)	6	9	50	225	–	275
6	9	4 (08)	4	5	–	135	–	135
7	5	7 (75)	5	0	–	75	60	135
8	0 (+15)	4 (01)	4	11	50	225	–	275
9	11	5 (21)	5	6	–	165	–	165
10	6	7 (63)	6	0	–	90	30	120
	Totals	57	47		£150	£1380	£300	£1830

The previous table shows that the new ordering policy is an improvement. In particular, there are fewer lost sales: 47 sales are achieved from a demand of 57 items. In general, there is a higher level of stock and this results in higher stock holding costs (a total of £1380 compared to the previous total of £930). Conversely, because of the increased stock levels there are fewer stockouts and the corresponding stockout costs are reduced (£300 compared to the previous total of £600). However, the total costs have increased using this new ordering policy (£1830 compared to the previous total of £1680).

At first sight this may lead us to think that the original ordering policy is better. However, this simulation has not included the actual income from sales of these items, and when this is taken into account it is likely that the policy of ordering in batches of 15 will prove to be more effective. For instance, the number of sales have been increased from 37 to 47 over the ten-day period. If each item earns £200, then there has been an increase in revenue of £2000 over this period. This would more than offset the small additional costs in stock holding costs. On the other hand, if each item only earns £2 then a different ordering policy may be called for.

As illustrated by the above arguments, care must be taken when analysing the results of the simulations. However, it can be seen that these simulations provide a clear picture of the processes, and could aid the manager in determining the most appropriate ordering policies in given circumstances. Further simulations could be carried out to compare the costs involved using a range of stock control variables. For instance, the table below shows the total costs incurred over a twenty-day period adopting different order quantities and reorder levels. The same sequence of twenty demand values has been used in each case.

	Total costs (£)				
	Order (batch) quantity				
Reorder level	5	10	15	20	25
5	3450	3405	3615	4675	5290
10	3440	3470	3845	5700	6430
15	3440	3470	3845	6050	6445
20	3415	3550	4750	6780	8205
25	3415	3550	4750	9230	8955
30	3415	3550	4750	9580	10 455

From this table it seems as though an order quantity of 10 with a reorder level of 5 will minimise the total costs. Therefore, this could be suggested as the best possible solution to this ordering problem. However, this is likely to be due to the relatively high stock holding costs (£15 per unit per day), which means that costs are kept low by simply keeping the level of stock at a minimum. However, with such a small reorder level it is likely that a high proportion of the demand will not be satisfied. This would usually be a totally unsatisfactory situation for most suppliers.

A clearer impression of the effectiveness of these policies can be obtained by incorporating the revenue with costs to estimate the profit obtained over the same period. The table below shows the profit values generated assuming that each item sold earns a gross profit of £100 excluding the stock holding costs described earlier.

	Net profit (£)				
	Order (batch) quantity				
Reorder level	5	10	15	20	25
5	750	3295	5585	4225	4110
10	1160	3630	5755	5400	3170
15	1160	3630	5755	5050	3955
20	1685	4550	6350	4920	3495
25	1685	4550	6350	2470	2745
30	1685	4550	6350	2120	1245

Again, the figures in this table have been obtained using the same sequence of randomly generated demand figures. A new set of values would yield different results. However, the values would be similar to those shown in this table. An average over a number of simulation runs could be used to generate a more realistic estimate of the expected profit in each case. Nevertheless, the table does indicate potential solutions to the problem in terms of maximising the profit. It can be seen that an order quantity of 15 produces a relatively consistent profit level for the complete range of reorder levels.

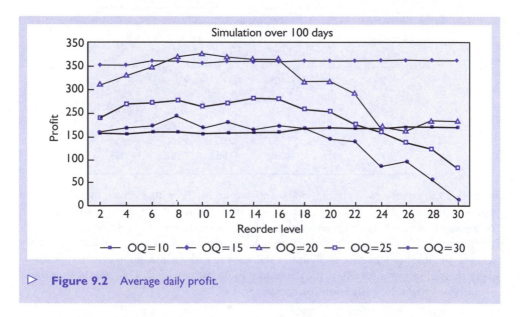

▷ **Figure 9.2** Average daily profit.

This is not surprising, since this is closest to the average demand over a three-day period which corresponds to the lead time for delivery of batches.

Such values could be illustrated to represent the effect of different values for the order quantity and reorder levels. Figure 9.2 illustrates a further simulation of this situation taken over 100 days. The graph shows the average daily profit obtained from the simulation of sales over 100 days for various values of the two variables. The reorder level is shown on the horizontal axis of the graph, with the average daily profit given on the vertical axis. The different lines shown indicate a number of values for the order quantities (OQ). Again, the graph shows that the order quantity of 15 is very consistent, with little variation related to the reorder level used. However, the graph shows that an order quantity of 20 increases the profitability, particularly for reorder levels of around 10. Further simulations would need to be generated using new demand values in order to confirm these findings.

9.9   Exercises: stock control simulations

1.(E) Use random numbers to simulate the demand of items over a ten-day period that conform to the following distributions:

(i)

Demand:	1	2	3	4
Percentage:	20	40	30	10

(ii)

Demand:	5	10	15	20	25
Percentage:	12	27	32	19	10

(iii)

Demand:	0	1	2	3	4	5
Percentage:	5	10	13	33	22	17

2.(I) The ABC electrical warehouse in New York stocks a range of electrical goods including hi-fi systems, CD players, washing machines and fridges. The daily demand for the Electroloop de luxe washing machine conforms to the following distribution:

Daily demand:	1	2	3	4	5	6
Percentage:	10	30	30	20	5	5

Stock is normally reordered when the level reaches six or below. At this stage eight washing machines are ordered, which take three days to be delivered.

Assuming an initial stock level of ten washing machines, use a suitable method to simulate the demand of these items over a 20-day period.

How likely is it that the ABC warehouse will run out of stock if they adopt this ordering policy?

3.(D) Consider the problem outlined in question 2, above. The following additional information is known:

(a) Each washing machine retails at $300.

(b) Each washing machine costs $150 for the ABC company to purchase from the manufacturer.

(c) Each batch order costs an additional $50 in administration and delivery costs.

(d) Each order that cannot be satisfied costs the ABC company $200 in loss of good will and customer satisfaction.

(i) Repeat the simulation required in question 2 using this additional information. Estimate the daily income and costs associated with this washing machine.

(ii) Would a better policy be to order ten washing machines when stock levels reach eight or below? Use a new simulation to investigate this.

(iii) What about other ordering policies? For instance, what if the company orders twenty washing machines when stock reaches ten or below? Simulate this over a ten-day period to demonstrate why such a policy might not be sensible.

9.10   Queuing problems

Simulation can be used to investigate problems involved in queuing. Such problems are common in any situation involving customers, items or orders arriving at a given point, and being processed in a specified order (such as the order in which they have arrived). For example, the following give a range of circumstances involving queuing problems:

(i) Customers arrive in a bank and form a single queue which feeds a number of service desks. The arrival rates of customers into the bank will determine the optimum number of service desks to have open at any specific point in time.

(ii) Orders from customers are delivered to a central location in a company and are then distributed by a group of employees to the appropriate departments within the organisation. It is crucial that these orders are processed quickly and efficiently, and the number of employees used in this function and the processes adopted can be considered as a queuing problem.

(iii) Finished products arrive at the end of an assembly line for dispatch to a central warehouse. There is a limited amount of space available to store these products before dispatch, and it is essential that the products are processed and delivered quickly. The products effectively form a queue at the end of the assembly line, which must be carefully monitored and controlled.

(iv) Cars arrive at a major road junction at a known rate. Traffic lights can be set to change at specified time intervals, in order to minimise the amount of traffic queuing and the waiting time for individual vehicles.

In all the above examples, simulation techniques will enable a detailed analysis of a given situation, and compare appropriate solutions to given problems. Such problems often involve keeping variables such as queue length, waiting times, and costs, to a minimum. In most analyses the information that should be considered includes vital details on arrival patterns, arrival rates, and 'service' times. The following examples give a range of queuing problems using simulation analysis techniques.

9.11	**Arrival rates**

The management of a large petrol station is concerned that customers are being lost because of the long waiting times sometimes required at their petrol pumps. Over a one-week period a careful study has been taken of the arrival of cars onto the garage forecourt. The arrival rates are shown in the table below:

Time between successive arrivals (minutes):	1	2	3	4
Percentage of customers:	60	25	10	5

It should be noted that the arrival rates are usually defined in this way. An alternative method would be to simply count the number of customers arriving in given periods. For example, the table below shows the number of arrivals of customers:

Number of customers arriving per minute:	0	1	2
Percentage of minutes:	55	35	10

Although this information can be useful, for simulation purposes it is much better to record the time between the arrival of successive customers (the inter-arrival times) rather than the number of arrivals in a given period. Thus, the first table showing inter-arrival times will be used to simulate the arrival of a number of customers. The table shows that following the arrival of one customer, there is a 60% chance of the next customer arriving in 1 minute, a 25% chance of arriving within 2 minutes, and so on.

Definition: *The inter-arrival time defines the difference between the arrival of successive 'customers' in a queuing situation.*

Random numbers can be used to simulate the arrival of successive customers. For example, using two-digit random numbers, the first 60 numbers (00 to 59) will be used to represent an inter-arrival time of 1 minute. The next 25 random numbers (60 to 84) will be used to represent an inter-arrival time of 2 minutes, and similarly for the remaining inter-arrival times as shown in the table below:

Inter-arrival times (minutes):	1	2	3	4
Percentage of customers:	60	25	10	5
Random numbers:	00–59	60–84	85–94	95–99

The table on p. 400 shows the arrival of the first ten customers at the petrol station. The random numbers used to simulate inter-arrival times are shown in brackets in the table.

The inter-arrival times simulated give the times between the arrival of successive customers. It is assumed that the clock is started at time 0, and it can be seen that the first customer arrives three minutes later. The second customer has an inter-arrival time of 1 minute, and therefore that customer arrives in the fourth minute. In general the actual arrival time of any customer is obtained by adding the customer's inter-arrival time to the preceding customer's arrival time. It can be seen from the simulation that ten customers have arrived in the first fourteen minutes.

Customer	Inter-arrival times	Arrival times
1	3 (89)	3
2	1 (07)	4
3	1 (37)	5
4	1 (29)	6
5	1 (28)	7
6	1 (08)	8
7	2 (75)	10
8	1 (01)	11
9	1 (21)	12
10	2 (63)	14

This information can then be used to investigate a number of different service methods. This type of problem is illustrated in the next example.

9.12   Service patterns

Clearly, in order to investigate queuing in a given situation, it is necessary to have information on the length of time taken to serve customers. The table below shows the length of time taken to serve customers at the petrol station previously described.

Service time (minutes):	2	3	4	5	6
Percentage of customers:	20	30	20	15	15

The service times can be simulated using two-digit random numbers as in the method previously outlined. For example, the first 20 random numbers (00 to 19) can represent a service time of 2 minutes. The table below shows the random numbers that will be used to represent given service times:

Service times (minutes):	2	3	4	5	6
Random numbers:	00–19	20–49	50–69	70–84	85–99

Thus, the service times for the first ten customers arriving at the petrol station are shown in the top table on p. 401. The random numbers used to simulate the service times are indicated in brackets.

The inter-arrival times and service times can be combined to investigate the queue length for this situation. The bottom table on p. 401 shows the arrival times and service times previously simulated together with the length of queue when each new customer arrives at the petrol station. The table assumes that only one customer can be served at any one time. This would be the scenario in a self-service petrol station with only one petrol pump, or an attended petrol station with only one member of staff on duty.

Customer	Service times
1	3 (34)
2	4 (65)
3	2 (11)
4	5 (80)
5	3 (34)
6	2 (14)
7	6 (92)
8	3 (48)
9	5 (83)
10	6 (91)

Customer	Arrival time	Queue length	Service time	Service IN	Service OUT
1	3	0	3	3	6
2	4	1	4	6	10
3	5	2	2	10	12
4	6	2	5	12	17
5	7	3	3	17	20
6	8	4	2	20	22
7	10	4	6	22	28
8	11	5	3	28	31
9	12	5	5	31	36
10	14	6	6	36	42

It should be noted that the queue length includes all customers who are **waiting** to be served. This includes the customer that has just arrived, but does not include any customer who is currently being served.

The arrival time (column 2) and service time (column 4) have previously been simulated using random numbers. The 'service IN' column gives the time when the customer starts to be served, and the 'service OUT' column gives the time when the customer has finished being served. For the first customer the 'service IN' will be equivalent to the arrival time, since there are no customers already being served. After the first customer, the 'service IN' time will be equal to the 'service OUT' time of the previous customer.

Definition: *Queuing problems can be investigated by simulating variables such as the inter-arrival times and service times of customers.*

The queue length (i.e. the number of customers waiting to be served) is obtained in the following way:

(i) Look at the arrival time for the customer, e.g. customer 5 arrives in the seventh minute.

(ii) By referring to the 'service IN' and 'service OUT' times of the preceding customers, find who is currently being served, e.g. in the seventh minute, customer 2 is still being served (since customer 2 has 'service IN' = 6 and 'service OUT' = 10).

(iii) The queue length can then be obtained as the current customer number minus the number of the customer currently being served.

Care must be taken over this, particularly when the arrival time of a customer coincides with the 'service OUT' (or 'service IN') of a previous customer. For example, customer 7 arrives in the tenth minute. At this time the second customer has just finished being served, and customer 3 has just commenced service. Therefore there are only 4 customers in the queue (including customer 7).

9.13   Waiting times

The simulation shown in the previous section could be used to analyse the waiting times for each customer. This is a critical variable in the queuing analysis and would be a useful indicator of customer satisfaction for the manager involved in this process.

The table below shows a simulation of the arrival and service of ten customers into the petrol station as outlined previously and includes an extra column giving the waiting times for each customer.

Customer	Arrival time	Queue length	Service time	Waiting time	Service IN	Service OUT
1	3	0	3	0	3	6
2	4	1	4	2	6	10
3	5	2	2	5	10	12
4	6	2	5	6	12	17
5	7	3	3	10	17	20
6	8	4	2	12	20	22
7	10	4	6	12	22	28
8	11	5	3	17	28	31
9	12	5	5	19	31	36
10	14	6	6	22	36	42

The waiting times calculated in this table are obtained by finding the difference between the arrival time and the 'service IN' time for each customer.

Using this simulation it can be seen that the situation in this petrol station will quickly get out of control. As the simulation progresses there are two striking circumstances. Firstly, the queue length is very quickly increasing: the tenth customer, for instance, joins a queue of six waiting to be served. Secondly, as a consequence of this, the waiting times for successive customers are rapidly increasing. The first customer has no waiting time whereas the tenth customer in this simulation must wait for 22 minutes before being served. Clearly, this situation cannot be allowed to continue. It is likely that customers will be lost since they will not be prepared to wait the increasingly excessive amounts of time. For the manager of this petrol station, a number of possible solutions are plausible. The most obvious one is that the number of customers that can be served at any one time should in some way be increased. For instance, the number of pumps available or staff employed could be increased. The simulation shown in the table below shows the situation where there are two pumps available. The same arrival times and service times are used in order to provide a direct comparison with the original situation, and thus to investigate any significant change in performance.

Customer	Arrival time	Queue length	Service time	Waiting time	Service IN	Service OUT
1	3	0	3	0	3	6
2	4	0	4	0	4	8
3	5	1	2	3	6	8
4	6	1	5	2	8	13
5	7	2	3	1	8	11
6	8	1	2	3	11	13
7	10	2	6	3	13	19
8	11	2	3	2	13	16
9	12	3	5	4	16	21
10	14	2	6	5	19	25

In this table, two customers can be served at the same time. Consequently, customers 1 and 2 arrive and are served immediately. Customer 3 arrives and must wait until one of the previous customers has finished being served. Thus customer 3 makes a queue of length 1 on arrival. Care must be taken when establishing the queue length when other customers arrive. In particular, it must be remembered that two customers are currently being served, and neither of these is included in the queue. Thus, for instance, customer 7 arrives at the tenth minute. At this time the two customers being served are customer 4 ('service IN' = 8, and 'service OUT' = 13) and customer 5 ('service IN' = 8, and 'service OUT' = 11). Therefore, all customers after customer 5 are currently in the queue. Thus, customers 6 and 7 are the two members of the queue.

The average waiting times per customer and average queue lengths per customer arrival are useful indicators of the performance in a given situation. For instance, the two situations previously simulated where one and two petrol pumps are available yield the following data:

Service situation	Average waiting time	Average queue length
One petrol pump	10.5 minutes	3.2 cars
Two petrol pumps	2.3 minutes	1.4 cars

Clearly, the waiting times and queue lengths are both reduced by having a second pump available for service. The situation for one pump is even worse than the average values in this table imply. As can be seen from the simulation, the waiting times and queue lengths are continually increasing. Consequently, a simulation over a longer period of time (for instance over the first twenty or more customers) would show an even wider difference between the two scenarios simulated here. Even with the two-pump situation there seems to be a slight, though perceptible, increase in the waiting times and queue lengths as time progresses. This may imply that the current situation requires three pumps in order to satisfactorily serve all customers arriving at the petrol station. It is left to the reader to simulate a situation in which three customers can be served at the same time.

9.14   Analysis of costs/revenue

In addition to considering variables such as queue length and waiting times it is obviously necessary to consider the potential costs and revenues involved. In the previous simulations it can be seen that if the number of service points (e.g. petrol pumps) is increased, then the number of customers that can be served, and therefore the potential revenue, is increased. However, there is a limit to the number of service points that can be introduced. Beyond a certain level, the costs of installing new service points are not justified by the possible increase in revenue. Consider the previous simulation, with the following additional information. Petrol is served by attendants at the petrol station. Each attendant is paid £5 per hour. The average contribution from each customer is £2. Furthermore, consider an added complication regarding customers arriving at the petrol station: If the queue length is 2 or more then any new customer arriving will leave without waiting to be served. This is an example of a more realistic situation, since in practice customers will not be prepared to wait indefinitely to be served with petrol.

The table below shows the new simulation, assuming two attendants are employed:

Customer	Arrival time	Queue length	Service time	Waiting time	Service IN	Service OUT	Contribution (£)
1	3	0	3	0	3	6	2
2	4	0	4	0	4	8	2
3	5	1	2	3	6	8	2
4	6	1	5	2	8	13	2
5	7	2	3	1	8	11	2
6	8	1	2	3	11	13	2
7	10	2	6	3	13	19	2
8	11	2	3	2	13	16	2
9	12	2**	–	–	–	–	–
10	14	1	6	2	16	22	2

In this simulation, the queue length is not allowed to exceed 2. In other words, if there are two already queuing when a new customer arrives then this customer will not wait. It is acceptable if the new arrival is the second customer in the queue. Thus, in the above table, customer 5 is the second in a queue, and similarly customers 7 and 8 both arrive when there is a car already queuing. Customer 9 arrives when there are already two cars in the queue. Therefore, customer 9 would have become the third customer in the queue. In this simulation such a situation is not permissible, and the assumption is that this customer will leave. The table shows this by placing ** in the queue length box. There is a queue of 2 already when customer 9 arrives, and this is indicated. The remaining boxes in this row are blank since there is no service time, waiting time or other variables to consider.

We see that after the first 22 minutes, nine customers have been served. (This is shown by the 'service OUT' time for customer 10.) Furthermore, the total contribution during this period is £18. One way of estimating the hourly contribution from this simulation would be to use the following multiplying factor:

Hourly contribution $= \frac{60}{22} \times £18 = £49$

It should be noted that a more accurate estimate could be obtained by simulating this situation over a longer period of time.

There are two attendants employed, each earning £5 per hour, giving a total hourly staff cost of £10. Therefore, the gross profit obtained is £39 per hour.

Clearly, a similar analysis could be carried out to consider the profitability of using more attendants in the petrol station. For instance in the above simulation, if three attendants were employed, the only significant difference would have been that customer 9 would have been served. This would have given an additional contribution of £2 over the 22-minute period at an extra cost of £5 per hour. It can be seen that the benefits of an extra attendant are marginal, and clearly the use of four or more attendants would not be required. This example illustrates how the use of simulation can provide additional management information in order to make decisions such as the use of appropriate manpower levels.

9.15 | Practical application

One section in Rednall is involved in providing on-line support and assistance in a range of software supplied and/or developed by the company. The frequency of telephone calls into this section is indicated in the following table:

Time between successive calls (minutes):	5	10	15	20	25
Percentage of calls:	15	26	33	17	9

Each call is answered immediately by a central switchboard, and the client is then transferred to the support service and asked to wait. Each enquiry is handled by a single member of the support team and takes a variable length of time as shown below:

Duration of call (minutes):	10	15	20	25	30
Percentage of calls:	5	20	30	35	10

Use simulation to determine the optimum number of staff who should be employed within this section. It should be noted that it is unsatisfactory for customers to have to wait for more than 10 minutes before they receive assistance.

As with the previous simulations, random numbers can be used to simulate these variables given. In particular, the following random numbers will be used:

Time between calls (minutes):	5	10	15	20	25
Random numbers:	00–14	15–40	41–73	74–90	91–99

Similarly, for the time taken to help the clients:

Duration of call (minutes):	10	15	20	25	30
Random numbers:	00–04	05–24	25–54	55–89	90–99

The Support Services Manager requires information on the amount of time clients usually wait for assistance, and at any single point in time, how many clients are waiting to be served. Simulation could be used to determine the required number of staff providing on-line support in order to provide a satisfactory and effective service.

The table below shows the simulation of a number of calls into the support service desk, assuming that only one person is available to provide assistance.

Client	Time between calls	Arrival time	Queue length	Service time	Waiting time	Service IN	Service OUT
1	20 (89)	20	–	20 (52)	0	20	40
2	5 (07)	25	1	20 (49)	15	40	60
3	10 (37)	35	2	30 (98)	25	60	90
4	10 (29)	45	2	20 (44)	45	90	110
5	10 (28)	55	3	25 (80)	55	110	135

The numbers in brackets indicate the random numbers used to generate the time between calls (inter-arrival times) and the service times.

It can be seen that after the first few clients there is an impossible situation here. The waiting times, and numbers of clients waiting to be served, are increasing rapidly. Very quickly there would be a situation where clients give up waiting, and eventually because of the poor service will look elsewhere for a more satisfactory support service. It is therefore clear that extra staff will need to be employed in this important area of customer service.

The simulation is repeated on the next page for the first fifteen calls assuming that two members of staff are available.

The situation here using two members of staff looks fairly stable. Occasionally there is a small queue of clients building up, but this is cleared at various stages. The maximum waiting time in this simulation is 10 minutes and almost half (7 out of 15) of the clients did not wait at all before receiving assistance. Clearly, the use of a third

Client	Time between calls	Arrival time	Queue length	Service time	Waiting time	Service IN	Service OUT
1	20 (89)	20	–	20 (52)	0	20	40
2	5 (07)	25	–	20 (49)	0	25	45
3	10 (37)	35	1	30 (98)	5	40	70
4	10 (29)	45	–	20 (44)	0	45	65
5	10 (28)	55	1	25 (80)	10	65	90
6	5 (08)	60	2	10 (04)	10	70	80
7	20 (75)	80	–	20 (42)	0	80	100
8	5 (01)	85	1	20 (37)	5	90	110
9	10 (21)	95	1	25 (87)	5	100	125
10	15 (63)	110	–	30 (96)	0	110	140
11	10 (34)	120	1	25 (85)	5	125	150
12	15 (65)	135	1	20 (46)	5	140	160
13	5 (11)	140	1	20 (51)	10	150	170
14	20 (80)	160	–	25 (73)	0	160	185
15	10 (34)	170	–	15 (10)	0	170	185

member of staff would improve the situation further, and would ensure that the large majority of clients received immediate assistance. A simulation on the basis of three members of staff would show this. The results of such simulations would enable a comparison to be made between different staffing levels. For instance, the end results could be summarised in the following table:

Number of staff	Average waiting times (minutes)
1	85
2	4
3	2

As can be seen from the table, an increase in the number of staff reduces the average waiting times. It is a matter of debate whether an increase in the number of staff over two employees significantly affects the waiting times. It remains a decision for the manager as to whether this would be a viable proposition in terms of the additional costs compared with the benefits.

Further simulations could take place in Rednall to consider the full range of calls into the central exchange. For example, information on the actual types of call and the appropriate department within Rednall to which they are directed would then enable an analysis of the overall system of customer care. For instance, the table below shows the percentage of calls into Rednall which have been directed to various departments over the past three months:

Departments:	Hardware	Software Development	System Development	Packages Advice
Percentage of calls:	10%	15%	20%	55%

A simulation of all the calls received by Rednall will then enable an analysis of the services provided in other areas in the company. This may involve a review of the staffing levels and a redistribution of the staff resources currently available.

9.16   Exercises: queuing problems

1.(E)   Customers arrive at a checkout in a supermarket at the rate shown in the table below:

Inter-arrival times (minutes):	1	2	3	4	5
Percentage:	40	30	10	10	10

It usually takes two minutes to serve each customer. Simulate the arrival of the first 20 customers at the checkout and record the queue length at the arrival of each customer.

2.(I)   Consider the problem outlined in question 1 above. The actual service times of customers can vary and conform to the distribution shown below:

Service times (minutes):	1	2	3	4	5
Percentage:	10	20	30	35	5

As before, simulate the arrival of the first 20 customers, and estimate the average queue length and average waiting time for each customer.

3.(D)   As an added complication, if on arrival there are already three customers waiting to be served, then the customer will go to another checkout. Carry out the simulation as in question 2, and estimate the average waiting time and average queue length during this period.

4.(D)   Customers arrive at a counter at the rate shown in the following table:

Inter-arrival time (minutes):	1	2	3	4	5	6	7
Percentage:	15	25	25	15	10	5	5

Each member of staff serves these customers at the following rate:

Service times (minutes):	2	3	4	5	6	7	8	9
Percentage:	5	10	10	15	20	20	10	10

(i) Assuming that only one member of staff is serving, simulate the arrival of 25 customers using the following information:
   (a) Each customer spends £15 on average.
   (b) If the queue is over 2, then customers will not stay to purchase any goods.
   (c) It is estimated that each customer who leaves without being served costs the company £30 in loss of earnings and good will.
   Use your simulation to estimate:
   (a) The average queue length.
   (b) The number of lost customers.
   (c) The total daily income (assume that the shop is open for ten hours per day).
   (d) The total net income (equal to income minus loss of goodwill costs).
(ii) Repeat the above simulation assuming that there are two members of staff serving at the counter.

9.17   Simulation of a normal variable

The previous examples have involved the simulation of discrete variables. Let us now consider applications which require the simulation of continuous variables such as those conforming to the normal distribution.

EXAMPLE 1

The daily sales revenue of a small company tends to be normally distributed with a mean of $10 000 and a standard deviation of $3000. The daily sales revenue can be simulated by using random normal deviates tables. The table below shows a sample of such values that have been computer generated. The numbers included are random values which are normally distributed with a mean of 0 and a standard deviation of 1.

−0.136	0.099	−2.479	0.451	−0.998	0.986	0.461	0.555	0.963	0.398
0.171	−0.321	−1.646	−0.781	0.635	2.054	1.722	0.246	1.560	−0.880
−0.037	−0.839	0.931	0.433	0.089	1.302	−0.129	−1.562	0.850	0.055
−0.941	1.615	0.134	1.464	−0.787	−0.533	−0.291	−1.177	2.211	0.241
0.757	0.155	0.350	−0.337	−0.001	0.030	0.203	−1.087	−0.855	0.562

The values in this table can be converted to simulate any normal variable by multiplying by the standard deviation and adding the mean value.

In order to simulate the daily sales in this example, a value is taken from the table multiplied by 3000 (standard deviation) and then added to 10 000 (the mean). Thus, the first value in the table (−0.136) generates a sales figure as follows:

Sales = −0.136 ∗ 3000 + 10 000 = £9592

Similarly, the sales over a ten-day period could be simulated as shown in the table below.

Day	Random number	Sales revenue (£)
1	−0.136	9592
2	0.099	10 297
3	−2.479	2563
4	0.451	11 353
5	−0.998	7006
6	0.986	12 958
7	0.461	11 383
8	0.555	11 665
9	0.963	12 889
10	0.398	11 194

Such a simulation could be used for considering a range of strategies on advertising, staffing and costs in order to make the most effective use of available resources.

EXAMPLE 2

A simple model has been developed to forecast the monthly fluctuations in the value of the Nikkei index based on previous changes in the Dow-Jones share index. The percentage monthly change in the Nikkei (N) can be estimated from the previous month's change in the Dow (D) as follows:

$$N = 1.3D - 0.4 + I$$

The variable I is an irregular variation that is normally distributed with a mean of zero and a standard deviation of 0.8. Using this relationship we can simulate the variations in the Nikkei based on previous changes in the Dow. For example, if in a given month the Dow index increases by 2%, then the model shows that the change in the Nikkei is $N = 1.3D - 0.4 + I = 1.3*2 - 0.4 + I = 2.2 + I$. The value of I can be simulated using the random normal deviates as shown in the previous example. The table on p. 411 shows the monthly changes of the Nikkei index based on this model.

The table shows the estimates of the variation of the Nikkei based on the previous changes in the Dow. Thus, the change in the Dow-Jones index in month 1 is used to estimate the Nikkei change in month 2. Similarly, the change in the Nikkei in the tenth month is based on the fluctuation in the Dow index in month 9. The values of D have been input into the table and all other values are obtained using the model stated earlier.

Month	Change in Dow index (D%)	Random number	Irregular variation (I)	Change in Nikkei (N%)
1	1.0	–	–	–
2	2.2	0.171	0.137	1.0
3	1.4	−0.321	−0.257	2.2
4	0.5	−1.646	−1.317	0.1
5	−0.5	−0.781	−0.625	−0.4
6	−1.0	0.635	0.508	−0.5
7	−1.2	2.054	1.643	−0.1
8	−0.5	1.722	1.378	−0.6
9	0.7	0.246	0.197	−0.9
10	–	1.560	1.248	1.8

Such a model could be tested in real life, by comparing the estimated values of N against the Nikkei changes when they occur. In fact, the model would initially be tested by using past data to examine how closely the estimates of N fit the actual values. In this way the model can be validated and modified in the light of new evidence. Again, the results of such a simulation could be used to investigate a range of investment strategies and test these without any risk involved. Having obtained a reasonable model, a potential investor could test out a number of investment approaches based on the changes to the Dow index, without any risk of financial loss.

9.18   Evaluation of simulation techniques

The use of simulation can be a valuable tool in management decision making. The application of a simulation approach to decision making has a number of advantages:

Coping with uncertainty. Simulation provides a means of dealing with uncertainty. For instance, uncertain variables may include future demand, competitors' prices, suppliers' delivery times, customer arrivals and interest rate changes. A complex simulation could be developed to incorporate a wide range of such variables.

Comparison of alternatives. The use of simulation enables the model to be applied a number of times in order to consider alternative strategies and explore their effects on a range of factors. For instance, we could consider the effect of different pricing strategies on demand.

Monitoring multiple outcomes. Complex simulation models can be utilised to record the performance of a range of factors such as profit, sales, costs and measures of customer service.

Consistency. The application of a simulation model involves a consistent, standardised method of considering a range of inputs. Without such a model it is easy to be subjective about any comparisons and thus any results could be erroneous.

Risk-free environment. The use of simulation is without any significant risk. Without simulation, a range of strategies could be tested by their use in real life. For instance, increase the price of a product and observe the effect on sales or demand, or reduce the number of staff and view the resulting customer service performance. Such a process would involve risks such as loss of revenue and deteriorating customer relations. The use of a simulation model would alleviate such risks.

Cost reductions. Simulation models are relatively inexpensive to operate. Following the development of a suitable model, a range of situations can be considered at virtually no cost in a relatively short space of time.

However, the use of simulation does have some drawbacks such as:

Model development costs. The building of complex models can be time-consuming and costly. Realistic models may involve a large number of variables with a significant range of possible outputs. To develop such a model may be prohibitive. In practice, it is better to build a simplified version of a model which can be tested and evolved into a practical tool.

Complexity. Practical simulation models can become incredibly complex and cumbersome. This can result in problems with the validation of such models, and difficulties in analysing the results from simulation runs. Such complexity results in the simulation model producing unreliable information which could be misleading to the unsuspecting manager.

9.19   Computer applications

From the examples covered in the previous sections it can be seen that the actual process of simulation, though relatively simple, involves a large number of repetitive steps, including simple arithmetic operations. Such a process is ideally suited for computerisation, and a range of bespoke packages (including SIMAN, Simlog, SIMULAB and Model Builder) is available which can be used for the simulation of specific problem areas in business and manufacturing. The type of simulations developed in this chapter can be successfully reproduced using a range of statistical or spreadsheet packages. Providing a package has the facility to generate random numbers, it can be adapted to simulate given problems.

The Excel and Lotus 123 spreadsheet packages have random number generators (using the function =RAND in Excel or @RAND in Lotus), and the following examples illustrate a range of simulations and corresponding outputs obtained from these types of package.

EXAMPLE 1

An example earlier in this chapter related to the demand for televisions from an electrical warehouse. The demand conformed to the following distribution:

Daily demand (number of TVs):	0	1	2	3	4
Percentage number of days:	10%	22%	37%	28%	3%

The daily demand can be simulated using a spreadsheet package. The table below shows the output from Lotus simulating the demand for televisions over a twenty-day period.

Day	Initial stock	Random number	Demand	Orders placed	Deliveries received	Closing stock	Unsatisfied demand
1	12	10	1	0	0	11	0
2	11	36	2	0	0	9	0
3	9	83	3	0	0	6	0
4	6	25	1	0	0	5	0
5	5	24	1	0	0	4	0
6	4	93	3	4	0	1	0
7	1	53	2	0	0	0	1
8	0	23	1	0	4	3	0
9	3	9	0	4	0	3	0
10	3	58	2	0	0	1	0
11	1	27	1	0	4	4	0
12	4	3	0	4	0	4	0
13	4	69	3	0	0	1	0
14	1	24	1	0	4	4	0
15	4	63	2	4	0	2	0
16	2	62	2	0	0	0	0
17	0	51	2	0	4	2	0
18	2	48	2	4	0	0	0
19	0	10	1	0	0	0	1
20	0	24	1	0	4	3	0

The table assumes specific values for a number of variables including the following:

(i) The initial stock level is 12.
(ii) The reorder level is 4 (i.e. a new batch of televisions is ordered when the stock level at the beginning of the day reaches 4 or below).
(iii) The televisions are ordered in batches of 4.
(iv) Delivery of a batch takes 2 days from ordering.

The spreadsheet package enables a detailed analysis and provides graphical output of selected data. Thus, the diagram shown in Figure 9.3 illustrates the level of stock over

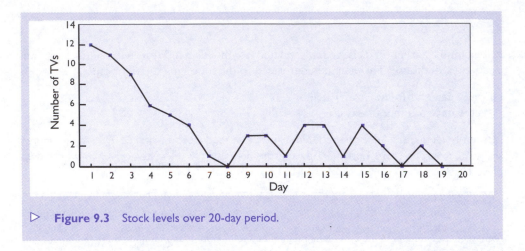

Figure 9.3 Stock levels over 20-day period.

the simulation period. It can be seen from the graph in Figure 9.3 that following the first few days when levels were high, the stock levels are fluctuating around zero. Although it is desirable to have minimal levels in stock, this indicates that there is a greater risk of a stockout, as demonstrated in the simulation where demands have not been satisfied on three of the 20 days considered.

One advantage of using a computer package to assist in the simulation process is the ability to change one or more variables and recalculate the process very quickly. This enables a range of scenarios to be considered by the manager in order to make an informed decision on the most appropriate ordering policy to adopt in this case. For instance, the spreadsheet package has been used again with a change in the order quantity. If the televisions are ordered in batches of ten, and all other variables remain the same, a simulation reveals the graph of stock levels over the 20-day period shown in Figure 9.4. In this illustration we see that there is a regular pattern of stock levels from

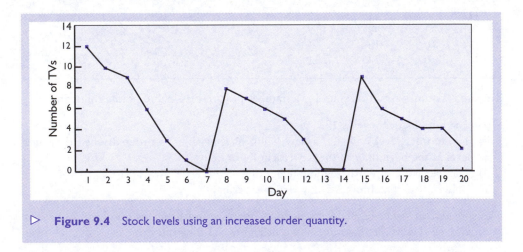

Figure 9.4 Stock levels using an increased order quantity.

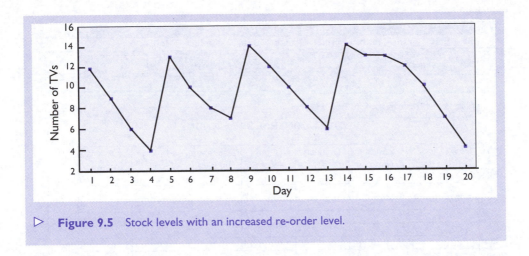

▷ **Figure 9.5** Stock levels with an increased re-order level.

the high levels when new batches arrive (days 8 and 15) to low levels preceding new deliveries. Unfortunately, there still seems to be a risk of running out of stock, even using the high batch quantities as simulated. Further changes in the ordering variables can be investigated such as a change in the reorder level. The graph given in Figure 9.5 shows the results of a simulation using a reorder level of 10 with a batch size of 10.

Using this ordering policy it can be seen that there is little risk of running out of stock. In fact, the stock levels are always relatively high, and further investigation may lead to a better ordering method using different order quantities and reorder levels.

Using the disk The disk accompanying this text has a file called STOCK.WK3 containing this simulation. Load Excel or Lotus 123 and retrieve this file. The cells J4 to K18 contain a number of variables relating to the simulation as shown in the screen displayed in Figure 9.6.

This STOCK spreadsheet can be used to generate other simulations such as those previously described. For example, consider changes in the reorder levels and batch sizes used as follows:

Simulation	Batch quantity	Reorder level
1	10	4
2	10	10
3	7	7
4	20	5

In order to perform the simulation, simply type in the new values for order quantity (in cell K15) and reorder level (in cell K18). Now press <F9> to recalculate all the formulae. You will see that a new set of random numbers are generated each time you

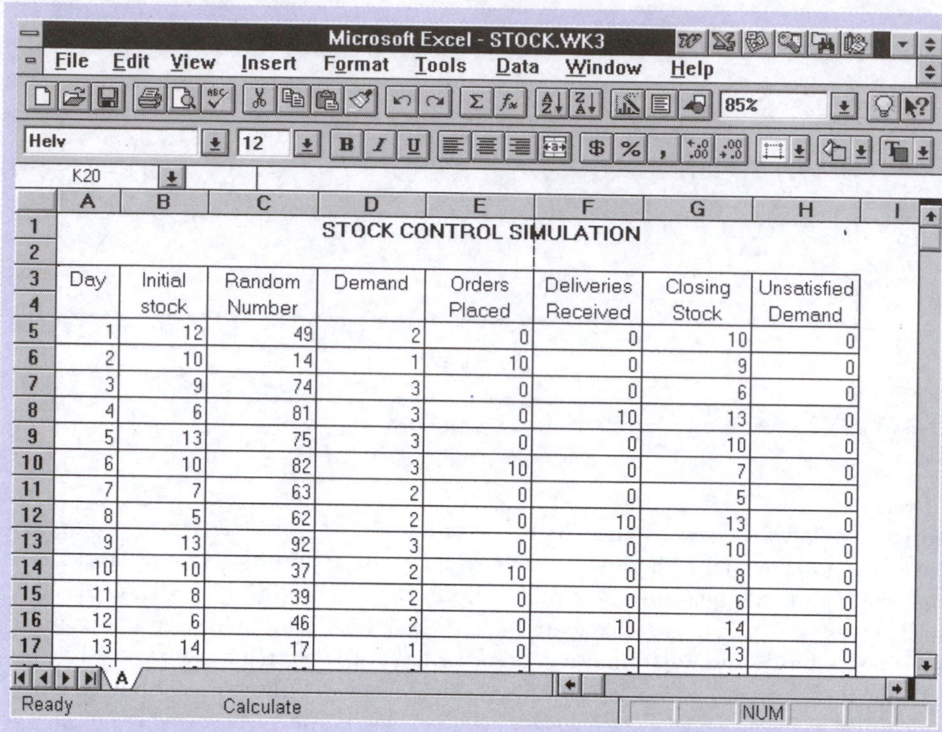

Day	Initial stock	Random Number	Demand	Orders Placed	Deliveries Received	Closing Stock	Unsatisfied Demand
1	12	49	2	0	0	10	0
2	10	14	1	10	0	9	0
3	9	74	3	0	0	6	0
4	6	81	3	0	10	13	0
5	13	75	3	0	0	10	0
6	10	82	3	10	0	7	0
7	7	63	2	0	0	5	0
8	5	62	2	0	10	13	0
9	13	92	3	0	0	10	0
10	10	37	2	10	0	8	0
11	8	39	2	0	0	6	0
12	6	46	2	0	10	14	0
13	14	17	1	0	0	13	0

▷ **Figure 9.6** Stock control simulation.

press <F9>. Following each simulation you can look at the graph displayed in the cells A26 to E34 and print out the results if required.

EXAMPLE 2

Consider the use of a computer simulation in queuing. Planes arrive in the air-space above an airport at the rate shown in the following table:

Inter-arrival times (minutes):	1	2	3	4	5	6	7	8
Percentage of arrivals:	5	15	30	25	10	5	5	5

The planes circle around the airport until they are given permission to land. Aircraft are landed in strict order of arrival into the air-space. Once given permission to land, the time taken to complete the landing and be clear of the runway ready for the next aircraft is given in the table below:

Time taken for completion:	4	5	6	7
Percentage of aircraft:	35	25	25	15

Simulate the arrival of the first 30 aircraft in the air-space above the airport.

The following spreadsheet shows the simulation of this problem. The table shown provides similar information to the simulations generated in the previous sections on queuing problems.

Aircraft	Rand. No.	I.A.T.	Arrival Times	Queue Length	Rand No.	Comp'n Time	Wait Time	Commence Landing	Complete Procedures
1	32	3	3	0	39	5	0	3	8
2	87	6	9	0	18	4	0	9	13
3	45	3	12	1	20	4	1	13	17
4	49	3	15	1	54	5	2	17	22
5	94	7	22	0	66	6	0	22	28
6	93	7	29	0	1	4	0	29	33
7	13	2	31	1	79	6	2	33	39
8	2	1	32	2	45	5	7	39	44
9	55	4	36	2	66	6	8	44	50
10	37	3	39	2	75	6	11	50	56
11	0	1	40	3	83	6	16	56	62
12	30	3	43	4	61	6	19	62	68
13	38	3	46	4	80	6	22	68	74
14	99	8	54	4	44	5	20	74	79
15	28	3	57	4	46	5	22	79	84
16	70	4	61	5	57	5	23	84	89
17	91	7	68	4	94	7	21	89	96
18	18	2	70	5	35	5	26	96	101
19	60	4	74	5	51	5	27	101	106
20	9	2	76	6	93	7	30	106	113
21	26	3	79	6	88	7	34	113	120
22	20	3	82	7	66	6	38	120	126
23	62	4	86	7	23	4	40	126	130
24	34	3	89	7	91	7	41	130	137
25	48	3	92	8	62	6	45	137	143
26	58	4	96	8	8	4	47	143	147
27	74	4	100	9	2	4	47	147	151
28	25	3	103	9	86	7	48	151	158
29	62	4	107	9	14	4	51	158	162
30	28	3	110	10	60	6	52	162	168

The spreadsheet shown here produces graphs such as that shown in Figure 9.7.

Using a package such as Excel or Lotus enables the speedy change of a range of variables used in the simulation. For example, if the completion times are changed to the following distribution:

Time taken for completion:	4	5	6	7
Percentage of aircraft:	50	35	10	5

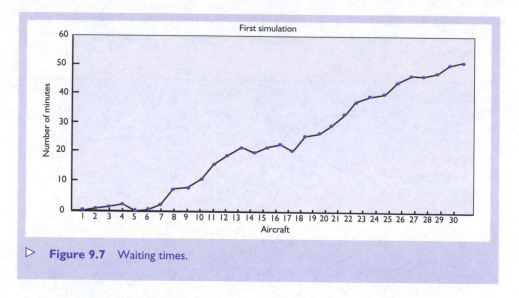

The improvement in completion times outlined in this table will produce the graph of waiting times as shown in Figure 9.8. It can be seen that waiting times, though still increasing for successive planes, are lower than the original values. Clearly, this is as expected, since any improvement in completion times should help the situation. In this way we can consider a range of scenarios very quickly, and obtain immediate feedback and analysis of results. For instance, consideration of alternative arrival patterns and servicing procedures is necessary in this practical example. One possible solution is the introduction of a second runway to improve the congestion problem. Simulation could be used to investigate this and to consider the economic benefits and viability of such a scheme.

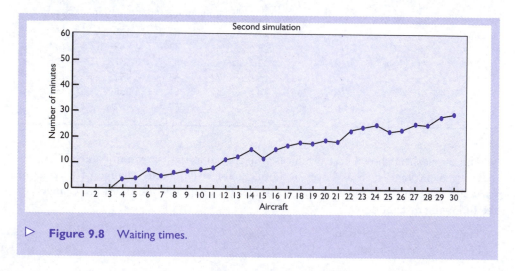

▷   **Figure 9.8**   Waiting times.

Using the disk Load the QUEUE1.WK3 file from the disk available with this text. This spreadsheet contains a simple simulation of the queuing problem for aircraft previously outlined. There are tables (so-called lookup tables) containing details of the specific arrival patterns and service times used in the simulation. The inter-arrival times used are as follows:

Inter-arrival times (minutes):	1	2	3	4	5	6	7	8
Percentage of planes:		5	15	30	25	10	5	5	5

Similarly, the service times (time taken for each plane to land and clear the runway area) are as follows:

Service times (minutes):	4	5	6	7
Percentage of planes:	35	25	25	15

Using the lookup facility in Excel or Lotus 123 it is preferable to refer to the cumulative percentages rather than the actual values. Thus the tables displayed in cells O4 to S13 in the QUEUE1.WK3 file give the cumulative values for each variable as shown in Figure 9.9.

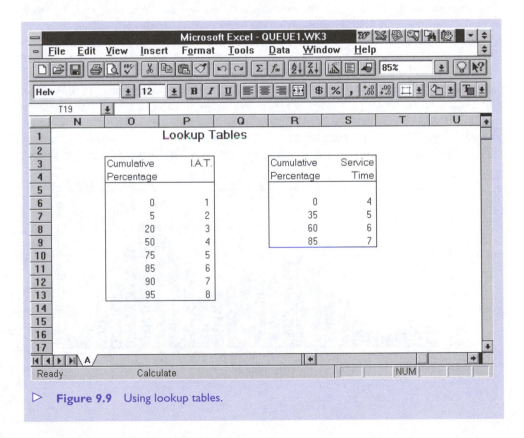

▷ **Figure 9.9** Using lookup tables.

By changing these cumulative values we can consider a variety of arrival patterns and service times.

EXAMPLE 3

Queuing simulations can often involve more complex distributions of arrival times. For example, consider the arrival of customers into a supermarket. The arrival patterns are likely to vary during different periods of the day. The customer arrivals at a particular supermarket are found to vary according to the distribution shown in Figure 9.10. The supermarket opens from 8.00 a.m. until 9.00 p.m. The graph in Figure 9.10 illustrates the number of customers arriving into the store in half-hour intervals on a given day. It can be seen that the two main peaks of customer arrivals occur during the evening and over the lunchtime period. The highest number of customer arrivals occurs during the periods around 6.00 p.m.

It can be seen that any realistic simulation of arrivals will need to take this variation into account. Thus, the distribution of inter-arrival times of customers will vary depending on the time of day. Clearly, this could have implications for staffing levels at the supermarket. It is likely that the management will require additional staff to work at peak times (i.e. at lunchtime and during the early evening sessions).

Further complications can occur by the consideration of customer numbers on different days of the week. The example previously outlined shows the customer numbers on a specific Thursday. The arrival patterns on other days may be significantly different. For instance, the Thursday and Saturday arrivals are illustrated and compared in the graph shown in Figure 9.11. The graph illustrates that there are major differences between the arrival patterns on the two days. The distribution of arrivals on Saturday is more uniform, rising to a peak around lunchtime, and tailing off gradually until closure of the store. Thus, any simulation would need to reflect

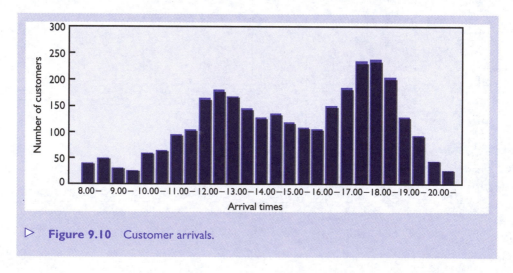

▷ **Figure 9.10** Customer arrivals.

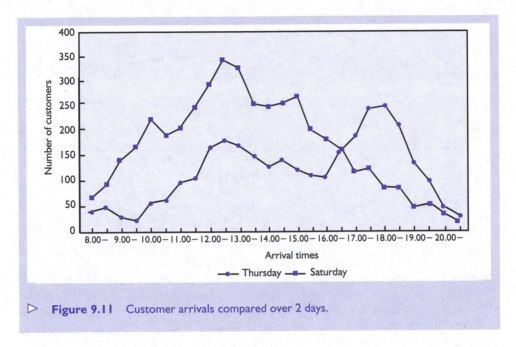

▷   **Figure 9.11**   Customer arrivals compared over 2 days.

the differences between the daily arrival patterns, and staffing levels would be adjusted accordingly.

The results of simulations in this area would include a comparison of different numbers of service points. For example, a consideration of the average waiting times and queue lengths based on changes in the number of cash tills open would provide useful information for management decision making. The graph in Figure 9.12 gives an indication of the customer waiting times compared with a variable number of

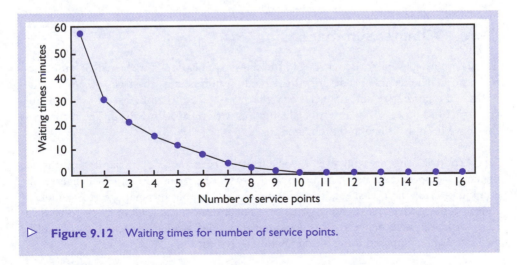

▷   **Figure 9.12**   Waiting times for number of service points.

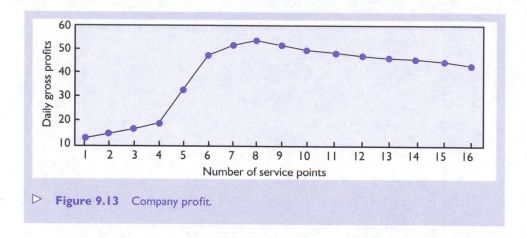

△ **Figure 9.13**   Company profit.

service points based on simulations. From this graph it can be seen that an increase in the number of service points will usually result in a reduction in customer waiting times. However, an increase above 10 service points makes little impression on the waiting times. At this stage, waiting times are very low and an increase in the number of service points is unnecessary. The graph in Figure 9.13 shows an analysis of the profit obtained in relation to the number of service points open. It can be seen from Figure 9.13 that beyond a certain number of service points the company's profit starts to decline. This is because there is a level beyond which the majority of service points are idle, and therefore these points (i.e. staff manning cash tills) are not fully utilised. Each member of staff costs a fixed sum of money, and the income generated from extra staff is not sufficient beyond a given number to justify the additional cost. The example here shows that the introduction of more than eight service points is not cost-effective.

9.20   Chapter summary

This chapter has summarised a range of business applications for the use of simulation techniques. The techniques described use random numbers as the basis of simulating a variety of quantitative and financial data. Such values can then be used to test possible strategies and processes in an artificial situation with no risks involved. The main areas that have been described in this chapter are:

Stock control. This area involves a consideration of a range of variables such as the demand for specific items, in addition to the rates of production and/or delivery. The combination of these elements in a simulation will enable the manager to examine a range of alternative stockholding situations. For instance, the level of stock to be held, re-order levels used, delivery times and frequency, and production schedules can all be evaluated and compared using the simulation techniques.

Queuing. Queues can build up in a variety of diverse situations such as customer service in retail and wholesale outlets, product bottlenecks from production and assembly lines, telephone calls received, and communication between computer network users and other equipment. In this topic area the variables that can be simulated include the arrival times, arrival frequency, service times and utilisation of multi-service points. Changes in one or many of these variables will dictate changes in the way 'customers' are dealt with. The service given to customers can be gauged by a range of statistics such as the average queue lengths, average waiting times, and average service times. The use of simulation methods can help the manager to make decisions on the most appropriate ways of improving service to customers.

Market simulations. A range of variables in the commercial and manufacturing sectors such as sales, demand, customer fluctuations, price changes, output, production quality control factors, and staff turnover can be simulated. These variables can often be modelled incorporating an unpredictable element which can be simulated using random numbers. In these situations the simulation of variables conforming to the normal distribution may be appropriate.

Other situations which have unpredictable components can be simulated in order to investigate possible alternative decisions and produce optimum solutions. Simulation is a powerful tool in situations where there are no appropriate analytical methods available. The simulation process has a number of advantages including the ability to analyse complex situations involving uncertainty with a range of potential outcomes. The method can be used to perform a detailed analysis at a reduced cost in a risk-free environment. The drawbacks of simulation include the difficulty and costs involved in developing a valid simulation model to cater for the complexities involved in most practical situations.

9.21   Further exercises

1.(I)   Patients arrive at an emergency centre in a large city centre hospital at the following rate:

Time between arrival of successive patients (minutes):	2	4	6	8	10	12	14
Percentage of arrivals:	5	10	12	23	27	16	7

An analysis of the time taken to handle each patient has been conducted over the past three months. The handling includes an initial interview with the patient, brief examination, diagnosis of possible problems, and redirection to the next phase in treatment. The next stage would normally involve the movement of the patient to areas such as the X-ray or scanner department, or transfer to another section in the hospital for specialist diagnosis and treatment. A junior doctor is generally used for the initial stage of the patient, and the table below shows the length of time taken for this stage based on the survey's findings.

Handling time (minutes):	10	12	14	16	18	20	22
Percentage of patients:	15	21	19	17	15	9	4

(i) Simulate the arrival of the first fifteen patients in the emergency centre assuming that there is only one doctor on duty to handle the initial stage of patient handling. Comment on this situation in terms of the patient care provided.

(ii) Assuming that two doctors are on duty, reproduce the simulation for fifteen patients, and estimate the average waiting times and average queue length.

(iii) Would the addition of a third doctor significantly help the queuing situation?

2.(I) A production line produces finished goods at the hourly rate shown in the following table.

Number of items produced (per hour):	25	26	27	28	29	30	31
Percentage of hours:	5	12	21	19	17	14	12

The finished goods are then individually taken to a handling area where they are stacked in preparation for transportation. Every four hours, a batch of 100 items is shipped to the central warehouse in another part of the factory on the same site.

(i) Simulate the arrival and transportation of these items over a 20-hour period. Assume that there are 50 items in the handling area at the beginning of the simulation. Evaluate the number of items in the handling area at the end of each hour and estimate the average number of items stored here.

(ii) Repeat the simulation assuming that batches of 100 items are shipped to the central warehouse when there are enough items available. Shipments of fewer than 100 items are not considered necessary. How does this affect the average number of items in the handling area? Also, does this new procedure drastically affect the frequency of shipments to the warehouse?

3.(D) The Central Stores in a large educational institution stocks a range of stationery for distribution to various Departments and Sections on request. Three items frequently required are Printer paper, Photocopying paper, and Overhead projector slides. These are kept in a separate store which is more convenient for distribution purposes. Departments telephone the store to place a request for these items, and if available the items are immediately sent to the appropriate locations. The rate of telephone calls received by the store is given in the table below:

Time between successive calls (minutes):	4	5	6	7	8	9	10
Percentage of calls:	13	7	10	25	23	17	5

Each telephone call involves the request of only one of the items in stock. The following table shows the percentage of calls requesting each of the items:

Items of stock:	Printer paper	Photocopier paper	Overhead slides
Percentage of calls:	25	55	20

Simulate the arrival of the next 20 telephone calls into the stores, assuming the following values:

(i) The number of items currently in stock are:

Items of stock:	Printer paper	Photocopy paper	Overhead slides
Number of items:	30	40	10

(ii) When an item is requested, a batch of 5 is normally sent to the appropriate department, unless there are fewer than this in stock, when the remaining stock is sent.

(iii) Every half-hour an automated stock control system checks the stock levels of each item and reorders the items from the central store when the stock levels are below 10. The following batch sizes are ordered:

Items of stock:	Printer paper	Photocopy paper	Overhead slides
Batch size:	80	120	40

(iv) The orders are normally delivered within 4 hours of ordering.

Your simulation should include an estimate of the average stock level for each item in the store, and a record of which, if any, items are unavailable so the Department's requests cannot be immediately dealt with.

4.(D) A medium-sized clothes retailer is reconsidering its ordering policy in respect of a range of jeans merchandise. Weekly demand for the Relis super jeans is distributed as shown in the following table:

Weekly demand:	10–14	15–19	20–24	25–29	30–34
Percentage of weeks:	15	35	25	15	10

(i) Simulate the demand over a fifteen-week period and estimate the average weekly demand. (Use the mid values of each range for the purposes of this simulation.)

(ii) Estimate the average weekly income and costs of Relis jeans by using the simulation values obtained in part (i), given the following information:

Retail price of a pair of jeans = £40,
Cost price = £25 per pair,
Batch size = 50 pairs of jeans,
Order cost = £40 per batch,
Re-order level = 40 pairs,
Lead time = 2 weeks,
Storage = £2 per pair of jeans,
Initial stock level = 90 pairs,
Cost of running out of stock = £10 per pair of jeans.

(iii) Repeat this simulation assuming that the lead time for batch orders is not constant, but conforms to the following distribution:

Lead time for orders (number of weeks):	1	2	3	4
Percentage of orders:	20	45	30	5

(iv) Discuss how simulation could be used to determine the best order quantity in order to maximise profit.

5.(D) The trading in 'derivatives' by the Barings Bank during the early 1990s has been introduced in a case study earlier in this chapter. In an analysis of the risks involved with this type of investment the following information is given.

Regular investments are made in the Nikkei 225 futures market. Such an investment yields profits (or losses) dependent on the performance of the Nikkei index. The table below shows the percentage change in this index on a weekly basis over the past year.

Percentage change:	−4%	−3%	−2%	−1%	0	+1%	+2%	+3%
Percentage of weeks:	3	10	15	15	20	20	15	12

On every investment of $1 million each week such changes in the Nikkei yield the following profit (or loss):

Percentage change:	−4	−3	−2	−1	0	+1	+2	+3
Profit/loss ($ millions):	−1.0	−0.6	−0.4	−0.2	−0.1	+0.2	+0.8	+1.5

(i) Simulate the changes in the Nikkei index over a twenty-week period, and estimate the profit or loss each week based on a $1 million investment. What is the average weekly profit/loss? What is the overall profit/loss over the twenty weeks?

(ii) The actual amount of investment each week is dependent on the following:

In week 1 invest $1 million.
On subsequent weeks, the investment is based on the previous week's percentage change as shown in the following table:

Percentage change:	−4	−3	−2	−1	0	+1	+2	+3
Investment ($ millions):	10	7	4	2	1	1	1	0

Using the previous simulated percentage changes in the Nikkei index, find the weekly investment, profit and loss figures over the twenty-week period.

(iii) Try to produce an investment strategy based on the previous week's percentage changes as illustrated in part (ii) of this question. For example, consider the alternative strategy described: Assume that $1 million is invested in week 1. Following this, if any loss occurs (i.e. there is a negative change in the previous week's value), then double the investment for the current week. Continue the doubling up of the investment until a gain is obtained; then revert to the $1 million investment. (This is a simplified version of what actually happened in the Barings' investments during early 1995. In an attempt to recoup previous losses on the market, an increasing amount of money needed to be invested.)

Test this new strategy by using the simulation process and find the overall profit/loss expected with such an investment plan.

6.(I) The Knophler Inc company in San Diego has developed a simple model to estimate the daily sales income for a specific product based on the product's unit price. For a unit price (P) between \$20 and \$100 the daily sales figure (S) is estimated to be:

$$S = 6000 - 20P + V$$

The value of V is an unpredictable variation which is approximately normally distributed with a mean of 0 and a standard deviation of \$1,000.

 (i) Based on a unit price of \$50, simulate the daily sales of this product over a 15-day period. Using this simulation, calculate the average daily sales revenue for this product over this period.
 (ii) Using a different unit price for this product, re-work the simulation and consider the effect on the sales revenue during the 15-day period.

7.(I) In a production line at the Christopher Ford cigarette manufacturer in Baton Rouge, Louisiana, a quality inspection has found that the weight of batches of 200 cigarettes produced is normally distributed with a mean of 100 grams and a standard deviation of 1.2 grams. Batches of 200 cigarettes weighing less than 98.5 grams are rejected and are recycled in the production. Simulate the production of the first twenty batches of 200 cigarettes and note which batches are rejected. How many batches have been rejected during this simulation? Investigate other quality control strategies such as rejecting batches of less than 99.5 grams or more than 101 grams. How would this affect the proportion of batches rejected? Compare your results against the expected number of rejects using the normal probability distribution described earlier in this book.

8.(D) The Rednall company, described in the case study at the beginning of this chapter, has a storage facility for a number of the most popular personal computers and peripheral hardware. The company has experienced problems with running out of stock and not being able to satisfy the demands of its clients. In this volatile and highly competitive market, clients' orders which cannot be met immediately are often lost to alternative suppliers. It is important, therefore, that Rednall attempts to have in stock the most popular models for immediate despatch to customers.

Consider the storage of the laptop computer SX486/33. The cost price of this item is £500 and Rednall sells it to clients at a basic price of £700, making a gross profit of

£200 per computer. Over the past year, weekly sales of the SX486/33 have conformed to the following distribution:

Weekly sales:	1	2	3	4	5	6
Percentage:	5	10	20	30	25	10

In terms of the administration and transportation costs it has been found to be cost-effective to order the computers from the manufacturer in batches of 10. Each order costs an additional £60 in administration, packaging and transportation charges. Currently, the company orders a new batch of computers when stock reaches eight or below. Stock levels are checked at the beginning of each week. Orders take three weeks to arrive. Thus an order placed in week 1 will definitely be included in the stock at the beginning of week 4.

Storage costs for these computers have been estimated to be £10 per computer per week.

Simulate the demand for this product over 12 weeks, assuming that the company has twelve laptop SX486/33s at the beginning of week 1, and determine during this period the following:

 (i) the total number of computers sold,
 (ii) the number of lost sales due to stockouts (assume that if an order cannot be satisfied immediately, it is lost),
 (iii) the total sales revenue,
 (iv) the average weekly profit.

Comment on this ordering policy and compare this with a reorder level of twelve laptop computers.

9.(D) Bottles are produced and packaged in batches of 1000 from a production line. The batches produced are immediately moved individually to a warehouse and arrive at the site at a rate of:

Inter-arrival times (minutes):	2	4	6	8	10	12
Percentage:	5	10	15	28	26	16

Lorries arrive at the warehouse regularly and are loaded up with batches from the single loading bay. The time taken to load each lorry is given in the table below:

Loading time (minutes):	10	12	14	16	18	20
Percentage:	30	35	20	8	5	2

 (i) Simulate the arrival and loading of the first fifteen batches in the warehouse.

Comment on this process. What is the average number of batches in the warehouse waiting to be loaded?

(ii) Assuming that two loading bays are available, so that two lorries can be loaded at the same time, carry out the simulation again and re-estimate the average number of batches waiting to be loaded. Are two loading bays sufficient to handle this production output? If not, how would you determine how many loading bays are required by the use of simulation?

10.(I) Calls from clients are received by the Rednall central telephone exchange at the following rate:

Time between calls (minutes):	1	2	3	4	5	6	7
Percentage of calls:	12	15	21	25	18	5	4

These calls are redirected to four main sections within the Rednall company. The following table shows the proportion of calls received by these departments:

Departments:	Hardware	Software development	System development	Packages advice
Percentage of calls:	10	15	20	55

The average time taken to answer a client's call varies from one department to another. The table below shows the times taken to complete calls into the four departments.

Departments:	Hardware	Software development	System development	Packages advice
Duration of calls (minutes):	12	10	20	8

Simulate the first twenty telephone calls into Rednall, and record the waiting times for the callers in each department, assuming that there is only one member of staff dealing with enquiries. What is the average number of callers waiting for assistance in each department?

11.(I) **Using the disk** The file called RATE on the disk contains a simulation in a production situation. The two tables shown give the production rates per hour of a given item, together with the demand rates for these items.

By experimenting with a variety of production and order rates consider the resulting change in the level of stock for the finished product.

(i) For example, consider the following distributions:

Production rate

No. produced per hour:	1	2	3	4	5	6	7	8
Percentage of hours:	5	5	20	30	20	10	5	5

Demand rate

No. of items required:	1	2	3	4	5	6	7	8
Percentage of hours:	15	30	25	15	10	5	0	0

(ii) Now try a new distribution for the demand such as:

Demand rate

No. of items required:	1	2	3	4	5	6	7	8
Percentage of hours:	5	15	25	20	10	10	10	5

What effect does this have on the stock levels?

(iii) Experiment with new distributions for the production and demand rates.

Project Management

CHAPTER OBJECTIVES

At the end of this chapter you will be able to:

▶ understand the applications of networks in project management

▶ draw networks based on information for individual activities

▶ use Gantt charts in the allocation of resources

▶ use probabilistic techniques in network analysis

▶ compare the main methods of network construction

Introduction

Network analysis incorporates a variety of techniques used to help plan and manage the scheduling of interrelated activities. These techniques can be particularly useful in project management, where the use of networks will help to monitor projects, allocate resources where appropriate and review costs. In practice, network analysis techniques are often more useful for complex projects involving many hundreds of activities. In these cases the application of computer-based network analysis packages is beneficial.

CASE STUDY   **The Gilford & Partners consultancy group**

The Gilford & Partners organisation provides consultancy services in structural and civil engineering projects. The company has headquarters in the UK, with subsidiary offices located throughout the world, including Los Angeles and Dallas, in the USA, Hong Kong, and Melbourne, Australia. Many of the company's more recent large civil engineering projects have taken place in the Australasia region. These projects have included the design and construction of bridges, tunnels, office and industrial buildings, and large-scale roadway construction.

The Gilford organisation has expertise in the full range of activities involved in such projects. The management and careful control of these multi-million dollar projects are crucial. Gilford & Partners would generally be contracted to complete a project within a certain timescale, and this imposes restrictions and presents resource allocation problems requiring strict adherence to timescales. For instance, a recent project for the Australian government involved the design and construction of a freeway in the outskirts of Sydney. Gilford & Partners were involved in the initial surveying of the land, site investigations, production of designs for the roadways and associated carriageways such as bridges, flyovers, slip roads and junctions. Following these early stages, the organisation was involved in writing planning applications and obtaining planning permission where necessary. The actual construction work was subcontracted to local building companies, with Gilford & Partners controlling and monitoring each stage in the process.

Gilford & Partners eventually agreed to a contract for this major project, including clauses on the completion time of a number of phases in the project as well as the overall completion time. The contract included penalties for the late completion of each stage, and bonuses for earlier completion of the full project.

Clearly, in these circumstances, it is vital to closely monitor the progress of such a project, and to determine if any stage is behind schedule. If stages do fall behind schedule, then the Project Manager will need to consider alternative approaches to attempt to rectify the situation and bring the project back within timescales, in order that no penalties are incurred. This may involve the reallocation of resources, such as the transfer of staff, or the use of additional staff where appropriate. Any tools and techniques that assist the manager in this complex process would be extremely beneficial. The use of networking in this type of project is now commonplace for organisations such as Gilford & Partners.

CASE STUDY   **Refitting the QE2 – a problem for Cunard**

A well publicised and controversial refurbishment of the QE2 cruise liner occurred between November 1994 and January 1995. The liner was virtually transformed by a major refurbishment of the public rooms and many passenger cabins on board. Some areas on the ship were completely redesigned, including the upgrading of the largest restaurant, and a complete change of an existing ballroom into a theatre-style performance area. Hundreds of cabins were totally refurbished, including the replacement of existing baths, toilets and showers with new suites. New electrical systems were installed, walls demolished, walkways redesigned, bars and public rooms redecorated, and carpets replaced.

A major element of the refit was carried out in Hamburg, Germany, with the remainder of the work scheduled to be completed during the return trip to Southampton, England. Such a refit involved the use of a number of German and British contractors, incorporating an enormous workforce of electricians, builders, plumbers, painters, decorators and cleaners. The total time scheduled in for the majority of this work was a period of eighteen days, sandwiched between scheduled cruises that had been prebooked by passengers.

In the event, the refurbishment took considerably longer than was scheduled. This resulted in a one-week 'Pre-Christmas cruise' being cancelled, and the following two cruises (an Atlantic crossing to New York and a Caribbean cruise over the Christmas and New Year period) being significantly disrupted with continuation of the refurbishment work. Indeed, problems for Cunard (the owners and operators of the QE2) did not end there. The vessel failed to gain the necessary safety certificate prior to sailing from New York, and was delayed by a further 36 hours during which time additional work was carried out to rectify the situation. These problems resulted in considerable losses by the Cunard Company, not only in lost revenue and compensation claims (estimated to be around $14 million) but also in poor public relations, loss of customer confidence, and diminished reputation.

Clearly, a major project of this type, incorporating the interrelationship of many tasks involving numerous skills, a variety of subcontractors and significant logistical problems, was ideally suited for the use of networking techniques. Whether appropriate techniques were effectively used can be evidenced by the string of complaints and recriminations following this major refurbishment. The problems of managing this type of project include estimating the duration of tasks, scheduling the complex range of diverse activities, and utilising different skills and expertise. Clearly, if one activity early in the project is delayed, then this has a 'knock on' effect which may multiply this delay many times before the project completion. Examples on networks relating to this case study will be introduced throughout the chapter.

10.1 Networks: activity on arrow notation

A network consists of activities and events. Each activity can be illustrated by an arrow. Events denoting the start and finish of each activity are illustrated by nodes (circles) and are usually numbered. Figure 10.1 shows one activity with nodes at the beginning and end.

This simple illustration of one activity could represent the following elements:

Activity A = transport goods from factory to warehouse.
Node 1 = start activity A, i.e. goods can be transported.
Node 2 = activity A finished, i.e. transport of goods completed.

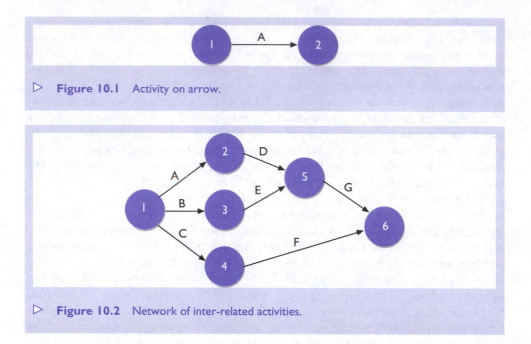

▷   **Figure 10.2**   Network of inter-related activities.

Such elements are grouped together in order to represent the interrelationship between activities.

Single events, represented by nodes, can indicate the start or finish of more than single activities. For instance, the diagram shown in Figure 10.2 shows node 1 indicating the start of three activities (A, B and C), and node 6 represents the completion of two activities (F and G).

It should be noted that other network notations can be used. In particular, most project management computer packages use the nodes, rather than arrows, to indicate activities. This notation will be explored later in the chapter.

10.2   Project networks: example

The network shown in Figure 10.3 illustrates some simple steps involved in organising a training course. This network diagram illustrates the various activities required to complete the project. Each activity is represented by an arrow on the diagram. Nodes (circles) are numbered and drawn to indicate the start and finish of each activity.

The network diagram clearly illustrates the relationships between the activities. For example, according to this diagram, applications for the course can only be processed after the course has been advertised. Furthermore, the course can only be run after the applications have been processed and the course documentation produced.

Using the network diagram enables the illustration of complex relationships between a range of activities.

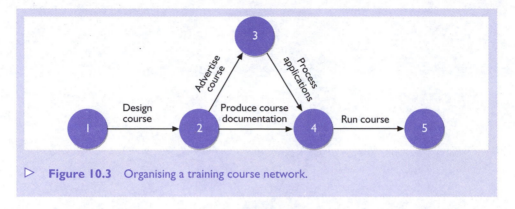

Definition: *A network is a diagrammatic illustration of the relationship between a group of activities.*

10.3   Drawing networks

In order to produce a network diagram the following information must be supplied:

 (i) a list of activities required, and
(ii) the interdependence between activities, i.e. which activities precede other activities.

EXAMPLE 1

Consider the following table, which gives a list of activities involved in a factory expansion scheme.

Activity	Preceding activity
A: Plan new site	–
B: Move to temporary premises	A
C: Build new plant	A
D: Train staff	B
E: Install machinery	C
F: Move production to new site	D,E

This table describes the precedence for each activity. For instance, activity A (plan new site) is preceded by nothing. Activity C is preceded by A. This tells us that the new plant cannot be built (activity C) before the new site has been planned (activity A). Activity F is preceded by both D and E. This implies that the production will be moved to the new site (activity F) only after staff have been trained (D) and machinery installed (E).

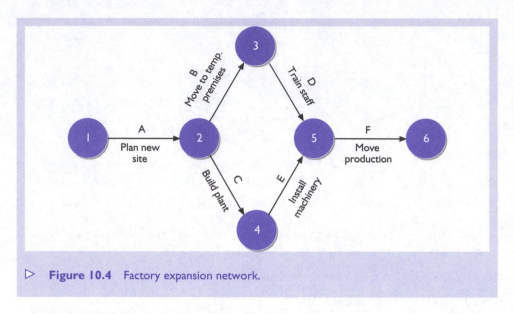

▷   **Figure 10.4**   Factory expansion network.

The network for this list of activities is drawn in Figure 10.4.

Note that on the network the activities (indicated by the arrows) are labelled, and the nodes, indicating the start and finish of activities, are numbered. The numbering of nodes is almost arbitrary. The only rule to be followed when deciding on node numbers is that for each activity the number of the start node should be **less** than the number of the finish node. These numbers can be used to represent (or describe) activities, and are essential when computerising the networking process. For example, activity A is node 1 to node 2 (1 to 2). Similarly, activity B is 2 to 3, C is 2 to 4, and so on.

EXAMPLE 2

Consider the first case study introduced at the beginning of this chapter. This concerned the structural engineering consultancy group, Gilford & Partners. The

	Primary activities	Precedences
A:	Initial survey & site investigations	–
B:	Design roadways	A
C:	Planning applications & permission	B
D:	Site preparation	B
E:	Construction of link roads	D
F:	Construction of main freeway	C,E
G:	Erection of signs, lighting, etc.	C,E
H:	Completion & hand over	G

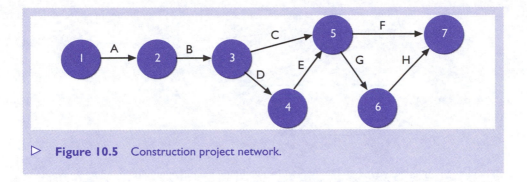

▷   **Figure 10.5**   Construction project network.

design and construction of a major freeway complex around the northern suburbs of Sydney involved a large number of interrelated activities. For the purposes of this example, this construction project has been split into a small number of primary activities. These activities are shown on p. 436 together with their precedences.

The network for this group of activities is illustrated in Figure 10.5. Note that activity A starts off the project, and that the completion of activities F and H defines the end of the project.

EXAMPLE 3

The 1994–5 QE2 refit introduced in the case study at the beginning of this chapter involved a significant refurbishment of many of the public areas on board the ship. This massive project was split down into a number of subprojects involving specific skills and expertise. The team of electricians involved in the project had a number of tasks as outlined in the table below.

	Tasks	Preceding tasks
A:	Remove existing fittings	–
B:	Clear and prepare areas	–
C:	Improve power source output	–
D:	Rewire sections	B
E:	Add additional power points	A
F:	Add new fittings	D
G:	Modify wiring configurations	B
H:	Change lighting arrangements	E
I:	Test lighting	C,G,H
J:	Test complete electrical system	F,I

The network illustrating these activities is given in Figure 10.6.

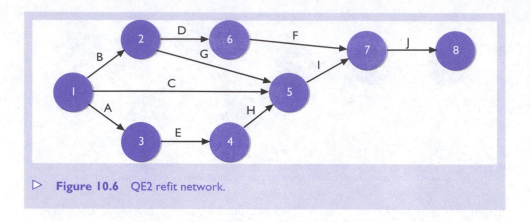

Figure 10.6   QE2 refit network.

10.4   Dummy activities

Occasionally, the relationship between activities cannot easily be illustrated because of their unusual dependencies. In some examples, dummy activities can be incorporated to illustrate the correct precedences. A dummy activity can be considered as an activity that requires no resources or time, and will be treated as such in any calculations.

EXAMPLE 1

Consider the following list of activities:

Activity	Preceding activity
A	–
B	–
C	B
D	A
E	A,C

One attempt at drawing a network of these activities could be that shown in Figure 10.7.

Note that in all networks, *one* node represents the start of the project, and one node the finish of the project. The diagram in Figure 10.7 is almost correct. However, the network does *not* illustrate the fact that E follows A and C, as given in the original table. In the illustration shown in Figure 10.7, the activity E only follows C.

In order to illustrate that activity E also follows A, a dummy activity (indicated by ----▸) is included as shown in the network in Figure 10.8.

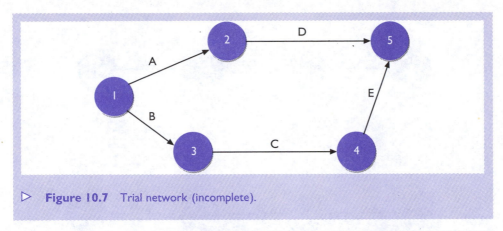

▷ **Figure 10.7**   Trial network (incomplete).

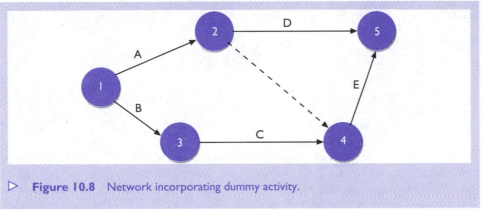

▷ **Figure 10.8**   Network incorporating dummy activity.

EXAMPLE 2

Consider the following list of four activities forming a small project:

Activity	Preceding activity
A	–
B	A
C	A
D	B,C

The network for this group of activities could be drawn as shown in Figure 10.9. Although this network illustrates the precedences accurately, it is not in an appropriate format. Activities B and C both start and finish in the same nodes, and this is not

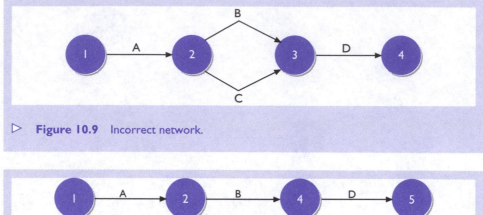

▷ **Figure 10.9**   Incorrect network.

▷ **Figure 10.10**   Use of dummy activity.

allowed in the construction of networks. This is because activities are often defined in terms of the beginning and end event numbers. Thus, activity A can be defined as $(1 \rightarrow 2)$. However, in the diagram shown in Figure 10.9, activities B and C cannot be distinguished in this way since they are both defined as $(2 \rightarrow 3)$. Thus, an alternative representation of these activities is required. To rectify this problem, a dummy activity can be inserted as shown in Figure 10.10. As can be seen, activities B and C start at the same node, but now finish in different nodes. Thus, B is defined as $(2 \rightarrow 4)$ and C as $(2 \rightarrow 3)$. Furthermore, the diagram still illustrates the correct precedences; in particular, the activities B and C follow A, and activity D follows both B and C.

EXAMPLE 3

It has been found that the list of activities defining the freeway construction project managed by Gilford & Partners has been incorrectly defined. The correct precedences are shown in the table on p. 441.

The network for this group of activities is illustrated in Figure 10.11. Two dummy activities are required in this network. Activities C and D commence at the same node in the diagram, and it is tempting to finish them both in the same node after which E and F commence. Two activities cannot start at the same node and finish at the same node, and therefore a dummy activity is included to avoid this. For the same reason, a dummy activity is included following activity F, so that E and F can run in parallel.

Primary activities	Precedences
A: Initial survey & site investigations	–
B: Design roadways	A
C: Planning applications & permission	B
D: Site preparation	B
E: Construction of link roads	C,D
F: Construction of main freeway	C,D
G: Erection of signs, lighting, etc.	E,F
H: Completion & hand over	G

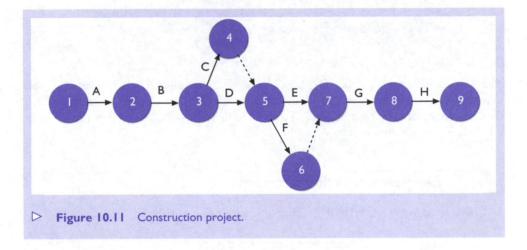

▷ **Figure 10.11**   Construction project.

EXAMPLE 4

A reconsideration of the electrical tasks involved in the QE2 refurbishment project has produced the following list of tasks and associated precedences.

Tasks	Preceding tasks
A: Remove existing fittings	–
B: Clear and prepare areas	–
C: Improve power source output	–
D: Rewire sections	A,B
E: Add additional power points	A
F: Add new fittings	D
G: Modify wiring configurations	A,B
H: Change lighting arrangements	E
I: Test lighting	C,G,H
J: Test complete electrical system	F,I

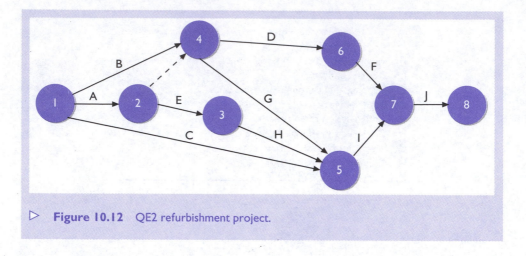

▷ **Figure 10.12**   QE2 refurbishment project.

The precedences for activities D and G have been modified. This results in a new network as shown in Figure 10.12 incorporating the use of a dummy activity. The dummy activity is required because D and G both follow the two activities A and B, whereas E only follows activity A.

10.5   Exercises: drawing networks

1.(E) Draw networks for each of the following groups of activities:

(i)

Activity	Preceding activity
A	–
B	–
C	A
D	B

(ii)

Activity	Preceding activity
A	–
B	A
C	A
D	B
E	D
F	C

(iii)

Activity	Preceding activity
A	–
B	A
C	–
D	C
E	A,D

(iv)

Activity	Preceding activity
A	–
B	A
C	A
D	A
E	B,D
F	E
G	C

2.(I)   A production consists of three stages, I, II and III.

Stage I involves the assembly of C and D.
Stage II involves the assembly of component B to components C and D.
Stage III involves adding component A to the stage II assembly.
Finally, the completed product is packed for shipping.

Using dummy activities if required, draw a network of the following activities:

Produce A
Produce B
Produce C
Produce D
Stage I
Stage II
Stage III
Packing

10.6   Time calculations

The total project duration is an important factor when managing projects involving many activities. The overall duration can be calculated from the network providing the duration of each activity in the project is known.

EXAMPLE 1

Consider a project consisting of six activities (A, B, C, D, E and F). The duration of each activity is given in the following table.

Activity	Preceding activity	Duration (weeks)
A	–	5
B	–	4
C	B	2
D	B	6
E	A,C	7
F	D	1

The network for this group of activities is shown in Figure 10.13. Note that the duration of each activity is indicated on the network. In addition, the nodes are numbered to ensure that for every activity, the start event number is less than the finish event number.

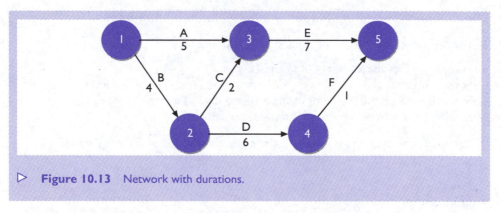

▷ **Figure 10.13** Network with durations.

In order to analyse the overall duration in this project it is necessary to consider the earliest and latest times at each of the nodes in the network. In order to accommodate these times in the diagram, each node in the network is split into three sections as indicated in Figure 10.14. Each node includes three values: the event number, the earliest event time, and the latest event time. The event numbering has already been discussed in earlier examples. The earliest and latest times at each event (i.e. at each node) are calculated as shown in the following sections.

The earliest event times are calculated as follows:

1. A zero is placed in the first event node in the project. This represents the time at the start of the project.
2. Subsequent earliest event times are calculated by adding an activity's duration onto the preceding earliest event time.

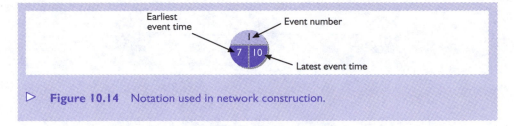

3. If two or more activities lead into an event, then the earliest time on each route is calculated and the largest value is used. Remember that a node indicates the finish of **all activities** leading into it. The earliest time at a particular node is determined by the longest route and therefore the largest value is used.

This process is called the 'forward pass' through the network. The earliest event times are indicated in the network shown in Figure 10.15. The earliest time in node 2 must be calculated before the value in node 3 can be obtained. Following this, nodes 3 and 4 must be calculated before the earliest time in node 5 is found. Node 5 indicates the end of the project.

At this stage, we see that the project can be completed at the earliest in 13 weeks. Now, the latest event times are calculated in each node as follows:

 (i) In the last node in the project, the latest event time equals the earliest event time. This seems logical since the latest finish time for the overall project should normally be the same as the earliest finish time. In other words, we would not want the project to last longer than is necessary. This value should be entered.
 (ii) Preceding latest event times are calculated by subtracting an activity's duration from the subsequent latest event time.
(iii) If two or more activities start from an event, then the latest time from each route is calculated, and the lowest value is used.

This process is referred to as the 'backward pass' and the completed network is illustrated in Figure 10.16.

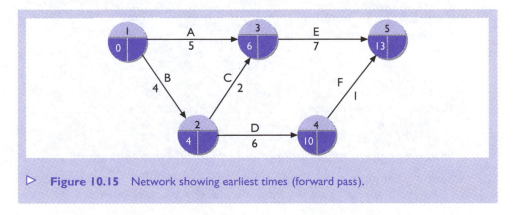

▷ **Figure 10.15** Network showing earliest times (forward pass).

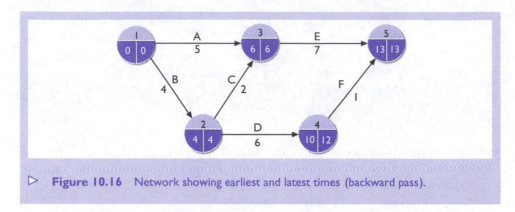

▷ **Figure 10.16**   Network showing earliest and latest times (backward pass).

Such a network is used in any further analysis of the group of activities. Note that in some circumstances, the earliest and latest times in the last node need not be equal. For instance, we may have a deadline for the project completion which is not equal to the earliest completion time. For instance, in the network shown in Figure 10.16, we may be asked to complete the project in 15 weeks. This value can then be used as the latest time in node 5, and all other latest times recalculated accordingly. However, without such additional information we will assume that all projects should be completed as early as possible, and thus the earliest and latest times in the last node should usually be the same.

EXAMPLE 2

The durations of the electricians' tasks in the QE2 refurbishment project have been estimated and are shown in the following table.

Tasks	Preceding tasks	Duration (days)
A: Remove existing fittings	–	2
B: Clear and prepare areas	–	1
C: Improve power source output	–	6
D: Rewire sections	A,B	5
E: Add additional power points	A	2
F: Add new fittings	D	3
G: Modify wiring configurations	A,B	3
H: Change lighting arrangements	E	2
I: Test lighting	C,G,H	1
J: Test complete electrical system	F,I	1

The network illustrating these activities is shown in Figure 10.17. Note that the dummy activities (with zero duration) are treated in the same way as any other activity when

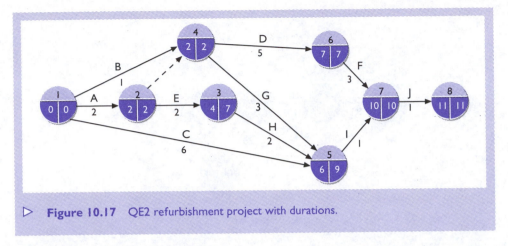

▷ **Figure 10.17** QE2 refurbishment project with durations.

determining the earliest and latest times at each node. The network shows that the electricians' part of the refurbishment can be completed in 11 days.

EXAMPLE 3

The table below shows an expanded list of the primary activities involved in the Gilford & Partners construction project introduced in the previous section. The table below incorporates extra activities and shows additional information on the duration of each activity in the project.

Primary activities	Precedences	Duration (weeks)
A: Initial survey & site investigations	–	6
B: Design roadways	A	8
C: Planning applications & permission	B	8
D: Environmental planning	B	7
E: Site preparation	B	10
F: Construction of link roads	C,E	30
G: Construction of main freeway	C,E	26
H: Erection of signs, lighting, etc.	F,D,G	7
I: Environmental landscaping	D,G	8
J: Completion & hand over	H,I	3

The network for this group of activities is illustrated in Figure 10.18. The earliest and latest event times are calculated in the same way as in the previous example. The project requires the use of two dummy activities as shown in the illustration.

Definition: *Each node in the network can be used to display the earliest and latest times for a given event.*

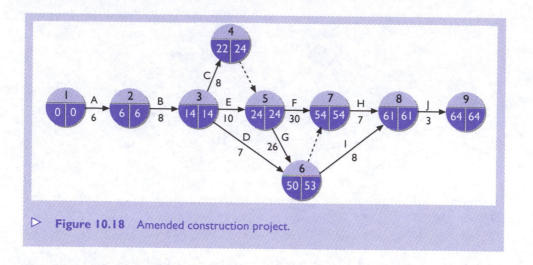

▷   **Figure 10.18**   Amended construction project.

10.7 Critical path analysis

Critical path analysis (CPA) involves identifying the route (or routes) through the network that specifically defines the overall duration. This can be achieved by calculation of earliest and latest event times as shown in the previous section. Activities on the critical path are referred to as **critical activities**. Such activities have no flexibility if the project is to finish on time. For instance, in order to finish the overall project on schedule, critical activities must start on time, and be completed in the time allowed.

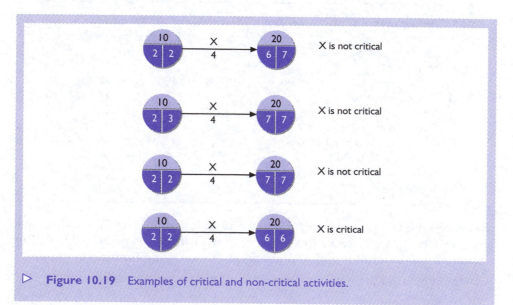

▷   **Figure 10.19**   Examples of critical and non-critical activities.

Any variation in the start time, duration, or finish time of a critical activity will invariably affect the overall project duration.

A critical activity can be identified in the network diagram as follows:

  (i) the earliest and latest start times are equal and
 (ii) the earliest and latest finish times are equal and
(iii) the difference between the start and finish times equals the activity's duration.

The diagrams shown in Figure 10.19 illustrate a range of circumstances in which an activity X may be critical or non-critical.

> **Definition:** *Critical path analysis (CPA) involves the use of networks in determining the 'critical' activities in the project. Critical activities have no flexibility, and must start and finish on time in order for the project to be completed on time.*

EXAMPLE 1

The diagram in Figure 10.20 illustrates one of the networks developed in the previous section. The critical activities are indicated on this diagram using the following notation:

Critical activity   ⟶‖⟶
Non-critical activity   ⟶

This network shows that the overall project duration is 13 weeks, and the critical path is B→C→E.

All other activities are not critical. For instance, activity A is not critical since it can start on day 0 and finish on day 6, giving a total of six days to perform an activity that only requires five days.

Overall, activities A, D and F are not critical. This implies that if the duration of any of these activities were reduced, this would not affect the total project duration. However, if the duration of any of the critical activities (B, C or E) changed, then the overall project duration would be affected.

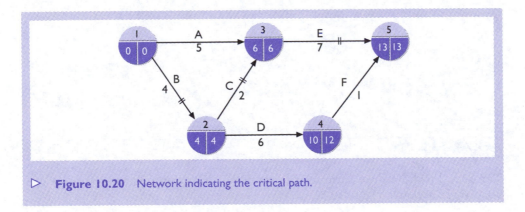

▷ **Figure 10.20** Network indicating the critical path.

| 10.8 | **Critical path analysis examples** |

EXAMPLE 1

Estimate the overall project duration and the critical path for the group of activities listed below.

Activity	Preceding activity	Duration (days)
A	–	5
B	A,C	4
C	–	3
D	C	3
E	B,D	2

Figure 10.21 illustrates the network for this group of activities. Note that a dummy activity is required when drawing this network in order to illustrate activity B following A and C, whilst activity D only follows C.

It should be noted that dummy activities need to be considered when evaluating the earliest and latest times in each node in the network. A dummy activity has zero duration.

The critical path for this group of activities is A, B and E. The other activities (C and D) are not critical. The overall project duration is found to be 11 days.

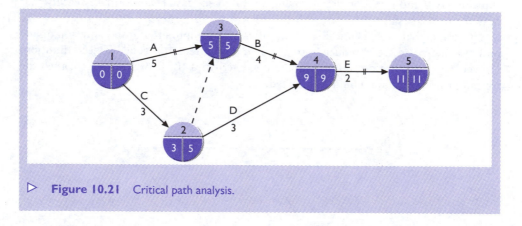

▷ **Figure 10.21** Critical path analysis.

EXAMPLE 2

The critical path for the electricians' project in the QE2 refurbishment (see also Figure 10.17) is indicated in Figure 10.22.

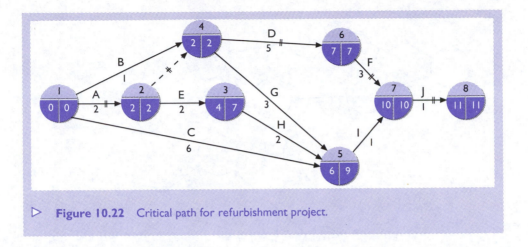

▷ **Figure 10.22**   *Critical path for refurbishment project.*

EXAMPLE 3

Similarly, the construction project network developed in the previous section has a critical path as illustrated in Figure 10.23.

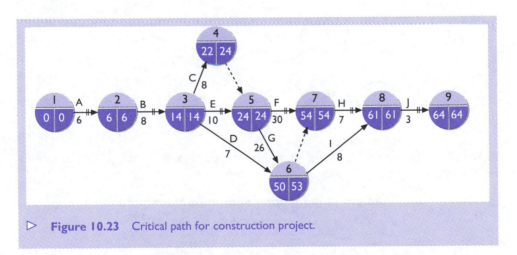

▷ **Figure 10.23**   *Critical path for construction project.*

10.9   Exercises: critical path analysis

1.(E)   Find the overall project durations and identify the critical paths for each of the following networks:

(i)

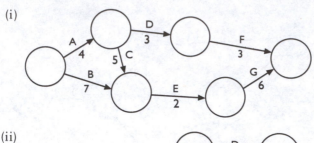

(ii)

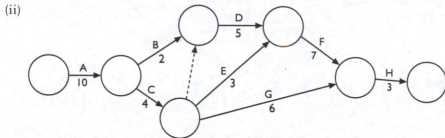

(iii)

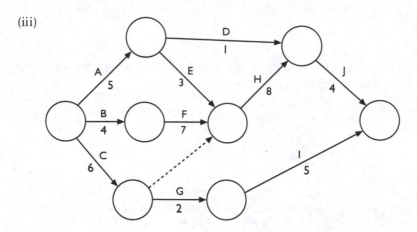

2.(I) Draw the networks, determine the critical paths and overall project durations for each group of activities given below:

(i)

Activity	Preceding activity	Duration
A	–	3
B	A	2
C	–	7
D	–	5
E	D	6

(ii)

Activity	Preceding activity	Duration
A	–	5
B	A	2
C	A	4
D	A	1
E	B	7
F	C	3
G	D	4
H	F,G	6

(iii)

Activity	Preceding activity	Duration
A	–	10
B	–	5
C	A	2
D	C	3
E	B	1
F	A,E	8
G	B	6

3.(I) (i) Estimate the overall project duration and identify the critical path for the factory expansion project summarised below:

Activity	Preceding activity	Duration (months)
A: Plan new site	–	8
B: Move to temporary premises	A	3
C: Build new plant	A	15
D: Train staff	B	10
E: Install machinery	C	4
F: Move production to new site	D,E	3

(ii) If the training of staff takes 20 months, would this change the overall project time? With this new duration for activity D, recalculate the earliest and latest times at each node in order to clarify this new situation.

| 10.10 | **Floats: definitions** |

A 'float' gives the amount of flexibility or spare time associated with each activity in the network. Critical activities have no flexibility and therefore have zero float. There are three different types of float that can be calculated:

Total float: The amount of time an activity can be delayed without affecting the overall project time.

This can be calculated for each activity in the network using the following formula:

Total float = Latest finish time – Earliest start time – Duration

Free float: The amount of time an activity can be delayed without affecting the overall project time and without affecting the start times of subsequent activities.

The free float can be calculated as follows:

Free float = Earliest start time of next activity – Earliest start time – Duration

Note: The earliest start time of next activity is normally equal to the earliest finish time of the current activity unless it is followed by a dummy activity.

Independent float: The amount of time an activity can be delayed without affecting the overall project time, and without affecting the start times of subsequent activities or the finish times of preceding activities.

The independent float can be calculated as follows:

Independent float = Earliest start time of next activity – Latest start time – Duration

These floats can be utilised in the analysis of flexibility in specific activities and may be useful in the reorganisation of activities in the project if and when required. Such information can be used to determine which activities can be rescheduled in order to create minimum disruption to the remaining activities and limit any increase in the overall project duration.

Definition: *The float shows the amount of flexibility for a given activity assuming that the project must finish at the earliest time possible. The total, free and independent floats indicate the amount of flexibility for a given activity based on their effect on previous and subsequent activities.*

10.11   Calculation of floats

The floats described in the previous section may need to be calculated for all activities in the network. However, to demonstrate the calculation of the float formulae, one specific activity will be illustrated.

EXAMPLE 1

Consider the activity X illustrated in Figure 10.24, where the duration is given in days. Note that this activity is part of a network and that other activities may start and finish at the two nodes illustrated. The diagram provides the following information on the activity X:

Duration = 5 days
Earliest start time = day 20   Latest start time = day 30
Earliest start time of
next activity (activity Y) = day 40   Latest finish time = day 50

The various floats use these values as follows:

(i) Total float = Latest finish time – Earliest start time – Duration

$$= 50 - 20 - 5$$

$$= 25 \text{ days}$$

This means that activity X can be delayed by up to 25 days without affecting the overall project time. (However, such a delay may affect the timing of preceding or subsequent activities.)

(ii) Free float = Earliest start of next activity – Earliest start time – Duration

$$= 40 - 20 - 5$$

$$= 15 \text{ days}$$

Activity X can be delayed by up to 15 days without affecting any subsequent activity and without affecting the overall project time.

(iii) Independent float = Earliest start of next activity – Latest start time – Duration

$$= 40 - 30 - 5$$

$$= 5 \text{ days}$$

Activity X can be delayed by up to 5 days without affecting preceding or subsequent activities, and without affecting the overall project time.

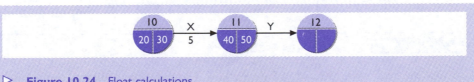

▷ **Figure 10.24** Float calculations.

EXAMPLE 2

Consider the diagram in Figure 10.25 showing part of a network. The diagram provides the following details relating to the activity S:

Duration = 4
Earliest start time = 5
Earliest start time of next activity = 13 (Note that the next real activity is U)
Latest start time = 12
Latest finish time = 20

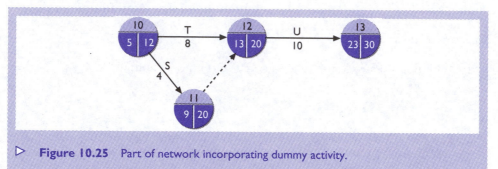

▷ **Figure 10.25**   Part of network incorporating dummy activity.

Thus, the floats are calculated as follows:

 (i) Total float = Latest finish time – Earliest start time – Duration
            = 20 – 5 – 4
            = 11

(ii) Free float = Earliest start of next activity – Earliest start time = Duration
            = 13 – 5 – 4
            = 4

(iii) Independent float = Earliest start of next activity – Latest start time – Duration
                = 13 – 12 – 4
                = –3

A negative value in any of these calculations indicates a zero float. Therefore, the independent float for activity S is zero.

10.12   Floats in a network: examples

EXAMPLE 1

Consider the network illustrated in Figure 10.26. The durations indicated are in weeks and the critical activities have been indicated. The floats for these activities are

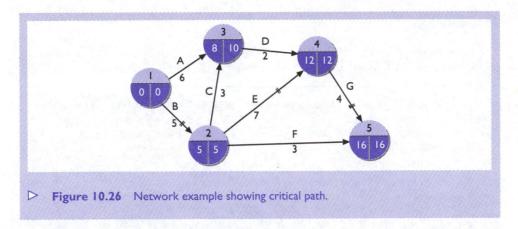

▷ **Figure 10.26**   Network example showing critical path.

calculated in the table below. The first six columns in this table are obtained directly from the network diagram. The float times are calculated using the methods outlined in the previous example.

Activity	Duration (weeks) ①	Earliest start ②	Latest start ③	Earliest finish ④	Latest finish ⑤	Total float ⑤ – ② – ①	Free float ④ – ② – ①	Independent float ④ – ③ – ①
A	6	0	0	8	10	4	2	2
B	5	0	0	5	5	0	0	0
C	3	5	5	8	10	2	0	0
D	2	8	10	12	12	2	2	0
E	7	5	5	12	12	0	0	0
F	3	5	5	16	16	8	8	8
G	4	12	12	16	16	0	0	0

Note: The earliest finish time given in column ④ is equivalent to the earliest start of the subsequent activity.

Consider activity A. This can be delayed by up to 4 weeks (as indicated on the total float) without affecting the overall project time. However, activity A can only be delayed by up to 2 weeks (indicated by the free float) without affecting the start time of subsequent activities. Activity C has a total float of 2 weeks, with zero free and independent floats. Thus, although the duration of activity C can be increased by up to 2 weeks without affecting the overall project duration, such a change will affect the timings for some of the preceding and subsequent activities. Conversely, in activity F, all the float times are equal (8 weeks), showing that this activity can be extended by up to 8 weeks without affecting the timings of other activities in addition to the overall project duration.

Notice that all the floats for the critical activities (B, E and G) are zero, indicating that any increase in the duration of these activities will affect the duration of the overall project.

EXAMPLE 2

The table below shows the calculation of floats for the activities in the construction project managed by Gilford & Partners illustrated in the previous sections.

Activity	Duration (weeks) ①	Earliest start ②	Latest start ③	Earliest finish ④	Latest finish ⑤	Total float ⑤ − ② − ①	Free float ④ − ② − ①	Independent float ④ − ③ − ①
A	6	0	0	6	6	0	0	0
B	8	6	6	14	14	0	0	0
C	8	14	14	24**	24	2	2	2
D	7	14	14	50	53	32	29	29
E	10	14	14	24	24	0	0	0
F	30	24	24	54	54	0	0	0
G	26	24	24	50**	53	3	0	0
H	7	54	54	61	61	0	0	0
I	8	50	53	61	61	3	3	0
J	3	61	61	64	64	0	0	0

Note: The Earliest finish values indicated by ** in column ④ of this table have been obtained by reference to the earliest start of the subsequent activities. For example, the network diagram illustrates that the earliest finish for activity C is at the 22nd day. However, this activity is followed by a dummy activity which need not be considered in this process. Following the dummy activity, the earliest start of subsequent activity (both E and F) is by the 24th day. Similarly, for activity G the earliest start of a subsequent activity (ignoring dummies) is in the 50th day.

Consider activity D in this table. Clearly, there is significant flexibility in when this activity can be carried out. The total float of 32 indicates that the activity can be delayed by up to 32 weeks, or the duration extended by this period and still the overall project can be completed on time. However, such a change in D will have some impact on other activities. This is shown by the free and independent floats both equalling 29. The activity D can be extended by up to 29 weeks without affecting any of the start or finish times of other activities in the project.

10.13   Exercises: floats

1.(E) Calculate the total, free and independent floats for each of the activities in the network illustrated below. (Duration given in days.)

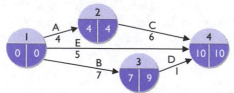

2.(I)   (i)   Draw a network of the following group of activities:

Activity	Duration (days)	Preceding activities
A	10	–
B	10	–
C	15	–
D	5	B
E	20	A
F	15	D,E
G	20	B

(ii)   Calculate the total, free and independent floats for each of these activities.
(iii) Owing to unplanned changes, activity D may take up to 10 days to complete. Comment on this with reference to the floats you have calculated for this activity.

10.14   Gantt charts

A Gantt chart provides a different way of illustrating a group of activities. It illustrates the start and finish times of each activity, and provides an easy method of seeing which activities should be taking place at any point in time. The Gantt chart is particularly useful in project management and resource scheduling.

Consider the network shown in Figure 10.27. (This example was introduced in Section 10.12.)

A Gantt chart from this network is drawn in the following way:

1. Draw a horizontal scale representing the duration starting at 0 and increasing up to the overall project duration (16 weeks in this example).
2. Illustrate all the critical activities along one line.

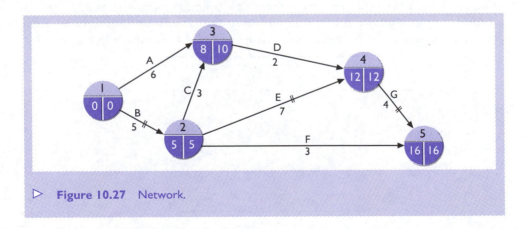

▷   **Figure 10.27**   Network.

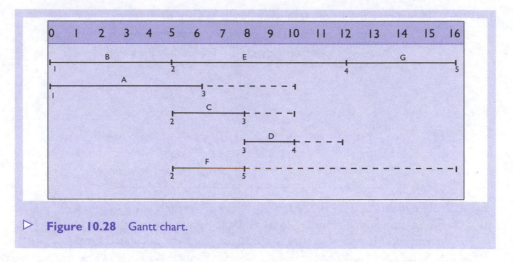

▷ **Figure 10.28** Gantt chart.

3. Illustrate other activities on separate lines using the earliest start time and duration for each activity and include an indication of the total floats (i.e. up to the latest finish time).
4. Indicate the nodes (event) numbers at the beginning and end of each activity.

The Gantt chart for the above example is illustrated in Figure 10.28. Note that the dotted lines | ------- | in the Gantt chart indicate the total float for each activity.

| 10.15 | **Resource scheduling** |

The Gantt chart enables a user to determine which activities are taking place in any specific period. This will help a manager to determine the resources required at specific points during the project. The resources can be illustrated using a resource histogram. Such a diagram may also enable the manager to consider alternative allocations of resources if *and when* problems arise with the programmed schedule.

For example, consider the activities illustrated in the Gantt chart above. Each activity requires a specific number of personnel in order to complete in the specified

Activity	Workforce required
A	2
B	1
C	3
D	2
E	2
F	3
G	1

time. The workforce requirement (e.g. number of employees required to complete each activity) is shown in the table on p. 460. It is assumed in this example that the workforce is a homogeneous group, and that the same expertise and skills are required for all activities in the project.

From the Gantt chart we can see which activities are taking place in each week. For instance, in weeks 1 to 5, activities A and B are in progress. In week 6, activities A, C, E and F are in progress. In weeks 7 and 8, activities C, E and F are in progress, and so on.

These activities can be related to resource requirements (e.g. workforce needed). For instance, the table shows that activity A requires 2 personnel, B requires 1 person, and so in weeks 1 to 5 (when both A and B are in progress) we require a workforce of 3 to complete the activities. Similarly, in week 6, when A, C, E and F are in progress, a maximum workforce of 10 is required.

Such an analysis of requirements can be extended to each week in the project. The workforce requirements can then be graphed as shown in Figure 10.29. We see that during week 6, we have a maximum workforce requirement of 10. In certain circumstances such a requirement may not be attainable. We could try to reduce this requirement by rescheduling the activities with reference to the Gantt chart. For example, activity F can be completed at any time up to week 16. If activity F is started at week 12 instead of week 5 then we have the amended workforce requirement

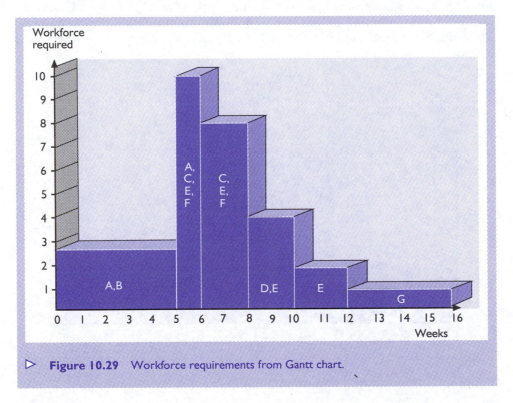

▷ **Figure 10.29** Workforce requirements from Gantt chart.

illustrated in Figure 10.30. This configuration now shows a maximum workforce requirement of 7. Similarly, changes in the start times of other activities may reduce the maximum requirement further. For instance, with a delay of 1 week in the start of activities C and D the maximum workforce requirement can be further reduced.

The basic approach here for the manager is to attempt to 'even out' the resource requirement (e.g. workforce) over the duration of the project. Consequently, we initially look at the 'peaks' in the requirements and try to reduce them by moving one or more activities. Critical activities cannot be moved without affecting the overall project duration. The Gantt chart shows how much each activity can be moved, by illustrating the total floats. However, initial reference to the free or independent floats may help in deciding which activities to reschedule. For instance, utilising the independent float for a given activity would be the first choice, since this not only preserves the overall project duration but also has no effect on other prior or subsequent activities.

It should not be assumed that the process of levelling the resources over the lifetime of the project is the only, or even the best, way of proceeding. For example, this may not be appropriate in the workforce scheduling shown in this section, since there is no reference to special skills that may be required to complete specific activities. For instance, training staff released from one activity may be of little use in road surfacing or brick laying! Furthermore, it should be noted that it is better that some resources are not evened out. For instance, with reference to financial resources, it could be that in order to improve cash flow, a company may prefer to make payments later in the project, rather than evenly stage the payments throughout the project.

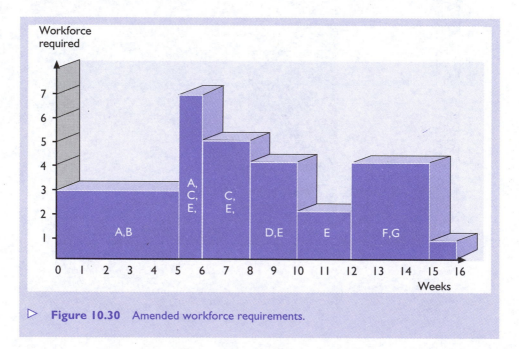

▷   **Figure 10.30**   Amended workforce requirements.

| 10.16 | **Exercises: Gantt charts and resources** |

1.(E) Draw a network and Gantt chart for the following groups of activities:

(i)

Activity	Preceding activity	Duration (days)
A	–	2
B	–	4
C	B	5
D	A,C	3
E	B	4

(ii)

Activity	Preceding activity	Duration (weeks)
A	–	4
B	A	3
C	B	1
D	A	6
E	A	2
F	C,D,E	5
G	E	7

(iii)

Activity	Preceding activity	Duration (weeks)
A	–	4
B	A	5
C	B	3
D	A	7
E	C	2
F	C	6
G	D,E	2

2.(I) (a) Draw a network of the following activities:

Activity	Preceding activity	Duration (days)
A	–	3
B	–	5
C	A	4
D	B	6
E	C,D	9
F	B	8
G	B	3
H	G	2

(b) Find the critical path and overall project duration.
(c) Draw a Gantt chart of these activities.
(d) Assuming that each activity requires one employee, draw a graph to represent the number of employees required during the period of the project.

3.(I)   The following table gives a list of activities involved in a project. The table includes the number of employees required to complete each activity in the time specified.

Activity	Preceding activity	Duration (weeks)	No. of employees
A	–	10	2
B	–	4	3
C	A	3	1
D	A	12	4
E	B	8	2
F	B	10	3
G	D,E	7	1
H	C	6	2
I	D,E	15	2
J	F,G	6	1

(a) Draw a network of these activities indicating the critical path and overall project duration.
(b) Draw a Gantt chart of these activities and produce a diagram of the workforce requirements during the lifetime of the project.
(c) What is the maximum workforce requirement? Can this requirement be reduced by changing the start time of any of the activities? If so, determine the minimum workforce required in order to complete the project on time.

10.17   Crash costs

In this section we will consider the possibility of reducing the duration of a project. In practice, this can sometimes be achieved by using extra resources (e.g. manpower/overtime) and will consequently involve additional costs. Such costs are called **crash costs**, and the process of reducing the duration is referred to as **crashing**.

Consider the following example:
The table on p. 465 gives the normal durations and costs together with crash durations and costs for each activity in a project.

(Note that the costs given are total costs for each activity, not *costs per week.)*

First, we can draw a network of this group of activities, assuming the normal durations as shown below. The network is illustrated in Figure 10.31, with the earliest and latest event times displayed.

Activity	Preceding activity	Duration (weeks)		Costs (£100s)	
		Normal	Crash	Normal	Crash
A	–	10	8	12	17
B	–	6	5	10	11
C	A	4	4	6	6
D	A	14	10	11	21
E	A	8	6	20	23
F	B,C	3	2	6	9
G	E,F	12	9	14	20

From the network we see that:

(i) The overall project duration is 30 weeks.
(ii) The critical path is A, E, G.

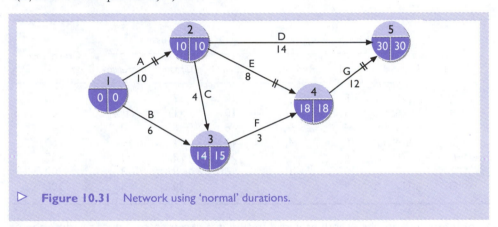

▷ **Figure 10.31**   Network using 'normal' durations.

The Gantt chart for this project is displayed in Figure 10.32.

Now consider the problem of reducing the duration (crashing) of this project. For instance, if we wish to complete the project in 28 weeks, how can we do this for a minimum extra cost?

Consider the cost of crashing each of these activities. For example, activity A can be crashed from 10 weeks (at a normal cost of £1200) down to 8 weeks' duration (at a cost of £1700). So, a two-week reduction involves an additional cost of £500. Therefore, a simplistic view of this situation would imply that a one-week reduction in the duration of activity A costs £250. In practice the costs of crashing may not be in direct proportion to the overall reduction period.

The first table on p. 466 shows the costs of crashing each of the activities. The weekly crash cost for each activity (given in the last column) is calculated by dividing the increase in cost by the number of weeks crashed.

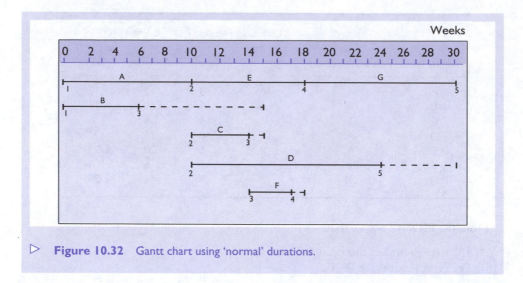

▷ **Figure 10.32**   Gantt chart using 'normal' durations.

	Duration (weeks)			Cost (00s)			
Activity	Normal	Crash	Reduction	Normal	Crash	Increase	Crash cost per week (£)
A	10	8	2	12	17	5	250
B	6	5	1	10	11	1	100
C	4	4	0	6	6	0	–
D	14	10	4	11	21	10	250
E	8	6	2	20	23	3	150
F	3	2	1	6	9	3	300
G	12	9	3	14	20	6	200

In order to decrease the overall project duration it is necessary to reduce the duration of one or more critical activities. A reduction in the duration of the non-critical activities will not have an effect on the overall project duration.

The critical activities are:

Activity	Crash cost per week (£)
E	150
G	200
A	250

The table shows the critical activities listed in ascending order of crash costs. From the table it can be seen that it is cheaper to reduce the duration of activity E than the other critical activities. Therefore, we would decide to reduce the duration of activity E down to 7 weeks (at an extra cost of £150).

A new network can be drawn using the new reduced duration for activity E as shown in Figure 10.33. Figure 10.33 shows that the project duration has been reduced to 29 weeks.

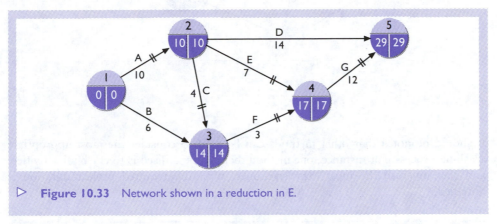

▷   **Figure 10.33**   Network shown in a reduction in E.

Notice that the activities C and F also become critical. This means that in order to reduce the project duration by another week, a reduction in activity E will not be enough. The path A→C→F→G will still take 29 weeks. Therefore it would be necessary to reduce one of the following activities:

   (i)   activity A (crash cost £250)
  (ii)   activity G (crash cost £200)
 (iii)   activities E and F (crash cost £150 + £300 = £450).

From these options it can be seen that the cheapest alternative is to reduce activity G. Therefore, in order to reduce the overall project duration we would reduce the duration of activity G down to 11 weeks (at an extra cost of £200).

A new network can be drawn using this new duration as shown in Figure 10.34. The project duration has now been reduced to 28 weeks.

Notice that crashing must be performed one week at a time, since reducing one activity's duration may result in others becoming critical. Consequently after each change a careful investigation of the new network is advisable.

To summarise the process of crashing a project down to an overall target duration:

   (i)   Draw a network of the activities and locate the critical path.
  (ii)   Consider the costs of reducing the duration of each critical activity. Find the cheapest activity to crash.
 (iii)   Reduce the duration of the cheapest activity.
 (iv)   Redraw the network and locate the critical path.
  (v)   Repeat (ii) to (iv) above until the required target duration is obtained or until no further reductions are possible.

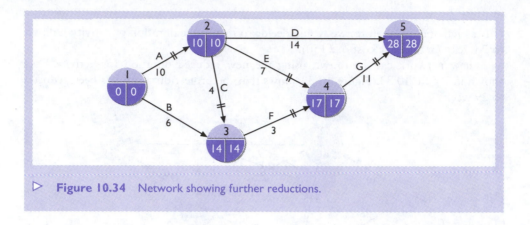

▷   **Figure 10.34**   Network showing further reductions.

It should be noted that other methods can be used to consider the most appropriate crashing process. For instance, one method that can be utilised is to crash all activities, and then uncrash the most expensive ones, until the required project duration is obtained.

10.18   Exercises: crashing

1.(I)   The table below shows a group of activities together with normal and crash times, and normal and crash costs.

Activity	Preceding activity	Duration (weeks)		Cost (£000s)	
		Normal	Crash	Normal	Crash
A	–	4	3	5	8
B	–	2	2	3	–
C	A	3	2	4	6
D	–	4	2	6	11
E	A	5	3	8	10
F	B,C	1	1	2	–
G	D	2	1	3	6

(i)   Draw a network based on these activities and determine the overall project duration.

(ii)   You wish to reduce the duration of the project by two weeks. How will you do this, and how much extra will it cost?

(iii)   Investigate further reductions in the overall project duration. What is the minimum achievable project duration based on this information? How much would such a reduction cost?

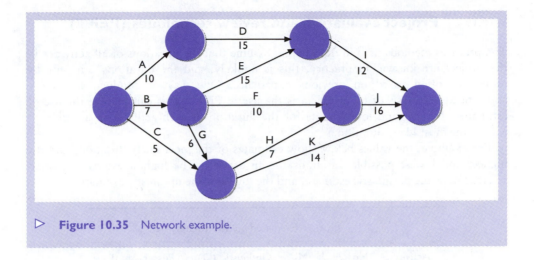

▷ **Figure 10.35** Network example.

2.(D) The network given in Figure 10.35 shows a group of activities with durations given in weeks. The maximum number of weeks each activity can be crashed together with the cost of crashing per week is given in the following table:

Activity	Maximum crash time (in weeks)	Crash cost per week (£)
A	2	250
B	3	150
C	1	300
D	4	400
E	5	120
F	2	250
G	1	300
H	0	–
I	3	175
J	4	180
K	5	240

(i) Find the critical path and overall duration of this project.
(ii) Determine the most cost-effective method of reducing the duration of this project by one week.
(iii) Furthermore, try to reduce the duration of the project by a further week. How much extra will this cost?
(iv) Without evaluating the cost, what is the minimum duration of the project?

| 10.19 | **Project evaluation and review techniques (PERT)** |

The previous methods used in this chapter assume that the durations of all activities in the project are known. In practice, this is unlikely, and the durations can only be estimated, often based on previous experience. One way of conducting a more sophisticated analysis of the problem is the use of PERT. This can involve the use of estimates of upper and lower limits for the duration of each activity, in addition to stating the most likely duration.

For example, the values below show estimates of the most likely duration, and the highest and lowest possible durations for an activity. The highest estimate is often referred to as the pessimistic estimate, and the lowest is the optimistic estimate.

	Estimated duration (days)		
Activity	Most likely (M)	Optimistic (O)	Pessimistic (P)
A	19	16	28

The expected (mean) duration of this activity can be estimated by a 'weighted' average of the three estimates as follows:

$$\text{Expected duration} = \frac{\text{Optimistic} + 4 \times (\text{Most likely}) + \text{Pessimistic}}{6}$$

$$= \frac{16 + 4 \times 19 + 28}{6}$$

$$= \frac{16 + 76 + 28}{6}$$

$$= \frac{120}{6}$$

$$= 20$$

Therefore, the expected duration of this activity is 20 days. This value would be used in the network analysis.

Furthermore, it is useful to estimate a measure of spread (the standard deviation) in order to analyse the potential spread in the duration of the full project. The normal distribution techniques described in Chapter 3 provide a method of estimating the standard deviation (σ) based on the range.

The 99.8% confidence limits are found to be approximately $\mu \pm 3\sigma$ as indicated in the diagram in Figure 10.36. Thus three standard deviations either side of the mean will virtually incorporate all of the values in the distribution.

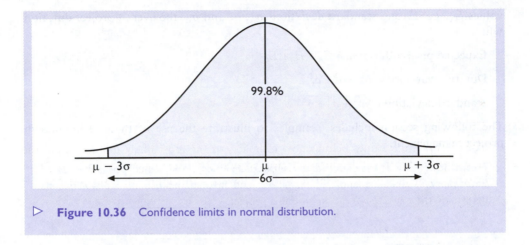

Therefore, the difference between the maximum and minimum values in this distribution is approximately 6 standard deviations. So a reasonable estimate of the standard deviation is determined as follows:

$$\sigma = \frac{\text{Range}}{6}$$

Thus, $$\sigma = \frac{\text{Maximum value} - \text{Minimum value}}{6}$$

This translates to the estimate of the standard deviation being found by

$$\sigma = \frac{\text{Pessimistic value} - \text{Optimistic value}}{6}$$

In the above example, this means that the standard deviation for activity A (denoted by σ_A) is:

$$\sigma_A = \frac{28 - 16}{6} = \frac{12}{6}$$

$\sigma_A = 2$ days

So, activity A has an expected duration of 20 days, with a standard deviation of 2 days. This type of analysis can be performed on each activity in the project.

The expected time and standard deviation of the overall project duration can be obtained by combining the expected values and standard deviations of all the critical activities. For instance, if activities A, B, C are critical with the expected values E_A, E_B, E_C and standard deviations σ_A, σ_B and σ_C, the overall project duration will have:

Expected project duration $= E_A + E_B + E_C$

Duration variance $= \sigma_A^2 + \sigma_B^2 + \sigma_C^2$

Standard deviation $= \sqrt{\sigma_A^2 + \sigma_B^2 + \sigma_C^2}$

The following section includes examples to illustrate the use of these techniques in project management.

Definition: Project evaluation and review techniques (PERT) incorporates ideas of uncertainty in the estimation of timescales and involve the use of probabilities to determine the expected durations within a project.

| 10.20 | **PERT examples** |

| **EXAMPLE 1** |

Consider the following group of activities:

Activity	Preceding activity	Estimates of duration (days)		
		Most likely	Optimistic	Pessimistic
A	–	9	8	16
B	A	8	7	9
C	–	4	3	5
D	C	5	5	5
E	C	8	7	15
F	E	3	2	4

The expected durations for these activities are calculated as follows:

Activity A: Expected duration $= \dfrac{8 + 4 \times 9 + 16}{6}$

$$= \frac{60}{6} \qquad = 10 \text{ days}$$

Activity B: Expected duration $= \dfrac{7 + 4 \times 8 + 9}{6} = 8 \text{ days}$

Activity C: Expected duration $= \dfrac{3 + 4 \times 4 + 5}{6} = 4 \text{ days}$

Activity D: Expected duration $= \dfrac{5 + 4 \times 5 + 5}{6}$ = 5 days

Activity E: Expected duration $= \dfrac{7 + 4 \times 8 + 15}{6}$ = 9 days

Activity F: Expected duration $= \dfrac{2 + 4 \times 3 + 4}{6}$ = 3 days

The network for these activities using the expected durations is shown in Figure 10.37. The critical activities as illustrated in the network are A and B.

In activity A: Expected duration $= 10$ days

$$\text{Standard deviation} = \dfrac{P - O}{6} = \dfrac{16 - 8}{6} = \dfrac{8}{6} = 1.33 \text{ days}$$

In activity B: Expected duration $= 8$ days

$$\text{Standard deviation} = \dfrac{9 - 7}{6} = 0.33 \text{ days}$$

The expected project duration $= 10 + 8 = 18$ days

with standard deviation $= \sqrt{\sigma_A^2 + \sigma_B^2}$

$$= \sqrt{1.33^2 + 0.33^2}$$

$$= \sqrt{1.778 + 0.11}$$

$$= \sqrt{1.88}$$

$$\sigma = 1.37 \text{ days}$$

These values can be used in any further analysis of the project. For example, to determine the probability of the project lasting longer than 20 days. This can be

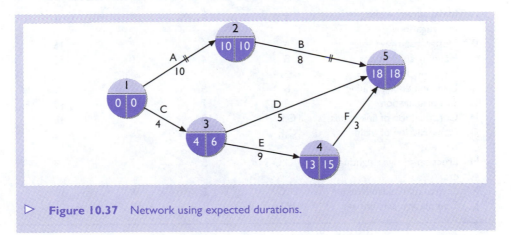

△   **Figure 10.37**   Network using expected durations.

considered, assuming that the project duration is normally distributed as follows:

Project duration mean = 18 days
Project duration standard deviation = 1.37 days

The distribution for the overall project duration is illustrated in Figure 10.38.

Probability that duration is over 20 days = area shaded.

Now, to estimate this area we calculate the standardised variate

$$z = \frac{20 - 18}{1.37}$$

$$= 1.46$$

Using normal tables, the area shaded = 0.072

Therefore this indicates that there is a 7.2% chance of the project lasting longer than 20 days. Further analysis could be carried out with regard to the possible variations in the overall project time.

EXAMPLE 2

Consider the construction project managed by Gilford & Partners introduced earlier in this chapter. Previously, we have considered specific estimates for the duration of each activity in this project. Now, consider a more realistic situation in which the duration of the activities have been estimated within a range of values. The estimates of the durations are given in the following table:

Primary activities	Precedences	Estimated duration (weeks)		
		Optimistic	Most likely	Pessimistic
A: Initial survey & site investigations	–	5	6	7
B: Design roadways	A	5	7	15
C: Planning applications & permission	B	4	8	12
D: Environmental planning	B	5	7	9
E: Site preparation	B	7	10	13
F: Construction of link roads	C,E	10	33	38
G: Construction of main freeway	C,E	20	26	32
H: Erection of signs, lighting, etc.	F,D,G	5	7	9
I: Environmental landscaping	D,G	5	8	11
J: Completion & handover	H,I	3	3	3

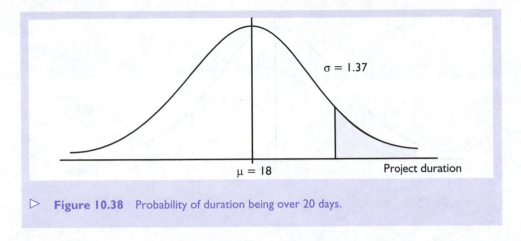

$\sigma = 1.37$

$\mu = 18$ Project duration

▷ **Figure 10.38**   Probability of duration being over 20 days.

These estimates enable us to estimate the expected duration for each activity using the formula:

$$\text{Expected duration} = \frac{O + 4M + P}{6}$$

Thus, the expected duration for each activity in this construction project is:

Activity:	A	B	C	D	E	F	G	H	I	J
Expected duration (weeks):	6	8	8	7	10	30	26	7	8	3

The critical path for this network is A, B, E, F, H, J (as shown in Figure 10.23).

The standard deviation for the critical activity durations can be obtained using the formula:

$$\text{Standard deviation} = \frac{P - O}{6}$$

Thus the critical activities have standard deviations:

Activity:	A	B	E	F	H	J
Stand. devn.:	0.33	1.67	1	4.67	0.67	0

Using these values enables us to determine the standard deviation for the overall project duration:

$$\text{Project duration s.d.} = \sqrt{0.33^2 + 1.67^2 + 1^2 + 4.67^2 + 0.67^2}$$
$$= 5.1 \text{ weeks}$$

The Project Manager at Gilford & Partners will be able to use this information to determine the likelihood of completing the project within a given period of time. This type of information could be vital in determining whether the contract offered is acceptable in terms of completion dates and potential penalties for late completion.

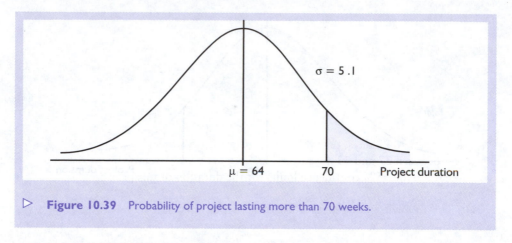

$\sigma = 5.1$

$\mu = 64$ 70   Project duration

▷ **Figure 10.39** Probability of project lasting more than 70 weeks.

For example, Gilford & Partners have been offered a contract which includes a penalty clause stating that if the project is not completed within 70 weeks then a penalty of £100 000 will be incurred, and each additional week over this target will involve a further £30 000 penalty. The chances of incurring a penalty given this situation can be determined by using the normal distribution as follows:

The project duration has an expected value = 64 weeks
with a standard deviation = 5.1 weeks

The diagram in Figure 10.39 illustrates the normally distributed project durations and shows the shaded area indicating the probability of the project lasting for longer than 70 weeks (when a penalty will be incurred).

Using normal tables this probability is found to be approximately 0.12. Thus, the Gilford & Partners company has a 12% chance of incurring a penalty under the contract offered. This may deter the company from proceeding and would almost certainly lead to further negotiations in order to review the project duration and reduce the penalties imposed.

10.21   Exercises: PERT

1.(I)   Assume that the overall duration of a given project is defined by the following three activities, G, F and M. The table below gives the estimates of the duration of each of these critical activities:

Activity	Estimated duration (in weeks)		
	Likely	Optimistic	Pessimistic
G	10	5	21
F	6	4	8
M	14	6	16

(i) Calculate the expected duration for each activity and thus obtain an estimate of the expected project duration.

(ii) Use the optimistic and pessimistic estimates of the activities' duration in order to determine the standard deviation for each critical activity. Use these values to obtain an estimate of the standard deviation of the overall project duration.

(iii) Assuming a normal distribution, estimate the probability that the project duration is:
   (a) more than 34 days,
   (b) less than 28 days, or
   (c) between 27 and 33 days.

(iv) What are the 95% confidence limits for the duration of this project?

2.(D) The following table gives a list of activities and estimates of the duration for each activity in terms of the most likely, most pessimistic (highest) and most optimistic (lowest) estimates.

Activity	Preceding activity	Estimate of duration (weeks)		
		Most likely	Pessimistic	Optimistic
A	–	19	29	15
B	A	10	12	8
C	–	16	18	8
D	–	8	9	7
E	D	4	4	4
F	A	32	36	16
G	B,C,E	12	14	10
H	D	21	22	14
I	F,G	43	48	20

(i) Obtain estimates of the expected duration of these activities.

(ii) Use these expected values in drawing a network of this group of activities.

(iii) Find the expected duration of the overall project and the standard deviation of this duration.

(iv) Assuming a normal distribution, estimate the probability of the project lasting:
   (a) longer than 95 days,
   (b) less than 87 days,
   (c) between 92 and 96 days.

10.22	**Networks: alternative method – activity on node**

In the previous sections in this chapter, we have used one particular method for drawing networks. This has involved illustrating activities by arrows, and start and finish events by nodes. An alternative method is to illustrate activities on the nodes. The arrows will then simply illustrate the precedences between activities. One advantage of this method is that it is unnecessary to incorporate dummy activities in the network. This approach is often adopted in computer packages on project management. Such packages will be explored in a later section in this chapter.

EXAMPLE 1

Consider the following group of activities:

Activity	Preceding activities
A	–
B	–
C	B
D	A,C
E	B

The network in Figure 10.40 is drawn using the standard method in which activities are illustrated by arrows.

The alternative method (illustrating the activities on nodes) is shown in Figure 10.41.

EXAMPLE 2

Similarly, consider the following group of activities:

Activity	Preceding activities
A	–
B	A
C	A
D	B,C

This collection of activities can be illustrated by either of the networks shown in Figure 10.42. Notice that the 'activity on nodes' method does not involve the use of dummy activities. This is one way in which the 'activity on node' approach to networks is simpler than the 'activity on arrow' method. However, complications in further analysis such as time calculations mean that new students to this subject often find that the 'activity on arrow' approach is easier for small manual networking problems.

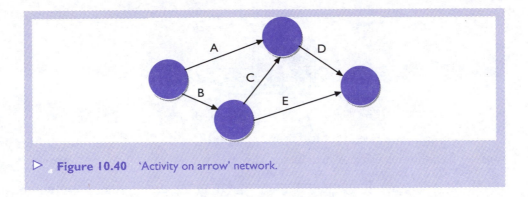

▷ **Figure 10.40** 'Activity on arrow' network.

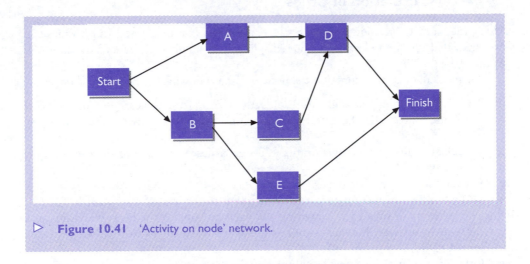

▷ **Figure 10.41** 'Activity on node' network.

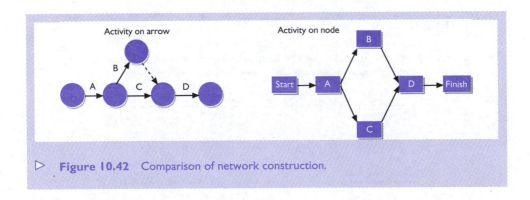

▷ **Figure 10.42** Comparison of network construction.

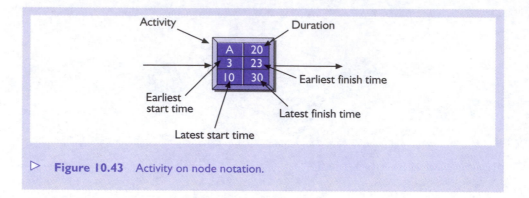

▷   **Figure 10.43**   Activity on node notation.

10.23   Calculation of times

Using the 'activity on node' approach, the earliest and latest start and finish times can be illustrated on the nodes. Each node is split into a number of sections as shown in Figure 10.43.

When calculating these times on the network, the following method should be used.

1. To calculate earliest start time for each activity copy from the earliest finish time of preceding activity. If there is more than one preceding activity, then copy the highest value.
2. To calculate the earliest finish time, add the earliest start time to the duration for each activity.
3. Repeat 1 and 2 for all activities.
4. In the 'Finish' node, copy the earliest finish time to the latest finish time.
5. The latest finish time of an activity is obtained by copying the latest start time of a subsequent activity. If there is more than one subsequent activity, then copy the lowest value.
6. Calculate the latest start time by subtracting the duration from the latest finish time.
7. Repeat 5 and 6 for all activities.

EXAMPLE 1

Consider a simple example involving the four activities as shown in the following table:

Activity	Preceding activity	Duration (weeks)
A	–	5
B	–	20
C	A,B	15
D	B	25

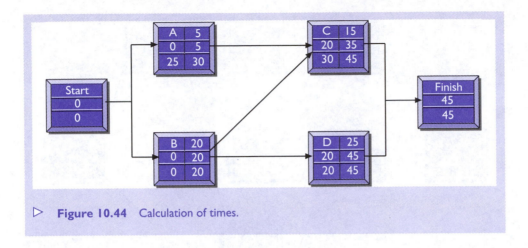

These activities are illustrated in the network in Figure 10.44. The reader may wish to compare this with a network drawn using the 'activity on arrow' method. It is often personal choice as to which method is preferred.

EXAMPLE 2

Using the 'activity on node' method draw a network of the following group of activities. Calculate the earliest and latest start and finish times and the overall project duration.

Activity	Preceding activity	Duration (weeks)
A	–	6
B	–	5
C	B	3
D	A,C	2
E	B	7
F	B	3
G	D,E	4

Using the 'activity on node' method we will obtain the network shown in Figure 10.45. This network shows that the overall project takes 16 weeks to completion.

Critical activities are those where earliest and latest start times are equal, and also earliest and latest finish times are equal. Consequently we see that the activities B, E and G are critical in the network.

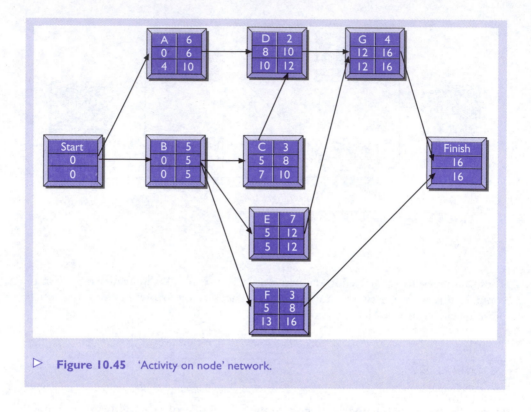

Figure 10.45   'Activity on node' network.

(**Note:** This group of activities has already been illustrated using an 'activity on arrow' network in Example 1 of Section 10.12. You may wish to compare the two methods of drawing networks by comparing these two illustrations.)

10.24   Exercises: 'activity on node' networks

1.(**I**)   Draw the network of the following lists of activities using the 'activity on node' method. Find the critical path and overall project duration for each group of activities.

(i)

Activity	Preceding activity	Duration (weeks)
A	–	10
B	A	5
C	B	3
D	C,E	4
E	B	6
F	C	12

(ii)

Activity	Preceding activity	Duration (weeks)
A	–	4
B	–	10
C	A,B	8
D	B	13
E	C,D	5
F	C,D	22

(iii)

Activity	Preceding activity	Duration (days)
A	–	8
B	–	4
C	–	2
D	A,B,C	5
E	C	6
F	D,E	7

10.25   Evaluation of network analysis

In the management of projects there are a number of key questions that need to be addressed. These include:

(i) How long will the project take to complete?
(ii) Is there likely to be any variability on this estimate?
(iii) When should individual activities start and be completed?
(iv) Which activities are critical in determining the completion time of the project?
(v) What flexibility is there in the remaining activities?

These questions can be investigated using the techniques of network analysis. The advantages of the networking approach are as follows:

▶ It provides relatively simple tools to enable the monitoring and control of complex projects.
▶ It helps to make decisions if the reallocation of resources is required.
▶ It provides a means by which the manager can check the progress of the project against targets.

However, there are some practical problems with the use of networks. These include:

▶ There are often difficulties in estimating the duration of activities within the project.
▶ The interdependence of some activities within a complex project can be difficult to determine.

▶ The analysis of a range of different resources required increases the complexity of the problem.

Nevertheless, such problems make the use of network analysis even more necessary, since any other less objective approach is fraught with dangers. The application of computer systems in the production of networks and associated analyses has helped to improve the level of sophistication possible in analysing specific projects.

10.26   Computer applications

The project management application is an increasingly competitive area for software producers. There are currently a large number of computer packages available on the market specifically related to project management and control systems. Many of these packages incorporate the techniques used within this chapter including the production of networks, Gantt charts and the evaluation of critical paths. Such packages include Microsoft Project, Project Manager Workbench, PERTMASTER, Harvard Project Manager, Hornet, and MacProject Pro.

The following examples illustrate a range of project management applications using the Microsoft Project package. In addition to the application packages, other software can be used for specific elements within project management. For instance, spreadsheet packages such as Lotus 123 and Excel can be used for the tabulation and illustration of data obtained from network analysis. Examples are included in this section demonstrating the use of Excel and Lotus 123 in this way. However, it should be noted that the subject-specific packages such as Microsoft Project and Project Manager Workbench provide a much more sophisticated analysis and presentation in the area of project planning.

EXAMPLE 1

The table below shows an amended list of activities involved in the Gilford & Partners construction project outlined earlier in this chapter. The table also includes the precedences for each activity, as well as the estimated duration of each activity in the project.

	Primary activities	Precedences	Duration (weeks)
A:	Initial survey & site investigations	–	6
B:	Design roadways	A	8
C:	Planning applications & permission	B	8
D:	Site preparation	B	10
E:	Construction of link roads	C,D	30
F:	Construction of main freeway	C,D	26
G:	Erection of signs, lighting, etc.	E,F	7
H:	Completion & hand over	G	3

These activities can be inserted into the Microsoft Project package, including estimates of the durations and details of the relationships between activities. The Microsoft Project package can produce a range of output based on the data entered, including an illustration of the overall network. The screen in Figure 10.46 shows part of the network diagram produced from this package. Only the first four activities can be seen on the screen illustrated. However, the user can zoom out to display the overall network if required. A full display of the network is not usually practicable, as most real projects will contain many dozens, if not hundreds, of separate interrelated activities. The activities are illustrated by the boxes in this diagram. The arrows simply indicate the relationships between the activities. This is an example of the 'activity on node' notation described earlier in this chapter. Each box gives a description of the activity, an activity number, the duration, and the earliest start and finish times. The network also highlights the critical path, by emboldening the critical activities and the arrows linking them.

Gantt charts can be produced based on the activities and relationships entered as shown in the screen in Figure 10.47. The Gantt chart produced assumes a given start date for the project indicated near the top of the graph. The project illustrated starts at the end of February 1995. Using the Microsoft Project package in a Windows

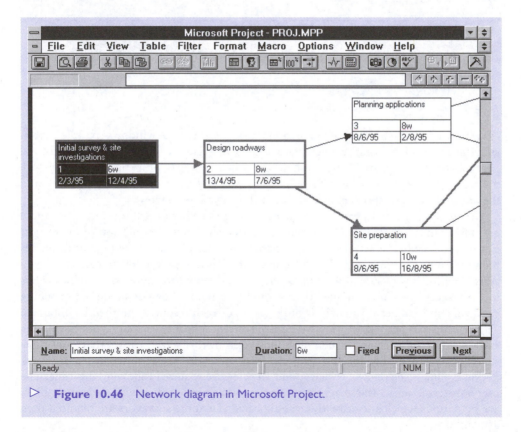

▷ **Figure 10.46** Network diagram in Microsoft Project.

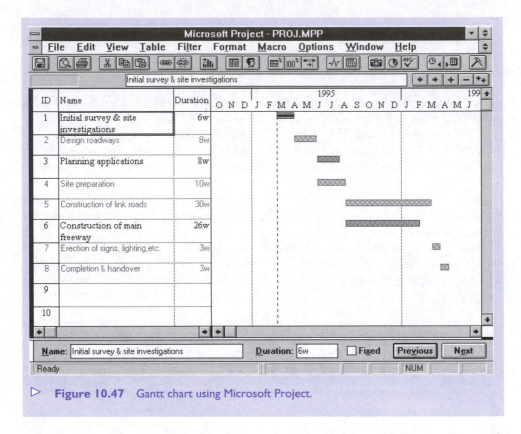

File   Edit   View   Table   Filter   Format   Macro   Options   Window   Help

Initial survey & site investigations

ID	Name	Duration
1	Initial survey & site investigations	6w
2	Design roadways	8w
3	Planning applications	8w
4	Site preparation	10w
5	Construction of link roads	30w
6	Construction of main freeway	26w
7	Erection of signs, lighting,etc.	3w
8	Completion & handover	3w
9		
10		

1995   199

O N D J F M A M J J A S O N D J F M A M J

Name: Initial survey & site investigations   Duration: 6w   ☐ Fixed   Previous   Next

Ready   NUM

▷ **Figure 10.47**   Gantt chart using Microsoft Project.

environment enables the display of a number of separate windows on the screen simultaneously. For instance, the screen shown in Figure 10.48 is split into two and contains the Gantt chart in the top half and a detailed view of a specific activity (site preparation) in the lower half. The user can select any activity in the top window and the appropriate view showing precedences will be displayed below.

Resource implications can be investigated using the Microsoft Project package and a graphical output illustrating the resource requirements over the duration of the project can be produced. The Project package enables the user to specify the type of resources required for each activity. For example, if the manpower resources are being considered, then different skills and expertise are required for different activities. Thus in the project previously outlined there would be a number of skills required including surveyors and builders. An analysis of the usage of each resource can then be obtained. The screen in Figure 10.49 shows the resource requirements for Surveyors during the early stages of this project. The graph illustrated in this screen shows that only three surveyors are available for this project. Two surveyors are required for a six-week period commencing on 26 February, and all three are required following this time. The user can scroll across this diagram to display other time periods and check that there are no periods which are currently over-allocated (i.e. more surveyors are required than available).

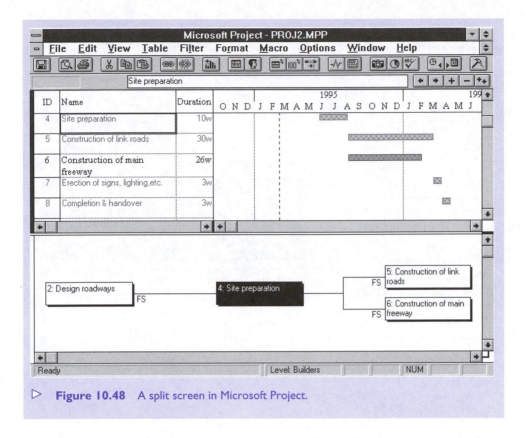

▷ **Figure 10.48**   A split screen in Microsoft Project.

EXAMPLE 2

Some analysis of the project outlined in the previous example could be achieved using a spreadsheet package. For instance, an obvious application is the calculation of float times for each activity as described in Section 10.11. The table below shows the results of the floats' calculations.

Activity	Duration (Weeks)	Earliest Start	Latest Start	Earliest Finish	Latest Finish	TOTAL FLOAT	FREE FLOAT	INDEP'T FLOAT
A	6	0	0	6	6	0	0	0
B	8	6	6	14	14	0	0	0
C	8	14	14	24	24	2	2	2
D	10	14	14	24	24	0	0	0
E	30	24	24	54	54	0	0	0
F	26	24	24	54	54	4	4	4
G	7	54	54	61	61	0	0	0
H	3	61	61	64	64	0	0	0

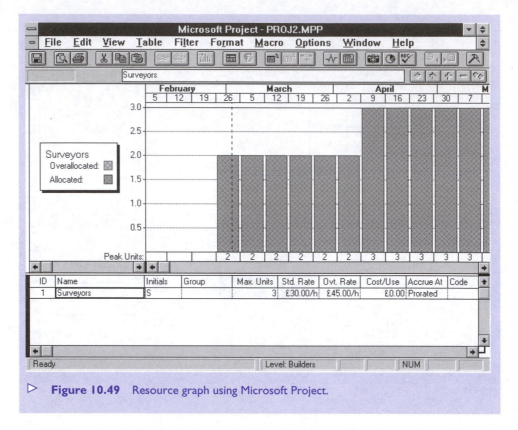

The first six columns are input by the user. The spreadsheet can then be used to calculate the specific float times as shown in the remaining three columns. The spreadsheet can also identify the critical activities as outlined in the table, simply by checking which activities have zero total float.

Using the disk   The disk included with this text contains a file called PRO-JECT.WK3. Load this file into the Excel or Lotus spreadsheet package. The spreadsheet shown in Figure 10.50 should be displayed. The table displayed in cells A3 to I12 shows details on a list of activities, durations and precedences as shown in the previous table. Try to change the duration of an activity and look at how the other float values are recalculated. In this file the cells containing the start and finish times have been deliberately protected so that a user cannot inadvertently change these values.

A second file called PROJECT2.WK3 contains the same data, with the cells containing start and finish times unprotected. If you wish, you can load this spreadsheet file and then change the values for the start and finish times in addition to altering the durations. Be careful when you do this. It should be noted that these values have been obtained from a previous network analysis, and so care should be

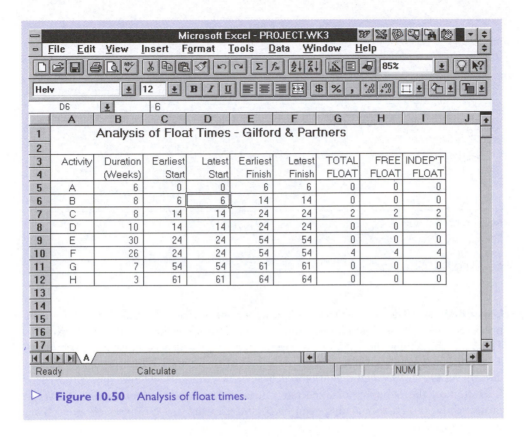

> Figure 10.50   Analysis of float times.

taken to input realistic numbers or the spreadsheet may yield impossible results. A more sophisticated spreadsheet could be produced that would check values on data input in order to ensure that only feasible numbers are entered. This would involve checks such as ensuring that the start times are less than the finish times, and the difference between these values is greater than or equal to the activity's duration.

EXAMPLE 3

The spreadsheet package can also be used to carry out some of the calculations involved in PERT analysis. For instance, the table below shows the output from a spreadsheet where the various estimates for each activity are used to estimate the expected values and standard deviation of the durations. Furthermore, if the critical activities are marked as shown, then the spreadsheet will automatically calculate the expected value and standard deviation of the overall project duration as shown in the table.

		PERT Analysis					
		Estimates of Duration (Days)					
Activity	Preceding Activity	Most Likely	Optimistic	Pessimistic	Expected Value	Standard Deviation	Critical Activities
A	–	9	8	16	10.00	1.33	1
B	A	8	7	9	8.00	0.33	1
C	–	4	3	5	4.00	0.33	
D	C	5	5	5	5.00	0.00	
E	C	8	7	15	9.00	1.33	
F	E	3	2	4	3.00	0.33	

Note: A "1" in colmn H indicates that the activity is critical
Duration of Overall Project
Expected value =   18
Stanard Deviation =   1.37

Using the disk   The file PROJECT3.WK3 contains a spreadsheet as illustrated in the previous table. The user can input values for the duration estimates in cells C5 to E10. The cells containing the list of activities and their precedences have been protected. Two further columns give the calculated values of the expected duration and standard deviation. The final column marks which activities are critical, and the cells B14 to D16 contain the estimates of expected values and standard deviation of the overall project duration. Further analysis can be conducted using the estimates obtained from this spreadsheet.

10.27   Chapter summary

This chapter has considered a range of techniques to assist in project management and planning. Primarily the techniques involve the use of network analysis. This process involves the following areas:

Production of network diagrams. Using the 'activity on arrow' or 'activity on node' notations to obtain a diagrammatic representation of the overall project and its constituent parts (activities).

Analysis of the critical path. This involves the estimation of individual activity durations, and a consideration of the degree of flexibility involved in each activity. The activities with no flexibility are considered to be critical. The duration of such activities cannot be changed without affecting the overall project duration. Other activities that do not have an immediate effect on the project duration are considered to be non-critical. Such an analysis of the individual activities is performed with the use of the network diagram.

Use of resources. The production of Gantt charts based on the network diagrams can enable the manager to determine the resource implications for a project. Thus the workforce requirements for the complete life of the project can be evaluated and planned. Lack of available resources can be dealt with by the rescheduling of activities with the aid of Gantt charts.

Crashing activities. The process of rescheduling a project may involve reducing the time allocated for specific activities. This process, called crashing, is likely to change the resource and cost implications of the project. Thus, the manager may consider which activities will be changed with reference to the resulting increases in costs, and their effect on the overall project. The manager is likely to wish to keep the crash costs to a minimum. Again, such an analysis can be performed with the use of networks and associated diagrams.

PERT analysis. In practice, it is often impossible to predict the exact duration of each activity in a project. For instance, in building projects, activities can be affected by a range of factors such as staffing, availability of equipment, and even the weather. In order to obtain a more realistic analysis of the project, the possible range of durations can be considered for each activity. The PERT analysis provides a probabilistic method of project analysis. Thus PERT can be used to consider the chances of a project lasting longer than a given period.

The use of computer packages in the management of large projects is becoming increasingly important. This chapter has described some of the facilities available in a specific project management package – Microsoft Project. In the absence of such software, a spreadsheet package can greatly assist in some of the calculations involved in project planning, and this has been described with the aid of examples.

In general, Networking techniques provide the manager with an extremely powerful tool in project planning and control. For many managers, this is the single most important area in quantitative techniques in terms of the management of staff and other resources.

10.28   Further exercises

1.(I) The Training & Development Manager of a large multinational financial organisation has been asked to develop and organise a new course for middle managers on business modelling. Initially, in order to provide an overview of the possible timing of such a course, the manager has produced a summary of the primary activities involved. The table below shows a list of activities involved in developing this training course:

  (i)   Draw a network of these activities (using the 'activity on arrow' approach) in order to illustrate the interrelationships between these activities.
  (ii) Find the critical path and overall project duration. Specify when the training course will be able to commence.
  (iii) Draw a Gantt chart of this project to illustrate the flexibility available in each activity.

Activity	Preceding activity	Duration (weeks)
A: Design course	–	4
B: Produce course documentation	A	6
C: Produce promotional leaflet	A	3
D: Advertise/promote course	C,F	2
E: Process applicants	D	2
F: Organise venue/facilities	A	1
G: Complete delegate list	E	1
H: Run course	B,G	2

(iv) Calculate float times for each activity. Describe how these times can be used in the management of the overall project.

(v) If the production of the course documentation actually takes nine weeks to complete, how will this affect the course timing? Redraw the network using this new time, and thus specify the amended start date for the course.

2.(I) The information below shows the tasks required in a recruitment campaign for new staff in the Reynolds & Patching Company, a manufacturing organisation based in the UK. The Recruitment Officer in the Personnel Division has outlined the main tasks necessary for the completion of this recruitment drive. The information provided includes details of each task required in this campaign together with estimates of the length of time required, and prerequisites for each task.

Task	Preceding tasks	Length of time (weeks)
A: Identify vacancies	–	3
B: Define job specifications	A	2
C: Design new literature/forms	B	2
D: Advertise posts	B	4
E: Receive & acknowledge applications	C,D	2
F: Organise assessors/interviewers	B	2
G: Set up aptitude tests	E	3
H: Process results/produce shortlist	F,G	1
I: Organise interviews	F,G	2
J: Appoint candidates	H,I	2
K: Candidates start job	J	8

(i) Draw a network to illustrate the activities involved in this recruitment campaign.

(ii) Estimate the length of time from the initial identification of vacancies before any new employee could start their employment.

(iii) What are the critical activities? Describe the significance of these activities.
(iv) Draw a Gantt chart for this recruitment campaign.
(v) If aptitude tests cannot be set up until after assessors/interviewers have been organised, would this affect the overall timing?

3.(I) The activities described below involve the development of a new company information system, from the initial appointment of a project team to full implementation of the system.

Activity	Preceding activity	Duration (weeks)	Cost (£)
A: Appoint project team manager	–	4	500
B: Define problem areas	A	3	1000
C: Collect relevant information	B	8	3000
D: Determine requirements	B	6	1500
E: Consider alternative solutions	D	4	1000
F: Evaluate alternative hardware	C,E	3	500
G: Develop software solutions	C,E	12	6000
H: Design manual solutions	C,E	8	3000
I: Install hardware/software	F,G	6	2500
J: Test-run computer systems	I	4	1000
K: Train staff	H,J	6	3500
L: Full implementation of system	K	4	800

(i) Determine the critical path and overall project duration for this project.
(ii) Draw a Gantt chart for this system development project.
(iii) Use the Gantt chart to draw a graph of expenditure assuming that the cost of each activity is paid for at the end of the activity.
(iv) Assuming that the staff training can commence after activities G and H, redraw the network diagram. How will this change affect the overall project time?

4.(D) Concern has been expressed in a local hospital that patients visiting the Casualty Department are not being dealt with quickly enough. The hospital management team has employed consultants to investigate current procedures. An initial review has revealed that the following activities take place.

(i) Draw a network of this sequence of activities using the most likely times and estimate the overall duration.
(ii) Using a PERT analysis, estimate the expected duration for each activity. Using these expected times, redraw the network diagram.
(iii) Estimate the standard deviations of the times of activities on the critical path, and hence the standard deviation of the overall duration.

| | | | Time estimates (minutes) | | |
Activity	Preceding activity	Most likely	Optimistic	Pessimistic
A: Patient check-in at reception	–	10	3	20
B: Wait for doctor to be available	A	30	15	75
C: Receptionist locates medical records	A	15	5	25
D: Initial patient check-up	B	20	15	30
E: Blood test	C,D	25	10	35
F: X-ray taken	C,D	45	20	60
G: Obtain blood test results	E	15	10	25
H: Obtain X-ray results	F	25	15	45
I: Final patient check-up	G,H	15	10	30
J: Provide diagnosis	I	20	15	30

(iv) Assuming a normal distribution, find the probability that the time taken between arrival at Casualty and obtaining a diagnosis is:
   (a) over 3 hours
   (b) under 2 hours
(v) Find the 95% confidence limits for the duration of this process.

5.(D)   The table below shows the activities involved in an expansion programme incorporating the opening of a second factory to increase production output. The programme involves transferring staff from the existing factory (factory A) to the new factory (factory B). The details of this programme are shown below, including the

| | | Duration (weeks) | | Cost (£000s) | |
Activity	Preceding activity	Normal	Crash	Normal	Crash
A: Recruit replacements for training staff	–	10	8	2	4
B: Train new recruits	A	8	4	3	5
C: New recruits replace training staff in A	B	2	2	1	1
D: Recruit new staff for A	C,H	10	8	2	3
E: Train new staff on A	D	6	4	5	7
F: Move training staff to B	B	3	2	1	2
G: Training staff trained on B	C,F	4	3	2	3
H: New machinery installed in B	A	15	12	12	21
I: Move staff from A to B	E,G	4	2	2	5
J: Train staff on B	I	8	5	5	8
K: Factory B start production	J	3	2	8	10

normal duration and costs plus crash duration and costs for each activity.

(i) Draw a network and locate the critical path for this project.
(ii) Determine the cost of 'crashing' each activity per week. Hence determine the best way of reducing the project duration by one week.
(iii) If you wish to reduce the project duration by a further two weeks how would this be done and how much extra will it cost?

6.(E) A project consists of six activities as shown in the following table. The duration for each activity has been estimated in terms of the most likely, maximum and minimum durations.

Activity	Preceding activity	Duration (days) Most likely	Maximum	Minimum
A	–	20	25	19
B	A,D	7	8	5
C	B	4	5	3
D	E	6	10	5
E	–	12	16	10
F	E	15	20	11

(i) Draw a network using the *expected* durations for each activity and locate the critical path.
(ii) Assuming that activities on the critical path could be achieved in the minimum time estimated, how will this affect the overall project duration?
(iii) Estimate the expected duration and the duration standard deviation of the overall project.
(iv) Assuming a normal distribution, find the 95% confidence limits for the project duration.

7.(I) **Using the disk** The file called NETWORK on the disk contains a spreadsheet similar to the file illustrated in Figure 10.50. The table has been designed to contain up to 26 activities labelled A to Z. From the network you can enter the appropriate values for the activity durations and event times. The spreadsheet will then automatically evaluate the values for the total, free and independent floats, as well as highlighting the critical activities.

You can use this file to calculate the floats for any list of activities. For instance, consider any of the networks drawn for the previous exercises in this section. Use the spreadsheet to evaluate the floats and highlight the critical activities.

(**Note:** In general, if there are more than 26 activities in the project, then this spreadsheet can be extended by copying the formulae entered in the three float columns to additional rows.)

Basic Mathematics

The aim of this section is to revise a range of mathematical techniques that, for many of the examples in this text, it is assume the reader has the required skills. If you have difficulty in understanding any of the following topics then it is advised that you study some basic mathematics texts in order to bring yourself up to the required standard. The following range of topics will be covered in this section:

▶ Percentages
▶ Ratios
▶ Powers and roots
▶ Arithmetic operations
▶ Substitution
▶ Simple equations
▶ Summation notation

Percentages

A percentage shows the relative size of a given value compared to the total. The following examples will illustrate the evaluation of percentages.

EXAMPLE 1

Percentages and fractions can be interchanged. For instance, 30% can be written as 30/100. This can also be written as a decimal = 0.3.

A decimal or fraction can be converted into a percentage by multiplying by 100. For examples, the decimal 0.65 as a percentage = $0.65 * 100 = 65\%$. Similarly, the fraction $\frac{3}{4}$ as a percentage = $\frac{3}{4} * 100 = 75\%$.

EXAMPLE 2

Consider a situation in which 20% of an individual's pay is taken in tax. If the employee earns £400 then the amount of tax paid is found as follows:

$$\text{Tax paid} = 20\% \text{ of } £400 = \frac{20}{100} * 400 = 0.2 * 400 = £80$$

So the employee pays £80 in tax from the £400 earned.

EXAMPLE 3

A company employs 200 staff, including 40 members in the Sales Department. 40 can be expressed as a percentage of the total workforce (200) as follows:

$$\text{Percentage staff in Sales Department} = \frac{40}{200} * 100$$
$$= 0.2 * 100$$
$$= 20\%$$

This shows that 20% of all employees work in the Sales Department for this company

Ratios

A ratio gives a comparison of one value with another and can be expressed as a fraction.

EXAMPLE 1

Each week a family spends $120 on food and $30 on electricity. The ratio of spending on food compared with electricity is 120 to 30. This is often written as $120:30$, although can be expressed as a fraction 120/30.

Using the fraction we can see that other forms are equally valid. For example, 120/30 is the same as 60/15 or 12/3 or 4/1, as well as many other combinations. Similarly, the ratio $120:30$ is the same as $4:1$. This means that for every $4 spent on food, only $1 is spent of electricity by this family.

EXAMPLE 2

An inheritance of £1000 is split between two people (James and Joanne) in the ratio $3:7$. This means that for every £3 received by James, Joanne obtains £7.

This can be expressed in a different way. For example, from the ratio given, James receives £3 out of every £10 of inheritance, or 3/10 of the total amount.

Consequently, James receives 3/10 of £1000 $= \frac{3}{10} * 1000 = £300$

Similarly, Joanne receives 7/10 of the total $= \frac{7}{10} * 1000 = £700$

EXAMPLE 3

An expenditure budget in a company is split between three divisions (Marketing, Production and Quality) in the ratio $12:3:5$. Out of a total budget of $40 000 we can evaluate how much each division is allocated. For example, the ratio shows that for every $12 in Marketing, Production receives $3, and Quality gets $5. Thus, Marketing obtains 12/20 of the total budget, Production 3/20 and Quality 5/20. Therefore, the divisions each receive:

Marketing $= \frac{12}{20} * 40\ 000 = 0.6 * 40\ 000 = \$24\ 000$

Production $= \frac{3}{20} * 40\ 000 = 0.15 * 40\ 000 = \$6000$

Quality $= \frac{5}{20} * 40\ 000 = 0.25 * 40\ 000 = \$10\ 000$

Powers and roots

The use of powers and roots is common in many of the formulae used in this textbook. A power of a number indicates how many times the number is multiplied by itself. The following examples illustrate the use of powers and roots to abbreviate complex calculations.

EXAMPLE I

Consider 4^2. This is read as 4 to the power 2 (or 4 squared).

Now 4^2 is the same as $4 * 4 = 16$

Similarly, 2^3 (2 to the power 3) $= 2 * 2 * 2 = 8$

and $3^4 = 3 * 3 * 3 * 3 = 81$

It can be seen from these examples that the number expressed in the 'power' gives the number of times the value is multiplied by itself.

EXAMPLE 2

If we have an expression in which a number is raised to a power, and then multiplied by the same number raised to another power, then the result can be obtained simply by adding the powers together. For instance, consider the following expression: $2^3 * 2^5$. This can be calculated by treating the two expressions separately, i.e. $2^3 = 2 * 2 * 2 = 8$, and $2^5 = 2 * 2 * 2 * 2 * 2 = 32$.

Therefore, $2^3 * 2^5 = 8 * 32 = 256$

Alternatively, the original expression could be obtained simply by adding the powers,

i.e. $2^3 * 2^5 = 2^{3+5} = 2^8 = 2 * 2 * 2 * 2 * 2 * 2 * 2 * 2 = 256$

Similarly, $3^2 * 3^4 = 3^{2+4} = 3^6 = 3 * 3 * 3 * 3 * 3 * 3 = 729$

EXAMPLE 3

The use of roots is necessary in a range of simple data analysis formulae. The square root of a number is a value that, when squared, gives the original number. This is much easier to calculate than it is to express in words!

Consider finding the value of $\sqrt{16}$.

The result of this is a number that, when squared, gives a result of 16. now we know that $4^2 = 16$. Therefore $\sqrt{16} = 4$.

Similarly, $\sqrt{9} = 3$ (since $3^2 = 9$),

$\sqrt{25} = 5$ (since $5^2 = 25$),

and $\sqrt{36} = 6$ (since $6^2 = 36$).

Finding the square root of other numbers generally requires the use of a calculator.

Arithmetic operations

The calculation of an arithmetic expression can only be carried out accurately by using a fixed order for the various operations involved. The acronym BEDMAS is a useful way of remembering the order of operations in such a calculation. This gives the initial letters of all the likely operations as follows:

1. **Brackets** – The contents inside brackets are always calculated first.
2. **Exponentiation** – This means raising to a power. Powers are calculated before any other arithmetic operations after the contents inside brackets are found.
3. **Division and multiplication** – Any divisions and products of values must then be calculated.
4. **Addition and subtraction** – Values should be added and subtracted as the final stage of the calculation of an expression.

The following examples show how the order of arithmetic operations indicated is adhered to.

EXAMPLE I

Consider the evaluation of the expression $4 + 6/2$.

The two operations, addition and division, should be performed with division first. So we calculate 6/2 first and then add to 4 as shown:

i.e. $4 + 6/2 = 4 + 3 = 7$.

Alternatively, the expression $(4 + 6)/2$ is calculated differently. The BEDMAS acronym shows that the contents of the brackets must be calculated before anything else. Thus, $(4 + 6)/2 = (10)/2 = 5$.

It can be seen from these two simple examples how the use of brackets can change the results of calculations.

EXAMPLE 2

Consider the calculation of the following expression:

$(3 * 4 - 2) * 3/(1 + 4)$

For this expression the contents of both sets of brackets should be calculated first. Inside the brackets it is still necessary to use the BEDMAS acronym. Thus, for the expression $(3 * 4 - 2)$ the product should be calculated before the subtraction.

So we have: $(3 * 4 - 2) = 12 - 2 = 10$

and $(1 + 4) = 5$.

Therefore, $(3 * 4 - 2) * 3/(1 + 4) = (10) * 3/(5)$

The division operation should be performed next, i.e. $3/5 = 0.6$

and so $(10) * 3/(5) = (10) * 0.6 = 6$

Similarly, the following expression is calculated as shown:

$$(5 * 8 - 6 * 3) * 20/(12 * 2 + 1) - 7 = (40 - 18) * 20/(24 + 1) - 7$$
$$= (22) * 20/(25) - 7$$
$$= 22 * 0.8 - 7$$
$$= 17.6 - 7$$
$$= 10.6$$

EXAMPLE 3

Finally, let us consider a calculation involving powers as follows:

$(4 + 2 * 3)^2/(3 + 3^2)$. The powers need to be calculated before other operations, except that the contents inside of brackets must be evaluated initially.

So the expression $(4 + 2 * 3)^2 = (4 + 6)^2 = 10^2 = 100$

and $3 + 3^2 = 3 + 9 = 12$

Therefore, $(4 + 2 * 3)^2/(3 + 3^2) = 100/12 = 8.333$

Substitution

Many analytical methods involve the substitution of values into algebraic formulae. The following examples illustrate a range of substitution problems involving simple algebraic expressions.

EXAMPLE 1

The expression below gives a method of calculating the value of y for given values of x:

$$y = 3(x + 1) + 2(2x + 3)$$

In order to obtain a value of y it is necessary to substitute in a specific value of x. For example, if $x = 5$ then substituting this into the expression we obtain:

$$y = 3 * (5 + 1) + 2 * (2 * 5 + 3)$$

Using the techniques described in the previous section we have:

$$y = 3 * (6) + 2 * (10 + 3)$$
$$= 18 + 2 * (13)$$
$$= 18 + 26$$
$$y = 44$$

Thus, we know that when $x = 5$ the value of $y = 44$.

Similarly, other values of x can be substituted into the expression in order to evaluate y.

EXAMPLE 2

Given an expression for S in terms of t as shown below:

$$S = (2t + 3)^2$$

The value of S when $t = 4$ is calculated as follows:

$$S = (2 * 4 + 3)^2 = (8 + 3)^2 = 11^2 = 121$$

Similarly, when $t = 3$ the value of S is:

$$S = (2 * 3 + 3)^2 = (6 + 3)^2 = 9^2 = 81$$

Other values of t can be substituted if required.

EXAMPLE 3

Given $A = \dfrac{2(3B - 2) + 6(5 - B)}{2B - 1}$

We require the value of A when $B = 4$. Substituting the value of B into the expression we obtain:

$$A = \frac{2*(3*4-2)+6*(5-4)}{2*4-1}$$

Remembering the order of arithmetic operations as outlined in the previous section this is calculated as follows:

$$A = \frac{2*(12-2)+6*(1)}{8-1}$$

$$= \frac{2*(10)+6}{7}$$

$$= \frac{20+6}{7}$$

$$= \frac{26}{7}$$

$A = 3.714$ to 3 decimal places.

Simple equations

Many techniques covered in this text, including correlation and regression in Chapter 3 and linear programming in Chapter 8, require the solution of simple linear equations as illustrated in the following examples.

EXAMPLE I

Solve the equation $5x + 2 = 17$

The way in which we solve this type of equation is to rearrange it until the unknown variable (such as x in this example) is on its own on one side of the equation, and an expression only involving numbers is on the other side.

The main rule when rearranging equations is that you must do the same to both sides of the equation. For example, if you add 2 to the left hand side of the equation then you must do the same to the right hand side. Similarly, you can multiply, divide or subtract a number providing you do it to **both sides** of the equation.

In this equation in order to isolate the term in x we must remove the $+2$ from the left hand side of the equation. We could do this be subtracting 2. Remember that this will need to be done to both sides as shown below:

Subtracting 2 from both sides of the equation we have:

$$5x + 2 - 2 = 17 - 2$$

This simplifies to $5x = 15$

Now to obtain x on its own we must divide by 5. Again, this is done to both sides of the equation as shown:

$$\frac{5x}{5} = \frac{15}{5}$$

Thus, we have $x = 3$ giving the solution of the original equation.

EXAMPLE 2

Solve the following equation:

$$(2x + 4) + (4x + 5) = 3x + 30$$

Now this equation can be solved by first combining all the 'like' terms together. In other words, try to collect all the terms in x together, and similarly all the constants (or numbers on their own) together.

For instance, the left hand side of the equation has terms in x ($2x$ and $4x$) which can be combined as shown:

$$2x + 4x + 4 + 5 = 3x + 30$$

Therefore we have:

$$6x + 9 = 3x + 30$$

Now let us try to collect all the terms in x together on the left hand side of the equation, with the constants on the right hand side. Again, using the techniques described in example 1 we can achieve this as shown below:

Subtract 9 from each side of the equation:

$$6x + 9 - 9 = 3x + 30 - 9$$

This then gives:

$$6x = 3x + 21$$

Now subtract $3x$ from each side of the equation:

$$6x - 3x = 3x + 21 - 3x$$

We are now left with:

$$3x = 21$$

Finally dividing both sides by 3 we have:

$$\frac{3x}{3} = \frac{21}{3}$$

This gives the solution of the equation $x = 7$

EXAMPLE 3

Solve the equation $\dfrac{(2x+4)}{(4-3x)} = \dfrac{5}{3}$

The complication in this equation is that there are terms in x on both the top and bottom lines of the expressions. First, this equation can be rearranged by moving all expressions to the top line as shown below:

Multiply both sides by $(4-3x)$:

$$\frac{(2x+4)}{(4-3x)} * (4-3x) = \frac{5}{3} * (4-3x)$$

The terms in $(4-3x)$ on the left hand side of the equation now cancel each other out and we are left with

$$(2x+4) = \tfrac{5}{3} * (4-3x)$$

Now multiply both sides of the equation by 3:

$$3 * (2x+4) = 3 * \tfrac{5}{3} * (4-3x)$$

The right hand side of the equation can be simplified by cancelling the 3 on the top and bottom lines:

$$3 * (2x+4) = 5 * (4-3x)$$

Now the numbers can be multiplied through the brackets as below:

$$3*2x + 3*4 = 5*4 - 5*3x$$

This simplifies to:

$$6x + 12 = 20 - 15x$$

Now collecting the 'like' terms together we have:

$$6x + 15x = 20 - 12$$

This gives the simple equation:

$$21x = 8$$

Finally, dividing through by 21 we obtain:

$$x = \tfrac{8}{21}$$

This can be written as $x = 0.38$ to 2 decimal places.

Summation notation

The summation notation is used in many statistical formulae. This notation is introduced in Chapter 1 of this text. However, if the reader is not familiar with the notation, it is useful to consider additional examples on the basic application of this method.

In general, the Greek letter Σ (pronounced 'sigma') represents a summation. Thus, if we see a formula including Σx, then this means that the sum of all values of x should be found. Similarly, $\Sigma y =$ the sum of y values, and $\Sigma xy =$ the sum of all the products x times y. The following examples illustrate this approach.

EXAMPLE 1

Consider the following table giving values of x and corresponding values of y.

x: 1   2   3   4   5

y: 2   5   4   8   11

Now the following summations can be found:

$\Sigma x = 1 + 2 + 3 + 4 + 5 = 15$

$\Sigma y = 2 + 5 + 4 + 8 + 11 = 30$

Similarly, we can obtain the product x times y as shown.

$xy: 1*2 \quad 2*5 \quad 3*4 \quad 4*8 \quad 5*11$

Thus, we obtain xy: 2   10   12   32   55

Therefore, the summation $\Sigma xy = 2 + 10 + 12 + 32 + 55 = 111$

EXAMPLE 2

From the data given in example 1, find the following values:

(i) Σx^2 (ii) Σy^2 (iii) $\dfrac{(\Sigma x)(\Sigma y)}{\Sigma xy}$

The calculations for each of these expressions are shown below

(i) In order to calculate Σx^2 it is necessary to evaluate the values of x^2 and then find the sum. The values of x^2 are as follows:

x^2: 1^2 2^2 3^2 4^2 5^2

i.e. x^2: 1   4   9   16   25

Thus, $\Sigma x^2 = 1 + 4 + 9 + 16 + 25 = 55$

(ii) Similarly, the value of $\Sigma y^2 = 2^2 + 5^2 + 4^2 + 8^2 + 11^2$

$$= 4 + 25 + 16 + 64 + 121$$

Therefore, $\Sigma y^2 = 230$.

(iii) We have already calculated the three summations included in this expression. From example 1 we know that $\Sigma x = 15$, $\Sigma y = 30$ and $\Sigma xy = 111$

Therefore, the expression $\dfrac{(\Sigma x)(\Sigma y)}{\Sigma xy} = \dfrac{(15)*(30)}{111} = \dfrac{450}{111}$

$$= 4.054 \text{ to 3 decimal places.}$$

Statistical Tables

Areas under the standard normal curve

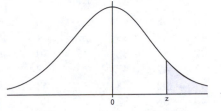

The tables give the area under one tail, as shaded:

z	0.00	0.01	0.02	0.03	0.04	0.05	0.06	0.07	0.08	0.09
0.0	0.5000	0.4960	0.4920	0.4880	0.4840	0.4801	0.4761	0.4721	0.4681	0.4641
0.1	0.4602	0.4562	0.4522	0.4483	0.4443	0.4404	0.4364	0.4325	0.4286	0.4247
0.2	0.4207	0.4168	0.4129	0.4090	0.4052	0.4013	0.3974	0.3936	0.3897	0.3859
0.3	0.3821	0.3783	0.3745	0.3707	0.3669	0.3632	0.3594	0.3557	0.3520	0.3483
0.4	0.3446	0.3409	0.3372	0.3336	0.3300	0.3264	0.3228	0.3192	0.3156	0.3121
0.5	0.3085	0.3050	0.3015	0.2981	0.2946	0.2912	0.2877	0.2843	0.2810	0.2776
0.6	0.2743	0.2709	0.2676	0.2643	0.2611	0.2578	0.2546	0.2514	0.2483	0.2451
0.7	0.2420	0.2389	0.2358	0.2327	0.2296	0.2266	0.2236	0.2206	0.2177	0.2148
0.8	0.2119	0.2090	0.2061	0.2033	0.2005	0.1977	0.1949	0.1922	0.1894	0.1867
0.9	0.1841	0.1814	0.1788	0.1762	0.1736	0.1711	0.1685	0.1660	0.1635	0.1611
1.0	0.1587	0.1562	0.1539	0.1515	0.1492	0.1469	0.1446	0.1423	0.1401	0.1379
1.1	0.1357	0.1335	0.1314	0.1292	0.1271	0.1251	0.1230	0.1210	0.1190	0.1170
1.2	0.1151	0.1131	0.1112	0.1093	0.1075	0.1056	0.1038	0.1020	0.1003	0.0985
1.3	0.0968	0.0951	0.0934	0.0918	0.0901	0.0885	0.0869	0.0853	0.0838	0.0823
1.4	0.0808	0.0793	0.0778	0.0764	0.0749	0.0735	0.0721	0.0708	0.0694	0.0681
1.5	0.0668	0.0655	0.0643	0.0630	0.0618	0.0606	0.0594	0.0582	0.0571	0.0559
1.6	0.0548	0.0537	0.0526	0.0516	0.0505	0.0495	0.0485	0.0475	0.0465	0.0455
1.7	0.0446	0.0436	0.0427	0.0418	0.0409	0.0401	0.0392	0.0384	0.0375	0.0367
1.8	0.0359	0.0351	0.0344	0.0336	0.0329	0.0322	0.0314	0.0307	0.0301	0.0294
1.9	0.0287	0.0281	0.0274	0.0268	0.0262	0.0256	0.0250	0.0244	0.0239	0.0233
2.0	0.02275	0.02222	0.02169	0.02118	0.02068	0.02018	0.01970	0.01923	0.01876	0.01831
2.1	0.01786	0.01743	0.01700	0.01659	0.01618	0.01578	0.01539	0.01500	0.01463	0.01426
2.2	0.01390	0.01355	0.01321	0.01287	0.01255	0.01222	0.01191	0.01160	0.01130	0.01101
2.3	0.01072	0.01044	0.01017	0.00990	0.00964	0.00939	0.00914	0.00889	0.00866	0.00842
2.4	0.00820	0.00798	0.00776	0.00755	0.00734	0.00714	0.00695	0.00676	0.00657	0.00639
2.5	0.00621	0.00604	0.00587	0.00570	0.00554	0.00539	0.00523	0.00508	0.00494	0.00480
2.6	0.00466	0.00453	0.00440	0.00427	0.00415	0.00402	0.00391	0.00379	0.00368	0.00357
2.7	0.00347	0.00336	0.00326	0.00317	0.00307	0.00298	0.00289	0.00280	0.00272	0.00264
2.8	0.00256	0.00248	0.00240	0.00233	0.00226	0.00219	0.00212	0.00205	0.00199	0.00193
2.9	0.00187	0.00181	0.00175	0.00169	0.00164	0.00159	0.00154	0.00149	0.00144	0.00139

Random sampling numbers

46	30	07	19	49	79	46	62
61	30	37	52	62	72	04	54
32	18	78	65	09	24	67	97
68	80	55	38	39	18	55	14
41	77	42	75	43	25	28	29
04	9	21	03	12	30	53	23
88	38	21	84	80	89	29	31
17	75	96	05	00	82	61	07
26	58	99	36	56	28	14	87
45	34	59	27	64	05	80	83
00	55	80	29	50	46	48	15
57	47	47	23	18	57	10	52
38	02	78	34	03	50	39	53
43	06	82	77	64	77	92	22
20	35	84	87	84	80	47	67
44	71	85	61	46	11	16	18
11	55	10	56	40	97	33	24
64	99	75	09	81	22	09	22
98	76	27	17	44	23	53	96
73	13	96	76	80	48	17	54
75	55	87	80	45	86	20	80
17	77	79	84	39	80	73	03
48	64	03	99	44	76	71	12
24	63	76	68	97	36	48	00
92	18	04	01	43	03	02	86
01	15	30	17	37	46	18	61
55	19	01	50	63	36	31	36
95	35	71	23	36	62	00	97
33	58	58	08	69	38	90	82
17	01	40	97	36	61	87	15
33	34	65	13	58	35	43	03
91	52	37	36	76	90	00	80
17	60	55	57	58	25	57	83
01	53	12	69	89	29	18	85
11	94	62	16	70	27	01	55
80	52	19	59	33	71	79	00
45	81	16	57	29	56	97	86
98	20	64	62	18	80	44	18
79	64	27	16	20	98	55	91
13	42	66	63	81	28	46	27

Answers

Answers to all odd numbered questions

CHAPTER 1
Section 4
1 (i)

Number of readers (10 000s):	90–	100–	110–	120–	130–	140–	150–
Number of days:	1	3	6	9	15	12	4

   (iii) Histogram for single set of data. Line graph for comparisons.
3 Line graph

Section 7
1 Mean = 2.117, Median = 2, Mode = 1
3 (i) Mean = £434, Median = £433, Mode = £375   (ii) Mean = 6.76, Median = 6.5, Mode = 5.3
   (iii) Mean = 11.67, Median = 10.2, Mode = 7

Section 11
1 (i) Range = 28, IQR = 6   (ii) Range = 29, IQR = 14
3 (i) Mean = 45.4, sd = 13.96   (ii) Mean = 6.06, sd = 2.25   (iii) Mean = 22.85, sd = 6.17
5 B closer to target but less consistent.

Section 15
1 (i) Bar   (ii) Pie   (iii) Histogram   (iv) Line
3 (i) Mean = 41, Median = 39.7, Mode = 36.4   (ii) Mean = 5.8, Median = 5.89, Mode = 5.6
   (iii) Mean = £5.01, Median = £4.90, Mode = £4.78
5 (i) Mean = 5.56, sd = 0.261   (ii) Mean = 24.25, sd = 2.48   (iii) Mean = 476.92, sd = 140.21
7 C is highest average, though A has most reliable production output.

CHAPTER 2
Section 3
1 a) 0.64, b) 0.04, c) 0.32
3 (i) a) 0.45, b) 0.9, c) 0.055, d) 0.405   (ii) a) 0.3025, b) 0.01, c) 0.18, d) 0.045, e) 0.495

Section 8
1 a) 0.009, b) 0.14, c) 0.024
3 (i) A; £31 000   (ii) A & B; £45 000

Section 11
1 (i) 0.3543,   (ii) 0.0159,   (iii) 0.8857
3 (i) 0.2440,   (ii) 0.7560,   (iii) 0.4744

Section 14
1 a) 0.3085, b) 0.1587, c) 0.3057, d) 0.7881, e) 0.8181
3 (i) a) 0.1335, b) 0.0478, c) 0.4215, d) 0.3130, e) 0.3209   (ii) 2 weeks

Section 18
1 (i) 122.4 to 357.6   (ii) 228.24 to 251.76
3 (i) a) 0.0661, b) 0.1294, c) 0.4210   (ii) 93.67 to 146.03   (iii) Yes, outside expected range.

Section 21
1 (i) a) 0.9, b) 0.96   (ii) a) 0.01, b) 0.004, c) 0.9216, d) 0.0768, e) 0.072
3 (i) a) 0.941, b) 0.886, c) 0.616   (ii) a) 0.9606, b) 0.0394
5 (i) a) 0.2119, b) 0.0026, c) 0.0228   (ii) 490.2 to 509.8 gms   (iii) 4.55%   (iv) 0.82%
7 Recommend purchase B if not successful then modify. Profit = 2.8 million

CHAPTER 3
Section 4
1 (i) 1,   (ii) −0.969,   (iii) 0.971

Section 8
1 (i) 0.588,   (ii) No

Section 11
1 (i) 1, $y = 3x + 2$ (ii) −0.968, $y = -1.5x + 13$ (iii) 0.530, $y = 0.8x + 2.6$
3 (i) 0.989   (ii) 6

Section 16
1 (i) 0.911, sig   (ii) $y = 0.134x + 2.647$, 5.3
3 (i) $y = 0.153x + 1.734$, 6 hours   (ii) 0.607
5 (i) 0.844

CHAPTER 4
Section 3
1 (i) £2000   (ii) £1080   (iii) £1300
3 (i) £4375.72   (ii) £2039.89

Section 6
1 (i) 6.17%, £106.17   (ii) 10.38%, £551.91   (iii) 7.12%, £1071.22
3 (i) £821.93   (ii) £873.44   (iii) £564.47

Section 9
1 £4418, £4152.92, £3903.75
3 (i) £2558.27   (ii) £5416.32   (iii) £1937.77
5 (i) £5092.61   (ii) £5434.72   (iii) £7886.77

Section 11
1 (i) 20%   (ii) 4.9%   (iii) 11.9%
3 (i) A: 15%, B: 42.6%

Section 14
1 (i) £600   (ii) £240   (iii) £157.50   (iv) £249.73   (v) £134.19   (vi) £2697.35
3 (i) $418.38   (ii) $308.39   (iii) $573.39
5 (i) a) £3903.75 b) $2190.42 c) £3779.14   (ii) a) 15.9% b) 9.1%
7 (i) $6793.40   (ii) $10 655.20   (iii) $995.40   (iv) $3669.40

CHAPTER 5
Section 5
1 (i) 100, 102, 104, 94.4, 89.6   (ii) 100, 102, 101.96, 90.77, 94.92
3 116.12

Section 9
1 (i) a) 115.39 b) 124.2

Section 11
1 (i) a) 125.71 b) 125.68

Section 13
1   (i) 110.57   (ii) 122.55
3   (i) 100, 107.36, 103.0   (ii) 100, 106.70, 101.11

Section 18
1   (i) 100, 107.5, 115.6, 116.9, 118.8, 126.3   (ii) 100, 107.5, 107.6, 101.1, 101.6, 106.3
3   (i) 120.2, 106.9
5   (ii) 102.99, 108.18   (iii) 102.99, 105.00

CHAPTER 6
Section 6
1   (iii) 40 patients
3   (ii) 4.5, 4.9   (iii) 3.8, 3.9. Moving averages preferred.

Section 10
1   (i) Trend: 6.7, 6.85, 7.0   (ii) Forecasts: 6.4, 7.4, 6.7
3   (ii) Multiplicative   (iii) 401, 349, 891

Section 17
1   (i) Trend: 19.2, 19.3, 19.4, 19.5, 19.6, 19.7, 19.8   (ii) Forecasts: 18.0, 18.1, 21.9, 22.5, 29.9, 16.5, 10.4
3   (i) 15.3, 16.2   (ii) 11.2, 11.8
5   (i) Forecasts: 295, 479, 356, 194. Ave error = -31 (ii) RMS = 45.7   (iii) Forecast ± 1.96 RMS

CHAPTER 7
Section 4
1   (iii) EOQ = 98   (iv) Monthly   (v) $980 + Unit costs

Section 8
1   (i) 693   (ii) 250   (iii) a) Costs = £14 429 b) Costs = £14 060

Section 11
1   (i) POQ = 727, 720 every 6 months

Section 13
1   (i) 37   (ii) 55   (iii) 73   (iv) 39, 59, 78

Section 18
1   (i) 154, £1541   (ii) 380, £1368   (iii) 1633, £735
3   (i) 27, $2343   (ii) Yes, total cost reduced to $512 175   (iii) 80
5   (i) 436   (ii) 1088   (iii) 2538
7   (i) $7562.50   (ii) EOQ = 95, Costs = $7040   (iii) Overall saving = $330   (iv) Yes, reduce costs by over $5000 per year.

CHAPTER 8
Section 6
3   (i) 14 & 8 (ii) 0 & 20

Section 9
1   (i) 10, 10; P = 70   (ii) 60, 0, 30; P = 840   (iii) 73.5, 3.9, 98.1; P = 1925.5

Section 11
	A	B	C	D
X	1	0	0	10
Y	2	0	11	0
Z	5	17	0	0

Section 14
1   (i)

	A	B	C
1	0	25	0
2	5	0	20
3	35	5	0

(ii)

	A	B	C
1	0	0	15
2	20	10	0
3	0	25	15

Section 18
1   40, 26; Profit = $2900
3   (i) 0, 42; £8400   (ii) 20, 32; £1168
5   117.6, 76.5, 0; $8940
7

	S	T	U	V
A	0	0	60	0
B	50	50	0	0
C	20	0	30	30

Total cost = £4450

CHAPTER 9
Section 9
1   Using random numbers 89, 07, 37, 29, 28, 08, 75, 01, 21, 63
   (i) 3, 1, 2, 2, 2, 1, 3, 1, 2, 3   (ii) 20, 5, 10, 10, 10, 5, 20, 5, 10, 15
   (iii) 5, 1, 3, 3, 3, 1, 4, 0, 2, 4
3   (i) Ave daily income approx $750, Ave daily costs approx $360   (ii) Reduction in number of stock-outs and slight reduction in order costs.

Section 16
1   Ave queue length approx 2.5
3   Ave queue length approx 2.3, ave waiting time approx 6 minutes

Section 21
1   (i) Ave wait time approx 60 minutes, ave queue length approx 4.4   (ii) Ave wait time approx 6 minutes, ave queue length approx 1   (iii) Wait time and queue length near zero
3   Out of stock for photocopy paper and overhead slides. Delivery time too long! Re-order levels should be increased.
5   (i) Loss approx $1000 per week; $20 000 over 20 weeks   (ii) Total investment approx $50 million. Loss approx $,000 per week
7   Number of rejects approx 2

CHAPTER 10
Section 9
1   (i) A, C, E, G: 17   (ii) A, C, D, F, H: 29   (iii) B, F, H, J: 23
3   (i) 30 months: A, C, E, F   (ii) No change

Section 13
1   B: TF = 2; D: TF = FF = 2; E: TF = FF = IF = 5. All others zero.

Section 16
1   (i) B, C, D; 12 days   (ii) A, D, F; 15 weeks   (iii) A, B, C, F; 18 weeks
3   a) A, D, I; 37 weeks c) Max requirement = 10 employees. Move C and F, requirement reduced to 6 employees.

Section 18
1   (i) A, E; 9 weeks   (ii) Reduce E by 2 weeks and C by 1 week. Total extra cost = £4000
   (iii) 6 weeks. Crash cost = £7000

Section 21
1   (i) G = 11, F = 6, M = 13, Total 30 weeks   (ii) sd = 3.21   (iii) a) 0.116 b) 0.268 c) 0.35
   (iv) 24 to 36 days

Section 24
1   (i) A, B, C, F; 30 weeks   (ii) B, D, F; 45 weeks   (iii) A, D, F; 20 weeks

Section 28

1   (ii) A, C, D, E, G, H; 14 weeks   (iv) B and F floats are 2 weeks. All others zero.
     (v) Increase duration by 1 week.
3   (i) A, B, D, E, G, I, J, K, L; 49 weeks   (iv) Reduce to 39 weeks.
5   (i) A, H, D, E, I, J, K; 56 weeks   (ii) Reduce D (£500) (iii) Reduce D by further 1 week (£500)
     and either A, E or J by 1 week (£1000)

Index